THE RED AND THE REAL

The Red and the Real

An Essay on Color Ontology

JONATHAN COHEN

OXFORD
UNIVERSITY PRESS

OXFORD
UNIVERSITY PRESS

Great Clarendon Street, Oxford OX2 6DP
United Kingdom

Oxford University Press is a department of the University of Oxford.
It furthers the University's objective of excellence in research, scholarship,
and education by publishing worldwide. Oxford is a registered trade mark of
Oxford University Press in the UK and in certain other countries

Reprinted 2014

British Library Cataloguing in Publication Data
Data available

Library of Congress Cataloging in Publication Data
Data available

ISBN 978-0-19-969223-1

For my son, Aaron Gabriel Cohen.

PREFACE

It was not always thus. Colour, if Tradition speaks the truth, once for the space of half a dozen centuries or more, threw a transient splendour over the lives of our ancestors in the remotest ages. Some private individual — a Pentagon whose name is variously reported — having causally discovered the constituents of the simpler colours and a rudimentary method of painting, is said to have begun decorating first his house, then his slaves, then his Father, his Sons, and Grandsons, lastly himself. The convenience as well as the beauty of the results commended themselves to all. Wherever Chromastites, — for by that name the most trustworthy authorities concur in calling him, — turned his variegated frame, there he at once excited attention and attracted respect. No one now needed to 'feel' him; no one mistook his front for his back; all his movements were readily ascertained by his neighbours without the slightest strain on their powers of calculation; no one jostled him, or failed to make way for him; his voice was saved the labour of that exhausting utterance by which we colourless Squares and Pentagons are forced to proclaim our individuality when we move amid a crowd of ignorant Isoceles.

— (Abbott, 1884, 39–40).

UPS, the UPS brandmark and the color brown are trademarks of United Parcel Service of America, Inc. All rights reserved.

— United Parcel Service web site.

Why Color Matters

A brief glance at recent philosophical journals, book catalogs, conference schedules, or graduate seminar offerings reveals that color has recently returned to its place at the center of philosophical inquiry after many years of receiving relatively scant attention from philosophers. Color had, of course, been of central importance at many periods in the history of philosophy (notably during the modern period), but it is fair to say that color had receded in philosophical interest and importance in recent decades. The current resurgence in philosophical work on color can be traced to a series of articles and monographs published in the late 1980s and early 1990s (e.g., Hardin, 1988; Hilbert, 1987; Thompson, 1995); one respect in which these works were so significant and stimulating to so many is that they showed how a large and exciting body of results drawn from the contemporary color sciences (including physics, colorimetry, computational vision, physiology, psychophysics, and evolutionary biology) bear on traditional ontological and epistemological questions about color. This was important and exciting news for philosophy and cognitive science more generally speaking. Here, for once, the oft-made promises of interdisciplinary research actually panned out: ideas from color science really did foster novel evaluations of old positions, and suggested new arguments and theories. Moreover, and perhaps more importantly in the long run, this work had the salutary effect of increasing the empirical sophistication of later philosophical discussion of color.

Recent philosophical work on color shows that these lessons have been largely taken to heart by academic philosophers. Why, then, should philosophers care about color in particular, when there are other pressing philosophical matters that deserve our attention?

A first reason is that colors are pervasive and salient features of the world as we ordinarily experience it: normal observers cannot help but notice that objects (in a very broad sense) appear to be red, green, and so on. If it is part of the job of an adequate ontology to account for the features we find in the world, then providing an account of colors is a necessary condition of success for such a theory. This is not to say that our ontology must take the reality of colors as a datum: it must be admitted that irrealism about *being red* is, at the very least, less inducing of blank stares than irrealism about tables and chairs. Rather, it is to say that our ontology must take the appearance of colors as a datum, for which one particularly simple and salient explanation is that colors are genuine features of the world.

Second, and notwithstanding the first point, colors are *prima facie* difficult to locate with respect to our best understanding of the fundamental physical properties in our world. There is good reason to think that *red, blue* and their ilk will not show up alongside and on a par with *mass, charge* and their ilk on the list of fundamental physical properties recognized by our best scientific accounts of the world. But if colors are not among the fundamental physical properties, then we need to find some other way of explaining how colors are related to them. Philosophers have defended a range of explanations of this sort — explanations involving supervenience, reduction, elimination, dualism, primitivism, and more. Providing an account of the nature of color, therefore, requires consideration of these notions, and evaluation of the theories that employ them.

In fact, the two reasons I have just given provide yet a third reason for being interested in color. If the first reason arose from the need to fit color into the description of the world given by our ordinary experience of it, then the second reason arose from the need to fit color into the description of the world given by our best scientific and theoretical description of it. Presumably, however, our ultimate explanatory goal is not to fit color into this or that proprietary description, but to find a single, unified description of the world that makes room for color *inter alia*. Color, then provides us with a specific instance of the general questions (emphasized, for example, in Sellars (1963)) about whether and how we can reconcile the description of the world given to us by our ordinary perceptual experience, on the one hand, and the description of the world given to us by scientific and philosophical inquiry, on the other.

But if color provides a specific instance of this general type of question, then a fourth reason for caring about color is that, plausibly, the general question is more fruitfully pursued in its specific form. Indeed, it seems reasonable to hope that the richness of both the ordinary and theoretical descriptions associated with color will be particularly conducive to answering this particular instance of the question, and that the answers arrived at will shed light on other instances of the problem that have attracted philosophical interest (e.g., instances concerning mental, aesthetic, and moral properties).[1] Of course, if the facts about colors turn out to be unlike the facts about (say) aesthetic properties in relevant respects, then that would potentially limit the extent to which lessons about the former are generalizable to the latter; but in so far as it is more fruitful to learn from what is known than to conjecture about what is not, it seems worth the effort to work out how the facts about color should influence our color ontology first, and then decide how far we want to extend our conclusions second. Either way, it seems to me, our general ontological purposes will be well served by our first attending to the nature of color properties.

Provenance

Although I have been thinking about color more or less continuously since 1997 (when I was introduced to the subject in Brian McLaughlin's graduate seminar on color at Rutgers), and have devoted a substantial proportion of my scholarly output to the topic, I have resisted writing a book on color for several years. For the most part, I resisted because it seemed (and still seems) to me that well-placed articles often have greater visibility and impact in academic philosophy than do books.

One day, however, I found that I could resist no longer. One reason for the change was that, once some of my ideas on color had been published in article form, I was lucky enough to see them criticized in print. This criticism has shown me some of the weaknesses of my positions, and has led me to rethink some commitments; consequently, I think I can now offer a richer and more complete defense of my ideas than I could before. Second, I began to tire of writing piecemeal defenses of my positions from one or another challenge, each containing more or less the same section 1 (in which I lay out the relevant views). Third, and more importantly, that these defenses have been pursued in such a fragmentary way has, I think, hidden the coherence, power, and generality of the entire package of views; the same fact has also had the effect of obscuring the relationships each component of the package bears to the others.

[1] I am by no means the first to make this suggestion. For example, Hume explicitly takes the metaphysics of color as a model for the metaphysics of value (*Treatise of Human Nature*, Book III, Part i, sec. I). Philosophers who have followed this recommendation include Harman (1977, 44ff.); Mackie (1977, 19–20); McGinn (1983, 146–155); McDowell (1985); Wiggins (1987*b*); and Wright (1992, 108ff.).

Taken together, these factors overwhelmed my resistance, and so I set out to produce the book you now have in your hands.

In view of this history, it has been my goal while writing the book to draw together several interconnected positions (e.g., the relationalist theory of color properties, the role functionalist version of relationalism, views about the semantics of color terms in natural language, commitments about the nature of color experience, and so on) into a single coherent account. I hope that each component in the resulting package derives some of its plausibility from the power of the whole of which it is a part. Nonetheless, I have done my best to make evident the relationship of each component to the others — both because I think the commitments can be (to a large extent) evaluated independently, and because I want to encourage partial alliances with my total view where possible. I want to preserve the possibility that readers might, for instance, agree with my arguments in favor of relationalism in Chapters 2–3, but favor some form of relationalism other than the role functionalist view I argue for in Chapter 7. I need all the alliances I can forge — partial or otherwise.

While the book draws on ideas from my earlier work on color relationalism and color functionalism (in particular, Cohen (2003*a*, 2004, 2006, 2010)), I've rewritten much of the overlapping material — something that involved, in several cases, changing my views substantially — and added much that is new.[2] I am grateful to the editors of the anthologies and journals in which those papers were published for allowing me to use this material.

Typographical Conventions

In this book I enclose expressions in single quotation marks (or sometimes corner quotation marks, when there are variables involved) to indicate that I am mentioning (rather than using) them (e.g., to talk about the word 'cat' as opposed to the kind *cat* or the individual members of this kind). I reserve double quotation marks for quoting material from other works. I use italics for property names (e.g., *being beautiful*, *being red for S in C*). I use small capitals for concrete thoughts, in order to distinguish them from their contents; thus, a COW-thought is a dated particular mental representation that has as its content the property *cowhood*.

[2] Part I of this book contains the most overlap with earlier work: portions of Chapter 1, most of Chapter 2.2, and some parts of Chapter 3 contain material from Cohen (2004) (although it has been greatly expanded and reworked). (As I think of it, if Cohen (2004) is a relationalist manifesto, then Part I of this book is something like a relationalist *Das Kapital*.)

ACKNOWLEDGEMENTS

It has been my great good fortune to have received so much extraordinarily useful input on the ideas in this book from so many smart people. Among those who have aided me in thinking through these matters, I am grateful to Ed Averill, Chris Barker, David Brink, Justin Broackes, Alex Byrne, Craig Callender, Ivano Caponigro, Nancy Cartwright, David Chalmers, Paul Churchland, Frankie Egan, Ione Fine, Justin Fisher, Jerry Fodor, André Gallois, Joshua Gert, Rick Grush, Larry Hardin, Benj Hellie, David Hilbert, Mark Kalderon, Janet Levin, Don MacLeod, Michael Martin, Mohan Matthen, Colin McGinn, Brian McLaughlin, Dana Nelkin, Ram Neta, Shaun Nichols, Adam Pautz, Agustín Rayo, Sam Rickless, Philip Robbins, Peter Ross, Robert Rupert, Mark Sainsbury, Brad Thompson, Sydney Shoemaker, Michael Tye, Eric Watkins, Michael Watkins, Mike Webster, and Wayne Wu. I thank all of them for their insight and assistance. In addition, I owe a special debt to the graduate students in my autumn 2006 seminar on color at the University of California, San Diego (Tim Jankowiak, Charlie Kurth, Liberty Jaswal, and Tarun Menon); these brave souls not only endured the seminar, but then met with me several times in winter 2007 to discuss a draft of the present monograph.[1] I also wish to express my gratitude to Jacob Stegenga for his work preparing the index, to two anonymous referees for Oxford University Press who gave me detailed comments that were immensely useful in carrying out revisions, and to Peter Momtchiloff, who has been a patient and helpful editor at every turn and who originally encouraged me to write this book. I am sure I have forgotten others to whom I incurred intellectual debts while writing this book; to them I owe not only thanks but apologies for my absent-mindedness.

One of the special benefits that comes with being an academic philosopher is the opportunity to present one's ideas to far-flung audiences consisting of clever interlocutors, who then provide immediate criticism and feedback at no charge. What's more, one's audience often compounds this generous deed by taking one to a nice dinner! I make a policy of availing myself of this arrangement whenever possible. In particular, I am grateful to have been able to exploit this practice to talk about material that found its way into this book before audiences at meetings of the American Philosophical Association (several times); Brown University; the CUNY Graduate Center; Florida State University; Kings College, London; Rutgers University; Simon Fraser University; the Southern California Philosophy Conference; the 2008

[1] In June of 2007, Liberty Jaswal was killed in a tragic hit and run accident in La Mirada, California. Liberty was much-admired as a person and valued as a philosophical interlocutor; I am thankful to have had the benefit of his insight in thinking about the topics contained in this book.

Syracuse Philosophy Annual Workshop and Network; Texas Tech University; the Third Biennial Margaret Dauler Wilson Conference; the University of British Columbia; the University of California, Berkeley; the University of California, San Diego; the University of California, Santa Barbara; the University of Kentucky; the University of Texas, Austin; the University of Tokyo; the University of Toronto; and the 2003 Workshop on Colour Ontology and Colour Science at the University of British Columbia.

I would like to thank two granting agencies for their support while I wrote this book: the UCSD Center for the Humanities, which provided me with a Humanities Faculty Fellowship during winter 2006, and the Warren and Chris Hellman Foundation for making me a 2005–2006 Hellman Fellow.

Finally, I convey my deepest gratitude to Liza Perkins-Cohen and to Aaron Cohen, who bring color to my world.

CONTENTS

FIGURES

1

INTRODUCTION: THE SPACE OF OPTIONS

Order and simplification are the first steps toward the mastery of a subject — the actual enemy is the unknown.

— Thomas Mann, *The Magic Mountain*, 5.

The main purpose of this book is to argue for a particular (role functionalist, relationalist) account of the nature of color properties. But before I can argue for the view I favor, I need to locate that view in the landscape of options, and say how it differs from competing accounts. Unfortunately, I have become dissatisfied with the usual ways of understanding the space of options. My first order of business, then, which I'll pursue in this chapter, will be to develop an alternative map of the terrain. To do that, I'll begin by presenting a more or less standard taxonomy (henceforth, the Standard Taxonomy) of the major alternative positions about color ontology (§1.1). Next, I'll raise some difficulties with the Standard Taxonomy, and indicate some directions in which we might proceed to refine our characterization of the options (§1.2). Following this, I'll introduce the distinction between relationalist and non-relationalist accounts of color, and offer reasons for thinking that this distinction captures many of the central disputes about color ontology better than does the Standard Taxonomy (§1.3). This will enable me to offer an alternative (if idiosyncratic) Refined Taxonomy of positions on color ontology (§1.4) that (among other advantages) makes clear the relationship of color relationalism to other views. With this new characterization of the options in hand, I'll be in a better position to join the debate between them in later chapters.

1.1 The Standard Taxonomy

I'll begin by outlining what I take to be a fairly Standard Taxonomy of positions about color ontology (cf. Byrne and Hilbert, 1997*a*, 2003); this Taxonomy is represented in Figure 1.1.

The Standard Taxonomy begins with a distinction between accounts on which there are colors (versions of color realism) and accounts on which there are not (versions of color irrealism/eliminativism).

Color irrealism denies the quotidian belief that things bear color properties, and thereby amounts to a serious revision of the naïve view. Of course, the color irrealist needn't deny that objects look colored —roughly, that they are represented by visual perception as bearing color properties. But she will claim that, if it does represent objects as having colors, visual perception is in this

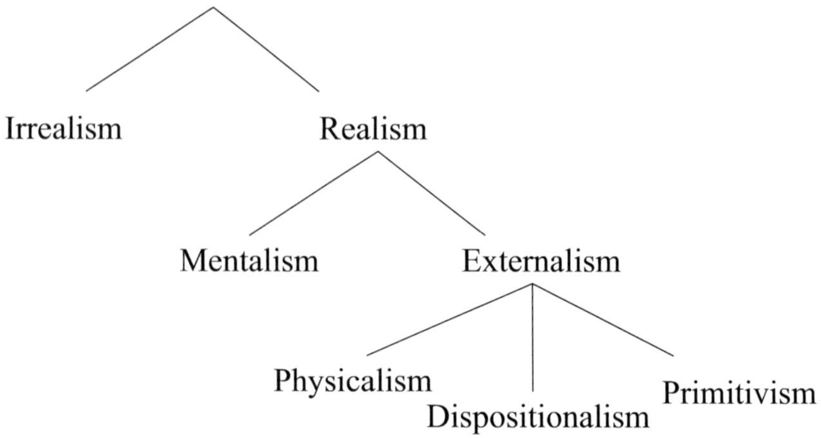

FIG. 1.1. The Standard Taxonomy of positions on color ontology.

respect erroneous. So understood, color irrealism could be fleshed out in at least the following (incompatible) ways:

- There are no properties at all. *A fortiori*, there are no color properties.
- There are properties, but colors do not figure amongst the properties that there are.
- There are properties, and color properties are among the properties that there are. But as a matter of (necessary or contingent) fact, nothing in the actual world exemplifies any color property.[1]

Despite its revisionary character, color irrealism has a long history in philosophy that is often traced to Democritus's famous exhortation that "by convention color exists, by convention bitter, by convention sweet but in reality atoms and void" (DK 68 B 9).[2] More recently, irrealism has been defended ably by authors including Hardin (1988); Boghossian and Velleman (1989, 1991); Maund (1995); Chalmers (2006).

Turning our attention next to realist views, the Standard Taxonomy distinguishes between what we might call *mentalist accounts*, according to which the bearers of colors are mental items (e.g., sense-data) and *externalist accounts*, according to which colors are exemplified by physical items (e.g., tables and chairs, but also mental items in so far as these are counted as physical). Mentalist theories of one form or another have a venerable history in empiricist

[1] I won't distinguish between these versions of irrealism in the present work except where it matters. It's also worth mentioning that there are a number of quite different, weaker uses of 'irrealism' in philosophical currency — uses on which some property or properties might count as unreal despite existing and having actual instances. (I discuss several of these uses in Chapter 5, when I turn to the question of whether color relationalism amounts to a species of irrealism.)

[2] However, Johnson (2008) contends that this passage represents only half of a Democritean dialogue between the senses and the mind in which, ultimately, the senses triumph; on this basis Johnston argues that the customary attribution of color irrealism to Democritus is incorrect.

theorizing about perception and knowledge, and have been defended relatively recently by Jackson (1977) and Perkins (1983).

However, the realist positions that have the widest contemporary following are all different forms of color externalism. The three traditional, and most popular, strands of realist externalism in the Standard Taxonomy are *color physicalism*, *color dispositionalism*, and *color primitivism*. I'll take these positions in turn.

Color physicalism is best understood by comparison to two forms of identity theories familiar from philosophy of mind: type- and token-identity views.[3] Recall that a type-identity (type-physicalist) theory about pain, for example, has it that the property *being in pain* is numerically identical to the (physical) property *undergoing C-fiber firing* (as it might be); this means, among other things, that the instances of the psychological property *being in pain* are, one and all, tokens of a single physical type. Type-identity theories of this sort are traditionally contrasted against token-identity (token-physicalist) theories. Views of the latter sort have it that every single token instance of *being in pain* is an instance of some or other physical type, but they deny that there must be one single physical type that embraces all tokens of *being in pain*. Significantly, both type- and token-physicalist theories about pain are compatible with the view that all properties are physical (whatever that comes to); hence, partisans of both theories can endorse the claim that pains are, one and all, physical.

Likewise, color physicalism is a position that instances of color properties are, one and all, physical. However, as in the case of physicalism about pain, color physicalists can be further divided into type- and token-physicalists. Type-physicalists identify colors with microphysical types (Armstrong (1968, chapter 12); Smart (1975); Jackson and Pargetter (1987); Lewis (1997)). In contrast, many self-identified color physicalists hold views according to which colors are dispositions to affect light in certain ways (Hilbert (1987); Matthen (1988); Byrne and Hilbert (1997*a*); Dretske (1995, chapter 3); Byrne and Hilbert (2003); Ross (1999); Tye (1995, 2000)). On such a view, there is no one physical constitution type that is shared by all instances of a given color (hence no chromo-physical type-identity claims are true), but every token instance of a given color is a member of some or other physical type that affects light in the requisite way.[4] In recent years, many color physicalists have been attracted by a specific form of token-physicalist positions according to which the dispositions at issue are characterized in terms of *spectral reflectance functions*, which map the

[3] Color physicalism has sometimes gone by alternative (and seemingly non-equivalent) labels, including 'color objectivism' and (adverting to the modern distinction among primary and secondary qualities of matter) 'primary quality theory of color'.

[4] Here as elsewhere, the distinction between type- and token-physicalism presupposes a particular inventory of physical types; I have tried to preserve the analogy with the standard story about pain by assuming that the inventory of physical types will not include functional properties such as that of being disposed to affect light in a certain way. If such functional properties are counted as physical types, then the view presented here as a form of token-physicalism will in fact be a kind of type-physicalism.

range of visible wavelengths to the interval [0, 1], and represent the proportion of reflected to incident light at each wavelength. Most physicalists who appeal to these functions (but not all — see Churchland (2009)) identify colors with *classes* of such functions, rather than with the individual functions themselves, in order to allow that perceptually indistinguishable but numerically distinct spectral reflectance distributions ("metamers") can count as one and the same color.[5]

We can move on now to dispositionalism, at whose core is the claim that colors are dispositions to affect perceivers. This core claim, however, requires considerable clarification: to fill out her view, the dispositionalist needs to say more about which perceivers, which circumstances, and exactly which effects in those perceivers in those circumstances, she has in mind. The many species of dispositionalism can be distinguished by the ways they fill in those blanks. For example, one canonical form of dispositionalism holds that red is the disposition to cause red sensations (/to look red) to normal observers in normal circumstances. I think it is safe to say that dispositionalism, in a suitably broad sense, is the received view about color ontology in philosophy: versions of it have been ascribed (controversially) to such as Galileo, Boyle, Newton, and Locke. More recently, forms of dispositionalism have been defended by McGinn (1983); Peacocke (1984); Johnston (1992).

Dispositionalism is counted by the Standard Taxonomy as a realist rather than an irrealist account of colors; this treatment makes sense if the relevant dispositions are genuine properties that actual objects genuinely exemplify. It is also an externalist view (in the sense defined above) on the assumption that ordinary tables and chairs (rather than any kind of mental objects) are the things that exemplify the dispositions to affect perceivers. Dispositionalism is unlike physicalism in many respects; perhaps most important among these, dispositionalism is unlike color physicalism in characterizing colors in terms that explicitly mention perceivers. That said, it is worth noting that, as unpacked above, dispositionalism is compatible with the token-physicalist claim that every token instance of a color property is a member of some or other physical type.[6] (I'll return to this point in §1.2.)

The final traditional strand of realist externalism about color in the Standard Taxonomy is color primitivism. This view holds that colors are genuine properties borne by actual ordinary extra-mental objects, but that they are primitive or *sui generis*. In order to remain an alternative to other realist externalist views, this must mean, minimally, that the essences of colors cannot be reduced to, i.e.,

[5] Byrne and Hilbert (2003) generalize the notion of a reflectance function to what they call a productance function, which maps each wavelength λ in the visible range to the proportion of emitted (i.e., reflected plus generated) to incident light of wavelength λ. So defined, productances collapse onto reflectances for non-emitting objects (e.g., matte surfaces), but make possible the treatment of colors of other objects (e.g., light sources, transparent volumes) as well.

[6] For that matter, dispositionalism is compatible with the type-physicalist claim that all the instances of each single color are of a common physical type (although this seems rather unlikely).

identified with, the things to which other views aim to reduce them. Thus, color primitivists maintain that colors are *not*, for example, physical or functional types or dispositions to affect perceivers. Color primitivists generally hold that the physical/functional types and dispositions to affect perceivers — the properties with which other externalist realists identify colors — exist (and are exemplified), but that they cannot be successfully identified with colors for one reason or another. Of course, primitivists can allow that colors are universally correlated with such physical/functional types or dispositions. Indeed, they can even allow that such correlations hold as a matter of nomological or metaphysical necessity, so long as they insist that these are mere correlations (universal and nomologically or metaphysically necessary though they be) between numerically distinct properties. Since they are color realists (at least, according to the Standard Taxonomy), and since they do not believe that colors are physical types or dispositions to affect perceivers, primitivists conclude that there are more properties in heaven and earth than are dreamt of in the philosophy of color physicalists and dispositionalists. Colors are, on this view, additional properties — properties over and above those called on in the metaphysical accounts of other realists — that must appear in a complete inventory of what there is.

In practice, and perhaps unsurprisingly, given primitivists' view that colors are primitive/*sui generis*, the characterizations of colors put forward by defenders of color primitivism have tended to be more in terms of what they are not (not physical types, not dispositions to affect perceivers) rather than what they are. Correspondingly, many (but not all) arguments offered in support of color primitivism turn out to be negative arguments targeting other views; after showing the problems with these other views, primitivism is then held out as a way of endorsing externalist realism without falling victim to the faults that attend other theories.[7] Recent years have seen a resurgence in the popularity of color primitivism: some form of the view is endorsed by Cornman (1971, 1975), Westphal (1987, 2005), Campbell (1993), Yablo (1995), Watkins (2002, 2005, 2008), Johnston (2002), Gert (2008), and (arguably) Stroud (2000).

1.2 Problems With the Standard Taxonomy

In my view, there are a couple of reasons for being dissatisfied with the Standard Taxonomy presented above.

A first problem with that taxonomy concerns the relationship of irrealism to other positions. On the Standard Taxonomy, irrealism is deemed incompatible with physicalism, dispositionalism, and primitivism: these last three views are all offered as forms of (externalist) realism. But that doesn't seem quite right. For, so long as one can be a color irrealist by holding that color properties are unexemplified, it is possible to combine color irrealism with

[7] See Byrne and Hilbert (2007*a*) for arguments against primitivism (together with a helpful history, summary, and classification of several forms of the view), and Watkins (2008) for responses to these arguments. I'll consider critically several arguments for primitivism in §3.2.2.

either physicalism, dispositionalism, or primitivism. For example, one might combine the primitivist thesis that colors are *sui generis* properties with the irrealist claim that nothing exemplifies such properties (the resulting position is called 'E-primitivism' — for eliminativist-primitivism, and contrasted with 'R-', or 'realist-' primitivism — by Byrne and Hilbert (2007*a*)). Likewise, one might combine the type-physicalist's claim that colors are identical with physical types with the irrealist idea that no actual objects exemplify those particular physical types to arrive at an irrealist form of physicalism. (I am not suggesting that this position is attractive — only that its presence in logical space deserves recognition.) Similar strategies make possible irrealist forms of dispositionalism and even color mentalism.[8] What this shows, I think, is that the realism/irrealism distinction is orthogonal to the choice between substantive theories of the nature of colors. On reflection, this lesson seems plausible: for staking a view on what sorts of things color properties are should not commit one, by itself, to a view on whether actual objects exemplify those properties or not. It is a defect of the Standard Taxonomy that it obscures this lesson.

An analogous problem arises with respect to the mentalist/externalist distinction. Just as the Standard Taxonomy errs in failing to recognize irrealist forms of mentalism and externalism, that taxonomy goes wrong in categorizing physicalism, dispositionalism, and primitivism exclusively as forms of externalism. Mentalism, it will be recalled, is the view that the bearers of color properties are mental entities rather than, say, cabbages and kings. But one might have thought that that claim about what individuals *bear* the colors should leave largely open the nature of the properties those bearers turn out to exemplify. In principle, a mentalist (*qua* mentalist) should be open to the claim that colors are primitive properties of mental entities, or physical properties of mental entities, or dispositional properties of mental entities, and perhaps more. The mentalism/externalism distinction is, like the realist/irrealist distinction, orthogonal to the choice between substantive theories of the nature of colors. And, again, this seems appropriate on reflection: mentalists and externalists differ over the matter of which individuals are colored, not over the matter of what their being colored consists in. Again, the Standard Taxonomy misleads by keeping this fact from view.

A third problem with the Standard Taxonomy involves the relationship between color physicalism and the physical. Now, color physicalism is often presented (not, as in §1.1, by comparing it to identity theories in philosophy of mind, but) merely as the view that colors are physical properties (e.g., Byrne and Hilbert (2004, 7); Ross (1999)). One difficulty is that this gloss is somewhat empty unless supplemented by a substantive characterization of the

[8] Despite its coherence, irrealist dispositionalism seems a particularly unattractive view, in that it seems to entail that actual, ordinary objects lack dispositions to look colored — something that, on the face of it, flies against the facts. Again, my point is not to advocate such a view, but only to make room for it in logical space.

physical (which is usually not supplied in such discussions). Moreover, if the notion of the physical is unpacked in any of the usual ways, many ostensible non-physicalists about color — e.g., dispositionalists and primitivists — will also claim that colors are physical properties. To see that this is true about dispositionalists, recall that dispositions are standardly thought to come with bases/grounds in virtue of which they are exemplified by objects (e.g., the vase might exemplify the disposition *fragility* in virtue of exemplifying a certain kind of irregular atomic structure), and that such bases are ordinarily taken to be physical.[9] Consequently, the relevant color dispositions will themselves count as physical for those who construe the relation between dispositions and their bases as one of type-identity (Armstrong (1968); Armstrong *et al.* (1996, chapter 1)), token-identity (Mumford, 1998) and plausibly even a functional relation (Prior, 1985). Likewise, there seems to be no obstacle to combining the conclusion that colors are physical with color primitivism so long as there can be primitive physical properties. Mass, charge, and (quark) flavor are often taken to be just such primitive physical properties; there is no obvious reason, then, why colors couldn't be treated in the same way. All this goes to show that (ontological) physicalists needn't be color physicalists.

It must be admitted that, lamentably, 'color physicalism' is an entrenched label in the Standard Taxonomy. However, we've seen that physicality doesn't end up drawing useful distinctions between ostensibly competing theories — it is, in effect, a taxonomic surd. Here too, then, the Standard Taxonomy is conducive to error.

A final reason for favoring a revised taxonomy comes from the observation that there is an element in dispositionalism whose interest outruns the specific claim that colors are dispositions. This is the idea — an idea I'll label *color relationalism* — that colors are constituted in terms of relations to subjects.[10] Of course, if colors are dispositions to affect subjects, it follows that colors are constituted in terms of relations to subjects. However, recent discussion has pointed out that there are also non-dispositionalist forms of color relationalism — views that, in principle, might allow us to keep what is worth having in dispositionalism without signing on to the whole dispositionalist package. Unfortunately, the Standard Taxonomy doesn't mention relationalism *per se* at all, and makes room for relationalism only by having a single node for dispositionalism. As I hope to show, color relationalism deserves more consideration than this.

For all these reasons, I think we would do better to replace the Standard Taxonomy with a more refined alternative. Before I come to this, however, I want to explain in more detail what is meant by the claim that colors are constituted in terms of relations.

[9] For more on the metaphysics of dispositions see McLaughlin (1995), Fara (2006).

[10] This idea has been brought out (to differing extents and in different ways) by such authors as Cohen (2004, 2007), Giere (2006), Matthen (1999, 2001, 2005), and Thompson (1995).

1.3 Relationalism Defined

The heart of color relationalism is the claim that colors are relational; in particular, the relationalist claims that they are constituted in terms of a relation between (*inter alia*) objects and subjects. Presumably, this view should be understood by way of contrast with the view that colors are non-relational properties of their bearers. Unfortunately, there is no uncontroversial account of the relational/non-relational distinction to which we can turn. On the other hand, I take it that we have a pre-theoretical grasp on the distinction that comes out in our agreement about paradigm cases: *being a sister* and *being 50 meters to the left of a philosopher* are relational properties, while *being cubical* and *having a mass of 50 kg* are standardly taken to be non-relational.[11] In saying that these paradigm examples of relational and non-relational properties express our pre-theoretical understanding of the distinction, I mean that we don't need a philosophical account of the relational/non-relational distinction to classify these properties as relational or non-relational; on the contrary, these classifications are data that any acceptable philosophical account of the distinction must respect (at least pending empirical reconsideration — see note 11), and therefore that we may use (even in the absence of an uncontroversial account of the distinction) as paradigms against which to compare new cases.

Moreover, we have a pre-theoretical grasp of what distinguishes relational from non-relational properties: roughly, a non-relational property of x is a property that x has (or lacks) regardless of the relations x bears to things other than x. This may not amount to a satisfactory analysis of non-relationality, depending on whether one thinks we have a prior satisfactory understanding of relations, and of the individuation of particulars (*inter alia*). But, again, this gives us an entry point for the discussion about whether particular properties, such as colors, are relational or not.

It is worth noting at this point that one sometimes finds in the literature (see Tye, 2000, 152) that the view that colors are relational is contrasted with the view that colors are *intrinsic* properties. Now, the antonym of 'relational' is obviously 'non-relational', rather than 'intrinsic', and this matters because it is controversial whether the relational/non-relational distinction coincides with the intrinsic/extrinsic distinction (and, of course, over the proper understanding of the latter; cf. Weatherson (2006)). However, there does seem to be a connection between the two distinctions that will be relevant. Namely, if an intrinsic property is characterized in a rough-and-ready way as "a property that a thing has (or lacks) regardless of what may be going on outside itself" (Yablo,

[11] Alas, these (paradigmatic!) examples of non-relational properties are controversial (as are more or less all examples of the non-relational). For one might reasonably claim that objects only have a shape by being related to a particular space, and that objects only have a mass by being related to a reference frame. Nonetheless, I think it is fair (and fruitful) to continue to use these traditional examples to mark out the relational/non-relational distinction, even if further investigation of the world ultimately forces us to relocate the traditional examples with respect to that distinction.

1999, 479), then intrinsic properties will also be non-relational.[12] For x cannot bear a relation to something other than x (hence cannot exemplify a relational property) regardless of what may be going on outside itself: at a minimum, x cannot bear a relation R to y (and hence cannot exemplify a relational property) unless y exists.[13] For this reason, we may find that claims about the intrinsicness of properties are germane to the debate over whether colors are relational.

To return to the main line of discussion, we can express the point of contention between relational and non-relational accounts of color in terms of the paradigm examples cataloged above: the question is whether *being red* is more like *being the sister of b* (i.e., a relation that yields relational properties when relevant parameters are filled in) or *being cubical* (i.e., a non-relational property for which there are no parameters in need of filling). And in view of our pre-theoretical grasp of the relational/non-relational distinction, we may express that question in this way. Suppose x is something red; then, as we modify things other than x, and thereby modify the relations x bears to other things, will x (necessarily) continue to be red? If so, then *being red* is non-relational; if not, it is relational.

Here a caveat is needed. In order to ensure that the relational/non-relational distinction draws the lines in places that are most important for discussions of color ontology, it is essential that we limit the scope of relationalism to those theories that construe colors in terms of relations to *subjects* (possibly *inter alia*). After all, many of the theories in the Armstrong–Hilbert tradition turn out to understand colors as constituted in terms of relations between objects and light (even if they hold that colors are not constituted in terms of relations to subjects), and it would drain relationalism of its classificatory utility if we were

[12] As Yablo notes immediately, this characterization is obviously circular, in that the variations we are allowed to make when testing a property for intrinsicness have to be variations that are extrinsic to the instance of our test property (lest all properties turn out to be extrinsic). However, the circularity of the characterization does not show that it is false (or, as Yablo argues, incapable of inspiring a non-circular account along the same lines).

[13] Three remarks about the conclusion that intrinsic properties are non-relational are in order.

Remark 1: Brian Weatherson has pointed out that there can be counterexamples in cases where the relational property in question is constituted in terms of a relation that, as it were, relates a thing to one of its proper parts. I propose to stipulate such cases out of consideration, since they seem not to overlap with the cases I'll be wanting to discuss in the present debate about color properties.

Remark 2: I take this conclusion to be neutral with respect to the different accounts of the intrinsic/extrinsic and relational/non-relational distinctions that attempt to cash out the rough and ready characterizations I have appealed to (e.g., it is agnostic between the accounts of intrinsicness presented by Lewis (1983*b*); Yablo (1999)). It may not, however, hold for those who take the intrinsic/extrinsic distinction to be identical with the essential/accidental distinction or the real/unreal distinction; but I take it that these uses of 'intrinsic' and 'extrinsic' are confused, and therefore I shall put them aside (Dunn, 1990).

Remark 3: My claim about *relational properties* is not in conflict with the view, defended in Langton and Lewis (1998), that some *relations* are intrinsic. According to them, a relation R is intrinsic "iff it never can differ between duplicate pairs" (343). But the *relational property* of bearing R to something is, on the understanding adopted above, a property of a single individual, not a pair; whether an individual x can exemplify this relational property depends on things other than x, and consequently the (arbitrary) relational property is not intrinsic.

to count these theories as relationalist. For the same reason, I won't count it a victory for relationalism about colors if it turns out that *all* properties are constituted in terms of relations; for, even if this view is right, we can still formulate the debate about color relationalism by asking whether the relations in terms of which color properties are constituted happen to be relations to subjects.[14] Thus, in my usage, 'color relationalism' will be reserved for the view that colors are constituted in terms of relations to subjects, rather than the more liberal view that colors are constituted in terms of relations (to any old relata) *per se*.[15]

I also want to remark briefly on the label 'relationalism'. Some writers have — perhaps in deference to the traditional terminology in metaethics — discussed the kinds of positions under consideration under the label of 'relativism' rather than 'relationalism' (e.g. Spackman, 2002). However, I want to keep these two labels separate as a way of distinguishing between importantly different positions. On my usage, color relativism is (roughly) the thesis that there are no colors *simpliciter*, but only colors for certain kinds of perceivers in certain circumstances (McLaughlin, 2003*a*; Jakab and McLaughlin, 2003). Significantly, color relativism leaves it open whether colors are constituted by a relation to perceivers; this is just to say that color relativism does not entail color relationalism. Although I'll return to color relativism in §3.3.1, my main concern here will be with the question of whether color relationalism is true.

Having set out the relationalist/non-relationalist distinction, I now want to urge that it is potentially useful in understanding the space of alternative views on color ontology: it crystallizes a central set of issues that divides the accounts, and does so while sidestepping problems that plague the Standard Taxonomy.

For one thing, it gives us a clean way of distinguishing between two prominent views in the discussion — those the Standard Taxonomy labels physicalist and dispositionalist views about color. The former sorts of views are non-relationalist: they construe colors as not constituted in terms of relations to subjects or minds, and so predict that molecular duplicates of red things will be red even in worlds where there are no minds (/perceivers).[16] So-

[14] One might hold the view that all properties are constituted in terms of relations if one held, with Shoemaker (1980), that properties are sets of causal powers, and one also held (as Shoemaker does not) that causal powers (and not simply their specifications) are relational.

[15] An exactly analogous complication arises in the formulation of dispositionalism as it occurs in the Standard Taxonomy. For while accounts in the Armstrong–Hilbert tradition deny that colors are dispositions to affect *perceivers*, they construe colors as dispositions to affect *light*. In order to keep such views from falling under the Standard Taxonomy's dispositionalist heading, writers have preferred to limit the term 'dispositionalism' to theories that make appeal to dispositions to affect subjects.

[16] Primitivism will also get counted a non-relational view (in so far as committing to the relationality of colors gives up on the primitivist's official vow of silence about the constitution of colors); but one can easily distinguish between primitivist and non-primitivist forms of non-relationalism if needed by just asking whether colors are primitive.

That said, there is arguably a relationalist cousin of primitivism according to which colors are constituted in terms of relations to subjects (hence this view counts as relationalist), but on which

called dispositionalist views, in contrast, are species of relationalism: they construe colors as constituted in terms of (dispositional) relations to subjects (and possibly other parameters, such as viewing conditions). On these views, molecular duplicates of red things could fail to be red in worlds where features not preserved by the molecular duplication are allowed to vary.[17] Making the distinction between these positions in this way also frees us from having to provide either a general characterization of the physical, or a specific characterization of the extant physical types. Additionally, it avoids the false suggestion that one of the two is more closely tied to a physical ontology. The centrality of these two positions in the history of philosophical debate about color gives us reason for wanting a way of distinguishing the two; that the relationalist/non-relationalist distinction answers that need with a minimum of complications suggests that it should figure prominently in the revised taxonomy at which we are aiming.

However, there is a further — and, to my mind, far more significant — benefit to taxonomizing positions in terms of the relationalist/non-relationalist distinction: such a classification separates out distinct commitments previously collapsed under the old labels, and thereby brings into view whole constellations of previously unconsidered positions. For example, this way of sorting views makes room (as the Standard Taxonomy does not) for non-dispositionalist forms of relationalism such as those defended by Cohen (2004); Matthen (1999, 2001, 2005); Thompson (1995).[18] Moreover, this categorization reveals the possibility of non-relationalist views that are hard to fit into the standard taxonomy, such as the view that colors are non-relational and non-primitive but non-physical (whatever that comes to), or non-relational but unanalyzable (*a fortiori*, not susceptible of analysis in terms of physical kinds). The relationalist/non-relationalist distinction, then, makes visible previously unseen philosophical positions, and thereby enlarges our view of the space of options; this, I suggest, is strong reason for giving the distinction a central role in any successor to the Standard Taxonomy.

the relations in question are themselves *sui generis* and beyond the reach of informative explication. As no one (to my knowledge) has endorsed or argued for this view, I won't have anything further to say about it in what follows.

[17] This does not commit the relationalist to the view that nothing is red in a world where there are no minds, because a relationalist can unpack the colors in terms of a dispositional relation (or some other relation that would be expressed in terms of a subjunctive conditional). On such a view, x can be red in w (where there are no minds) if x *would* be appropriately related to the minds in w, assuming there were any. (This is also not to say that relationalists *must* take this line; for example, arguably Locke did not intend his relationalism to be understood in terms of subjunctive conditionals (see Rickless, 1997, 307ff.).)

[18] As I shall discuss in §8.1, the role functionalism of Cohen (2004) might or might not ultimately differ from dispositionalism, depending on how we understand the metaphysics of dispositions. However, the main point in the text stands regardless of how this shakes out, since the relationalist accounts offered by Matthen and Thompson are importantly different from dispositionalism given any plausible understanding of dispositions.

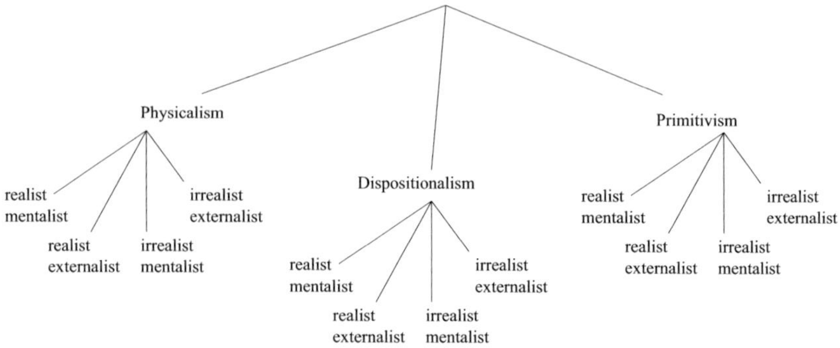

FIG. 1.2. Pruning and grafting the Standard Taxonomy.

1.4 Towards A Refined Taxonomy

So far I have set out the Standard Taxonomy (§1.1), pointed out several of its shortcomings (§1.2), put forward the distinction between relationalist and non-relationalist accounts of color, and then made a case for appealing to this distinction as one useful element in an improved characterization of the disputed terrain (§1.3). In this section I want to add to this single useful element to arrive at a new (and idiosyncratic) classification of positions that will guide us through the rest of this work. I'll do this by beginning with the Standard Taxonomy, and then apply some judicious pruning and grafting until we arrive at a Refined Taxonomy.

A first refinement is motivated by the finding (from §1.2) that some distinctions represented by choice points at relatively high nodes in the Standard Taxonomy (see Figure 1.1) turn out to be orthogonal to other choices represented lower in the tree — e.g., this is true of the realist/irrealist distinction. Since there seem to be both realist and irrealist versions of every position, our Refined Taxonomy should locate the choice between realism and irrealism not in a single node at the top of the tree (as in the Standard Taxonomy) but at every individual terminal node. For the same reason, the mentalist/externalist choice, too, should be represented at every terminal node. To do this, we should prune away from the Standard Taxonomy the realist/irrealist and mentalist/externalist distinctions (as well as the terminals that are their immediate daughters), and graft on to the remaining terminals (for physicalism, dispositionalism, and primitivism) branches corresponding to those recently pruned distinctions. The result of this pruning and grafting is represented in Figure 1.2.

Although this intermediate result represents progress over the Standard Taxonomy, further refinements are still needed. For one, as argued in §1.3, there is much to be gained from reorganizing the first layer in the taxonomy of Figure 1.2 in terms of the relational/non-relational distinction. We should, at the same time, replace the unhelpful label 'physicalism' with the heading 'identity theory' that more clearly brings out what is distinctive about the relevant view (its identification of colors with microphysical or non-subject involving

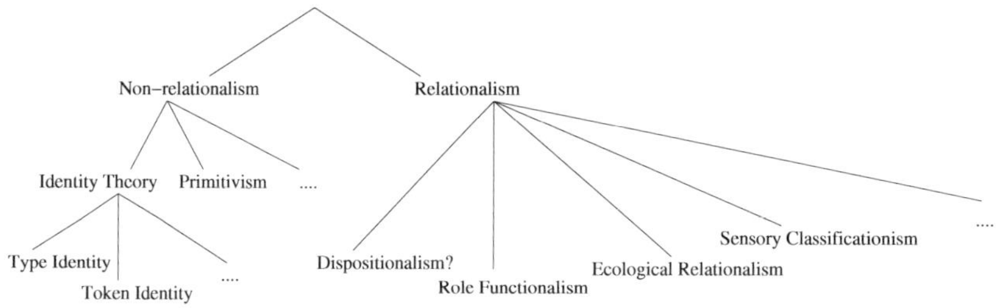

FIG. 1.3. A Refined Taxonomy of positions on color ontology. Every terminal node is ±realist and ±externalist.

functional kinds), and we should distinguish between its alternative (type and token) forms. In addition, we can and should now make room for the full variety of views that fit under the relationalist heading (a partial list of such views, which will be discussed in Chapters 7–8, would include role functionalism, ecological relationalism, and sensory classificationism; as discussed in note 18, dispositionalism might or might not remain a separate node in the taxonomy, depending on further commitments about the metaphysics of dispositions). Similarly we should add entries for distinct forms of non-relationalism (and distinct forms of the type-identity view). Making these changes gives us the Refined Taxonomy represented in Figure 1.3.[19]

This Refined Taxonomy seems to me a substantial advance over its Standard predecessor; nonetheless, it remains incomplete in (at least) two important respects.

The first is that it leaves room for as-yet-undiscovered forms of both relationalism and non-relationalism (and, for that matter, physical/functional identity theories) about color — hence the ellipses under the nodes for those views.[20] This open-endedness is, I think, unavoidable once we free ourselves from the more limited set of choices made available by the Standard Taxonomy.

A further form of incompleteness in the Refined Taxonomy is that, like any such organization of pure positions, it will inevitably fail to do justice to various

[19] To prevent the figure from becoming too cluttered I have omitted branches sprouting from every terminal node to represent the available choices on the realist/irrealist and mentalist/externalist dimensions (as in Figure 1.2). To capture these additional dimensions of variation, every terminal node should be understood to be parametrized ±realist and ±externalist.

[20] As an example of a novel non-relationalist view, it is worth mentioning the complex form of non-relationalism of Shoemaker (1994*b*, lecture III). While Shoemaker holds that our experience of colors represents relational properties, he argues (on the basis of concerns for relational theories addressed in Chapter 4 of this work) that these relational properties cannot be identified with objects' colors (254ff.; see also Shoemaker (1994*a*, 2000*a*,*b*); Thau (2002)). Shoemaker instead maintains that colors are *non-relational*, so is a non-relationalist about color. He claims that color experience represents *both* the (non-relational) color property *and* the corresponding relational property — he calls the latter a 'phenomenal property' or an 'appearance property'. Unsurprisingly, my view is that this doubling of properties represented by experience is implausible (and unnecessary, in light of the arguments in Chapter 4).

hybrids. One such hybrid is the disjunctive view that a particular color can be exemplified by both mental entities (say, experiences) and non-mental entities (say, ripe tomatoes) (see Maund, 1981, 1995; Rosenthal, 1999; Brown, 2006); since this view straddles a distinction (the mentalist/non-mentalist distinction) in the Refined Taxonomy, it doesn't find a natural location therein. A second hybrid account not easily accommodated by the Refined Taxonomy is the deflationary (nihilist?) view that there is no substantive matter for color ontologies to disagree about, but only the boring and verbal issue of what deserves to be labeled a color property (Dennett (2003); Giere (2006, 123–125)).[21] Alas, these (and perhaps other) hybrid positions fail to find a home in the Refined Taxonomy. On the other hand, these views can at least be described in terms of their relationships to other positions that are represented (and hopefully can be described better than they would have been in terms of the Standard Taxonomy).

Notwithstanding these defects, I submit that the Refined Taxonomy outlined in this section gives a useful way of organizing the issues that divide accounts of color ontology.

1.5 Looking Forward

With this organization of the alternative positions in place, let me now say how I intend to proceed in the rest of this book. In Part I I'll present an extended argument for color relationalism based on the phenomenon of perceptual variation. I'll begin to do this in Chapter 2 by laying out this argument in several different forms, and explaining how it motivates color relationalism. Next, in Chapter 3 I'll consider and respond to a series of challenges against the argument from perceptual variation; I'll find these challenges unsuccessful, and therefore urge that we should learn to live with color relationalism. In Part II I'll turn from arguing in favor of relationalism to defending it from objections. Thus, in Chapter 4 I consider how a relationalist can account for the semantics of linguistic color ascriptions (and related topics); in Chapter 5 I address a series of challenges to the color relationalist's ontology; and in Chapter 6 I offer a relationalist treatment of the phenomenology of color. My goal in this part of the book is simultaneously positive and negative: I hope to show both that the topics considered do not pose insuperable challenges to

[21] For the record, I find both these hybrid views unappealing. The first posits an ambiguity in color terms that is simply not supported by the evidence of standard tests for lexical ambiguity. And it seems to me simply false that the ostensibly competing views about color ontology are in agreement about the substantive facts; for one example among many, relationalist and non-relationalist theories make conflicting predictions about the results of molecular duplications (see §1.3).

At any rate, I am inclined to think that we should consider these and other hybrid positions only after such time as more straightforward first-order positions are shown to fail. As such, my best defense against them will be a good offense: if I can clearly articulate and defend from objections a first-order position about what colors are (as I aim to do in this book), then there will be no need to resort to meta-philosophical hybrids.

color relationalism, and that indeed relationalism contains the resources needed to give plausible treatments of each. Finally, Part III will be devoted to the choice between various forms of color relationalism. Thus, in Chapter 7 I'll present the role functionalist view that I favor, and in Chapter 8 I'll argue that role functionalism is preferable to other forms of relationalism.

What of the further, and orthogonal questions of realism/irrealism and externalism/mentalism? Although these issues won't be my main concerns in what follows, my default assumption will be that an adequate color ontology should be realist and externalist.[22] My reason for this default assumption is, in large part, one of rational conservatism. Irrealism and mentalism are (self-consciously) highly revisionary views that even their proponents regard as positions of last resort: this is why writers tend to embrace those views only after convincing themselves that all forms of realism/externalism are untenable.[23] Therefore, if I can make plausible a realist and externalist account of colors, as I hope to, then the mere availability of that account will substantially diminish the attraction of irrealism and mentalism.

So much by way of taxonomy and definition. The more interesting question, which I'll begin to address in Chapter 2, is why anyone should believe that colors are relational.

[22] I shall, however, consider arguments for irrealism in greater depth in §3.2.

[23] Famously, early 20th-century defenses of mentalism (e.g., by Price, Moore, and Russell) rested on the so-called argument from illusion and its variants. I think it is fair to say that most contemporary philosophers would reject this argument (for canonical responses, see Austin (1962); Jackson (1977)); and with the rejection of this motivation, mentalism about color has become a decidedly minority view. For relatively recent arguments against construing sense-data specifically as the bearers of color properties (as opposed to general arguments against positing sense-data in the first place) see Hardin (1988, 96–109).

PART I

THE CASE FOR COLOR RELATIONALISM

2

THE ARGUMENT FROM PERCEPTUAL VARIATION

> Upon examination, I find only one of the reasons commonly produc'd for this opinion to be satisfactory, viz. that deriv'd from the variations of those impressions, even while the external object, to all appearance, continues the same. These variations depend upon several circumstances. Upon the different situations of our health: A man in a malady feels a disagreeable taste in meats, which before pleas'd him the most. Upon the different complexions and constitutions of men: That seems bitter to one, which is sweet to another. Upon the difference of their external situation and position: Colours reflected from the clouds change according to the distance of the clouds and according to the angle they make with the eye and luminous body. Fire also communicates the sensation of pleasure at one distance, and that of pain at another. Instances of this kind are very numerous and frequent.
>
> — Hume, *A Treatise of Human Nature*, Book I, part iv, Of The Modern Philosophy.

Having set out a characterization of the distinction between relational and non-relational theories of color in Chapter 1, I now want to present what I take to be the core argument for relationalism: the argument from perceptual variation. I'll present this argument in stages. First (§2.1) I'll give a particular instance of that argument intended to establish the relatively narrow conclusion that colors are best construed in terms of a relation to viewing circumstance. Next, I'll attempt to generalize from that instance to a much more general argument form (§2.2), which I can then apply (§2.3) to a number of independent instances. In every instance, I'll argue, the evidence favors a relational, rather than an anti-relational, conception of color. In §2.5 I'll take stock of where we are.

2.1 An Illustrative Instance

To my mind, the most important argument for color relationalism is based on consideration of wide interspecies, interpersonal, and intrapersonal variations with respect to color perception. This is an old argument, variants of which show up in the works of Heraclitus and Protagoras, in Plato's *Theaetetus*, in great moderns such as Galileo, Locke, Berkeley, and Hume, and, more recently, by philosophers such as Bennett (1968) and McGinn (1983). In discussing my own version of the argument (henceforth, the argument from perceptual variation), I'll be emphasizing that the very same considerations can be applied again and again across different sorts of variations; consequently, it may be that "the" argument from perceptual variation is best thought of as a collection of instances of a common form. I take this fact to be significant, since I think the recurrence of identical considerations across different sorts of variation puts pressure on us to favor a uniform reaction in each case — a lesson that, as we'll see, many philosophers have failed to observe. However, I think the argument is (at least initially) most easily appreciated by consideration of its specific instances; accordingly, I'll begin to present the argument in this section by setting out one such instance, and then attempting to draw more general morals in later sections.

As a first concrete case of perceptual variation with respect to color, consider Figure 2.1 (an achromatic example) and Figure 2.2 (a chromatic example).[1]

FIG. 2.1. The two center gray squares have equal reflectances, but the one against the lighter background appears darker than the one against the darker background.

In Figure 2.1, the two central gray squares are intrinsically (hence non-relationally) qualitatively identical, so let us pretend that we have a single gray square, placed against two different backgrounds (this pretense is innocuous: the effect can be reproduced with a single gray square against two backgrounds, as you can convince yourself with the aid of scissors and glue). But most people report that the central gray square looks different in respect of color depending on the background against which it is placed — in particular, they report that the central square looks darker when placed against a light background (as in the right half of Figure 2.1) than when placed against a dark background (as in the left half of Figure 2.1). We have, then, a variation in perceptual effects (in respect of color) of a single object (the gray square).

Similarly, in Figure 2.2, the two central strips are intrinsically (hence non-relationally) qualitatively identical, so we can pretend that there is just one strip, placed against two backgrounds. The strip looks noticeably different in respect

[1] Readers of achromatic copies are encouraged to consult Hurvich (1981, chapter 13) and Albers (1963, chapter VI) for chromatic examples. (Among the most compelling examples in Albers (1963) are Studies VI-2.1, VI-3.1, VI-3.2, and VI-4.2.) In any case, the argument is not limited to achromatic examples, even if your copy of this chapter is.

FIG. 2.2. The two center strips are qualitatively identical, but there is an obvious difference in their color appearance. (See color plates.)

of color depending on the background against which it is placed. Once again, there is a variation in perceptual effects (in respect of color) of a single object (the central strip). Of course, this is not yet a very wide amount of variation — so far I have provided only two different variants. But I can generate more variants easily, as in Figure 2.3. (The set of perceptual variants can be expanded

FIG. 2.3. The center gray patches have equal reflectances, but they have different perceptual effects depending on the background against which they are placed.

even more widely by the same method; I'll stop here, as I take it the general point is clear enough by now.)

In each case of variation considered, there is variation in the way that the stimulus looks (in respect of color) to a single subject. On a more or less standard view of the visual system as visually representing the world, this entails that, in each case, there is a set of variant representations of the color of the stimulus.[2] Now consider the following question: can we select one amongst these perceptual variants that should be regarded as veridically representing the color of the object (where this would mean that the other variants are representing the object's color erroneously)? Consider Figure 2.3 once again; the identical gray central patch has a variety of perceptual effects, depending on the background against which it is placed. Suppose, for *reductio*, that color is a non-relational property. If so, then the central gray patch has a single color, irrespective of the background against which it is placed. It follows that at most one of the perceptual effects can veridically represent the color of the patch. But which one, and why? Notice that the question here is intended metaphysically, rather than epistemically: it is not 'how do ordinary perceivers know which of the varying perceptual effects veridically represents the color of the patch?', but 'what makes it the case that one of the varying perceptual effects (as opposed to the others) veridically represents the color of the patch?'.

It is just this question, I suggest, to which it is difficult to imagine a well-motivated, principled, and non-question-begging answer. That is to say, it is hard to imagine what, other than stipulation, could make it the case that one of the backgrounds (to the exclusion of others) is such that when the stimulus is viewed against that one, it is visually represented as bearing the color that it has. Of course, we may be able to say a lot about each of the backgrounds — we can talk about their size and shape, the composition of the inks (/lights) that compose them, their ecological roles, and so on. But, precisely because we can adduce these sorts of facts about every one of the patches, it is unclear how these facts could add up to a reason for favoring one variant perceptual representation of the patch over others.

Of course, making this point requires more than simply registering my own inability to come up with an answer (which might, after all, be due to the inadequacies of my own imaginative capacities). Let me consider, therefore, a possible answer that has at least some promise, and suggest why it is unsatisfactory.

The initially promising answer I have in mind turns on the use of reduction tubes, which block out surrounding objects from the field of view, thereby eliminating simultaneous contrast effects. After all, a critic might suggest, if all of the surrounds have an equal claim to generating variants that veridically represent the stimulus, then perhaps the key is to view the central patch without any surround at all, and thereby sidestep the perceptual effects of different surrounds altogether. Moreover, we could then say that a perceptual variant obtained without the use of the reduction tube would count as veridical just in case it perceptually matched the perceptual effect of viewing the stimulus through a reduction tube.

[2] For dissent from the idea that visual perception represents the world in this way, see Smith (2002); Travis (2004).

Unfortunately, this move seems to have a number of untoward consequences which, I suggest, should prevent us from endorsing it.

First, it will follow that surfaces in the vast majority of ecologically valid settings will not look to the vast majority of ecologically valid observers to have the colors they in fact have, in so far as contrast effects are ubiquitous in ordinary color perception.

Second (as a limiting case of the first problem), a specification relying on the use of reduction tubes will have the consequence that nothing will ever have any of the contrast colors. Contrast colors are colors whose appearance depends essentially on contrast effects — colors that cannot appear in the absence of contrast. Contrast colors include many we encounter everyday (outside the psychophysics laboratory), such as brown, olive, pure white, and pure black. That these colors disappear when contrast is eliminated is a striking fact: subjects are often surprised that brown objects, when viewed through a reduction tube, appear either orange or yellow (Hardin, 1988, 70). Similarly, the black hat of the villain depicted on the screen appears much darker when the television is on than does the very same region of screen after the television has been turned off, even though the relevant local region of the screen is illuminated in the same way whether the television is on or off. Thus, if we insist that the true colors of objects are revealed only in viewing situations where contrast effects are precluded by the use of reduction tubes, we are forced to the counterintuitive consequence that nothing is brown, olive, pure black, or pure white.

Third, we should notice that, far from eliminating perceptual variation, the appeal to reduction tubes introduces further dimensions of perceptual variation, this time due to the variety of possible reduction tubes: the way a given patch looks in respect of color will vary substantially as a function of the materials and surface characteristics of the interior of the reduction tube through which it is viewed.[3]

All this is to say we have made no progress on the problem of delimiting the range of perceptual variation; as shown by its counterintuitive consequences, the current proposal of eschewing backgrounds altogether, just as much as the choice of any particular background, amounts to an *ad hoc* stipulation. But if so, then the present response to the argument from perceptual variation does not (contrary to its advertised aims) offer us a way to avoid both perceptual variation and stipulation, and therefore is ineffective as a response to the argument from perceptual variation.

Suppose it is right, then, that there is no principled criterion for favoring any one variant over the others — that is, suppose that any reason for favoring a particular variant would have to be stipulative. In this situation, I suggest, it is preferable to avoid such unmotivated stipulations altogether by achieving an ecumenical reconciliation (if possible). This is not because stipulation is

[3] I am not aware of any systematic psychophysical investigations of these effects.

never justifiable; rather, and much more cautiously, it is because we should avoid stipulation unless we are forced to it by independent and unavoidable pressures, *a fortiori*, that we should avoid it when there are available non-stipulative alternatives.

But, on reflection, we should notice that there *is* a live non-stipulative alternative to the need to single out a particular variant at the expense of the other. In particular, we can achieve the needed reconciliation by giving up the initial supposition that colors are non-relational in favor of the view that colors are relational. In the present case, this would mean accepting that colors are constituted in terms of a relation to background configurations (or, more generally, to objects seen simultaneously). For if colors were so constituted, we could easily accommodate the observed range of perceptual variation: we could say that the central patch in Figure 2.1 exemplifies one color when placed against the light background on the left half of the figure, and a different color when placed against the dark background on the right half of the figure (*mutatis mutandis* for Figures 2.2 and 2.3). Thus, at this final step of the argument we see that the relationalist can accept the observed perceptual variation without making *ad hoc* stipulations (while, as we saw, the anti-relationalist cannot). Accordingly, to the extent that *ad hoc* stipulation should be avoided when possible, we should favor relationalism.

2.2 The Master Argument Form

As I have said, it seems to me an important fact about the argument from perceptual variation that it applies uniformly to so many different sorts of variation. Now that we have seen one particular instance of the argument at work in §2.1, we are in a position to characterize the argument in a general way — as an argument form with multiple instances.

This form, as I will understand it, consists of the following steps.

(1) There are multiple, psychophysically distinguishable, perceptual effects (in respect of color) of a single color stimulus.

(2) There is no independent and well-motivated reason for thinking that just one of the variants catalogued at step 1 is veridical (at the expense of the others).

(3) Given that there is no well-motivated reason for singling out any single variant as veridical (at the expense of the others), an ecumenical reconciliation of the variants is preferable to an unmotivated stipulation in favor of just one of them.

(4) The best way to implement such an ecumenical reconciliation between apparently incompatible variants is to view them as the result of relativizing colors to different values of certain parameters, which is just to admit that colors are relations between objects and those parameters.

Before generalizing the argument from perceptual variation, I want to say something about the kind of justification appropriate to each step, the vulnerabilities to which each is subject, and the strategies with which I hope to answer those vulnerabilities.

Premise (1) is straightforwardly empirical, and can be established by pointing to relevant psychophysical results. The main threat to the instances of (1) is that they, like all empirical claims, are always subject to reassessment in the light of further findings. Although such objections concerning the empirical adequacy of instances of (1) should be evaluated on a case by case basis by the standards of contemporary psychophysics, this sort of evaluation is beyond the scope of the present work. That said, I think it is fair to say that the results I'll be appealing to in making my case are more or less settled in the relevant scientific circles, so I'm well within my rights in making these appeals. In any case, our best defense against these worries in the mean time is to appeal to a wide variety of results drawn from the best current science.

I regard premise (2) as broadly empirical as well, but as one that requires a more complicated, inductive defense. Generally, my strategy will not be to argue that there is any inconsistency in the thought that one perceptual variant is veridical at the expense of the others; I'll claim only that it's hard to see what (besides *ad hoc* stipulation) could make this the case. The most important way of making this claim seem persuasive is to consider, in each instance, initially promising ways of settling on a single variant to the exclusion of others, and argue that these (and foreseeable alternatives) are unsuccessful. I've examined some of these instance-specific proposals in the context of a specific instance of the argument in §2.1, and shall continue to do the same in other instances in §2.3. However, in addition to these local objections to (2), there are a number of more general considerations that might be put forward as reasons for thinking that there is a single veridical variant in cases of perceptual variation; I'll address these considerations in §3.1.

We can arrive at (3) as the result of an inference from (2) that depends on two ideas. The first, which was mentioned briefly in Chapter 1 and which I shall defend in greater detail in §3.2, is that we should favor a realist over an irrealist account of color if that is possible. The second is a general principle of non-deductive reasoning to the effect that we should take measures to avoid *ad hoc* stipulation when possible — a principle I take to be well-advised, despite its not conferring demonstrative force. I must admit that this principle (like other principles of non-deductive inference) is ill-understood and certainly defeasible. Alas, I have nothing to add in its defence. Despite that, I think we are well-advised in using the principle in particular cases (bearing its defeasibilty in mind) unless someone can show us why we should not in those cases; in any case, this is how I shall proceed.

Finally, we can endorse (4) on the basis of the commitment to ecumenicism represented by (3) if we can show that relationalism provides us with a form of ecumenicism that is more attractive than its alternatives. There are two significant types of objections to this inference from ecumenicism to relationalism. The first is that the inference could be blocked by defending alternative, non-relationalist, forms of ecumenicism. A number of philosophers have put forward views that can be understood as favoring this sort of a response; e.g., McGinn (1996); Byrne and Hilbert (2003, 16–17, 56–57). I'll argue against this type of objection in §3.3 by critically examining the envisaged non-relationalist forms of ecumenicism and finding them unmotivated or otherwise unattractive. The other, much broader type of objection to (4) that I'll consider alleges that relationalism carries unacceptable costs. My general strategy regarding this final type of objection will be to develop a version of relationalism over the next several chapters whose costs are less than they might appear, and, in any case, worth paying.

This completes my general overview of the argument from perceptual variation. With this overview in hand, we are now in a position to appreciate the force of the argument's instances.

2.3 The Argument Generalized

In §2.1 I gave one concrete instance of the argument from perceptual variation (that concerning simultaneous color contrast). And in §2.2 I presented the general form of the argument. At this point I want to extend the argument form to a number of independent factors. In each case, I shall argue that there is a wide and ineliminable range of perceptual variation (with respect to color) as we modify the factor in question, and (relying on the pre-theoretical grasp of the relational/non-relational distinction discussed in Chapter 1) therefore that the color of x is a relation between (*inter alia*) x and that factor.

I regard the shared form of the multiple instances of the argument form as mutually reinforcing: seeing that the similar situation arises across a range of different kinds of variation should lead us to favor a pattern of response to each that can be applied to the rest. It is, to my mind, a significant advantage of relationalism that it lends itself to such a general treatment.

I'll organize the factors of variation that I consider under three headings: inter-species differences (§2.3.1), interpersonal differences (§2.3.2), and intrapersonal differences (§2.3.3).

2.3.1 *Inter-species Differences*

Pigeon visual systems are tetrachromatic — they use four (functionally individuated) channels to encode color information, and therefore an arbitrary color can be perceptually matched for a pigeon by a linear combination of four appropriately chosen primaries.[4] In contrast, normal human visual systems are trichromatic — they use three (functionally individuated) channels to encode color information, and therefore an arbitrary color can be perceptually

[4] There is some dispute about whether pigeons have tetrachromatic or pentachromatic visual systems (Thompson, 1995, 145–146), but all that will matter for the purposes to which I'll be putting pigeons is that the dimensionality and receptoral structure of their visual system is different from those of typical human beings. This claim is uncontroversial whether pigeons turn out to be tetrachromats or pentachromats.

matched for a human being by a linear combination of three appropriately chosen primaries. Because of this difference, there are pairs of surfaces that are perceptual matches for human visual systems but not for pigeon visual systems. This entails that there is a difference between the way at least one surface of the pair (call it 'surface *S*') looks to pigeon visual systems and the way it looks to human visual systems. Thus, we have established an instance of premise (1).

In the face of this instance of perceptual variation, our next question is the following: which of the perceptual variants under consideration veridically represents the color surface *S*? The four choices in logical space are these: (i) confine our attention to human visual systems, declaring that how things look to pigeon (and other) visual systems is irrelevant to the colors of objects; (ii) defer to the pigeons, holding that the way things look to them determines the true colors of objects; (iii) declare that neither we nor the pigeons are the true arbiters of color, and instead select a different standard; (iv) adopt the ecumenical policy that both sorts of visual systems are right, and that one and the same object can have more than one color property.[5] Considered by itself, option (i) seems objectionably chauvinistic, while, considered by themselves, (ii) and (iii) seem unduly modest. This is not to say that the chauvinism following upon (i) or the modesty following upon (ii) or (iii) is incoherent, but only that these choices are revisionist with respect to quite a lot of ordinary and scientific talk about color (for example, just the sorts of apparently coherent questions about what colors pigeons see I'm asking here).

Part of the reason that options (i), (ii), and (iii) seem revisionary is that, although we may be able to say a lot about the workings of pigeon and human visual systems, it is unclear how these facts could add up to a reason for favoring one variant perceptual representation of surface *S* over others. After all, there is a lot to say about the workings of *both* the visual systems resulting in variants between which we are trying to choose, so the situation remains symmetric with respect to the variants even after pointing to these sorts of facts.

One response would be to insist that, if forced to choose between (i)–(iv), we should be inclined toward the chauvinist alternative (i) on the grounds that it gives pride of place to the visual systems and properties we care about most. Hilbert gives expression to this motivation in writing that,

> discussions of color ontology, as well as a large part of color science, are, after all, primarily concerned with a property that human beings perceive, reflect on, and talk about. If it turns out that this property is not perceived by some other kinds of organisms that is neither surprising nor a challenge to the adequacy of our accounts of this property of particularly human interest (Hilbert (1992*a*, 39); Hilbert (cf. 1992*b*)).[6]

[5] Because option (iv), as stated, combines commitments that are in principle detachable, this list of options leaves room for the following further possibility: (v) adopt the ecumenical policy that both sorts of visual systems are veridical even though objects have only one color property (in one place at one time). I'll consider (and argue against) one way of fleshing out this possibility in §3.3.3.

[6] I quote Hilbert here because he puts clearly a consideration that might be used to motivate response (i). However, Hilbert does not himself endorse (i); instead, he favors a non-relationalist version of response (iv) discussed in §3.3.2.

But this answer comes with serious costs. For one thing, *pace* Hilbert, much of color ontology and color science are primarily directed toward the properties that organisms *other* than human beings perceive.[7] Accepting chauvinism, therefore, has the revisionary result that much of what has passed for color ontology and color science (and, for that matter, our more casual talk about color) is not about color after all. This choice would not only revise our taxonomy of fields of inquiry, but also the impression presumably underlying that taxonomy that the properties perceived by pigeons and other non-human organisms are, even if not the very same properties we perceive, at least properties of the same kind — in a word, that they are *colors*.

Moreover, it must be said that the appeal to our own interests and preferences that underlies the present defense of chauvinism falls short of what we normally require of principled justifications. Pointing to our parochial interests does not, it seems to me, so much *justify* our siding with (i) so much as restate that the variant validated by (i) is one that arises in our sort of visual system. This is, I suggest, not to advance on the problem of saying why that variant is veridical to the exclusion of others. For this reason, I think that accepting (i) — at least, for the reason now being considered — is not just revisionary, but stipulative (as opposed to principled) as well. Since I take it that there is even less hope of providing a principled justification for the sort of modesty of choices (ii) or (iii), I believe we have now said enough to establish an instance of premise (2).

Having said this much, it is a relatively short step to (3) — the conclusion that we should favor the ecumenical choice (iv) over the stipulative alternatives (i)–(iii). I suppose I agree that if we were forced to settle a zero-sum dispute between our own particular interests and those of the pigeons, the (human) theorist should stipulate in favor of our interests rather than pigeon interests, even if that means accepting some costs. But, crucially, we are *not* in the situation of having to settle a zero-sum dispute of this kind. For nothing has been said to rule out option (iv). If, as maintained before, we should avoid stipulative revisionism unless we are forced to it, then option (iv) provides just the alternative we have been seeking.

To complete this instance of the argument form, then, we need only to show how accepting relationalism provides us with a way of implementing the ecumenical option (iv). The relationalist conclusion suggested by the case under consideration is that colors are constituted in terms of relations to kinds of visual systems (where the latter are typed as finely as the species in which they occur). The thought here is that if x looks green to a visual system of kind

[7] To be fair, much of the philosophical work that I have in mind (e.g., Matthen, 1999, 2005; Thompson, 1995; Thompson *et al.*, 1992) was published after or just before the Hilbert (1992*b*) paper from which I'm quoting. On the other hand, there is an immense scientific literature on comparative color vision that predates Hilbert's remarks.

K, x *is* green for a visual system of kind K.[8] Thus, we can accept the observed range of interspecies variation without need for revisionary stipulation: we can hold that one and the same object can be simultaneously green for your visual system and not green for the visual system of the pigeon on your window ledge.

2.3.2 *Interpersonal (Between-Subject) Differences*

In section 2.3.1 I applied the argument from perceptual variation to differences in color perception between members of different species (across visual system types). Now I want to apply the argument form to variations between members of a single species (who share a visual system type); in particular, I shall focus attention on perceptual variation between human beings.

First, there are among human beings non-negligible number of anomalous trichromats, dichromats (both protanopes and deuteranopes), and (much more rarely) monochromats, achromatopes, and (possibly) some tetrachromats.[9] Moreover, even within each of these functional classes, there are significant differences in the numbers of each type of receptor, in their peak sensitivities, and in the ratios of these types of receptors.[10]

In addition to these differences in the organization of receptors in members of our species, there are interpersonal differences (even among non-anomalous trichromats) in the filtering yellow pigment of the macula and the lens of the eye (Hurvich (1981, 113–116); see also the striking photographic evidence of this phenomenon in Werner (1998, 7) and in cone absorption spectra (Boynton, 1979, 384). As noted by Clark (1993, 164–170) and Hurvich (1981, 222–223), these sources of variation result in a non-trivial distribution of the loci for unique green between 490 and 520nm even among non-anomalous trichromats.[11]

[8] For the record, accepting this material conditional does not require identifying the properties *looks green to S* and *is green for S*. Compare: it is true that if x is a sister, then x is female, but it does not follow that the properties *being a sister* and *being female* are identical.

[9] Anomalous trichromats have trichromatic visual systems, but the spectral sensitivity of one of their three channels is shifted relative to normal subjects. Dichromatic visual systems encode color information only along two independent channels: human dichromats who lack functioning L-cones are called protanopes, while those who have no functioning M-cones are called deuteranopes. The remaining sort of dichromacy, in which S-cones do not function, is known as tritanopia, and is much rarer than both protanopia and deuteranopia. Monochromats encode color information only in one channel, and are responsive only to differences in brightness/lightness (not hue or saturation). Achromatopes are those who, due to damage to the visual cortex, are unable to make color discriminations at all.

See Sacks (1996) for one attempt to explicate for normal trichromats what the visual world is like for achromatopes. On this subject also see Byrne and Hilbert (2009); Broackes (2009).

[10] These results have been confirmed by several lines of converging research, including psychophysical methods (Rushton and Baker, 1964; Pokorny *et al.*, 1991; Cicerone and Nerger, 1989; Vimal *et al.*, 1989), spectral electro-retinograms (Jacobs and Neitz, 1993; Jacobs and Deegan, 1997), microspectophotometry (Bowmaker and Dartnall, 1980; Dartnall *et al.*, 1983), messenger RNA analysis (Yamaguchi *et al.*, 1998; Hagstrom *et al.*, 1998), and retinal densitometry (Roorda and Williams, 1999).

[11] So-called unique colors are are those that appear perceptually uncomposed. There are four such colors: unique green is that shade of green that appears neither bluish nor yellowish; unique

Finally, there are various non-receptoral abnormalities of color vision due primarily to damage to areas of the visual cortex, known collectively as central achromatopsia.

Once again, these differences result in a range of perceptual variants, this time between the effects produced by a single objectively specified stimulus in different human visual systems. For example, it can happen that subject S_1's visual system represents a spectral light of 505nm as being greenish without being bluish or yellowish, while subject S_2's visual system represents the very same spectral light as being greenish and also bluish. This completes the current instance of premise (1) of the argument from perceptual variation.

Now, to proceed to premise (2) we must ask which of these conflicting representations of the color of the spectral light is veridical. As before, there are four possible choices: (i) we can declare that S_1 is correct and S_2 is incorrect; (ii) we can side with S_2 to the detriment of S_1; (iii) we can insist that neither S_1 nor S_2 veridically represents the color of the light; or (iv) we can admit that both visual systems are veridical. And, as in earlier instances of the master argument, I suggest that (i), (ii), and (iii) are all unmotivated and stipulative, and therefore advocate the ecumenical choice (iv).

Now, there is in the literature a standard response to these considerations — a response that attempts to give a principled motivation for favoring one of (i), (ii), or (iii). This response, which is advocated in some form by Locke, Peacocke (1984, 60), Wright (1992, 136–137), and Harman (1996), holds that (the visual system of) a subject S that represents the color of x does so veridically just in case S's representation of the color of x matches with the representation of x's color by a standard observer of S's kind. Supposing that S_1 and S_2 are members of a common species (in the case at hand, they are both human beings), it is not unreasonable to hold that the relevant kind is that common species. On this view, then, we should choose among (i)–(iv) by asking whether one, the other, both, or neither, of S_1's and S_2's representations of the spectral light match that of the standard observer for human beings.

red is that shade of red that appears neither bluish nor yellowish; unique blue is that shade of blue that appears neither reddish nor greenish; and unique yellow is that shade of yellow that appears neither reddish nor greenish). All colors that are not unique in this sense (e.g., all shades of green other than unique green, all shades of orange) are labeled binary: they appear perceptually composed from a linear combination of unique hues.

Alternatively, we can think about the unique/binary distinction as applying (not, or not in the first instance, to colors, but) to color experiences. Put this way, the claim would be that there is a phenomenal distinction between those color experiences that are phenomenally composed (e.g., most experiences of green, all experiences of orange) and those color experiences that are phenomenally uncomposed (e.g., certain experiences of green, red, blue, and yellow).

On either construal, we can define the spectral locus of unique green for a given observer as that spectral frequency at which monochromatic light appears unique green — i.e., appears neither bluish nor greenish to that observer.

There is a non-trivial distribution for loci of all of the unique hues (unique green, unique red, unique blue, and unique yellow) although the standard deviation of the distribution is largest for unique green.

(We'll have occasion to return to the unique/binary distinction in later chapters.)

Of course, the strategy at hand will succeed only if there is a non-stipulative specification of what counts as a standard observer for human beings (if it is to be applied more generally, this strategy presupposes the possibility of a non-stipulative specification of what counts as a standard observer for an arbitrary species). One reason for optimism on this front comes from the intuition that certain observers in our own species are *deficient* (and not merely *alternative*) judges of color: for example, the U.S. Navy's refusal to accept even anomalous trichromats with perfect visual acuity as naval pilots presumably reflects an intuition that anomalous trichromats are seeing colors incorrectly, rather than just differently.[12] Of course, these intuitions, by themselves, cannot give us a full specification of what counts as a normal perceiver. However, there are at least two ways in which one might hope to elaborate these intuitions into a more complete specification.

First, one might hold that such standards are set by numerical majority: that an observer counts as a standard observer if his visual system is sufficiently like (in the right respects) the visual systems of a majority (or a weighted majority, or whatever) of members of the species. This proposal has the defect that it pushes back, rather than resolves, the problem of specifying a standard: now we owe a non-stipulative specification of the relevant dimensions for comparing visual systems, as well as a non-stipulative specification of the threshold for judging that two visual systems are sufficiently alike. Moreover, even putting these problems aside, a number of writers have noted that adverting to the larger sub-population leaves open the possibility that the standards could change because of mass micro-surgery or selective breeding.[13] But if the veridicality of a perceptual variant turns on its matching against the perception of a standard observer, this would mean that a perceptual variant that erroneously represented the color of x at t_1 could come to represent the color of x veridically at t_2 in the absence of any intrinsic change in x — a result that would surely be unacceptable to those who take colors to be non-relational properties.

A second way in which one might hope to elaborate intuitions about standard observers might appeal to some of the more elaborate specifications of standard perceivers designed for particular scientific and industrial purposes. The best established and most frequently used candidate specification of this sort is the CIE 1931 Standard Observer (cf. Wyszecki and Stiles, 1967), constructed by the CIE for the purpose of standardizing descriptions of the

[12] This intuition seems to have been shared by the officer at the Brooklyn Navy recruiting office who took my call; as she put it, "Honey, if you're color blind, it just ain't happening."

[13] The by-now standard case, which I believe originates in Bennett (1968, 105–107), involves phenol, which apparently tastes bitter to about seventy percent of the population and is tasteless to about thirty percent of the population. Is phenol bitter or not? As Bennett points out, if one answers that phenol is bitter on the grounds that it tastes bitter to a larger sub-population, then we could change the properties of phenol — we could make it go from being bitter to not being bitter — by mass micro-surgery or selective breeding. (Cf. Bennett (1971, chapter IV); McGinn (1983, 9–10); Jackson and Pargetter (1987, 71–72).)

color-matching properties of lights.[14] The CIE 1931 Standard Observer is in fact a set of triples (tristimulus values) corresponding to a range of spectral lights; each triple specifies coefficients for three selected primaries such that the resulting linear combination will perceptually match the corresponding spectral light for a so-called average observer. The average observer in question is, as it happens, a construction formed by averaging the results of actual observers from two different experiments.[15]

Unfortunately, there are reasons for doubting that the CIE 1931 Standard Observer will serve the purposes at hand. First, as noted by Hardin (1988, 76–82), the CIE 1931 Standard Observer, like other scientific and industrial specifications that have been articulated, is a statistical construct drawn from a range of actual individuals, but that differ significantly from most (perhaps as many as 90% of) human visual systems (Evans, 1948, 196–197); therefore, fixing the colors by appeal to such standards would commit one to the unpalatable conclusion that the color discriminations of most (perhaps as many as 90% of) human visual systems are erroneous. Second, specifications like the CIE 1931 Standard Observer are stipulatively chosen for particular purposes (mathematical convenience, industrial standardization). While this makes those standards entirely appropriate for use in the context of those purposes, it means that they are stipulative — they are explicitly stipulated to serve (mathematical, industrial) purposes. Which is to say that appeals to these standards cannot be, as we had hoped, non-stipulative ways of deciding between a range of perceptual variants. This lesson is reinforced by the plurality of standards itself (for example, we have seen that even for the restricted purposes of colorimetric matching, the CIE recommends different standards for stimuli under 4 degrees and stimuli over 4 degrees of visual angle). Each standard is clearly appropriate to the particular purposes for which it was designed, but clearly inappropriate for use in a range of other purposes one might have (including purposes for which users felt the need to invent distinct standards), and therefore not plausible as the fully general understanding of normality that one would need to respond to the argument from perceptual variation.

For these reasons, it would seem that the usual specifications of standard observers for species will not provide a non-stipulative response to the argu-

[14] The CIE (Commission International de l'Eclairage) is an international organization responsible for recommending standards and procedures for light and lighting.

[15] The CIE 1931 Standard Observer is used for purposes involving stimuli small enough that they fall within the fovea (roughly 2 degrees of visual angle). The data underlying this specification come from independent investigations by Guild and Wright; the CIE 1931 Standard Observer was calculated from these data by first transforming the two sets of results into a common coordinate system and then averaging the transformed values.

Investigators have found that the CIE 1931 Standard Observer is inadequate for many experiments involving larger stimuli; for this reason, the CIE recommends the use of another standard — the CIE 1964 Standard Observer — based on work of Stiles, Burch, and Speranskaya, for stimuli of more than about 4 degrees of visual angle.

See MacAdam (1997) for details concerning these standards.

ment from perceptual variation. Moreover, since these are our best motivated standards, it's extremely doubtful that some other specification will serve us better in this context; appeals to less motivated standards are *ipso facto* more stipulative, and therefore less persuasive as responses to the argument from perceptual variation. Consequently, there seem to be good reasons for endorsing the current instance of premise (2) of the argument from perceptual variation.

Moreover, and once again, we can rely on general canons of non-deductive reasoning to take us from (2) to (3). Namely, it is reasonable to think that, in the absence of a non-stipulative criterion that makes one of the variants under consideration veridical at the expense of the others, it is preferable to treat the variants uniformly. But given that a uniform rejection of all variants seems unduly skeptical (and given that we are taking color irrealism to be a position of last resort), there is good reason for preferring the ecumenical option (iv) that accepts the veridicality of all variants.

Finally, we can move from (3) to (4) by showing how relationalism makes good on ecumenicist aspirations. It does so by allowing that, if an object x looks green to a subject S, then x is green for S. Accepting this principle allows that a single stimulus can, at one and the same time, be green for a first subject S_1 and fail to be green for a second subject S_2. As before, there is no need to choose which one of these subjects represents the stimulus veridically; on the contrary, we can admit that both do.

2.3.3 *Intrapersonal (Within-Subject) Differences*

I've applied the argument from perceptual variation to cases of variation between members of different species (§2.3.1) and between members of a given species (§2.3.2); in this section I want to apply the same argument to cases of perceptual variation (with respect to color) within subjects.

That there is such intrapersonal perceptual variation will be familiar to anyone who has ever put on or removed tinted sunglasses, adjusted the lighting in a room, or been surprised by changes in the appearance of garments once removed from the flattering viewing conditions of the store. In all these cases, there is a range of perceptual variants, this time between the effects produced by a single objectively specified stimulus in a single human visual system, across variations in the viewing conditions. For example, my visual system represents a certain garment one way under the viewing conditions C_1 inside the store, and another way under the viewing conditions C_2 outside the store. Here again, we have an instance of premise (1) of the argument from perceptual variation.

As usual, we can now ask how to choose between the variants. Which of my conflicting representations of the color of the garment, for example, is veridical? And why? Just as in earlier instances of perceptual variation, there are four possible choices: (i) we can declare that the representation in C_1 is correct and that that in C_2 is incorrect; (ii) we can side with the representation in C_2 to the detriment of the representation in C_1; (iii) we can insist that neither the representation in C_1 nor that in C_2 veridically represents the color of the garment; or (iv) we can admit that both of the representations (that in C_1 and that in C_2) are veridical. And, just as in earlier cases, I suggest that (i), (ii), and (iii) are all unmotivated and stipulative, and therefore advocate choice (iv).

But, as in the instance of perceptual variation concerning between-subject (within-species) variations, there persists an intuition that we might give a motivated, non-stipulative reason for favoring one of options (i)–(iii). For it seems plausible that some viewing conditions are just not conducive to the veridical perception of colors. This is why, for example, we chide (rather than simply disagree with) the museum-goer who neglects to remove his sunglasses; similarly, we would be foolish (and not just eccentric) to choose a tie to match a suit without first turning on the lights. Once again, such intuitions suggest that we might attempt to specify some set of canonical or standard conditions for perceiving colors, and then choose between (i)–(iv) by asking whether one, the other, both, or neither, of the representations of the color of the garment in C_1 and C_2 matches the representation of the color of the garment in standard conditions.

But once again, it is doubtful that there is the kind of non-stipulative specification of standard conditions for color perception that this strategy demands. It is true that, as in the case of standard observers, there are scientific and industrial recipes for standard conditions (see American Society for Testing and Materials, 1968; Judd and Wyszecki, 1963; Kelly and Judd, 1976; Wyszecki and Stiles, 1967); but, once again, these are ill-suited to our purposes.

To see why, consider one of these recipes — one whose notion of standard conditions comes from the instructions for the use of Munsell color chips.[16] The instructions state that "the samples should be placed against a dark achromatic background and 'colors should be arranged under North Daylight or scientific daylight having a color temperature of from 6500 degrees to 7500 degrees Kelvin. Colors should be illuminated at 90 degrees and viewed at 45 degrees, or the exact opposite of these conditions' " (Hardin, 1988, 68).

While these conditions are adequate for standard uses of the Munsell chips, they cannot be taken as a specification for standard conditions more generally speaking. For one thing, the instructions ignore many factors variation in which generates further instances of perceptual variation: for example, they say nothing about the state of adaptation of the subject, other objects perceived by the observer prior to or after observation of the stimulus, or the relative proportions of the visual field occupied by the stimulus. Second, the instructions also provide no guidance at all about how to choose between variants in other sorts of conditions under which we are inclined to say that veridical color perception occurs (e.g., conditions where the background is not dark and achromatic, or where perceptual grouping effects influence the perceptual representation

[16] The Munsell color system is a widely used set of color samples (chips); these samples are used as standards in terms of which the colors of test samples can be described (see Munsell, 1946; Munsell Color Company, 1976).

of the color of the stimulus. This last point is especially significant because there are many objects — including paradigm colors-bearers — whose colors cannot be perceived in Munsell-specific conditions, such as stars, neon tubes, and rainbows.[17] Further, the Munsell-inspired conditions are not amenable to perceiving the colors of directionally reflective materials, materials whose color is dependent on use, or translucent materials: these conditions could assign only one of what seem to be equally plausible candidates for the color of directionally reflective materials, and could not assign any well-defined color to materials whose color is dependent on use or to translucent materials. Of course, we could answer some or all of these complaints by clinging to the specification from the Munsell instructions if we are willing to declare that the problematic phenomena are all color-illusions; however such declarations will seem disturbingly *ad hoc*.

One reaction to the difficulties just considered is the thought that, given the range of different situations in which we want to attribute colors to objects (veridically), an adequate understanding of normal conditions will have to be disjunctive. On this view, we could divide objects into different types, and then specify standard conditions for each type — one set of conditions for opaque surface colors, another for volume colors, a third for film colors, a fourth for self-luminous colors, and so on. Of course, our assessment of this proposal will depend on the details in terms of which it is carried out, including, in part, our view about how well-motivated are the types it recognizes. However, if its types look anything like the usual candidates in terms of which color science is now carried out (e.g., surface color, volume color), the proposal will be only as good as its criteria for settling on a single variant in instances of perceptual variation with respect to surface colors and the like — which is to say that it is not very good at all. Moreover, the disjunctive proposal now under consideration would face the question why the types it recognizes count as a species of a common genus; but it is hard to see what answer is available to the disjunctivist.

[17] Perhaps this limitation is one of practice rather than principle in certain cases, but arguably it is necessarily insuperable in others, such as that of the rainbow.

It is not obvious that rainbows have any definite location; if not, then the proposal at hand is necessarily inapplicable to rainbows. Suppose, therefore, and not unreasonably, that a rainbow has the location of the water drops refraction through which is responsible for its appearance. When light strikes the water/air interface at the front of a drop, it is dispersed by wavelengths — longer wavelengths are bent less than shorter wavelengths. If the angle between the refracted light and the normal to the drop surface is greater than a critical angle (48° for water), the light is then reflected off the back of the drop, and refracted/dispersed again when it passes through the front of the drop, at which point it can go on to strike local visual systems. The total angle from the incoming light path to the eye (with the back of the drop at the apex) is 40° at the violet end and 42° at the red end of the rainbow (cf. Descartes' classic account in the *Meteorology*, Discourse 8, and, for a more modern treatment, Humphreys (1964, 476–500).) Consequently, on the present supposition about the location of rainbows, no rainbow can be viewed at an angle of 45 degrees or an angle of 90 degrees. Moreover, since this restriction on viewing angles appears to be necessary, appealing to counterfactuals about how things *would* have looked in standard conditions won't resolve this difficulty.

Other proposals for selecting amongst variants fail even more obviously. Should we select the variant corresponding to the condition in which maximum visual resolution occurs? That is potentially relevant to a favored choice along some relevant dimensions of variation (illumination, viewing angle, visual field size) but not others (background, illumination, perceptual grouping); and in any case, variation in size of the receptive fields of retinal neural units suggests strongly that, even for relevant dimensions, there is no single point of maximum resolution (Hardin, 1988, 71). Likewise, while we may have greater visual resolution in daylight than at night, this leaves a large range of intrapersonal perceptual variation as a function of changes in illumination; and this remains so even if we restrict ourselves to the CIE standard illuminants (ostensibly the best candidates for a principled choice of standard conditions of illumination).[18]

Given these considerations, it seems that the standardized specifications of standard conditions designed for use in particular laboratory or industrial purposes will not provide a non-stipulative response to the argument from perceptual variation. And once again, since such scientific and industrial standards are our best motivated candidates, it seems unreasonably optimistic to think that a more successful specification of standard conditions is in the offing. Consequently, it seems unreasonably optimistic to think that an appeal to standard conditions can provide principled reasons for singling out one intrapersonal variant at the expense of others.

Given the failure of the appeal to standard conditions, it would seem that we are justified in accepting the present, intrapersonal instance of premise (2) in the argument from perceptual variation. And, given (2), we can once again arrive at the relevant instance of (3) by appealing to the general principle that, given the choice, ecumenicism is preferable to unmotivated stipulation.

The relationalist response to the intrapersonal instances of perceptual variation mirrors the relationalist response to the other instances we have already encountered. Namely, the relationalist suggests, we should accept that if x looks green to a subject S in a circumstance C, then x is green for S in C. Once again, this permits us to accept the full range of observed perceptual variation without having to make unmotivated choices between the variants: we can say that one and the same stimulus is green to S in a first condition C_1 and nonetheless not green to S in a second condition C_2 In so far as relationalism provides a consistent way of accepting the ecumenicism that, I have argued, we have reason to accept, this gives us reason to endorse the intrapersonal instance of (4).

[18] The CIE has specified several standard illuminants for laboratory and industrial use in terms of their relative spectral power distributions. The most important of these are standard illuminant A, standard illuminant B, standard illuminant C, and standard illuminant D_{65}.

2.4 Applications

So far in this chapter I have argued from considerations about perceptual variation to the conclusion that we should accept a relational understanding of colors. As it happens, there exist several puzzles about color in the philosophical literature that turn on perceptual variation phenomena. Perhaps it is unsurprising, given the view's facility in dealing with perceptual variation, that relationalism provides an elegant and unified resolution of all these puzzles. In any case, I share Russell's view that theories should be adjudged (at least partly) on the basis of their capacity for dealing with puzzles (Russell, 1905, 206), and therefore take relationalism's success at dispatching the puzzles of this section as an important point in its favor.

2.4.1 *Averill's Trilemma, Hilbert's Puzzle*

First, relationalism offers a uniform and attractively simple solution to a pair of related puzzles pressed in Averill (1985) and Hilbert (1987). Averill and Hilbert both appeal to cases of perceptual variation, although they use them to motivate very different conclusions; what unites these two authors is that the puzzles they raise from such cases (and, therefore, the motivation for the conclusions they draw from the puzzles) dissolve immediately if relationalism is true.

2.4.1.1 *Averill's Trilemma* Averill's version of the puzzle builds from the observation that "objects that reflect very different combinations of wavelengths of light can appear to be the same color to normal human beings looking at these objects in sunlight" (Averill, 1985, 12). He then uses this fact to formulate a trilemma:

> ...suppose that the paints in two pots, A and B, appear to normal humans to be the same shade of yellow in sunlight; and suppose that the paint in pot A reflects only light from the red and green parts of the spectrum and the paint in pot B reflects only light from the yellow and blue parts of the spectrum (the large majority of which will be light from the yellow part of spectrum). A figure is painted on a canvas with paint from pot A, and the background is filled in with paint from pot B. The canvas now appears to be a uniform shade of yellow to normal human beings looking at it in sunlight. What is the color of this canvas? Clearly the following three statements are inconsistent:
>
> **(a)** The canvas is a uniform shade of yellow.
>
> **(b)** This uniform shade of yellow is one distinct color.
>
> **(c)** The figure on the canvas is different in color from its background.
>
> ...How should the trilemma be resolved? (Averill, 1985, 12–13)

It should be clear that this trilemma revolves around a case of perceptual variation: the appearance of figure and background vary independently when subjected to different illumination, such that figure and background are indistinguishable (in respect of color) under sunlight illumination I_1, but distinguishable (in respect of color) under a different illuminant I_2 (without loss of generality, we may suppose this different illuminant is comprised of "only light from the red and green parts of the spectrum," so that the pot A figure reflects some portion of the incident illumination but the pot B

ground does not). The appearance of the canvas under I_1, presumably, is what motivates premise (a), while the appearance of the canvas under I_2, presumably motivates premise (c). The putative inconsistency, of course, comes from the introduction of premise (b): if the uniform shade of yellow is "one distinct color," then it would seem that either that one distinct color is shared by figure and background, or that it is not. But saying that figure and ground are alike in color appears incompatible with premise (c), while saying that figure and ground are unlike in color appears incompatible with premise (a).

But the relationalist will insist that the appearance of inconsistency, and therefore the trilemma, depends on requiring a choice that we need not and should not make. In particular, she will point out, the difficulty disappears once we make explicit the relational nature of the color properties ascribed in (a)–(c). According to the relationalist, the indistiguishability of figure and background under illuminant I_1 justifies us in accepting (not premise (a), but)

(a′) The figure and background of the canvas are uniform in color (i.e., they share a color): they both exemplify *yellow for S in C_1*.

Likewise, the distinguishability of the figure and background under I_2 motivates (not premise (c), but)

(c′) The figure and background of the canvas are not uniform in color (they fail to share a color): the figure does, but the background does not, exemplify the color *yellow for S in C_2*.

And now, of course, premise (b) is unproblematically compatible with both (a′) and (c′) — it says, correctly, that 'this uniform shade of yellow' (namely, if the demonstrative is anaphoric on the earlier material, the color that (a′) ascribes) is one distinct color. Indeed, that color is one distinct color that the regions both exemplify, and both manifest, in C_1 (as per (a′)). It is also true that there is some other color that they fail to share and that only one of them manifests in C_2 (as per (c′)).

If, as the relationalist maintains, colors are constituted in terms of relations to (*inter alia*) viewing conditions, then this is just what we should expect: changing the viewing condition (by changing the illumination) changes the color that each region manifests, so that the two regions can manifest a shared color in one condition but not in another. The relationalist answer to the trilemma, then, is to say that its three premises are, once suitably marked with the needed and independently motivated relativizations (cf. §2.3), perfectly compatible.

In contrast, this strategy of response to the trilemma is not available to an anti-relationalist. This strategy requires holding that x and y can simultaneously share one color property (*yellow for S in C_1*) and fail to share another color property (*yellow for S in C_2*). But, so long as the intrinsic makeups of x and y are held constant between C_1 and C_2 (as required by Averill's case), an anti-relationalist will not be able to secure this result, since, for her, the question whether x and y share a color property is answered determinately by whether x and y have a particular intrinsic property. On the other hand, Averill (1985) argues persuasively against resolutions of the trilemma that deny either (a) or (c), and accounts involving a repudiation of (b) (such as Averill's own proposal) seem to require the counterintuitive claim that things can be the same shade but be different colors.

Thus, an anti-relationalist response to the trilemma requires denying at least one of (a), (b), and (c), where each of these denials has serious *prima facie* costs. In contrast, the relationalist can answer the trilemma while accepting all of its component claims, once these have been modified to reflect the relational nature of the colors. Accordingly, I prefer relationalism over anti-relationalism in so far as I prefer simple, independently motivated solutions over serious *prima facie* costs.[19]

2.4.1.2 *Hilbert's Puzzle* Hilbert (1987, chapter 5) uses a similar puzzle to argue for his anti-relationalist account of color and against a relational (dispositional) account.[20] Hilbert's version of the puzzle revolves around metamers — pairs of surfaces that have distinct surface spectral reflectance distributions, but that are perceptual matches for a given observer and a given viewing condition. Metamers have long been cited as an objection to the identification of colors with surface spectral reflectance distributions. Hilbert formulates the puzzle to respond to that objection, thereby defending the identification between colors and surface spectral reflectance distributions.

As Hilbert notes, members of a metameric pair that are perceptual matches (for an observer) under one illuminant I_1 must be perceptual mismatches (for that observer) under a different illuminant I_2. For the members of a metameric pair can be perceptual matches under all illuminants only if they have the very same spectral reflectance distribution (in which case they are called isomers); but isomers are identified in color by both Hilbert's theory and ordinary perception, so they are not challenges to the individuations made by the theory. Thus, he suggests, we are faced with a choice point: should we, or should we not, claim that the two surfaces are alike in color? We can insist (on the strength of their matching for some observer under I_1) that the metameric pair share a

[19] Averill (1992) uses the same sort of puzzle to motivate what he calls a "relational account of color." This account, which is related to my account of the same name, resolves these puzzles along the lines that I am proposing. That said, Averill's relationalism differs from mine in several respects; perhaps the most important of these is that Averill considers fewer sources of perceptual variation than I have discussed in §2.3, and consequently relativizes colors to far fewer parameters than I have argued is necessary. Second, Averill is much more confident than I am in the possibility of a non-stipulative account of 'normal observer' and 'optimal viewing conditions' (Averill, 1992, 557–558), hence in ruling out difficult cases (such as rainbows) as color illusions. And third, Averill gives no account of the relation between colors, construed as relational properties, and our ordinary, apparently unrelativized color attributions (as I shall in Chapter 4).

[20] It is worth noting that Hilbert's account is in fact relational along the single dimension of viewing distance: the surface spectral reflectance distributions he identifies with colors are relativized to viewing distance (Hilbert, 1987, chapter 2). Nonetheless, I count this view as an anti-relationalist account since it takes colors not to be constituted in terms of a relation to subjects. See Chapter 1.

color, or we can say (on the strength of their not matching for the same observer under I_2) that the two fail to share a color. Hilbert thinks everyone needs to make this choice, and points out that either choice involves attributing an error to the individuations made by ordinary perception: if the two share a color, then the appearance in I_2 that they do not is erroneous, but if the two fail to share a color, then the appearance in I_1 that they do is erroneous. Given this set of alternatives, Hilbert claims, it is preferable to attribute the error to the appearance in I_1: after all, if the appearance of difference in I_2 is an illusion, it is a case where an illusory apparent difference reveals an intrinsic difference between the surfaces — and that, claims Hilbert, sounds more like a veridical appearance than an illusion! Hence, for Hilbert, the case provides justification for the policy of making color distinctions between metameric surfaces, and thereby vindicates the identification of colors with surface spectral reflectances.

But, from the relationalist perspective, it seems that Hilbert's puzzle errs in just the place that Averill's trilemma goes wrong: both cases present a choice between two conflicting judgments (made in different circumstances) about whether a certain pair of surfaces share a color, and then forces us to choose between those judgments. As I have argued, this is a choice that we ought to refuse to make.[21] As in the case of Averill's trilemma, it is a mistake to choose between holding that the surfaces always share a color (because they are a perceptual match in I_1) and holding that they never share a color (because they are not a perceptual match in I_2). Instead, we should hold that both (i) the surfaces share a color in I_1 and (ii) the surfaces fail to share a color in I_2. In this way, we can respect *both* of the intuitions whose rejection strikes us as unpalatable. Once again, relationalism provides a simple and well-motivated alternative to a forced choice between unpalatable alternatives.[22]

[21] In fairness, I should note that Hilbert briefly considers the option of endorsing both judgments, as I am suggesting, but rejects it on the strength of an objection I'll consider in more detail in Chapter 4. Namely, he alleges that relationalism is unacceptably revisionary because it makes no room for erroneous color attributions:

> We commonly take colors to be relatively stable properties of objects. In particular, we take the color of an object to be independent of the illumination under which it is viewed. Colors in our common sense ontology are illumination-independent properties of objects. The stability of colors and in particular their illumination independence is reflected in the distinction between real and apparent colors. [On the option considered] there is no distinction between real and apparent colors. The apparent color at any given time is the real color of the object at that time (Hilbert, 1987, 88).

However, as I shall argue in Chapter 4, the relationalist can account for the intuitions of illumination-independence and the distinction between real and apparent color that Hilbert adduces. Namely, she can explain these as intuitions about ordinary color ascriptions — viz., as intuitions about the colors things have, given the tacitly presupposed relativizations at work in ordinary thought and talk about color.

[22] As explained in the main text, I think the most serious problem with the argument under consideration is its insistence on choosing between (what even Hilbert would regard as) *prima facie* unattractive options; I've been urging throughout this chapter that one should respond to such

2.4.2 *Homogeneity*

A further benefit of a relational view of color is that it sheds light on the status of a historically important intuition about the homogeneity of colors over their spatial extent. There is good news and bad news about this intuition. The bad news is that the intuition, when understood in the most natural and direct way, is pretty clearly false. The good news is that color relationalism clears the way for a modified version of the intuition that is true, and shows how the attraction of the false version might have arisen through confusion with the true version. It seems to me a virtue of relationalism that it clarifies matters in this way and preserves as much of the notion of homogeneity as is worth keeping.

The *locus classicus* for the homogeneity intuition is the following famous passage from Sellars:

> ...there is no trouble about systems having properties which its [*sic*] parts do not have *if these properties are a matter of the parts having such and such qualities and being related in such and such ways*. But the case of a pink ice cube, it would seem clear, cannot be treated in this way. It does not seem plausible to say that for a system of particles to be a pink ice cube is for them to have such and such imperceptible qualities, and to be so related to one another as to make up an approximate cube. *Pink* does not seem to be made up of imperceptible qualities in the way in which being a ladder is made up of being cylindrical (the rungs), rectangular (the frame), wooden, etc. The manifest ice cube presents itself to us as something which is pink through and through, as a pink continuum, all the regions of which, however small, are pink. It presents itself to us as *ultimately homogeneous*... (Sellars, 1963, 26, original emphasis).

Initially, we might attempt to represent the Sellarsian intuition as follows:

(H_1) If x is pink, then every proper part of x is pink (*mutatis mutandis* for the other colors).

However, (H_1) must be modified: as Berkeley (*Three Dialogues between Hylas and Philonous*, First Dialogue) and Locke (*Essay Concerning Human Understanding*, II.xxiii.11) both point out, microscopes show us that blood, which appears red when seen with the naked eye, contains proper parts that are colorless (cf. Russell (1912, 10), Lewis (1997, 341)). One might plausibly respond to this observation by pointing out that, while there are proper parts of (red) blood that are not red, these parts are not visible in the circumstances under which blood is ordinarily observed, and under which the color *red* is ascribed to it. On the other hand, one might think, the intuition that (H_1) attempts to express is that only parts visible in the same circumstance in which the whole is visible must share a color with the whole. Perhaps, then, the way to assimilate the lesson of the

hard cases by refusing to choose. However, putting this point aside and spotting the assumption that we must choose, it seems to me that the grounds Hilbert proffers for making the choice beg the disputed question. He proposes to side with one of the apparently conflicting perceptual judgments at the expense of the other on the grounds that one of them fits better with the intrinsic difference in spectral reflectance distributions of the two surfaces. But it is unclear why our color attributions should respect this difference in intrinsic properties unless we are already assuming that colors are intrinsic properties, and thereby begging the question against the relationalist.

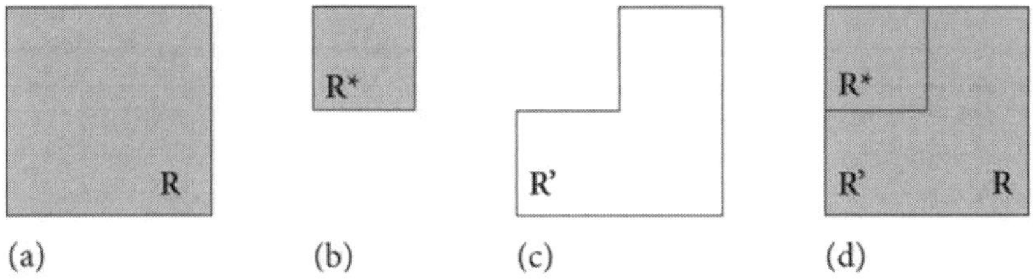

FIG. 2.4. (a) Square R. (b) Subregion $R^*(\subseteq R)$. (c) Subregion $R'(\subseteq R)$, such that $R' \cap R^* = \{\}$. (d) $R = R^* \cup R'$. (See color plates.)

microscope is to replace (H_1) with a suitably restricted formulation, containing explicit relativizations to reflect points made above; thus,

(H_2) if x is pink for S in C, then every proper part of x that is visible to S in C is pink for S in C (*mutatis mutandis* for the other colors).

Whatever we ultimately conclude about the homogeneity of color, there is surely something plausible in the intuitions supporting it that is worth preserving. After all, quite apart from what Sellars says about the matter, it is hard to see why the observation of colorless parts of blood under a microscope would have been surprising (which it undoubtedly was) were not some such intuitions in place.

However, there are cases, related to some we have already considered in the course of arguing for relationalism, that might seem to raise trouble for the homogeneity intuition (understood as (H_2)). The initially problematic case I have in mind is based on the general principle underlying contrast effects (see §2.3.3). Consider square R, which is pink for S in C (see Figure 2.4). Suppose that R is composed (exhaustively) of two subregions R^* and R' (Figure 2.4 b–d). Now suppose we separately attend to subregions R^* and R' in turn. When we attend to R^* on its own — without attending to its complement in R (viz., R'), it remains pink (Figure 2.4b). In contrast, when we attend to R' on its own — without attending to its complement in R (viz., R^*), it ceases to be pink (Figure 2.4c). (We may suppose, for the sake of concreteness, that it becomes clear; all that matters for the point of the case is that it ceases to be pink.) That is, the color of R' depends systematically on whether it is being viewed together with R^* (Figure 2.4a) — in which case it is (stably) pink — or on its own (Figure 2.4c) — in which case it is (stably) not pink. Finally, when we turn our visual attention to all of R once again (Figure 2.4d), both components R^* and R' are pink. If such a case is possible, it might seem a threat to (H_2): R' is a proper part of R that is visible in the same circumstance in which R is visible (and to the same subject), but (at least sometimes) R' fails to share the color *pink* with R.[23]

[23] Presumably one could raise largely the same puzzle by appeal to the homogeneity of colored regions with respect to their temporal parts instead of their spatial parts. I'll put this complication

Should we, on the basis of such cases, jettison the initially plausible principle (H_2)? We should not. For the resources relationalism makes available permit us to describe the case in a way that is compatible with (H_2).

Consider R again. When we attend to R, ordinarily we are also attending to R', which is, after all, one of R's proper parts. Indeed, one may wish to claim that there is some sort of in-virtue-of relation at work here — that we always attend to a region in virtue of attending to its proper parts. But I don't want or need to hold my contention hostage to a substantive metaphysical claim of this generality; all I need for present purposes is that, in at least many typical cases, it is true that we attend (at a given time) to both a region and one of its proper parts. To say this is to say that there is some viewing condition in which we are attending to both R and R'; call this condition C_1. Now consider the situation in which we attend to R' without the rest of R, viz., one in which we attend to R' without attending to R^*; call this condition C_2. Clearly C_1 and C_2 are not identical, since C_1 but not C_2 is a condition under which we attend to R. Therefore, given a relationalist understanding of colors, it is open to us to suppose that R' could exemplify a certain color for S in C_1 and fail to exemplify that color for S in C_2.[24]

I propose to describe the case by saying that R' exemplifies *pink for S in C_1*, but that it fails to exemplify *pink for S in C_2*.[25] Of course, R and R^* have the property *pink for S in C_1* as well. Thus, one of R's color properties distributes over its proper parts R^* and R', as demanded by (H_2). What about the property *pink for S in C_2*? Neither R nor R^* is visible in C_2 — neither of them looks any way at all in C_2, so neither of them has any color constituted in terms of a relation to C_2 (although they both have in C_2 colors constituted in terms of a relation to C_1). And the setup of the case ensures that R' fails to exemplify *pink for S in C_2*. Consequently, the other of R's color properties under discussion distributes over its proper parts R^* and R'; once again, (H_2) is respected.

aside in what follows, since it seems to me that the temporal version adds nothing of independent interest.

[24] Objection: the relationality here seems *ad hoc*: there is no principled *a priori* reason to think that the present difference between C_1 and C_2 reflects a variation in any parameter of a relation in terms of which colors are constituted.

Response: The suggestion should be assessed on the same principled, broadly empirical grounds employed regarding other parameters throughout §2.2. Colors should be construed as involving a relation to a parameter just in case, with all other factors fixed, a change in the relevant parameter can produce a difference in the colors things look to have to a given visual system (and there is no well-motivated, theory-independent reason for setting aside changes in that parameter). If the case under discussion is possible, the presence of R^* contiguous to R' is just the sort of difference that makes a difference to how things look to S.

[25] When viewed in C_2, does R' exemplify *pink for S in C_1*? Yes, it does; but, while it is in C_2 rather than C_1, it does not manifest this property; instead, while in C_2, R' manifests a color property that is constituted in terms of a relation to C_2. Consequently, as we move between the two viewing conditions, we do not destroy and reconstitute this color of R', but merely make it manifest or not manifest.

This description, I suggest, not only preserves (H_2) against the case under consideration, but also sheds light on (H_2) itself and the conclusions it licenses and does not license. (H_2) is true, but we must remember that our specifications of the viewing conditions must take account of other things we are viewing simultaneously — a conclusion we had already reached on independent (empirical) grounds in §2.3. (H_2) tells us that if x is pink for S in C, then every proper part of x that is visible for S in C is pink for S in C. This licenses us in concluding, from the fact that R is pink for S in C_1, that R' is pink for S in C_1. What this does *not* license is the conclusion that R' is pink for S in C_2, or in any other arbitrary circumstance.

Relationalism, then, provides a description of the case that respects intuitions about homogeneity, and also has lessons to teach about the way in which such intuitions should be understood. I count these as further benefits for the view.

2.5 Conclusion

Here's where we are. So far I've presented a class of empirical phenomena, showed how these phenomena put pressure on anti-relationalism, and showed how adopting color relationalism gives an attractive and unified way of accommodating all of these results. I've also showed how relationalism provides solutions to outstanding puzzles in the literature.

But much work remains to be done. Our next task, which will occupy Chapter 3, will be to consider and respond to a number of objections to the argument from perceptual variation. Having thus shored up the argumentative support for relationalism, we'll next turn to the task of defending relationalism (as opposed to the argument from perceptual variation given in support of that view) from objections in Chapters 4–6.

3

VARIATION REVISITED: OBJECTIONS AND RESPONSES

It should be clear by now that object color is not physical light radiation itself, that it is not something that inheres in objects, having to do exclusively with the chemical makeup of the object, nor is it only the nervous excitation that occurs in the eye and brain of an observer. In our perception of object color all these elements are involved....

— (Hurvich, 1981, 52).

Undisputedly, the concept of human color vision involves both a subjective component, as it refers to a perceptual phenomenon and an objective one.... We take this subtle tension to be *the* essential ingredient of research on color perception....

— (Mausfeld *et al.*, 1992, 47).

In this chapter I want to consider and respond to three classes of objections to the argument from perceptual variation presented in Chapter 2 — each class consisting of objections to a premise or inference of that argument.[1]

The objections in the first class (§3.1) target premise (2). They attempt to show, in different ways, that in instances of perceptual variation there is after all a distinguished variant that veridically represents the color of the stimulus — and that this is true even if we have no motivated reason for favoring any particular variant over the others. A second class of objections (§3.2) accepts premise (2), but rejects (3) on the grounds that we would do better to think that *none* of the perceptual variants represent the colors of objects veridically, because objects have no colors. (This class of objections, then, is grounded in the color irrealist position described in §1.1.) The third class of objections I'll examine (§3.3) consists of attempts to accept the ecumenicism recommended by premise (3) of the argument without acceding to the relationalist conclusion (4).

My primary aim in responding to the objections in these three classes is to strengthen the case for relationalism. In addition, however, discussing these objections will also throw into greater relief the connections between relationalism and other views that have shown up in the literature, and, I hope, will make possible a clear-eyed assessment of the merits and drawbacks of each.

3.1 A Favored Variant?

A crucial element in the argument for relationalism presented in Chapter 2 is the claim that, in cases of perceptual variation, there is no single variant

[1] There is no class of objections corresponding to premise (1), since I take this premise to be empirically well-established and not seriously contested by anyone.

that is uniquely veridical (a claim I labeled as premise (2) in presenting the argument). So far I have tried to defend this premise principally by arguing that the most natural ways of selecting particular variants from their competitors in individual instances of variation carry unacceptable costs. Seeing how and why several of these individual attempts fail has a cumulative importance that goes beyond the particular cases in which they come up: their collective effect is to provide what seems to me a powerful inductive defense of the disputed premise as a general matter.

However, some critics of relationalism and the argument from perceptual variation have urged that this style of defense is unpersuasive. This is because, they say, notwithstanding the inadequacy of the particular attempts canvassed, there is or at any rate may be a favored variant in cases of perceptual variation after all. Below I'll consider and respond to some reasons they have offered in support of this contention.

3.1.1 *An Epistemic Diagnosis*

A first reason for doubting premise (2) in the argument from perceptual variation rests on the thought that the difficulty is merely epistemic. The critic insists that, even if we are unable to find non-stipulative reasons for favoring a particular variant at the expense of others, there is a fact of the matter — unknown to us, and for that matter, possibly unknowable by us — about which variant is veridical. Perhaps, that is, our inability to single out a distinguished variant reveals only our epistemic shortcomings, and not the true metaphysical situation. If so, then the argument from perceptual variation, as I have presented it, falters at premise (2).

Byrne and Hilbert have advanced versions of this point in several places, and especially in response to interpersonal cases of variation concerning unique hue loci (see §2.3.2). For example, they write that,

> From the fact that we have no good reason to believe, of any chip, that it is unique green, it does not follow that we have no good reason to believe that there are any unique green chips. That would be like arguing that we have no good reason to believe that Professor Plum has been murdered, on the ground that there is no particular person who is clearly the culprit (Byrne and Hilbert (2003, 17); cf. Byrne and Tye (2006), Tye (2006*a*, 3)).[2]

[2] In other places Byrne and Hilbert have also offered a more direct criticism of the alternative, metaphysical, diagnosis of perceptual variation by suggesting that the difficulty in imagining a principled choice among variants isn't particularly difficult after all:

> ... it really isn't that difficult [to imagine what could make it the case that one variant is veridical at the expense of the others]. Presumably it is not puzzling why the chip looks true blue [unique blue] to John and greenish blue to Jane. That *would* be puzzling if John and Jane were in the same brain states, but (we may safely suppose) they aren't: they differ in many visually relevant respects. On the side of the chip, presumably it is not puzzling why it is unique blue and not greenish-blue. That *would* be puzzling if the chip didn't interact with light (for example), but it does; it is an ordinary opaque uniform chip. Putting the two together, what "makes it the case" that John, not Jane, is perceiving

Byrne's and Hilbert's primary aim in this passage is to argue against the inference from perceptual variation to the irrealist conclusion that *none* of the variants veridically represents the stimulus, rather than the ecumenicist conclusion that *all* of the variants do. Still, I take it that the Professor Plum analogy is potentially applicable to both irrealism and ecumenicism: the point is that, even if we are unable to motivate a choice amongst variants, there might nonetheless be a favored variant.[3]

In a related vein, they compare the same instance of perceptual variation to a case of representational variation where neither the irrealist's nor the ecumenicist's inference looks tempting. This case involves a population of intelligent, reasonably accurate, but not precisely calibrated thermometers to each of whom the ambient temperature seems to be some number of degrees Fahrenheit:

> Some think the temperature is 69°F, while others think it's 70°F, and yet others think it's 71°F.... Since they don't have other ways of measuring temperature, they have no "independent method" of determining whether the temperature right now is exactly 70°F, or even whether it's pretty high. Still, some of these thermometers are perceiving the temperature correctly and others are not (Byrne and Hilbert, 2004, 9).

Here again, I take it that the intended force of the analogy is that the phenomenon of perceptual variation with respect to color allows for the existence of a single variant that is uniquely veridical.

Similarly, Barry Stroud attempts to lessen the force of considerations about perceptual variation with respect to color by comparing that sort of variation against representational variation with respect to shape and species properties:[4]

> What colour you see when you see an object on a particular occasion does, of course, depend on the condition you are in and the circumstances in which you find yourself.... But that is true of the perception of all properties. Whether you get a perception of something ovoid from an ovoid object or a perception of an elephant from an elephant equally depends on your current state and the perceptual conditions. Alleged

the chip correctly, is that it looks true blue to John, greenish-blue to Jane (no problem so far) and the chip *is* true blue, not greenish blue (likewise, no problem) (Byrne and Hilbert (2007*b*, 88–89); cf. Byrne (2006, 337)).

Unfortunately, this response is unhelpful as it stands. It is of course correct (and not difficult to imagine) that a variant counts as veridical iff (i) it represents the color of the chip as being some way, and (ii) the color of the chip is indeed that way. That amounts to a correct statement of what it means for a variant to be veridical. But it does nothing to explain what makes it the case that one variant meets this condition at the expense of the others. Byrne and Hilbert have supplied vocabulary in terms of which we can re-raise the question they purported to be answering; but they have done nothing to answer it.

[3] In Byrne's and Hilbert's presentation, the problem is to choose between suspects rather than representations. Switching from material to formal mode, we can think of the case as one in which we choose between hypotheses of the form 'x murdered Professor Plum'. On this latter construal, the case is one in which, like cases of perceptual variation with respect to color, we are faced with a choice between variant representations. In what follows I'll switch freely between material and formal modes in talking about the cases.

[4] Stroud's criticism echoes Berkeley's complaint that Locke's secondary quality account of color is no more or less acceptable as an account of color than as an account of, say, shape.

facts of "perceptual relativity" do not support a distinction between colours and certain "primary" or "real" properties which objects are said to have on their own, independently of all human perception (Stroud, 2000, 174).

Or, again, Kalderon (2007*b*) criticizes a variant of the argument from perceptual variation (from Chalmers (2006)) as relying on the "anti-realist" principle that, "If there is no reason to suppose that one and not the other of the perceivers is misperceiving the color of the object, then it is not the case that one and not the other of the perceivers is misperceiving the color of the object" (19). Kalderon rejects this principle on the grounds that it "immodestly assumes that the limits of the world correspond to the limits of human intelligibility" (19). He thinks this immodesty is unwarranted, and so rejects the inference from (1) to (2) in the argument from perceptual variation.[5]

Anti-relationalists take these considerations to motivate an epistemic diagnosis of instances of perceptual variation with respect to color. On this diagnosis, we should concede about such cases that we lack compelling reasons for believing any variant to be uniquely veridical. Indeed, we might even concede for the sake of argument that the phenomenon of variation always undercuts everyone's reasons for believing any variant to be uniquely veridical. However, the epistemic diagnosis has it that there *is* some uniquely veridical variant that merely happens to elude our epistemic reach.

The epistemic diagnosis of the phenomenon of perceptual variation deserves our consideration as a coherent alternative to the more metaphysical diagnosis I have offered — viz., the diagnosis according to which the explanation for our inability to select a uniquely veridical variant is that there isn't one. Indeed, the coherence of the epistemic diagnosis is something I was careful to make room for throughout my presentation of the argument from perceptual variation. The crucial question for our purposes is whether this coherent alternative response is warranted in the case at hand, as the anti-relationalist maintains. It will come as no surprise that I think it is not.

One possible reason for rejecting the epistemic diagnosis is that it results in an unacceptable form of skepticism. Thus, Hardin urges that physicalists such as Byrne and Hilbert should be reluctant to accept such "unknowable color facts," lest they end up restoring the sort of veil of perception between us and the world that, one might have hoped, a physicalist ontology held the promise of sweeping away (e.g. Hardin, 2004, 35). However, I am not convinced that such epistemological motivations are all that essential in motivating color physicalism, or, for that matter, that unknowable color facts are otherwise objectionable. That said, I think there are other reasons for being dissatisfied with the epistemic diagnosis.

The most powerful reason, I think, comes from reflection about the analogies used to motivate that diagnosis. As we have seen, the case for the

[5] As Kalderon (2007*b*, 20) goes on to note, this criticism is compatible with the acceptance of cases of blameless (veridical) perceptual variation (see Kalderon (2007*a*) and §3.3.2 below).

epistemic diagnosis of perceptual variation with respect to color rests largely on consideration of other cases of representational variation involving who murdered Professor Plum, the ambient temperature, shape, and so on. Let me just accept that the epistemic diagnosis of the cases discussed by these critics is overwhelmingly and obviously the right one: it would plainly be the wrong reaction to conclude from the evidence available in these cases that no one or everyone murdered Professor Plum, that none or all of the thermometers veridically represent the ambient temperature, or that none or all of us are correct in representing objects as elephants or as ovoid. But it's not at all clear how this conclusion should bear on our assessment of perceptual variation cases involving color.

I can imagine two ways in which an anti-relationalist might attempt to extend lessons from the Professor Plum/temperature/elephant/ovoid cases to the color cases discussed in Chapter 2:

Defensive Strategy: On this version, the force of these additional cases is to make the metaphysical diagnosis of perceptual variation with respect to color seem less attractive. The additional cases demonstrate that our inability to single out a favored variant is compatible with the existence of a favored variant. Consequently, by drawing our attention to these cases, the anti-relationalist intends to warn us against accepting the metaphysical diagnosis (that there is no uniquely veridical variant) merely on the strength of the phenomenon of variation itself.

Offensive Strategy: The aim of citing the additional cases, on this version, is the more ambitious one of convincing us to adopt the epistemic diagnosis instead of the metaphysical diagnosis in cases of perceptual variation with respect to color. The idea is that, since the epistemic diagnosis is obviously appropriate and the metaphysical diagnosis is obviously inappropriate in the additional cases, parity of reasoning should lead us to extend an epistemic diagnosis to cases of perceptual variation with respect to color.

I'll first consider the Offensive Strategy, and then return to the Defensive Strategy.[6]

3.1.1.1 *The Offensive Strategy* I am unpersuaded by the Offensive Strategy for two reasons.

First, there are significant disanalogies between the factors controlling intuitions in those cases and the color cases, so the appeal to analogy at work here is unconvincing. The factors driving the intuitions in favor of the epistemic diagnosis in the additional cases are different, but I think these factors are unavailable in the color case.

[6] I should mention that, in independent conversations, Byrne and Hilbert have emphasized that their discussions of Professor Plum and the thermometers were intended to carry forward the Defensive, rather than the Offensive, Strategy.

Take the Professor Plum case first. The best explanation of our acceptance of the epistemic diagnosis of the Professor Plum case would cite our general (tacit) understanding of how people act and behave, which seems to underwrite the following banal conclusions:

1. Professor Plum is unlikely to have ended up in his present unhappy position (keeled over in the ballroom, knife protruding from his back) had some person or other not murdered him.
2. It is possible that someone might have murdered Professor Plum without making it the case that we possess evidence that they carried out that action.

The first of these banal conclusions creates a presumptive prejudice to the effect that Professor Plum was murdered, and the second explains away potential counter-considerations engendered by our lack of evidence about specific individuals. In combination, then, our background knowledge makes the epistemic diagnosis an attractive reaction to representational variation in the Professor Plum case. In contrast, I suggest that our background knowledge about color and color perception is far less elaborate and articulated in the relevant respects than our background knowledge about the way people move and behave. This is not to say that there is no such background knowledge (folk color psychophysics, if you like), but only that it doesn't do the analogous relevant things in cases of perceptual variation with respect to color that folk psychology does in the case of Professor Plum. In particular, in the context of cases of perceptual variation with respect to color, our background knowledge about color both fails to establish a presumptive prejudice in favor of a uniquely veridical variant, and fails to override the counter-considerations engendered by our lack of evidence in favor of any particular variant.

I think the temperature, elephant, and ovoid cases work slightly differently. What makes the epistemic diagnosis attractive in the temperature case is the widely held (and true) belief that a temperature property such as *being 70°F* has a natural essence (involving a particular mean molecular kinetic energy of the ambient atmosphere) such that the possession of this essence is constitutive of being 70°F; that is, there is a representation-independent essence for this temperature property that serves as a truth-maker (/falsity-maker) of the conflicting representations.[7] Much the same is plausible about Stroud's elephant and ovoid cases: in both of these cases there are good reasons to think we are committed to the existence of underlying essences

[7] Our commitment to such essences is beautifully documented by Chang (2005). See, for example, his discussion of the 17th- and 18th-century quest for physical fixed points for calibrating the measurements of temperature (8–39) and of the 18th- and early 19th-century dispute between advocates of air, alcohol, and mercury thermometers as the arbiters of disputes about temperature (57–84). Significantly, almost all of the disputes Chang recounts took place prior to the late 19th-century development of an explicit theory of just what essence was being measured by thermometers, which means that the participants in these disputes were committed to the existence of such an essence even before knowing just what it was.

(a natural essence in the case of *being an elephant*, an abstract essence in the case of *being an ovoid*) that serves as a truth-maker (/falsity-maker) of conflicting perceptual representations. But it is doubtful that we are equally committed to the existence of a representation-independent essence of *being red* that could serve as a truth-maker (/falsity-maker) of conflicting perceptual representations. For one thing, the range of inductive causal generalizations we are willing to make about *being red* seems far smaller than the corresponding range for *being 70°F*; in so far as these inductive generalizations are driven by our belief in an underlying constitutive natural essence, this gives us reason for doubting that we are as committed to the existence of an essence for *being red*. For another, our treatment of cases where surface cues and (alleged) essences clash reveal a commitment to an essence of *being 70°F* that is absent for *being red* (even assuming we are ignorant about what the alleged essences are). If a research scientist's *being 70°F*-instance-detector and the surface appearances disagree about whether some object exemplifies the temperature property in question, I think we would be prepared to side with the detector (assuming we have no background reason for being especially distrustful of either source of evidence) (again, see Chang, 2005). Whereas, I suggest, a research-scientist whose *being red*-instance detector classified as red an object that persistently looked green can expect to receive the reaction that his detector has simply locked onto the wrong property (again assuming we have no background reasons for being especially distrustful of either source of evidence).

In sum, the factors that are plausibly responsible for our sense of the appropriateness of an epistemic diagnosis in the range of cases of representational variation where it is appropriate seem to be either absent or, at least, far less powerful in cases of perceptual variation with respect to color. For this reason, the clear superiority of the epistemic diagnosis over the metaphysical diagnosis in the former cases should not compel us to accept the epistemic rather than the epistemic diagnosis in the latter cases.[8]

My second reason for being unsympathetic to the Offensive Strategy is that, even if the analogy between the cases were stronger than I think it is, there are yet other analogous cases of representational variation where the metaphysical diagnosis is clearly superior to the epistemic diagnosis; I take this to show that the appeal to analogy ultimately fails to give us clear direction about how to treat the cases under dispute. As an example of representational variant where the epistemic diagnosis is implausible, consider a case involving the representation of a particular joke as exemplifying or not exemplifying the property *being humorous*. Suppose that Byrne's and Hilbert's intelligent

[8] In empirical investigations of these kinds of cases, Shaun Nichols and I have found that subjects' view of the matter largely confirms the view I have recommended here (Cohen and Nichols, 2007). In particular, undergraduate subjects are significantly more likely to think there is a distinguished variant in cases of (interspecies) representational disagreement about shape than in cases of (interspecies) perceptual disagreement about color. I'll discuss these results in more detail in §5.3.1.

thermometers are given the powers of cocktail party conversation; and suppose that they all hear a particular joke being told at one of their soirées. Some think the joke is humorous, while others think it is not humorous. Since they don't have other ways of ascertaining whether jokes are humorous, they have no "independent method" of determining whether the joke is humorous. I take it that, in this case, it would be a mistake to insist that some of the conversants are representing whether the joke is humorous veridically while others are not. Or, in other words, it would be a mistake to apply an epistemic reading to this case.

The moral seems to be this. While there are some cases of representational variation where the epistemic diagnosis is appropriate and the metaphysical diagnosis is inappropriate (e.g., the temperature case, the Professor Plum case) there are other cases of representational variation where the situation is exactly the reverse. If that's true, then merely pointing to the existence of cases where intuition points in one direction or another is insufficient to compel a verdict about disputed cases of representational variation (such as the color cases). This provides us with a further reason for rejecting the Offensive Strategy.[9]

3.1.1.2 *The Defensive Strategy* What, then, of the Defensive Strategy?

I am happy enough to accept its lesson that the mere fact of variation in any case is compatible with the existence of a uniquely veridical variant, and that therefore the metaphysical diagnosis is not ensured in the particular cases of perceptual variation with respect to color. Indeed, I myself have emphasized this point in presenting the argument from perceptual variation as non-deductive, and in characterizing the epistemic diagnosis as a coherent alternative.

However, it is just not true that the argument from perceptual variation depends on accepting the metaphysical diagnosis (that there is no uniquely veridical variant) merely on the strength of the phenomenon of variation itself. On the contrary, the conclusion that there is no uniquely veridical variant was reached by appeal to the phenomenon of variation together with an inductive case against the viability of claiming the unique veridicality of any particular variant. What we observed was that, in instance after instance of variation with respect to color, the most promising attempts to single out a uniquely veridical variant required stipulations that are ultimately unacceptable. Moreover, it should be emphasized that the considerations leading to these judgments were, in every instance, local to the particulars about color perception. This

[9] Byrne (2006) complains that citing the example of *being humorous* in this dispute begs the question against the theorist who favors an epistemic diagnosis. But citing this case is no more (and no less) question begging than citing the cases (such as the intelligent thermometers case) where the epistemic diagnosis is plausible. The point is that both sorts of cases of representational variation exist: those in which the epistemic diagnosis is plausible, and those in which it is not. This is why, as I have said, pointing to the existence of either sort of case is insufficient, by itself, to resolve the issue of whether the epistemic diagnosis is appropriate in cases of representational variation with respect to color (or any other cases where this is in dispute).

is significant in the present context, where, because there are both cases of representational variation where an epistemic diagnosis is appropriate and cases where it is not, it is unclear how much scope we should allow ourselves in applying morals from one case of representational variation to others.

Since I have argued for the metaphysical diagnosis of perceptual variation cases not only by appeal to the phenomenon of variation, but also by an inductive argument making reference to the variants found in the particular cases under study, it seems to me that the case I have presented does not fall into the error that the Defensive Strategy warns us against. Ultimately, then, I think the epistemic diagnosis remains a coherent alternative response to the cases of perceptual variation under dispute, but one that is insufficiently motivated when compared against the metaphysical diagnosis I have recommended.

3.1.2 *Color Constancy*

Another way in which critics have urged the thought that there might be a favored variant in cases of perceptual variation involves an appeal to color constancy.[10] Suppose a subject visually perceives the scene depicted in Figure 3.1 — i.e., a coffee cup on a table, partially in direct sunlight and partially in shadow.[11] Clearly the regions of the coffee cup (and the table) that are in direct sunlight are perceptually distinguishable for the subject from the (qualitatively identical) contiguous regions of the coffee cup (and the table) that are in the shadow, which is just to say that there is perceptual variation in respect of color for the qualitatively identical regions of the coffee cup. The subject will normally judge, however, that these perceptually distinguishable regions are of the same color — despite the perceptual variation, she will ordinarily judge that the two adjacent regions have one color rather than two.

This is true not only of cases where the two regions are presented simultaneously, as in Figure 3.1 (cases of simultaneous color constancy), but also of cases where an object is perceived in successive presentations between which there is a change in illumination (cases of successive color constancy), such as that depicted in Figure 3.2.[12] Here, too, the regions of one object (say, the banana) in the two different photographs are perceptually distinguishable for the subject — i.e., there is perceptual variation in respect of color for the qualitatively identical regions of the coffee cup. But, once again, subjects will normally judge that these perceptually distinguishable regions are of the same color.

A critic of the argument from perceptual variation might use these facts to motivate an objection to the treatment of perceptual variation I have rec-

[10] The arguments of this section are defended in more detail by Cohen (2008).

[11] It will be important here that the subject is visually perceiving a coffee cup, not a photograph of the coffee cup (notwithstanding the arguments of Walton (1984), I take it that when a subject sees a photograph of x, she does not ordinarily see x as well (Cohen and Meskin, 2004)). I am using Figure 3.1 to *depict* the stimulus — I am not using it *as* the stimulus.

[12] I am grateful to David Hilbert for supplying and allowing me to use the photographs that make up Figure 3.2.

FIG. 3.1. Partially sunlit coffee cup. (See color plates.)

ommended. Namely, she will point to the judgment that there is one color rather than two in cases of simultaneous and successive color constancy, and will take that judgment to suggest that, in the present case, at most one of the two perceptual variants is a veridical representation of the shared color of the regions (even if we do not know which).

Moreover, because the argument from variation involves generalizing from instances, this criticism also threatens the treatment of perceptual variation cases I have urged more generally speaking. For, the critic will suggest, if the phenomenon of color constancy makes us think that there is a favored variant despite the the perceptual variation in Figure 3.1, this can serve to motivate the thought that there is a (possibly unknown) favored, uniquely veridical variant in other cases of perceptual variation. And if this conclusion really is motivated, then premise (2) of the argument from perceptual variation will fail.

By way of responding, I want to point out the objection turns crucially on having a partial view of the data about subject judgments in cases of color constancy. It is true that subjects will judge (when asked one way) that the adjacent regions have one color rather than two. On the other hand, the regions are obviously discriminable, and it is hard to say how they are discriminable except in respect of something like their color, which suggests that there is some important sense in which subjects will judge that the two regions are not alike in color (this second sort of judgment has been studied quantitatively by Arend and Reeves (1986); Arend *et al.* (1991); Troost and deWeert (1991); Cornelissen and Brenner (1995); Bäuml (1999)). So it looks as if the neutral thing to say

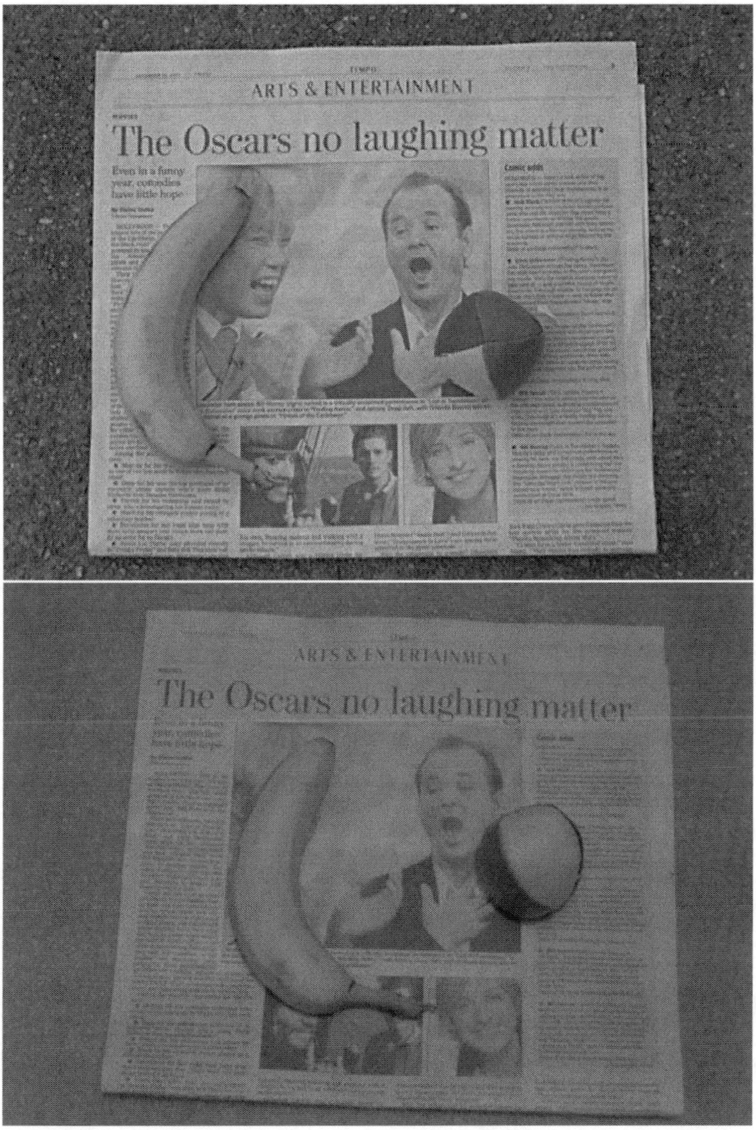

FIG. 3.2. Common objects under different daylight illuminants. (See color plates.)

is that subjects in color constancy experiments actually make two different judgments: they judge not only that the two regions of interest are (in some sense) alike in color, and also that the two regions are (in some sense) not alike in color. Now, it is not obvious how we should ultimately make sense of these apparently conflicting judgments. However, I submit, we should not respond to the situation by refusing to acknowledge that there is a perfectly good sense in which the adjacent patches are judged not to share a color. But that is just what the present objection amounts to — the point of the objection is that, despite the perceptual variation with respect to the adjacent regions, the judgment that the two share a color requires us to favor at most one of the variants at the expense of the other. This insistence seems unmotivated, however, when considered in light of the simultaneously offered judgment that the two regions fail to share a color. The point, then, is that the present objection suggests that at most one variant in color constancy cases is veridical only if we take a selective view of the data.

But if we take a more complete view of the data, then we are not forced to understand subject judgments in a way that favors one variant over others. In particular, I suggest that we should understand the judgment that the adjacent regions share a color as answering this question: would region R_1 (presented under illumination I_1) share a color appearance with region R_2 (presented under illumination I_2) if, contrary to fact, both regions were presented under the same illumination — namely, both under I_1 or both under I_2? On this construal, the subject's judgment is not a judgment to the effect that the regions are occurrently manifesting a common color, but rather to the effect that the regions share a color that one of them is not occurrently manifesting. That is, the subject judges that, although the sunlit region looks different (in respect of color) from the region in shadow, the two regions would look the same (in respect of color) were they both viewed under sunlight. (Of course, the two regions also share another color — namely, the color that either of them would exhibit in shadow but that only the currently shadowed region currently manifests.)

The understanding I have sketched does justice to subjects' judgment that the regions share a color — viz., the judgment on which the objection we are now considering turns. However, this understanding also leaves room for accepting the additionally observed subjects' judgment that the contiguous regions fail to share a color in some other sense. Namely, we can understand the latter as the judgment that the adjacent regions are unlike in the colors that they are occurrently manifesting. Thus, the present construal provides an account of subject judgments in color constancy experiments that (unlike the traditional construal considered first) respects the full range of data.

And now we may notice that, on the present construal, the subject's judgment gives no reason for believing that (as alleged) at most one of the perceptual variants is a veridical representation of the colors of objects. For, as noted, not only do the regions share the color that the sunlit region is currently manifesting, but they also share the color that the shadowed region is currently manifesting. That is to say, the regions share both of the colors represented by the perceptual variants; consequently, the judgment that they share a color in no way impugns the veridicality of either (currently manifested) perceptual variant.

The upshot of this discussion, then, is that subject judgments in color constancy cases do not, by themselves, give us any reason to believe that one variant in such cases is veridical (at the expense of the other); this result only follows given a certain understanding of the judgments in question, and in particular an understanding that is hard to reconcile with the full range of data about the cases. But if the phenomenon of color constancy fails to motivate a choice of a favored, uniquely veridical variant in the cases depicted in Figures 3.1–3.2, it also fails to motivate the more general conclusion that there is a favored, uniquely veridical variant in other instances of perceptual variation. For this reason, I take it that the argument from perceptual variation withstands considerations about color constancy.

3.1.3 *Alien Modalities*

Yet another consideration that might be used to argue that there is a favored variant despite our inability to specify it — and therefore to deny premise (2) of the argument from perceptual variation — relies on an appeal to alien modalities. The thought here is that our difficulty in choosing amongst variants could be remedied if only we had some further, non-visual, sensory modality for forming perceptual representations of the colors of objects — call this imagined modality 'color shmision'. Color shmision would be relevant to our purposes because it could serve as an independent standard against which we could check the multiple variants supplied by color vision, and thereby decide which of those variants is veridical: a perceptual variant of color vision will count as veridically representing the color of its object if and only if color shmision represents the object as having that very color. Of course, we lack color shmision; but the point of the objection is that there must be a fact of the matter about the color that shmision would represent objects as having, and that we can appeal to that fact of the matter (even if it is epistemically unavailable to us) to choose one of the perceptual variants supplied by color vision as representing the real color of an object.[13] By way of analogy, this objection supposes that we possessors of color vision but not color shmision are like the proverbial blind men and the elephant: color vision supplies us with a range of conflicting reports about the world, and it is only our lack of shmision that prevents us from having an independent check on, hence way to adjudicate between, the different things that color vision tells us.

[13] I take something like this objection to be at work in the following passage:

There is one final worry, which can be brought out by noting that in the shape case we have independent tests for whether someone is perceiving a shape correctly. In the color case, there is no such test. As it stands, the best evidence for a Munsell chip's having a certain color is that the majority of those with normal color vision see the object as having that color. The lack of an independent test is partly due to the fact that colors are not perceived by any other sensory modality... (Byrne and Hilbert, 2003, §3.4).

There are a number of problems with this objection. For one thing, it is not clear why color shmision should not also be subject to perceptual variation. Note that we cannot just stipulate a modality that (without perceptual variation) veridically represents the true colors of objects without begging the question against the relationalist, who believes that there is no non-relational color of objects to be veridically represented by an imagined modality not subject to perceptual variation. The question at issue is then: why should we believe that there is a modality for the perception of colors that is not subject to perceptual variation? Of course, if there is perceptual variation for color shmision too, then this modality cannot provide a standard against which to judge the deliverances of color vision. For in this case color shmision will have increased the number of candidates between which we have no way of deciding, rather than providing us with a criterion by which to settle on one of them. Just as the introduction of more blind men won't help the unfortunates in the proverb to discern the character of the elephant, color shmision won't help color vision unless the former is not subject to perceptual variation as well.

However, suppose for the sake of argument that color shmision does deliver a single verdict — that it is not subject to perceptual variation, but represents the colors of objects in just one way. Even so, we have no guarantee that the representation of color delivered by color shmision will agree with any of the representations of color delivered by color vision.

First suppose it does not. In this case, there seems little point in taking color shmision as the standard against which to settle the perceptual variation in respect of color vision; for, here again, color shmision will not adjudicate between the perceptual variants, but will add one more voice to the clamor. One might respond at this point by suggesting that, precisely because each representation of color vision fails to match with the representation of color shmision, *all* of the perceptual variants supplied by color vision are incorrect (just as all of the blind men in the proverb are incorrect about the character of the elephant). But it is unclear why we should side in this way with color shmision and against color vision. We have not been given any reason for investing color shmision with a better claim to represent the colors of objects (better in the sense that we are willing to rule representations of color vision veridical or erroneous on the grounds that they match or fail to match the deliverances of color shmision, but we are not willing to use color vision as a test for color shmision in the same way), merely because it delivers a single representation rather than many. Indeed, if the representations of color shmision fail to agree with all the representations of color vision, I think we would be justified in wondering whether the former modality should count as representing the colors of objects at all, rather than some other sorts of properties accessible only to shmision — whether, in this case, it would be more apposite to call the imagined modality 'shmolor shmision' (in which case it would clearly be wrong to take the deliverances of this modality as settling cases of perceptual variation with respect to color).

On the other hand, suppose that the representation of color delivered by color shmision agrees with one and only one of the varying representations of color delivered by color vision on a single occasion. And suppose no special skeptical worries about the reliability of color shmision are in play. Still, it is hard to see why we should think of color shmision as certifying certain of the deliverances of color vision, unless we are also prepared to say the same thing about the yet additional modality of color shmusion, whose representations of color may or may not agree with any of those delivered by color vision or those delivered by color shmision. Now, since it is possible that color shmision and color shmusion can disagree in their representations of the color of an object (and if they don't, we still must consider the representations delivered by color shmeesion, etc.) it may be these two imagined modalities each certify distinct representations produced by color vision. But in this case, our appeal to extra modalities does nothing to resolve the conflict between perceptual variants delivered by color vision. The extra modalities may provide more than one vote for some of the variants, but this hardly settles the conflict. To return to our analogy, if each of the proverbial blind men recruited friends to investigate just that part of the elephant that he himself felt, we would wind up with two votes for snake-like, two for rope-like, two for wall-like, and so forth, but we would be no closer to the truth about the character of the elephant.

To sum up, I am inclined to think that the appeal to color shmision does not block the argument from perceptual variation that we have been reviewing. Color shmision may be, like color vision, subject to perceptual variation, in which case it will provide no assistance in the face of worries about the perceptual variation of color vision. If it is not, it may not agree with any of the deliverances of color vision, in which case it is irrelevant to the decision between the variants delivered by color vision. And even if it does agree with color vision, we have no reason to endorse its deliverances rather than those of other imagined modalities which do not.

3.1.4 *Perfect Psychosemantics*

Psychosemantics is the theory of what it is in virtue of which our thoughts refer to (parts of) the world; if traditional, linguistic semantics is the theory of word-world relations, the psychosemantics is intended to be the analogous theory of thought-world relations. Although the topic of psychosemantics might, at first blush, seem to be remote from the present concerns about color ontology, it has sometimes been alleged that the argument from perceptual variation that we have been considering depends in a certain way on psychosemantic matters — or, at least, on the unsatisfactory status of extant psychosemantic theorizing. In particular, some writers (e.g., Byrne and Hilbert (2003, 8); Byrne and Tye (2006, 252)) have held that the appeal of premise (2) in the argument from perceptual variation rests on our current state of psychosemantic ignorance — on our not yet having in hand The One True Psychosemantics (henceforth, TOTP).

This complaint begins with what is a generally accepted (but, as it turns out, highly demanding) adequacy condition for psychosemantic theories: it is generally accepted that a successful psychosemantic theory will have to distinguish cow-caused COW-thoughts from our horse-on-a-dark-night-caused COW-thoughts (and all the rest of our COW-thoughts), and say that the former are veridical but the latter are not.[14] Similarly, critics of the argument from perceptual variation seem to be suggesting, an adequate psychosemantics must distinguish those UNIQUE-GREEN representations that are caused by *bona fide* instances of unique green (hence are veridical) from those caused by other things (hence are erroneous). Likewise, presumably, an adequate psychosemantics must distinguish those BLUISH GREEN representations caused by *bona fide* instances of bluish green from those caused by other things, e.g., instances of unique green.

Suppose this is all correct, and suppose that you represent a 500nm spectral light as unique green but that I represent it as bluish green. Then, even though it has not yet been formulated, we are now in a position to know that TOTP would provide what we need to make a principled choice amongst the representational variants: TOTP would tell us that your representation of the light is veridical and that mine is not (as it might be). Alas, we are not yet in possession of TOTP, and so cannot now give an explicit answer to the question about which variant is uniquely veridical, hence cannot now give a constructive refutation of premise (2). On the other hand, the suggestion seems to be, the contention that there is no explicit answer to that question to be given is an over-reaction — it inflates the unsettled state of current psychosemantics into a reason for endorsing premise (2).

It must be admitted that the state of play in psychosemantics is unsettled; unfortunately, I don't see that this helps those who would deny premise (2). The claim that the apparent force of the premise results from inadequacies in existing psychosemantic theories might be taken in two ways, neither of which (in my view) successfully undercuts premise (2). On the one hand, it might mean that, in assessing whether there is a distinguished variant in cases of perceptual variation we consult existing but inadequate psychosemantic theories to see whether they provide grounds for singling out just one variant, see that they don't do this (because of their inadequacies), and therefore conclude that there is no such distinguished variant. On the other hand, it might mean that the shortcomings in existing psychosemantic theories lead us to give up on the hope of ever finding TOTP — a theory that would both avoid those shortcomings and (*ex hypothesi*) say enough to single out a favored variant in cases of perceptual variation. I'll consider these readings in turn.

On the first disambiguation, the claim that the premise depends on problems in existing psychosemantic theories is just implausible. To see this, sup-

[14] See Fodor (1990*b*) for a discussion of this adequacy condition, and the difficulty it poses for several psychosemantic theories.

pose that we had a psychosemantic theory that *did* generate a clear prediction about whether there is a single veridical variant — either to the effect that there is no such single variant, or to the effect that some particular variant is the distinguished, uniquely veridical one. It seems to me that, just because it made this clear prediction, this imagined psychosemantic story would be no less controversial than the disputed matter of color ontology: since many who have considered these matters believe that such a prediction would be erroneous, they would regard any psychosemantics that licensed that prediction as *ipso facto* unacceptable. This shows that it is not the case that the argument works by consulting such theories, finding that (because of their inadequacies) they fail to favor clearly any one variant over others, and consequently giving up on the search. Rather, the problem is that nothing *else* — in particular, nothing that could make for data for a psychosemantic theory — favors any one variant over others: not pre-theoretical intuition, nor theoretical physics, nor theoretical psychophysics, nor any combination of these, nor anything else that comes to mind. Only a prior commitment to an anti-relational theory of color generates that prediction. Thus, it is not true that the argument from perceptual variation depends on the failures of existing psychosemantics in the present understanding of that claim.

On the second disambiguation, the suggestion would be that all sides are committed to there being an answer to the argument from variation after all. Of course, it is conceivable that there is no TOTP, and that our thoughts fail to hook onto the world; but this outcome would surely be regarded as a massive catastrophe by all parties to the present debate, and in any case there's no reason to think that this outcome would depend on or be made more likely by the denial of (2). On the contrary, the difficulties concerning current psychosemantic theorizing are (more or less) orthogonal to disputes about color ontology, so shouldn't be taken as special problems for the denier of (2). In any case, the thought goes, anyone who accepts psychosemantic realism of any sort — and that means everyone in the present dispute — is committed to there being principled veridicality conditions that would favor one representational variant over others, contrary to (2). But this means that all parties to the present dispute are committed to the existence of a non-stipulative response to the argument from perceptual variation, whether or not we now know what that response would look like.

That, at any rate, is the second disambiguation of the claim; unfortunately, it is hard to see why it should be true either. After all, it is uncontroversial that there are properties subject to representational variation such that — notwithstanding what the eventual discovery of TOTP might reveal — there is no distinguished, uniquely veridical variant. To return to an example discussed above, it is deeply implausible that there is a uniquely veridical variant in the case where Pam says my joke is humorous but Sam says it is not. While different psychosemantic theories will treat this situation in different ways that it is beyond the scope of this book to review, what matters for us is that no one does or should take the situation to entail the failure of psychosemantics. Psychosemantics does not demand that one of Sam's or Pam's response to the joke is veridical at the expense of the other. But then it would seem that whatever pattern of response one favors for treating *being humorous* is in principle available for application to *being red* as well.[15] That is, if psychosemantic realism survives the absence of a distinguished variant with respect to *being humorous*, it will also survive the absence of a distinguished variant with respect to *being red*.

3.1.5 *Determinables and Determinates*

A final objection to the argument from perceptual variation that I want to mention in this section, based on the view of Gert (2006), is that premise (2) should be accepted only in cases of variation involving fine-grained determinate colors such as *unique red*, but not in cases of variation involving coarse-grained categorical colors such as *red*.[16] The idea, then, would be to endorse the application of the argument from variation to determinate colors (and so to endorse relationalism about these colors), but to reject the application of the argument to determinable colors (and so to endorse anti-relationalism about these colors).

The most obvious drawback to the view considered is its non-uniformity; I take it that, other things equal, an account that treats colors uniformly is preferable to one that treats them non-uniformly.[17]

[15] Of course, one could block this move by finding some difference between the two properties (presumably there are plenty) and arguing that that difference requires distinct treatment of the properties by an adequate psychosemantics. It's hard to evaluate this objection without knowing (i) exactly what difference is alleged to make the difference, and (ii) what sorts of differences matter to an adequate psychosemantics. Still, even without knowing these things, notice that this form of objection depends on marking metaphysical distinctions between the two properties (prior to the appeal to psychosemantics); but since the metaphysics of *being red* is exactly what is in dispute between the two sides, the objection threatens to beg all of the relevant questions.

[16] This response is an extension of ideas from Gert (2006) — that paper is not, in the first instance, addressed to the argument from variation *per se*. Rather, Gert's aim is to argue that, in so far as there are public language words for the determinable colors, and in so far as a kind of ostensive account of learning for the use of these terms is correct, we have reason to be "realists" (i.e, anti-relationalists) about the determinable color properties that answer to those terms, whereas we lack similar motivation for "realism" about determinate colors. This, he thinks, justifies treating determinate and determinable colors in different ways.

Although I won't address this argument directly, I would just mention that, in my view, Gert's attempts to draw substantive conclusions about the metaphysics of color from (alleged) facts about the learning of color terms is unjustified. I'll say more about this in connection with Gert (2008) in §3.2.3.2.

[17] An anonymous referee points out that the view suffers from the further defect that (at least without appeal to further apparatus) it seems unable to secure the plausible claim that

Necessarily, if x is red then x is some determinate shade of red.

For the embedded conditional will be false in worlds where x exemplifies the non-relational property *red* but is not related to subjects in the way required for it to bear any relational determinate color.

On the other hand, one might be prepared to live with this differential treatment of different colors if one could point to differences in the data about perceptual variation with respect to fine-grained determinate colors on the one hand and coarse-grained categorical colors on the other. In particular, one might attempt to justify the differential treatment of fine-grained and coarse-grained colors by showing that there is more, or more significant, perceptual variation involving the former than the latter. Thus, some have admitted that, while there is clear and compelling evidence of blameless interpersonal variation in the spectral locus for unique red, which can then be used to argue for relationalism about *unique red*, there is far less, or far less compelling, evidence of blameless interpersonal variation with respect to the determinable color *red*.[18] But if there is less clear evidence of variation with respect to *red*, then the argument from variation with respect to *red* will be correspondingly less powerful.

Alas, this attempted justification fails for empirical reasons. There simply is not the dearth of evidence of interpersonal perceptual variation with respect to *red* and other categorical, determinable colors that the objector alleges. It is true that recent philosophical discussion of perceptual variation has revolved disproportionately around variation in unique hues (of which there is indeed clear and compelling evidence). But there is also clear and compelling evidence of perceptual variation with respect to *red, blue, orange,* and so on, for which it seems no less *ad hoc* to stipulate that one variant is uniquely veridical. For example, when Malkoc *et al.* (2005) asked normal subjects to sort chips into categorical color types corresponding to the four unique hue terms ('red', 'green', 'blue', 'yellow') and four binary hue terms ('orange', 'purple', 'blue-green', 'green-yellow'), they found that there are chips that look red to some normal human perceivers and (not red but) orange to other normal human perceivers (when all perceivers are in the same controlled perceptual conditions). Likewise, there are chips that look blue to some normal perceivers and purple to other normal human perceivers; and there are chips that look yellow to some normal perceivers and orange to other normal perceivers, etc. (This is particularly clear from figure 4 in Malkoc *et al.* (2005).) This result shows not only that subjects vary in their choice of focal instances of categorical color terms (although that is true), but that a chip that is assigned to the term 'red' by one subject — hence, presumably, looks red to that subject — is assigned to (not 'red' but) 'orange' by another — hence, presumably, looks orange to that other subject. In other words, there is intersubjective variation (between psychophysically normal human trichromats) in the coarse-grained determinable colors that subjects represent a single chip as bearing, just as there is intersubjective variation in the fine-grained determinate colors that subjects represent a single chip as bearing.[19]

[18] A version of this thought is presupposed by Tye (2006*a*,*b*) and criticized by Cohen *et al.* (2006*a*,*b*).

[19] While accepting the general point that there is interpersonal variation in color perception with respect to categorical, determinable colors (e.g., *red*), Byrne and Hilbert find the appeal to Malkoc

In short, there seems to be clear and compelling evidence of perceptual variation with respect to *red* and the other determinable, categorical colors, just as there is for *unique red* and other determinate colors. And the variation with respect to the former looks to be equally blameless in both sorts of cases. Therefore, if the evidence of variation leads to a relationalist conclusion about the determinates, exactly analogous reasoning based on exactly analogous evidence leads to a relationalist conclusion about the determinables. I conclude that the present route to the denial of (2) is unsuccessful.

3.2 Color Irrealism?

In §3.1 we contemplated a range of strategies for denying premise (2) in the argument from perceptual variation and found them unsatisfactory. In this section I want to consider ways of rejecting premise (3). The strategies I have in mind all turn on the thought that (as noted in Chapter 2) one can consistently respond to instances of perceptual variation by denying that *any* of the perceptual variants in such cases veridically represent the color of the stimulus. Because perceptual variation is rampant, and seems possible in more or less any perceptual setting, the least *ad hoc* and therefore most plausible version of this view would involve the claim that *no* perceptual representations of color are veridical. Perhaps the most common reason offered for thinking that that is true is that it follows from the the irrealist (/eliminativist) view that (actual, ordinary) objects lack colors altogether.

Interestingly, the ecumenicist who accepts (3) and the irrealist who denies (3) share the virtue of consistency in their treatment of distinct perceptual variants: the ecumenicist consistently accepts all variants, while the irrealist consistently rejects all variants. That irrealism is consistent in this way strikes me as a benefit of the position; in particular, this consistency seems preferable to the kind of unmotivated (and perhaps unmotivatable) inconsistency at work in the denials of premise (2) discussed in §3.1. Moreover, irrealism has a venerable philosophical ancestry that makes the position worthy of respectful attention.

et al. (2005) (by Cohen *et al.* (2006*a*)) of questionable value in making this point. For, they say, "Malkoc et. al. used a color-naming protocol and the within-subject variability was almost as large as the between-subject variability. This suggests that subjects found the naming task difficult and complicates the interpretation of the results" (Byrne and Hilbert, 2007*b*, note 5).

This is puzzling in several respects. For one thing, Malkoc *et al.* (2005) don't report within-subject variation for the specific result at issue (that represented in figure 4). For other tasks, they address this issue indirectly by reporting correlations between repeated settings of the same hue: if all the variability were within-subjects, this correlation would take the value 0, while if all variation were between-subjects, the correlation would be 1. They report (2158) that such correlations were in all cases significant, which is to say that there was statistically significant between-subject variation. Additionally, Malkoc *et al.* (2005) address the worry about large within-subject variation by separately analyzing settings for the most consistent subjects, and report that for these the correlations in repeated settings reached 0.8 (indicating between-subject variance roughly twice that of within-subject variance). (I am indebted to Mike Webster for discussion of these points.)

Thus, I don't see that the interpretation of these results is complicated in the way and for the reasons that Byrne and Hilbert suggest.

However, as I remarked when first setting out the irrealist position in Chapter 1, irrealism comes with the *prima facie* cost that it flies in the face of naïve belief. Put bluntly, it is a notable part of the manifest image that colors are exemplified by actual, ordinary objects — fruits, lights, tables, chairs, etc., and that we learn something about the world when we visually perceive the colors of those objects. There is, then, Moorean pressure to reject irrealism about color that must be counted a significant strike against the view. That said, it is not obvious that this strike is decisive; for it is consistent with the recognition of this pressure that there might be overriding considerations that make irrealism ultimately worthy of acceptance.

As I see it, then, the main issue in assessing the current, irrealist route to the denial of (3) is whether there are such overriding motivations in favor of the position. In the remainder of this section I'll consider critically possible motivations for the view. I'll conclude that none of them suffices to overcome the Moorean pressure it faces, and therefore that the irrealist threat to the argument from variation is unsuccessful.

3.2.1 *Irrealism by Elimination*

Proponents of color irrealism have often attempted to motivate their views by arguing against their opposition (Hardin, 1988; Boghossian and Velleman, 1989, 1991; Maund, 1995). Typically, that is, these authors have either argued that substantive forms of color realism are unsuccessful, or that nothing satisfies conditions that properties would have to satisfy in order to count as (exemplified) colors. However, in the context of the Moorean pressure against irrealism described above, this sort of argument is unsatisfying. For it amounts to admitting that irrealism should only be adopted at such time as all other alternatives are decisively shown to be unacceptable — it makes irrealism a position of last resort. And since refutations in philosophy are almost never decisive, this would mean that we may have to wait an awfully long time to be in a position to accept irrealism.

Moreover, and even more importantly, I believe that there is a defensible realist theory of color — one that is internally consistent and that meets the desiderata we have reason to accept. This is, of course, the relationalist, role functionalist theory of color that I'll be defending in the present work. If I am right in judging this realist position to be defensible (or, for that matter, if there is any other defensible form of realism), then I suggest that the Moorean pressure already described gives us reason to prefer that view over color irrealism.

3.2.2 *Irrealism by Way of Primitivism*

Recently, Pautz (2006*b*) has proposed a novel line of support for irrealism that might be thought to provide a more persuasive counter to the Moorean pressures against it, and that runs through the premise that color primitivism is true. Primitivism is, of course, an important and interesting position on the nature of color in its own right; but here I want to focus more narrowly on primitivism *qua* possible motivation for color irrealism. This motivation starts with the thought that, as noted in §1.2, one can consistently combine color primitivism with irrealism: one can do this by holding, on the one hand, that colors are primitive properties (hence the primitivism), and, on the other, maintaining that these properties are not exemplified by actual, ordinary, extramental, objects (hence the irrealism). Given the consistency of this position, Pautz (2006*b*) argues for irrealism by contending that, amongst primitivist views, irrealist primitivism is preferable to realist primitivism.

There are several reasons one might think this is so.[20]

A first is that, as Pautz notes, irrealist primitivists avoid the embarrassing doubling of physical and primitive properties at object surfaces that realist primitivists must accept. Moreover, Pautz argues that the realist primitivist's doubling of properties brings in its wake an unlovely profusion of brute modal truths linking the physical (e.g., reflectance) properties and primitive colors:

> ...on one elaboration, [realist primitivism] postulates, for every minimal shade C, a brute necessity of the form 'Necessarily, x has C iff x has R', which asserts a strictly necessary connection between the reflectance property R and the wholly distinct primitive color C. There is no more basic, general necessary truth relating primitive colors and reflectances from which each of these necessary truths may be derived. Each is a kind of surd modal truth... (Pautz, 2006*b*, ms35).

Clearly, however, the irrealist primitivist has no need for these surd modal truths; given her claim that the primitive colors are unexemplified, the need to posit necessary connections between them and (exemplified) physical properties doesn't arise.

In a similar spirit, Chalmers (2006, 68) argues that realist primitivists lack an adequate treatment of perceptual variation. Chalmers is moved by considerations of symmetry to deny that any variant in such cases is uniquely veridical, as per premise (2) of the argument from perceptual variation. Given this view, and if we accept that at least some variant is veridical, we will be inclined on grounds of symmetry to accept that all variants are veridical. But he points out that, given primitivism and some natural assumptions about how extensive cases of actual and possible variation are, this leads to the conclusion that *every* object exemplifies *every* primitive color. Chalmers takes this conclusion to be unacceptable, and therefore urges us to reject the realist primitivism that leads to it. But of course this conclusion does not follow from irrealist primitivism; for the proponent of that view, who denies the veridicality of all perceptual variants, avoids the slippery slope before it begins. On these grounds, Chalmers invites us to conclude, primitivists about color should be irrealist primitivists.

Another argument for the same conclusion might be drawn from considerations about causal/explanatory exclusion familiar from debates about non-

[20] For the record, I'm presenting these arguments rather than endorsing them. I should also mention that some realist primitivists (e.g. Watkins, 2002, 2005, 2008; McGinn, 1996) have offered responses to these and similar considerations that I won't try to evaluate here.

reductive materialism in philosophy of mind (Kim, 1989*a*, 1998). The thought here is that, while x's color should figure in the causal explanation of why x looks red (as it might be) to S in C, the physical properties of x (together with the physical laws) amount to what is in principle a sufficient causal explanation of that effect. Therefore, if, as the realist primitivist maintains, x exemplifies a primitive color property that is not identical to any of x's physical properties, then that primitive color is *not* (on pain of overdetermination) what causally explains x's looking red to S in C. But in that case it just seems mistaken to claim that we visually detect x's color, as opposed to its distinct physical properties; and, indeed, if we are committed to thinking of that claim as mistaken, then it is much better to simply eliminate the extra primitive properties, thereby embracing irrealist primitivism.[21]

There is much more that should be said about these arguments but that I won't attempt to say. For our limited purposes of assessing the inference from (2) to (3) in the argument from perceptual variation, it will suffice to note that such considerations might reasonably be held to support irrealist primitivism over realist primitivism. Thus, if we can additionally find reasons to embrace primitivism, then combining these reasons with the arguments above will justify us in rejecting premise (3) of the argument from perceptual variation.

3.2.3 *Motivating Primitivism*

The outstanding issue for the contemplated reaction, then, is whether there are convincing reasons to accept color primitivism. After reviewing the options, I will suggest that there are not.[22]

3.2.3.1 *Motivating Primitivism by Epistemic Access* One reason sometimes offered in support of primitivism is that that view, precisely by denying that there is more to be said about the essences of the colors, a primitivist metaphysics of colors would grant us full epistemic access to the nature of colors in our mere perceptual acquaintance with their instances. Something like this sentiment seems to underlie Russell's oft-quoted remark that,

> the particular shade of colour that I am seeing ... may have many things to be said about it.... But such statements, though they make me know truths about the colour, do not make me know the colour itself better than I did before: so far as concerns knowledge of

[21] Hardin (1988, 60–61) argues roughly in this way against the primitivism of Cornman (1975). The argument from causal/explanatory exclusion is discussed critically in Byrne and Hilbert (2007*a*). In Chapter 7 I respond to a parallel argument against role functionalism about color that would, if correct, disarm the present motivation for irrealist primitivism as well.

[22] Obviously I cannot survey all of the possible motivations for primitivism, and therefore will focus on what I take to be some of the most important or prominent proposals.

One interesting motivation that I won't explore here is that based on considerations of the causal contributions made by colors (as opposed to the physical properties on which colors supervene) offered by Watkins (2008). My reason for ignoring this motivation for primitivism is that, because unexemplified properties lack causal powers, it works (at best) as a motivation for *realist* primitivism (as Watkins is aware). Hence, it can't serve to motivate irrealist primitivism as a way of rejecting premise (3) of the argument from perceptual variation.

the colour itself, as opposed to knowledge of truths about it, I know the color perfectly and completely when I see it and no further knowledge of it itself is even theoretically possible (Russell (1912, 47); cf. Moore (1903, 7, 10); Strawson (1978, 224); Campbell (1993, 178ff); Johnston (1992)).

I find it hard to muster sympathy for this motivation; I don't see why we should expect perception to furnish epistemic access to the essences of colors (or any other properties).[23] More to the point, however, it seems to me that the present line of motivation for primitivism is not available to the irrealist primitivist. According to the irrealist primitivist, colors lack actual instances; if so, then of course we have no perceptual contact with the colors of objects. Consequently, the irrealist primitivist is in no position to hold that perceptual contact with instances of colors delivers anything at all. But since we are interested in motivating primitivism only in the context of further reasons that have been offered for accepting irrealist rather than realist primitivism, this means that the present motivation can't do what it is intended to do.

3.2.3.2 *Motivating Primitivism by Modal Quietism* Gert (2008) argues for primitivism on the grounds that non-primitivist theories of color unavoidably make modal commitments that a proper understanding of colors should leave unresolved.[24]

Gert's argument begins with the allegedly uncontroversial assertion that (primary) color terms, when taught at all, are taught ostensively.[25] Now, successful acquisition of these terms brings about the result that competent users largely agree (borderline cases aside) about whether these terms apply to mundane objects in mundane circumstances. In contrast, Gert claims, the acquisition process does *not* ensure that competent users agree about whether these terms apply to objects in remote counterfactual scenarios (scenarios in which light behaves differently, in which objects interact with light differently, in which the human visual system operates differently). Rather, he says, competent users — viz., those who have the dispositions to use the terms in their correct, interpersonally stable, semantically licensed, ways — do not agree about the application of such terms to objects in remote counterfactual scenarios. Since competent users are, by definition, those in command of the facts that fix semantic values, Gert takes this to show that whatever fixes semantic values is similarly uncommitted about the application of (primary) color terms to objects in remote counterfactual scenarios.

But Gert argues that this conclusion undermines all non-primitivist accounts of color, since, together with the natural assumption that color terms denote

[23] I'll return to the question of what and how perceptual acquaintance and perceptual phenomenology can disclose about property essences in Chapter 6.

[24] Gert (2006) himself advocates color realism, so presumably would reject the use of his case for primitivism to motivate color irrealism that we are contemplating.

[25] For the record, I think there is more room for disagreement than Gert allows about how central a role ostension plays in the acquisition of color terms; but since I don't believe this ultimately matters to the success of his argument, I'll let this pass.

color properties, they all entail commitments about the applicability of color terms to objects in such circumstances. For every non-primitivist theory of color reductively identifies colors with some or other nature. And given that 'red' and other color terms pick out color properties, it will follow from each of these theories that 'red' and other color terms denote these natures rigidly or non-rigidly. But then any non-primitivist theory will entail answers to questions about whether 'red' and other color terms apply to objects in remote counterfactual scenarios.[26] The answers given will differ depending on the non-primitivist theory in question, the counterfactual scenario in question, and whether or not the semantics for color terms is taken to be rigid or not. Still, on any set of choices, there will be such modal entailments — entailments which, according to Gert, go beyond what is licensed by the semantics of color terms.

Primitivism escapes this difficulty because it doesn't offer any informative explication of the nature of the referents of color terms. Consequently, primitivism will tell us no more about the application of color terms in remote counterfactual scenarios than that 'red' applies to things that are red, 'blue' applies to things that are blue, and so on. Because these commitments are so minimal, they stay within what is licensed by the semantics of color terms. Gert takes this to show that non-primitivist theories of color do, and primitivist theories of color do not, have unacceptable modal consequences, and therefore that we should prefer primitivism to non-primitivism.

In my view, this argument for primitivism is unpersuasive. It is indeed plausible, as Gert contends, that in learning color terms we acquire a disposition to apply them to the right actual objects in ordinary, actual circumstances. But it can't be right that that is *all* that is fixed by the acquisition process. After all, it is beyond question that (whatever ostension is or is not doing in the acquisition process) the dispositions one acquires when one becomes semantically competent with color terms (among others) extend to novel cases not found in the learning environment. For those dispositions must extend to some cases not found in any so-far encountered circumstances, and indeed to some counterfactual circumstances. Were this not so, we would be utterly incapable of functioning linguistically with respect to any new, unencountered, or counterfactual environments — which, thank goodness, we manifestly are not.[27] I take this to suggest strongly that semantic competence

[26] Just to have an example of how this goes, suppose we adopt an identity view according to which *red* is a class of productances one (or more) of which is actually exemplified by ripe raspberries, suppose we take 'red' to denote this class rigidly, and consider a world β in which the physics of light and surfaces is as it actually is but where human visual systems respond very differently to light, such that ripe raspberries look to subjects in β the way ripe limes look to subjects in the actual world. On these choices, 'red' applies to ripe raspberries in β, since the term denotes in all worlds (*a fortiori*, in β) a property that ripe raspberries in β have.

[27] Regarding counterfactual environments in particular, it is worth mentioning that, *pace* Gert, there appears to be significant interpersonal agreement between diverse thinkers about applications of concepts/words (which explains, among other things, why thought experiments in philosophy are ever effective).

with words/concepts *does* have implications for some fact patterns that fall outside the learning scenario, that are unencountered by actual speakers, and that are non-actual.[28]

Gert's reflections do raise an important question about the acquisition of semantic competence: viz., how, given the restricted range of data and teaching methods (ostensive or otherwise) at work in the learning situation, do language learners acquire the dispositions they do — dispositions that, as I have said, appear to extend to novel and even counterfactual cases? This is a special case of the general problem of understanding language learning in the face of the poverty of the stimulus (/primary linguistic data) that has been emphasized by Chomsky (1965) (and many others).[29] This is, I take it, a very good, and currently unresolved, question. And it is one that can be reasonably asked about the acquisition of many different linguistic elements — not just color terms. But the point to notice is that, while this remains an important outstanding question about language learning, the current lack of universally accepted answers to it should not be taken to show that we *don't* acquire dispositions to project terms beyond the limited cases encountered in the learning scenario. (Indeed, the question is interesting and important exactly because it presupposes that we *do* project beyond the limitations of the learning scenario.) Returning to the case of interest, then, it would seem inappropriate to infer from the limitations in the cases encountered in the learning of color terms to the conclusion that we lack altogether dispositions to project these terms to new or counterfactual fact patterns.

Now, it must be admitted that the capacity of even cooperative and (by the usual standards) competent speakers to project color terms/concepts to new cases presumably weakens, and eventually gives out altogether, as the imagined cases become more and more remote from actuality. But, precisely because the same is true for virtually all terms/concepts — including kind terms/concepts, about which it is generally thought that there *is* a determinate fact about their applicability or otherwise to even remote counterfactual scenarios, this fact shouldn't be taken to show that there is no fact of the matter about whether color terms/concepts apply to imagined counterfactual cases. Rather, what it shows is just that our dispositions eventually cease to provide useful evidence about the matter at hand. Luckily, however, we can formulate the worry Gert raises without relying on speaker dispositions unduly. This is because Gert's non-primitivist opponent is someone who thinks that our color terms latch onto one rather than another property — viz., a property that is picked out by the analysans occurring in the non-primitivist theory of color

[28] Indeed, given the complexity and lability of the actual/non-actual boundary, it would be deeply surprising to find that semantic competence gives out exactly at the boundaries of the actual.

[29] An analogous special case is the so-called problem of motherese: how does the language learner come to acquire English or Swahili, as it might be, as opposed to the syntactically simpler fragment of the relevant natural language typically pronounced with exaggerated intonation and slower than normal pacing by parents during early language learning?

favored by that opponent. The heart of Gert's question, it seems to me, is a puzzle over how it could be that our color terms latch onto one such property rather than another, given that the candidates coincide in their extensions within the learning scenario and perhaps even in all actual cases. That is, Gert is asking how it could be that subjects manage to acquire terms that latch onto property P_1 rather than property P_2, given that P_1 and P_2 come apart in extension only in cases found outside the learning scenario (and perhaps only in remote counterfactual cases).

Again, I think there is a good, and unresolved, question here; however, and also again, I don't think it is plausible to infer from our lack of possession of an answer to the conclusion that the question has no answer. That is, I don't see that there is reason to believe that our color predicates *don't* latch onto one rather than another property despite the coincidence in those properties' extension to actual cases. After all (and *pace* Quine (1960) and the Wittgenstein of Kripke (1982)), it appears that semantics can distinguish between properties that are not only coextensive in the actual world (*a fortiori*, in the language learning scenario), but in all metaphysically possible worlds (hence, 'rabbit'/RABBIT means *rabbit* and not *undetached rabbit part*), or even in all logically possible worlds (hence, 'triangle'/TRIANGLE means *triangle* and not *trilateral*). Moreover, it appears that normal human beings can acquire a semantic competence that makes those fine-grained distinctions between properties, despite the limited character of the language-learning scenario. As I say, it is a hotly disputed question that I won't attempt to resolve here how semantics makes these sorts of distinctions, and how speaker-hearers acquire such a semantics. Nonetheless, I contend that, unless one is prepared to accept radical semantic indeterminacy quite generally, one should also reject the contention that 'red' is semantically indeterminate between non-primitivist theoretical precisifications in the way that Gert suggests it is.

Where Gert's argument for primitivism goes wrong, it seems to me, is in inferring from the presence of outstanding questions about the acquisition of the semantics for color terms, on the one hand, to metaphysical quietism about color properties, on the other. It seems to me that this inference is invalid for reasons that are not specific to color in any way. Speaking quite generally about a wide range of predicates/concepts, it is the job of the (alas, insufficiently understood) semantics to ensure that those terms/concepts are connected with the right properties and individuals, and it is the job of the (alas, insufficiently understood) process of semantic acquisition to bring about that connection in individual heads. In contrast, it is the entirely separate job of the (also, alas, insufficiently understood) metaphysics to tell us how the properties and individuals are constituted. To demand that the constraints at work in the acquisition process do all of these jobs is just to demand too much. As I say, the distribution of explanatory labor I am suggesting appears to be at work for a wide range of predicates/concepts. Thus, acquisition of competence with 'water'/WATER must bring about a connection between that word/concept and a certain stuff, but doesn't specify that that stuff is constituted in terms of hydrogen (although it is). Likewise, acquisition of competence with 'humorous'/HUMOROUS must bring about a connection between that word/concept and a certain property, but doesn't specify that that property is constituted in terms of causing a certain syndrome in appropriately situated cognizers (although it is). Similarly, acquisition of competence with 'red'/RED must bring about a connection between that word/concept and a certain property, but fails to specify how that property is constituted. But I suggest that this is no reason for thinking there is no correct, informative, non-primitivist account of how the latter property is constituted.[30]

3.2.3.3 *Motivating Primitivism by the Elimination of Alternatives* There is a final, and perhaps currently more common, motivation for primitivism that might be employed *en route* to color irrealism, and so to the denial of (3) in the argument from perceptual variation. This motivation for primitivism can be thought of as a grand argument by elimination that is itself comprised of a lot of little arguments to the effect that primitivism succeeds where other theories fail — viz., that primitivism meets important desiderata for a theory of color better than its competitors. Although I cannot engage in a full-fledged comparison for each such desiderata that might be thought relevant and damaging to any non-primitivist alternative, a few examples should give the flavor of this style of argument by elimination.

For a first, consider the problem of explaining the structural similarity and difference relations between colors — e.g., that every shade of red is more similar to orange than it is to any shade of green. Some have argued that identity theories are incapable of explaining this phenomenon, since the physical properties identified with the colors by such theories appear not to stand in the relevant relations (Hardin (1984); Hardin (1988, 66); Boghossian and Velleman (1991); Thompson (1995, 128–130, 135–139); Maund (1995, 42, 141)).[31] If one is persuaded to abandon identity theories by such arguments, then primitivism might seem a more attractive alternative. For the primitivist can treat the relevant relations as primitive resemblance relations between fundamental properties (just as we treat, say, resemblances between mass properties and resemblances between charge properties as fundamental).

Analogously, many have thought that relationalist views are susceptible to a range of complaints that leave color primitivism unscathed. For example, some have held that since many relationalists understand colors as constituted in terms of a relation to color experiences, if it should turn out that the best theory

[30] At one point Gert (2008, 8) suggests that while there *could* be a fact of the matter about the applicability of color terms to remote counterfactual scenarios, the burden lies on the opponent to demonstrate that in fact there is one. But since the metaphysics seems to go beyond what can be discerned in the constrained predicate-learning scenario for such a wide range of properties, I suggest that the burden instead falls on Gert to show us that this familiar pattern breaks down in the case of color.

[31] For responses, see Cohen (2003*b*); Byrne (2003).

of color experience understands the latter in terms of the colors presented by those experiences, the relationalist understanding of colors is objectionably circular (Boghossian and Velleman, 1989). But this threat does not appear to arise for primitivism: proponents of that view do not propose to understand the nature of colors in terms of any substantive analysans at all, and therefore do not run any risk of having an analysis that turns out to be be viciously circular. Or, again, many authors have argued that relationalism is at odds with our phenomenal experience of colors as non-relational, and have taken this claim to motivate a (non-relationalist) primitivist theory of color (McGinn, 1996). As one final example, some have taken relationalism to be incompatible with the intuition that, by exemplifying one color, ordinary objects are necessarily precluded from exemplifying others (Pautz, 2006*b*): for if x bears one color-constitutive relation to one subject in one circumstance, this seems entirely compatible with x's bearing many other color-constitutive relations to a second subject in a second circumstance. In contrast, the primitivist can explain the intuition that there is necessary exclusion of one color by another as an instance of a familiar kind of incompatibility between different determinates of a single determinable: the thought would be that primitive *blue* excludes primitive *yellow* in exactly the same (brute) way that the primitive physical property *positively charged* excludes the primitive physical property *negatively charged*.

The argumentative strategy now under consideration is one that cobbles together a series of such challenges against non-primitivist views, and concludes that only primitivism emerges unscathed. Unfortunately, I find this piecemeal form of argument by elimination for primitivism unsatisfactory.

First, and most importantly, it seems to me that the argument by elimination fails on its own terms. For, as I hope to demonstrate over the course of this book, the individual components of the argument are unpersuasive against at least one non-primitivist theory of color. In particular, I respond on behalf of relationalism to the circularity objection in §6.4, to the criticism of phenomenal inaccuracy in §§6.1–6.3, and to the worry about exclusion in §4.4.2 and §5.3.1. If my defenses succeed, then there is a non-primitivist alternative left standing, so we are not justified in accepting primitivism.

Moreover, I worry that the primitivist's proffered explanations of at least several of the relevant desiderata are too thin to warrant acceptance. For example, the primitivist avoids the relationalist's trouble about regress not by offering an informative metaphysics of color that is free of regress, but rather by saying nothing at all — or, more charitably, by supposing that the nature of colors is not further explicable in any non-chromatic terms. Similarly, the contemplated primitivist explanation of the structural relations between colors and the exclusion of one by another is not given by derivation from features of colors, but simply posited as bare modal truths. In fairness, it is plausible that there are some bare modal truths about the world, and I have no argument that truths about color exclusion and color similarity could not be among them. On the other hand, it strikes me as preferable to avoid appeals to such bare modals whenever possible, lest we trivialize the project of explanation. Given that the primitivist's explanations are so underconstrained, I worry that its benefits are just those of theft over honest toil, and submit that we should prefer to live by honest toil at least to the extent that that is possible.

3.2.4 *Overcoming The Irrealist Challenge*

We have seen that, while color irrealism might provide grounds for denying premise (3) of the argument from perceptual variation, that view is itself undermotivated. Neither the argument for irrealism by elimination of alternatives nor the arguments for irrealism that run through primitivism about color are convincing. At the same time, color irrealism is decisively at odds with beliefs about the world lying at the heart of the manifest image. Although I allow that there could be reasons for abandoning that part of the manifest image, I don't see that the arguments offered in favor of irrealism rise to the level we should require of such a sweeping revision. Since the Moorean pressure against irrealism is not, in my view, countermanded by sufficiently powerful and offsetting considerations in its favor, it is reasonable to reject the position, and with it the challenge it poses to premise (3).

3.3 Ecumenicism Without Relationalism?

The final class of objections I wish to consider in this chapter begins where the objections of §3.2 leave off. Proponents of objections in this final class accept about the relevant instances of perceptual variation that there is no uniquely veridical variant, as per premise (2) of the argument. More than this, they are willing to accept on these grounds an ecumenical response that accepts the veracity of all (or at least multiple) variants, as per claim (3) of the argument. However, they suggest, we can accept this kind of ecumenicism without embracing relationalism, contrary to the argument's conclusion (4). In this section I'll consider three ways of fleshing out this suggestion, and find them wanting.[32]

[32] In addition to the views I'll discuss at greater length in this section, it is worth mentioning here that one can read McGinn (1996) as advocating realist primitivism as another way of accepting (3) but not (4) of the argument from perceptual variation. Here McGinn accepts that objects differ in their perceptual effects on subjects (as per premise (1)), that there is no principled way of choosing one variant that represents the object to the exclusion of others (as per (2)), that we should respond to this situation by accepting a plurality of properties that are exemplified by objects (as per (3)), and even that such properties are best construed as constituted in terms of (dispositional) relations between objects, perceivers, and viewing circumstances (as per (4)). However, he argues on phenomenological grounds that colors cannot be identical to these relational (dispositional) properties (thus he repudiates the dispositionalism of McGinn (1983)), even though the latter properties are indeed (necessarily) borne by colored objects. He concludes, instead, that colors are primitive properties that *supervene* on the relational properties. One's assessment of this view will, presumably, turn largely on one's sympathy to the phenomenological arguments McGinn brings to bear against relationalism, which I'll address in Chapter 6.

3.3.1 *Non-Relationalist Relativism*

In §1.3 I distinguished between color relativism — roughly, the idea that there are no (non-stipulative) colors *simpliciter*, but only colors for certain kinds of perceivers in certain circumstances (McLaughlin, 2003*a*; Jakab and McLaughlin, 2003) — and color relationalism — roughly, the idea that colors are constituted in terms of relations to perceivers. Color relativists hold that objects can simultaneously exemplify distinct relativized colors. Consequently, in cases where x looks unique green to S_1 in C_1 and looks bluish green to S_2 in C_2, relativists are in a position to say that both representations of x's color can be veridical — they can both be veridical if x (simultaneously and all over) exemplifies both the color *unique green for* S_1 *in* C_1 and the color *bluish green to* S_2 *in* C_2. This is just to say that color relativists can accept the ecumenicism of premise (3) in the argument from perceptual variation. However, as we have seen, color relativism does not entail color relationalism; indeed, color relativism (by itself) is extremely non-committal about the metaphysical constitution of the relativized color properties it recognizes.

Therefore, if there are viable non-relationalist forms of color relativism, these views will represent ways of blocking the inference from (3) to (4), hence ways of resisting my case for relationalism. Our question will be: are there any?

The metaphysically non-committal quality of color relativism can make it seem somewhat difficult to assess on metaphysical grounds. However, we can get at the critical metaphysical issues by asking about the source of the relativity in question. In particular, we can approach this issue by considering a range of non-color examples where there we encounter the relevant kind of relativity, and ask whether colors fit any of these models.

As far as I can tell, there are just two kinds of cases where it seems natural to relativize properties to subjects. First, there are properties that are constituted by a relation to subjects. Thus, something can be to the left of me but not to the left of you (by bearing a spatial relation to me but not you); someone can be my sister but not yours (by, in part, bearing a certain genetic relation to me but not you); and someone can be my teacher but not yours (by bearing a certain pedagogical relation to me but not you). Second, there are properties that are not constituted by a relation to subjects, but that are constituted by their realizing a certain functional role that itself involves a relation to a subject. Thus, something can be a carburetor for you but not for me (by realizing the functional role of mixing fuel and oxygen in some device appropriately related — say, by the ownership relation — to me, but failing to realize that functional role in any device appropriately related to you); something can be a can-opener for me but not you (by realizing the functional role of opening cans appropriately related to me, but failing to realize the functional role of opening cans appropriately related to you).

With these examples in mind, let us return to the question of how a color relativist should explain the relativity of colors.

Adopting the first model would involve claiming that colors are constituted in terms of relations to subjects. In other words, it amounts to accepting color relationalism. Thus, the first model for understanding the relativity of colors is not a way of resisting the inference from (3) to (4) — hence, not a way of resisting color relationalism — after all.

The second, model, however, is more promising for the purposes at hand; and, indeed, it is the form of non-relationalist relativism that has received the most support (e.g., this is the view defended by Jackson (1996); McLaughlin (2003*a*)). The color relativist who takes colors to be the realizers of certain subject-involving functional roles (e.g., the role of disposing their bearers to look a certain way to certain subjects in certain conditions) has a good explanation of the relativity of colors that does not commit her to color relationalism. She can explain the relativity of colors by noting that an object's material makeup can realize a subject-involving functional role with respect to one subject but not another — e.g., the object's material makeup might realize the role of disposing its bearers to look unique green to S_1 in C_1 but not the role of disposing its bearers to look unique green to S_2 in C_2. At the same time, this account does not commit the color relativist to relationalism; for it is left entirely open by this account that the properties realizing the relevant functional roles are not even partly constituted in terms of relations to subjects.

Because it identifies colors with the realizers of certain functional roles, the view under consideration is a kind of realizer functionalism. I should say immediately that this sort of realizer functionalism is, in my view, the most promising alternative to relationalism about color. However, I do not think the view merits our acceptance. I'll have to delay a full presentation of my reasons for this verdict to §7.2. There I'll attempt to explicate the realizer functionalist position more fully than I can here in the course of distinguishing it from the (related but distinct) role functionalist account of color that I'll defend in Chapter 7. As a preview of that later discussion, however, I want to mention briefly three objections to realizer functionalism that I'll bring out more fully in §7.2 and that, to my mind, show that view to be ultimately unacceptable.

The first such objection is that realizer functionalism cannot provide a satisfactory account of what is necessarily common to distinct instances of a given color property. Realizer functionalists hold that what makes a token material configuration an instance of a color property is that it realizes a certain functional role. Of course, they allow that tokens of different material configuration types might realize the very same functional role, and thereby qualify as distinct instances of the very same color. What is common to the distinct instances of the color, then, is the (relational) functional role that they realize. However, and crucially, realizer functionalists are committed to holding that this relational functional role is not part of the essence of the color property (that is why the view does not qualify as a species of color relationalism). Indeed, that the token material configurations realize this common relational functional role is, apparently, a contingent rather than necessary feature of each of them. That is, of each material configuration token, it is contingent that that token realizes the subject-involving functional role in question; in worlds with different laws, or different kinds of subjects/visual systems, these material configurations would play different subject-involving functional roles, or perhaps no subject-involving functional roles at all. Thus, realizer functionalists must explain what is common to instances of a given color property in terms of something that is inessential to that color, and only contingently exemplified by its instances. I'll argue in §7.2.2 that this is less than we should demand from a theory of colors.

My second objection to realizer functionalism is that the view is unable to secure certain necessary features of the colors that come out in such modal propositions as the following:

Necessarily orange is binary.

Necessarily orange is more similar to red than to green.

For, according to the realizer functionalist, colors are the realizers of the relevant subject-involving functional roles — certain material structures. Now, the best explanation of why some such material structure is binary rather than unique, or occupies its role in the similarity space of colors, is that that material structure is contingently connected with a phenomenal state in subjects that is phenomenally composed and stands in a position in a phenomenal similarity space. But since the material structure in question is only *contingently* connected with the mental state that has these properties, it has its status as binary rather than unitary and its role in similarity space only contingently. Therefore, I'll urge in §7.2.3, realizer functionalists are committed to denying that these features hold of the colors as a matter of necessity.

My third reason for doubting realizer functionalism about color turns on the question of whether color terms designate rigidly or not. Realizer functionalists are committed to saying that color terms designate non-rigidly. For they take those terms to designate the realizers of certain functional roles, and it seems that the realizers of those roles can vary substantially between possible worlds (for example, as a function of the laws, the physics, and the visual systems of each world). But, as I hope to demonstrate in §7.2.4, there are several reasons for believing that color terms designate rigidly.

To repeat, my over-brief remarks here should be treated only as previews of the arguments to be developed more fully in §7.2. However, it will be my contention that these criticisms, once developed fully, make realizer functionalism an untenable account of the nature of color.

Moreover, for reasons discussed above, I do not see any other way of understanding color relativism that avoids commitment to color relationalism. Therefore, I want to conclude that color relativism does not ultimately block the inference from ecumenicism to color relationalism (from (3) to (4) in the argument from perceptual variation), and therefore that it does not undermine my case for color relationalism in the way envisaged.

3.3.2 *Selectionism*

3.3.2.1 *Exposition and Elaboration* A second version of a non-relationalist ecumenicism that I want to consider — a view termed 'selectionism' by Allen (2009) — has recently been defended by Kalderon (2007*a*,*b*), Allen (2009), and Mizrahi (2007). In this section I'll lay out the view, and then say why I find it to be an ultimately inferior species of ecumenicism.[33] [34]

Selectionists accept the ecumenicism of premise (3), and consequently accept that a stimulus can bear multiple colors (all over, at a single time). But they deny that colors are constituted in terms of relations between subjects and objects. Selectionists agree that the phenomena of perceptual variation have important lessons to teach about color and color perception. Namely, they take these phenomena as reason for believing that different visual systems, in different circumstances, are selectively sensitive to different colors that the stimulus bears. However, they urge that once we see that this is the true lesson of perceptual variation, the temptation to construe colors as constituted in terms of a relation to subjects or circumstances evaporates.[35] Kalderon (2007*a*) follows Burnyeat (1979) in associating this selectionist account with Heraclitus, and contrasts it against relationalism (which, again following Burnyeat, he characterizes as Protagorean):

> The relation between object, perceiver, and circumstances of perception does not determine the color of the object (in the way that it would if colors were relational) so much as it determines the perceptual availability of that color. Thus the relation between the chip, Norm, and the circumstances of perception, does not determine that the chip is unique green; rather it determines the perceptual availability of unique green for Norm. Moreover, the relation between the chip, Norma, and the circumstances of perception does not determine that the chip is yellowish green; rather, it determines the perceptual availability of yellowish green for Norma. On the [Heraclitean] pluralistic hypothesis,

[33] I have been aided considerably in thinking about the material in this section by comments from an anonymous referee.

[34] Despite its interest, I have not represented selectionism anywhere in the Refined Taxonomy of views about the nature of color in Chapter 1. This is because, as noted by Kalderon (2007*a*, 577), this view is to a large extent agnostic about the nature of color; it is pretty clearly consistent with a variety of non-relationalist accounts. Indeed, for that matter, one could even imagine a variant of the view that is consistent with (multiple forms of) relationalism — this would be a view on which objects simultaneously exemplify a plurality of color properties constituted in terms of relations to one single observer and one viewing condition, as well as a plurality of color properties constituted in terms of relations to a second single observer and a second viewing condition, and so on. (It is unclear why one would accept such a view: its selectionism and its relationalism both purport to answer the very same ecumenical need, so it is hard to see why anyone would bother to embrace both commitments.) In any case, given that our present interest in selectionism is prompted by a search for non-relationalist forms of ecumenicism, I'll treat selectionism as a competitor to relationalism in what follows.

[35] Indeed, Kalderon (2007*a*) suggests that the possibility of a non-relationalist ecumenicism shows that "the alleged relational nature of the colors plays no role whatsoever in resolving the paradox [of perceptual variation]" (583). While I agree with Kalderon that ecumenicism (rather than relationalism *per se*) is the key to resolving what he calls "the paradox" about perceptual variation, I'll be arguing that Kalderon's preferred ecumenical alternative is unsatisfying, and therefore hold that relationalism is after all essential to resolving worries about perceptual variation because it is the most plausible form of the needed ecumenicism.

the chip is multiply colored — it is unique green all over and yellowish green all over at the same time; it is just that the perceptual availability of these sensible qualities is determined by different relations between the chip, perceivers, and circumstances of perception. According to the color pluralist, then, the [relationalist] conflates the conditions for perception of a color for the perceived color (Kalderon, 2007*a*, 577).

Since selectionism rests so heavily on the notion, it is worth asking just what it means to say that a visual system "selects" one property of an object rather than another. As I understand it, selection is nothing more than selective representation. Thus, the idea is that a single object might exemplify a range of properties, but that a visual system confronted with that object might represent only some of these properties — perhaps only a single one — rather than all of them. This construal allows the desirable result that S could select P rather than P' even in an object that exemplifies both properties, and even if, as a matter of contingent fact, all actual objects that exemplify P also exemplify P'. So far, so good.

However, on encountering selectionism for the first time, one might reasonably wonder how the view can account for the facts of color incompatibility — e.g., the incompatibility that holds between unique green and yellowish green. Of course, the traditional explanation of the incompatibility involves holding that, necessarily, nothing is both unique green and yellowish green (all over and at the same time). But this traditional explanation is unavailable to anyone who endorses an ecumenical response to cases of interpersonal perceptual variation with respect to the spectral locus of unique hues (*qua* instance of the more general phenomenon of perceptual variation): ecumenicism about such cases just amounts to the thought that one spectral light bears (all over and at the same time) both of the colors ascribed to it (as it might be, unique green and yellowish green). As we have seen, relationalist ecumenicists have an alternative explanation of the incompatibility. Namely, just as in their treatment of all other cases of perceptual variation, they hold that subject S_1 represents the stimulus as *unique green for* S_1 *(in* C_1*)*, whereas subject S_2 represents the stimulus as *yellowish green for* S_2 *(in* C_2*)*, and maintain that colors only stand in exclusion relations if they are constituted in terms of the same relata. Thus, relationalists can explain the incompatibility in question (without compromising their ecumenicism) by holding that, necessarily, nothing is both unique green to S in C and yellowish green to S in C (all over and at the same time). However, this relationalist explanation of the incompatibility is unavailable to selectionists, since it turns crucially on construing colors as constituted in terms of relations to subjects.

Thus, unless they wish to abandon the ecumenical response to the case of perceptual variation at hand, selectionists owe an alternative explanation of the incompatibility.[36] I think there is such an alternative account available to the

[36] One possible alternative reaction, endorsed by Allen (2009) would be to hold on to an ecumenical/selectionist response to interspecies cases of perceptual variation, but a different

selectionist, although it will involve something of a departure from the naïve gloss on the incompatibility. Instead of treating the incompatibility between the two colors as a prohibition on their simultaneous exemplification by an object (as per the traditional or relationalist treatments), the selectionist can claim that the "incompatibility" in question is a prohibition on any normal visual system's simultaneously ascribing both to an object. That is, for the selectionist, the incompatibility should be understood as a (broadly) psychological limitation on certain kinds of property representations, rather than a metaphysical limitation on certain kinds of property exemplifications. On this view, then, the incompatibility at issue is to be explained by the fact that, for any normal subject S, necessarily nothing is represented by S as unique green and represented by S as yellowish green (all over and at the same time).

Now, one might object to this strategy simply on the grounds that it is a revisionary understanding of the incompatibility. But this objection seems unpersuasive. For one thing, since the relationalist explanation of the incompatibility is also distinct from the traditional explanation, the complaint of revisionism is not one that relationalists (such as the present author) are particularly well-placed to make. More importantly, however, it strikes me that what the proposed selectionist explanation revises (likewise for the proposed relationalist explanation) — viz., the traditional explanation in terms of property exemplification — is reasonably regarded as a theoretical gloss on the data rather than anything mandated by the facts themselves. And I take it that revisionism about a theoretical gloss can be acceptable if (as the selectionist and relationalist will maintain is true in the present case) they provide compensatory explanatory gains elsewhere.

A second, but also ultimately unpersuasive, worry about the proposed selectionist strategy for explaining color incompatibilities is that it is committed to treating the interpersonal variation case ecumenically (while rejecting relationalism), so is committed to the idea that one stimulus can be both unique green and yellowish green; and one might think that this commitment can

response (e.g., something like the epistemic diagnosis discussed in §3.1.1) to cases of interspecies perceptual variation. A similar hybrid position is advocated by Byrne and Hilbert (2003, 2004):

> Since a single surface falls under many different reflectance types . . . , there need not be any conflict between color appearances across species. Goldfish and human beings see objects as having different colors, but reflectance physicalism gives no reason to suppose that if one species is right, then the other must be wrong (Byrne and Hilbert (2003, 16); cf. Bradley and Tye (2001)).

This strategy of response seems awkward given the structural similarity between the different forms of perceptual variation. Of the authors cited, only Allen (2009, 25–26) attempts to give any indication about why he favors different responses to different instances of what seems to be a common pattern of results (and, indeed, as Allen is aware, the reasons he offers for this preference turn on contentious assumptions about property individuation). Given the apparent structural similarity between interspecies, intraspecies, and intrapersonal cases of perceptual variation, it seems to me that, in the absence of some uncontroversial and persuasive reasons to the contrary, a uniform treatment of the cases is to be preferred.

be shown to lead to contradiction (cf. Hardin, 2006, 343). For assume, as per standard usage of the technical term, that what it is to be unique green just is to (i) exemplify *green*, (ii) lack *yellowishness*, and (iii) lack *bluishness*, whereas what it is to be yellowish green is to (i) exemplify *green* and (ii) exemplify *yellowishness*. Then it might seem that the selectionist is committed to allowing (unacceptably) that such things can simultaneously both exemplify and not exemplify *yellowishness*. But the selectionist can evade this contradiction by disputing the nature of the claimed connections between *unique green* and *yellowishness* (and between *yellowish green* and *yellowishness*). She might claim that *yellowishness* is in the first instance a a property of colors (thus, a property of properties of objects), and only derivatively a property of objects. The view would be that x is yellowish just in case some color of x is yellowish. On this construal, what follows from the selectionist's allowing that x bears both *unique green* and *yellowish green* is not that x both bears and lacks *yellowishness*, but rather that (i) one of x's colors bears *yellowishness*, (ii) another of x's colors lacks *yellowishness*, and (iii) x bears *yellowishness* (from (i), and in spite of (ii)). This combination of results is not contradictory, and well-suited to the selectionist position that objects have multiple colors simultaneously. Thus, as far as I can tell, selectionism contains the resources to answer the worries about color incompatibility that we have been discussing.

3.3.2.2 *Selectionism and Postreceptoral Perceptual Variation* There is much to admire in the selectionist view on offer; most significantly from my perspective, of course, is that the selectionist joins the color relationalist in endorsing both (2) and the ecumenical premise (3) of the argument from perceptual variation. That said, I find this view ultimately inferior to relationalism, and therefore not a threat to my claim that relationalism is the most attractive form of ecumenicism.

The most serious problem for selectionism, in my view, involves cases of intersubjective postreceptoral differences discussed by Shoemaker (2003) and Pautz (2006*c*, 2008).[37] These cases are challenges to selectionism because, if it is to remain a competitor to color relationalism, selectionism needs to say that

[37] There is one more worry about selectionism that I regard as potentially serious but not decisive. This worry is that selectionism seems to demand a large number of (non-relational) properties of objects: one that is selected by every visual system type and in every visual circumstance corresponding to each (veridical) perceptual variant we can produce. To anticipate the discussion in §5.1, a proliferation of relational properties of x is unproblematic, in so far as there are presumably large numbers of relata to which x can be related. On the other hand, it might well seem ontologically profligate to proliferate non-relational properties of x in the way that selectionism requires. (This worry is especially pressing for versions of selectionism that take color properties to be primitive.)

Allen (2009, 17ff.) attempts to defuse this worry by suggesting that (i) one might limit one's selectionism to interspecies cases, and (ii) there could turn out to be less interspecies perceptual variation than feared in the animal kingdom. As already mentioned (note 36), I find the non-uniformity represented by (i) a significant cost. Moreover, (ii) strikes me as implausible given what we now know about the differences between visual systems in different species.

That said, I think the most serious difficulties for selectionists lie elsewhere.

the color properties that are candidates for selection/representation are non-relational (physical or primitive) properties (this commitment is emphasized clearly in the Kalderon quotation that appears at the beginning of this section). But given that assumption, it is difficult to see how a proponent of selectionism can describe the cases adequately: in particular, it is difficult to see how selectionists can secure the plausible result that subjects in such cases differ in the color properties they select/represent.[38]

An instance of such problematic case is offered by Pautz (2006*c*). Pautz asks us to imagine two subjects, Maxwell and Twin Maxwell, who agree in their receptoral responses to color stimuli, but who differ in their postreceptoral responses to color stimuli. Maxwell is an actual perceiver who counts as normal by the standard psychophysical tests. Twin Maxwell is a non-actual perceiver who evolved in a different environment, who also counts as normal by the standard psychophysical tests, and who is exactly like Maxwell in the receptoral structure of their visual systems: they have not only the same proportions, but the very same number of each (functionally individuated) type of retinal photoreceptor. Given that visual systems respond to the non-relational properties selectionists propose to identify with colors via the activity of their photoreceptors, there is already some temptation to think that Maxwell and Twin Maxwell (/their visual systems) will represent/select the very same non-relational properties of objects (I'll argue for this more fully below). Nonetheless, it is consistent with the envisaged scenario that the visual systems of Maxwell and Twin Maxwell differ in their postreceptoral organization.[39] Consequently, when Maxwell and Twin Maxwell view x, their visual systems may end up in distinct chromatic response state types as a result of their having selected x's very same non-relational property P — for example, it might be that Maxwell's visual system enters into a state of type S_M, while Twin Maxwell's visual system enters into a state of type S_{TM}.

[38] Shoemaker and Pautz use these cases to argue that the subjects in question have phenomenally distinct experiences, and that this cannot be accounted for by those who hold that (i) the phenomenal character of experience supervenes on the representational content of experience, and (ii) the representational content of the relevant visual experiences supervene on the non-relational properties represented by the subject (Dretske, 1995; Tye, 1995). In the interest of simplicity, I'll put (i) and further issues about the phenomenal character of experience aside. My contention will be just that the subjects in question represent different contents, and that this cannot be reconciled with (ii).

[39] Objection: If the two subjects have the same receptoral structure but different postreceptoral structure, then at least one of them is a non-normal perceiver.

Response: Although this will depend on the understanding of normality in place, it is hard to imagine that any reasonable understanding of normality would require subjects with identical receptoral organization to be identical in postreceptoral structure. Certainly if 'normal' is understood in terms of the usual psychophysical criteria, then there is no such requirement. It is plausible that receptoral organization puts constraints on postreceptoral organization; but it is implausible that these constraints are consistent with only a single normal postreceptoral phenotype.

One kind of postreceptoral variation that is common amongst actual subjects, and that therefore provides a realistic model for the kind of variation imagined between Maxwell and Twin Maxwell, involves variation in the operation of the postreceptoral opponent channels that are at the center of the canonical "opponent process" explanation of the unique/binary distinction (viz., of subjects' judgments that certain colors (/color experiences) are uncomposed and others composed).[40]

Suppose, then, that Maxwell and Twin Maxwell differ in their postreceptoral opponent process responses (but not their receptoral responses to color stimuli). If so, then when Maxwell and Twin Maxwell are both presented with the same color stimulus (or qualitatively identical but numerically distinct color stimuli, since they are in numerically different worlds), then even though their visual systems will both select the very same non-relational property P exemplified by the stimulus, they will differ in their verdicts about whether P is unique or binary. In particular, we may suppose that the selection of P activates two

[40] Recall that the unique/binary distinction presented in §2.3.2 is based on phenomenological observations about subjects' color experiences (although, as noted, the distinction can be understood as applying to either colors or color experiences). A related phenomenological observation is that reddishness and greenishness are not found together in any binary combination. Likewise for bluishness and yellowishness. In this sense, reddish and greenish form what is called an opponent pair; bluish and yellowish form another. These claims about the structure of color experience are supported not only by direct introspection, but by an impressive collection of hue-cancellation and color naming results (Boynton *et al.*, 1964).

(Significantly, the standard understanding of the framework outlined here is in tension with the claim that, at least in certain constrained circumstances, reddishness and greenishness are phenomenologically compossible (Crane and Piantanida, 1983). However, the interpretation of these heterodox results is highly controversial; at the very least, it seems safe to say that the unusual combinations they report fail to occur in naturalistic settings. Accordingly, I'll put this challenge aside in what follows.)

The opponent channels are neurocomputational mechanisms proposed by the so-called (and widely accepted) opponent process theory to explain the phenomenological effects just described. Opponent process theory proposes that color appearances are encoded at the postreceptoral level (i.e., this encoding is computed from the output of retinal cone cells) along three independent informational channels: red–green, yellow–blue, and white–black. These channels have an opponent organization: a positive state of activation (firing rate higher than base rate) on the red–green channel means that the stimulus looks reddish rather than greenish, where a negative state of activation (firing rate lower than base rate) on the same channel means that the stimulus looks greenish rather than reddish.

Opponent process theory explains the unique/binary distinction by treating chromatic color appearances in terms of the activity on the opponent channels. It correctly predicts that there are exactly four chromatic unique color experiences that occur just when one of the two chromatic channels is neither positive or negative (is firing at base rate). For example, unique red experiences occur when the blue–yellow channel is at base rate and so makes no contribution, but the red–green channel is in a positive state of activation; likewise, we have blue/yellow experiences when the red–green channel is at base rate and so makes no contribution, but the blue–yellow channel is in a positive or negative state of activation. When, however, both chromatic channels are not at base rate, they both make a contribution to the experience; consequently, the experience is phenomenally composed. The opponent structure of the channels also explains why reddish/greenish and bluish/yellowish (and no others) are phenomenally opponent pairs.

For a more complete (and canonical) presentation of opponent process theory, see Hurvich (1981).

different opponent process channels in Maxwell's visual system, but only one opponent process channel in Twin Maxwell's visual system. If this occurs, Maxwell will judge that the color of the stimulus is binary (composed), while Twin Maxwell will judge that the color of the stimulus is unique (uncomposed). Moreover, given that (as is widely held) color similarity judgments between stimuli are computed on the basis of postreceptoral responses in the visual system, Maxwell's state S_M and Twin Maxwell's state S_{TM} will fall into different similarity orderings; consequently, Maxwell and Twin Maxwell will differ in the ways in which they sort qualitatively identical color stimuli. For these reasons, it seems that subjects who differ in the postreceptoral ways in which Maxwell and Twin Maxwell differ will have different behavioral dispositions with respect to the sorting, discrimination, and recognition of colors. Although these behavioral differences may be too subtle to emerge in ordinary settings, they are exactly the sort of differences that can be revealed by standard comparative psychophysical techniques in controlled settings.

With this setup in hand, it is now easy to state the problem posed for the selectionist by the case of Maxwell and Twin Maxwell. On the one hand, the most plausible characterization is that Maxwell's visual state S_M and Twin Maxwell's visual state S_{TM} differ in representational content. However, on the other hand, it appears that, given any of a wide class of popular psychosemantic theories, the selectionist will be forced to say that S_M and S_{TM} do not differ in the non-relational properties they select/represent. I'll argue for these points in turn.

First, why believe S_M and S_{TM} differ in representational content? The most obvious answer is that S_M and S_{TM} differ in how they characterize (a small piece of) the world. S_M characterizes the world as a world in which P is binary/composed, while S_{TM} characterizes the world as one in which P is unique/uncomposed. This is to say, first, that both states characterize the world — i.e., that they have representational contents, and, second that they *disagree* in how they characterize the world — that their content is different.[41] A further reason for thinking that S_M and S_{TM} differ in their representational content is that it is hard to see how to explain the behavioral differences between Maxwell and Twin Maxwell without that supposition.[42]

[41] N.B.: Plausibly there is no difference between what Maxwell's *receptors* represent and what Twin Maxwell's *receptors* represent. My contention is that there is (perceptual) variation between what the state of Maxwell's visual system represents and what the state of Twin Maxwell's visual system represents. I take it that it would be unreasonable to insist that sensory representation ends at the receptors.

[42] Objection: We might explain the behavioral difference without supposing S_M and S_{TM} differ in content. By analogy, Oedipus behaves one way if he represents Jocasta under a mode of representation he would linguistically express as 'Mommy', and behaves a different way if he represents the very same individual under a mode of presentation he would linguistically express as 'my wife'. This shows that the inference from the presence of a behavioral difference to a difference in content is invalid.

Thus, the most plausible description of the case is that S_M and S_{TM} differ in what they represent. But it's not at all obvious that selectionists can agree with that description of the case. For, given any of a wide variety of accounts of representation that selectionists might (and, in fact, do) accept, it is *prima facie* hard to see how selectionists can avoid concluding that both S_M and S_{TM} agree in representing the very same non-relational property P that causes each of them. Exactly how this plays out will depend on the details of our theory of representation. But the basic problem for all such theories is that S_M and S_{TM} are caused by the very same non-relational property P, and that Maxwell and Twin Maxwell can be made as alike as one wants in the criteria that are plausible candidates for constituting the representational relation.

For a representative example, consider the view of Tye (1995, 2000), according to which a state s represents F just in case s causally covaries with F in "optimal conditions" — conditions in which (confining ourselves to representation in the visual system),

> the various components of the visual system [are] operating as they were designed to do in the sort of external environment in which they were designed to operate. Here, there is no interference — no genetic abnormalities to throw things off, no peculiarities in the outside setting. Everything is as it should be (Tye, 2000, 138).

It certainly appears that both Maxwell's and Twin Maxwell's visual system are operating in optimal conditions in this sense if anything is. Maxwell and Twin Maxwell are psychophysically normal perceivers looking at an ordinary colored object under ordinary visual conditions. Nothing is interfering with their visual perception — we can stipulate that no evil demons, inverting lenses, or other trickery are at work in the case. And since it is a matter of empirical fact that there are postreceptoral differences of the sort under discussion between pairs of subjects neither of whom suffers from any genetic abnormality, we may suppose with no loss of generality that both Maxwell and Twin Maxwell do not either. Each of their visual systems is operating in the environment in which it evolved (as one says, in the environment in which it was designed to operate). Admittedly, these environments may differ from one another. But since, as Tye (2006*a*, 176) himself allows, the plurality of observation conditions under which our visual systems evolved makes it extremely implausible that the external environments under which normal observers were designed to operate by evolution are fixed at all uniquely, this gives no reason for supposing that either system is operating in a non-design environment, or that there is anything relevantly peculiar about either environment. It looks, then, as if S_M in Maxwell and S_{TM} in Twin Maxwell both covary with the non-relational

Response: The contemplated strategy succeeds only if there is a difference between Maxwell and Twin Maxwell in the mode of presentation under which they (/their visual systems) represent the very same content. While I'll argue against this proposal more generally in §3.3.3, for now I'll be content to point out that the proposed analysis is at odds with the ordinary description of the case as a disagreement about the color of the stimulus (rather than a mode of presentation of the stimulus).

property P in conditions that are optimal in the required sense.[43] Therefore, given this theory of representation, both S_M and S_{TM} represent P — they have a common representational content.

Moreover, and significantly, this result does not appear to be isolated to Tye's psychosemantics; on the contrary, and as Pautz (2006*c*, 220–228) argues convincingly, it appears that the same conclusion follows from many other extant theories of content (including the indicator psychosemantics endorsed by Dretske (1995), the asymmetric dependence psychosemantics of Fodor (1990*c*), the input-output psychosemantics of Armstrong (1999); Davies (1993), the success psychosemantics of Papineau (1993), and the consumerist psychosemantics of Millikan (1989)). The broad lesson seems to be that we can, consistently with the supposition that Maxwell and Twin Maxwell differ in their postreceptoral response but not their receptoral response to P, describe the situation so that the two are alike in all the respects that going psychosemantic theories take to be content-constitutive. If this is true, then it appears that selectionists who endorse any such theory of representation (and as a matter of fact, that means all selectionists) cannot secure the needed result that Maxwell's and Twin Maxwell's visual systems differ in what they represent.

I can imagine several ways in which selectionists might respond to this line of objection.

First, selectionists might attempt to escape the trouble by denying that their view together with standard psychosemantic theories leads to misdescription on the grounds that the standard psychosemantic theories are too schematic to make any prediction at all about the cases (Byrne and Tye, 2006, 252). Unfortunately, for reasons I have already given, I think this claim is false. As far as I can tell, while it is true that available psychosemantic theories don't make assignments of representational content to every imaginable state, we can consistently elaborate our description of the case of Maxwell and Twin Maxwell to the point that these theories do seem to make predictions about the contents

[43] Objection (cf. Byrne and Tye, 2006, 252): Either P is a unique hue or it is not. It was part of the description of the case that S_M represents P as binary while S_{TM} represents P as unique (viz., not binary). Therefore, one or the other of these states represents P non-veridically. But then this gives us reason for saying that one of the two visual systems is operating in non-optimal circumstances; for we can say that a circumstance C is optimal for a visual system only if that visual system has veridical representational contents in C.

Response: First, it is dialectically inappropriate to assume that P's being unique and P's being non-unique are mutually exclusive cases. For relationalists will take the case as showing precisely that a given external physical property P could realize a color that is unique for Maxwell and realize a different color that is binary for Twin Maxwell; if so, then both representations can be veridical. But if that is true, then the proffered reason for taking one of the circumstances in question to be non-optimal falls apart. Second, this objection leads to regress: since representation is being understood in terms of optimality, we can't also understand optimality in terms of non-veridicality — viz., false representation (cf. Pautz, 2006*c*, note 5). To escape from this regress and make the present objection persuasive, selectionists owe an independent reason for believing Maxwell or Twin Maxwell fails to be in optimal circumstances. Given that we seem to be able to elaborate the case in a way that makes the two subjects alike in all of the respects that seem to be relevant for optimality, it is hard to imagine what would count as such a reason.

of S_M and S_{TM}. And when we do so, it seems to me that these theories, when combined with selectionism, converge in predicting (wrongly) that the states are alike in their content.

Second, selectionists might regard the problem as a temporary result of the shortcomings of extant psychosemantics (Byrne and Tye, 2006, 252ff.). They might claim that, while the most plausible current psychosemantic theories plus the assumption that S_M and S_{TM} represent a non-relational property do yield the incorrect result that Maxwell and Twin Maxwell agree in what they represent, this result could be avoided by the adoption of a better (perhaps future) psychosemantics. Of course, no one is now in a position to rule out this outcome. On the other hand, it is telling that (not one, but) many of the most widely supported psychosemantic theories lead to the same trouble for the selectionist; in particular, this makes it seem somewhat unlikely that the trouble lies with the psychosemantics rather than selectionism. Given this state of play, it is not sufficient for selectionists to claim that there *might* be a psychosemantics that saves their view (that is true, but not a compelling defense of anything). Instead, it seems to me, the burden is squarely on selectionists to elucidate a psychosemantics whose combination with selectionism clearly does not lead to misdescription of the cases, and then show that it is equal to or better than the (admittedly incomplete) psychosemantic proposals we now know about and whose combination with selectionism does lead to misdescription of the cases. Until that burden has been discharged, I think we are justified in taking the cases at issue to cast doubt on selectionism.

A third avenue of response for the selectionist would be to insist flatly that the problematic cases are metaphysically impossible, and so simply don't arise. Kalderon, in particular, seems inclined toward this response on the grounds that, unlike the cases of perceptual variation discussed earlier, cases of postreceptoral variation are merely hypothetical:

> One might wonder what exactly we are being asked to imagine. The relevant case is so far underdescribed, we lack an explanation of the source of perceptual variation. While we can clearly conceive that the ... difference is due to further visual processing, without a further explanation of the source of the perceptual variation, we cannot *distinctly* conceive this. And if we cannot clearly and distinctly conceive this, we so far lack a reason to believe this to be genuinely possible. The worry, while genuine, is too weak, however. While we may so far lack a reason to believe that it is possible that the ... difference is due to further visual processing, this is not yet to claim that there could be no such reason. Further argument is required (Kalderon, 2007*b*, 14–15).

I confess that this last response strikes me as desperate. While I'm not sure what would be required to raise the relevant conception to Kalderon's standards for distinctness, it seems to me that the conceived case is in fact pretty well described. For one thing, the general structure of the case (which involves distinct post-receptoral responses in two different subjects even in optimal circumstances) just seems to me not that hard to conceive of clearly and distinctly. For another, on the best (and widely accepted) "opponent-process" accounts, the unitary/binary distinction provides an actual example of interpersonal differences in postreceptoral processing of a given color stimulus. It is true that, as Kalderon (2007*a*, 586) and Byrne and Tye (2006, 243) point out, the details of opponent-process theory (and in particular its neural implementation) remain poorly understood. Nonetheless, the form of the explanation it supplies is not only clearly and distinctly conceivable, but (despite the worries about the details and lack of neurophysiological confirmation) "by now universally accepted" (Jameson and Hurvich, 1989, 187). If so, then the general hypothesis that postreceptoral processing affects our perceptual representation of color — a hypothesis of which opponent-processing theory is a specific instance — is likewise clearly and distinctly conceivable. In the face of these considerations, it seems to me unreasonable to deny the possibility of the problematic cases in order to save selectionism.

Given all this, it seems to me that the most promising response to the challenge posed by the cases is to give up the selectionist's insistence that the properties that are candidates for being represented are restricted to non-relational properties. If we give up this insistence, and instead allow that the color properties represented by S_M and S_{TM} are relational properties, then we have no trouble finding a distinction between the representational contents of these states, and so can preserve the pre-theoretically plausible description of the case. In particular, the thought would be that Maxwell's visual system represents (as it might be) *orange to Maxwell in* C, while Twin Maxwell represents the property (as it might be) *red to Twin Maxwell in* C'. Since these properties differ, the relationalist can describe the case as involving a representational difference, as is plausible. Indeed, the relationalist can go on to assimilate the case to other instances of perceptual variation, and can extend her ecumenicism to the case. As in other instances of perceptual variation, the claim would be that Maxwell's and Twin Maxwell's perceptual representations of the color of x can differ and yet both be veridical, since Maxwell represents a relational property constituted in terms of a relation to Maxwell, while Twin Maxwell represents a relational property constituted in terms of a relation to Twin Maxwell.

The lesson seems to be, then, that relationalists, unlike selectionists, have a satisfactory description of the case — and one that fits smoothly within their general ecumenical treatment of perceptual variation. At the end of the day, then, it seems to me that selectionism should be rejected in favor of relationalism. For, despite its considerable attractions, the inability of selectionism to deal satisfactorily with cases of postreceptoral perceptual variation makes it, at best, an inferior species of ecumenicism to the relationalist view I have proposed. This is (in part) why I claim that relationalism is the most attractive form of ecumenicism, as per premise (4) of the argument from perceptual variation.

3.3.3 *Modes of Presentation*

A further way to block the interpretation of perceptual variation that I have recommended involves an appeal to what we might call perceptual modes of presentation.[44]

To see what this suggestion amounts to, consider the following familiar, non-perceptual case of representational variation. Suppose that you think of Venus as a certain heavenly body that is visible at thus and such position in the morning sky, while I think of Venus as a certain heavenly body that is visible at such and thus position in the evening sky. Following tradition, let it be that we linguistically express our respective ways of thinking about Venus by the labels 'the Morning Star' (you) and 'the Evening Star' (me). Now suppose we both see Venus at some indeterminate time of day and in some indeterminate location in the sky, and that this leads you to utter the demonstrative ascription (MS) and me to utter the demonstrative ascription (ES):

(MS) That [pointing at Venus] is the Morning Star.

(ES) That [pointing at Venus] is the Evening Star.

Grant, as seems plausible, that both utterances (understood as dated token linguistic productions, together with their completing demonstrations) succeed in demonstratively picking out Venus, and ascribing some property to it. Our utterances, then, vary in what they represent about x. How should we respond?

There is, of course, a standard Fregean response to this case indoctrination into which is the first intellectual event of graduate school in philosophy for many students. On this response, (MS) and (ES) both ascribe one and the same property to Venus — the property *being Venus*, but do so under distinct modes of presentation corresponding to the two distinct senses, or ways of thinking about the one planet. We can think of the surface forms of (MS) and (ES), then, as reflecting two different factors: the individuals and properties that Frege thought of as referents (the individual Venus, the property *being Venus*), and the modes of presentation of these referents. Given this apparatus, the easy and familiar diagnosis of the case under consideration is that (MS) and (ES) are not in conflict because the difference in the predicates they ascribe to Venus is a difference between two modes of presentation of one property. That is, the two ascriptions *agree* in the property they ascribe to Venus, and only disagree in the mode of presentation under which that one property is presented. But since, for Frege, the truth value of the unembedded ascriptions (MS) and (ES) is determined completely by the relevant referents (and the relations between them), and without taking account of modes of presentation, the difference that exists between (MS) and (ES) is not of the right sort to make a difference to their truth values. It follows from this understanding, then, that (MS) and (ES) cannot differ in truth value after all, and so do not conflict.

44 Versions of this view are defended by Block (1999), Shoemaker (2006), and Thompson (2006, 2009); the view has also been suggested to me in conversation (independently) by Dana Nelkin, Ram Neta, Mark Sainsbury, and Michael Watkins.

I expect it is becoming clear by now how this completely familiar idea from philosophy of language might be pressed into service in responding to perceptual variation with respect to color. Consider the interpersonal variation with respect to spectral loci for unique green discussed in §2.3.2. We found that, when presented with a single stimulus such as a 490nm spectral light, S_1 might endorse ascription (U_1), while S_2 might endorse (U_2), and that there seems to be no motivated reason for accepting either representation of the light to the exclusion of the other.

(U_1) The light [demonstration of 490nm light] looks unique green.

(U_2) The light [demonstration of 490nm light] looks bluish green.

In response, I recommended that we cease thinking of (U_1) and (U_2) as disagreeing about whether or not the light bears a single, non-relational property (*being unique green*) in favor of the view that the property ascribed by the first is different from the property denied by the second: the proposal was that (U_1) ascribes the property *looking unique green to* S_1 while (U_2) ascribes the property *looking bluish green to* S_2. The advertised advantage of this solution is that, since the latter two properties are obviously compatible, it shows how we can accept both representations of the one stimulus without having to make unmotivated choices between them.

But the Fregean resolution of the apparent the conflict between (MS) and (ES) suggests an analogous approach to that between (U_1) and (U_2) that, like the solution I have recommended, allows us to accept both representations without having to make unmotivated choices between them. The suggestion would be that we should reconcile (U_1) and (U_2) not by taking them to differ in the properties they ascribe/withhold to the light, but only in the mode of presentation of some one color property — where here we are extending the notion of modes of presentation from the domain of conceptual representations (where they are at least more familiar to philosophers) to that of perceptual representations (where they are less familiar). Thus, we could say, *being unique green* (to S_1) and *being bluish green* (to S_2) are not two different color properties that the light has at one time, but two different modes of presentation of the single color that the light has — one mode for the presentation of that color to S_1 and a different mode for its presentation to S_2. If applied consistently to cases of perceptual variation with respect to color, the strategy here might be thought to disarm the resolution of these cases I have suggested, and hence the case for relationalism.

There are a number of things that should be said in response to the present, Frege-inspired proposal.

To begin, I think it is fair to ask to be told more about perceptual modes of presentation and how they function.[45] It is not that the conceptual modes of

[45] The only source I know of that attempts to do needed work of explaining perceptual modes of perception is Thompson (2009).

presentations invoked in cases like that involving (MS) and (ES) are so well-understood as to need no further explanation. But if conceptual modes are in need of further explanation, at least it is true that there's a large literature devoted to supplying that further explanation. If anything, the trouble with conceptual modes of presentation is that too many options have been defended to permit an easy decision: they have been variously held to be individual concepts, general properties, percept tokens, stereotypes, prototypes, Kaplan-inspired characters, public language expression types, Mentalese expression types, functional roles, causal chains between Mentalese names and individuals, and more.[46] Since the literature has contained much less discussion of perceptual modes of presentation, those who would invoke them in response to cases of perceptual variation with respect to color incur the debt of explaining what they amount to.

A second comment about the Frege-inspired strategy is that, even if it can be fleshed out adequately, it seems to be seriously at odds with ordinary usage (cf. Tye (2000, 103–104); Pautz (2006*c*, 238)). A report such as (U_1) would ordinarily be characterized a report of the *color* experienced by the subject — not the way in which the color is presented. To the extent that we are inclined to respect this characterization, we have reason for rejecting the view under consideration.

A third comment is that the plausibility of the Frege-inspired strategy varies between instances of perceptual variation; in particular, it tends to have more of a ring of intuitive plausibility in intrapersonal cases than in interpersonal cases.[47] For example, I think the idea is at least superficially attractive to describe cases involving a single stimulus under different illuminants as presenting (to one visual system) a single color property under distinct modes of presentation corresponding to the difference in illumination. In contrast, it seems to me less plausible to apply the same reaction to, say, cases of interpersonal variation in spectral hue loci such as that involving (U_1) and (U_2), in so far as that reaction requires denying that *being unique green* and *being bluish green* are color properties (and instead claiming them to be modes of presentation of a color property).[48] I suppose one could react to this situation by either (i) confining the strategy to intrapersonal cases, while accepting relationalism (or some other view) of other cases, or (ii) applying the strategy uniformly across cases of perceptual variation, intuitions to the contrary notwithstanding. Option (i) has the disadvantage that it leaves us with

[46] This list is from Schiffer (1992, 511).

[47] For what it is worth, Thompson (2006, 2009) motivates the suggestion by starting with intrapersonal cases.

[48] Why insist that *being unique green* and *being bluish green* are color properties? First, they are obviously visually accessible properties of some sort, but don't fall under any other headings of visually accessible properties: they are not textures, not shapes, not sizes, etc. Second, they seem to obey the laws of color mixing, etc., that arguably implicitly define the colors, and seem to have clear positions in the various color spaces. I suggest that these are as good uncontroversial criteria for being a color as we have.

a non-general and incomplete answer to worries about perceptual variation. Moreover, there is an obvious threat that, if the moves enlisted to complete the treatment of perceptual variation can apply uniformly to intrapersonal cases as well (as can, for example, the relationalist strategy I have advocated), they would leave the Fregean strategy without a job to do. If option (ii) at least carries the benefits of uniformity, it also carries the *prima facie* cost of conflicting with intuition.

It should also be noted that the Fregean proposal we are now considering will have important implications for the general issue of the contents of experience — implications that many (including many of the most prominent critics of the argument from perceptual variation) have been unwilling to accept. I have been assuming throughout that color experiences visually represent, that they have truth-conditional content. Indeed, I have been assuming that they have as their representational or truth-conditional content that particular individual bits of the world (e.g., lemons, tables, chairs) bear particular color properties. But, of course, adopting the Fregean proposal under consideration will force us to understand these representational contents in a way that makes room for the needed modes of presentation, as well as individuals and properties. The resulting, enriched view is traditionally labeled "Fregean," and traditionally contrasted against the so-called "Russellian" view that understands contents of experience exhaustively as structured complexes of individuals and properties.[49] I do not wish to enter here into the dispute between these two competing conceptions of the content of experience. Rather, my present point is just that the Fregean response we are now considering will be unavailable to anyone unwilling to side with the Fregean conception and against the Russellian.[50]

But the most serious worries about the Fregean strategy, in my view, emerge from considering disanalogies between cases where the strategy most plausibly finds a home, one the one hand, and the disputed cases of perceptual variation with respect to color, on the other.

To see this, first consider a case of perceptual variation with respect to shape where, I think, a version of the Fregean proposal is extremely plausible. To take an example familiar from early twentieth century philosophy of perception, many have held that a round dinner plate can be perceptually represented as oval when seen from certain angles. On the other hand, the same dinner plate is perceptually represented as round when seen from other angles. It is plausible to describe this sort of perceptual variation by saying that the visual representation of the dinner plate is a joint product of (i) the non-relational

[49] For general discussion of these and other conceptions of the contents of experience, see Siegel (2005). The Fregean view is defended by Chalmers (2004) and Thompson (2009); while the Russellian view is defended by Thau (2002) and Tye (1995, 2000).

[50] This is no idle speculation: many of those most resistant to the argument from perceptual variation are staunch Russellians about representational content (e.g. Byrne and Hilbert, 1997*b*; Byrne, 2002; Tye, 2000). Consequently, these authors need something other than the Fregean response to ground their resistance.

shape of the object, and (ii) a mode of presentation of the non-relational shape of the object to the subject — viz., the viewing angle at which the shape is presented to the subject. As I say, I think the Fregean analysis of this case is, at the very least, plausible. However, it seems to me that there are crucial disanalogies between this case and cases of perceptual variation with respect to color that should dissuade us from applying the Fregean strategy to the latter.

The proposal is that each of the variants in the shape case represents the very same (non-relational) shape of the dinner plate under a distinct mode of presentation (i.e., viewing angle). Now, among these various modes of presentation it so happens that there is one, α, that is distinguished from its competitors in this sense: when objects are presented under α, subjects will reliably represent those objects as round if and only if they are round (assuming they are undistracted and cooperative, the lights are up, putting aside borderline cases, assuming the objects are not too big or too small, and so on). Namely, α is the head-on viewing angle. There is, in other words, a distinguished mode of presentation such that, when objects are presented under it, whether or not those objects are instances of *being round* is revealed to subjects.

Moreover, I suggest that this is no mere inessential feature of the case. On the contrary, the availability of a distinguished, revelatory mode of presentation for *being round* is part of what we mean in saying that it is (like other shape properties) something to which we have visual access. Of course, I am not claiming that the visual accessibility of *being round* is constitutive of the property, or that we have infallible access to its instances. My claim is only that normally sighted subjects can distinguish the clearly round things from the clearly non-round things when circumstances are favorable.

I assume we want to say that color properties are similarly accessible to visual perception in favorable circumstances. Therefore, we should apply the Fregean strategy to cases of perceptual variation with respect to color only if we think that, in these cases too, there is a distinguished mode of presentation in the same sense. For example, in the intrapersonal instance of perceptual variation with respect to color as a function of background (see §2.1), we should apply the Fregean strategy only if there is some distinguished mode of presentation under which the stimulus is visually represented as an instance of *being red* if and only if it is an instance of that property (again, putting aside borderline cases, assuming the subject is attentive, cooperative, and so on).[51]

The problem is that there is no good reason to believe that there is such a distinguished mode of presentation, and substantial reason to doubt it. Indeed, it is evident that the arguments against the existence of a uniquely veridical variant from Chapter 2 can easily be recast as arguments against the existence of a distinguished mode of presentation. For exactly the reasons that it is hard

[51] To repeat, I am being generous in focusing on intrapersonal instances; it seems to me even less plausible that any one mode of presentation could be distinguished in anything like the required sense in interpersonal cases (such as that involving (U_1) and (U_2)), much less interspecies cases.

to motivate a non-arbitrary choice of a single, uniquely veridical variant, it is hard to motivate a non-arbitrary choice of a single mode of presentation as revealing the instancehood or non-instancehood of color properties. Namely, it seems that any considerations that could be used to favor one such mode of presentation could be set against equally forceful considerations that favor another such mode of presentation.

I take this to show that the Fregean strategy is unsatisfactory as a response to the argument from perceptual variation. Ultimately, it just relocates the worries we had faced before accepting the strategy. Whereas without the strategy the anti-relationalist was faced with the need to choose a single uniquely veridical variant from the observed range, with the Fregean strategy the anti-relationalist is faced with the need to choose a single revelatory mode of presentation from the observed range. With respect to both choices, and for the same reasons, it is hard to envision a motivated, non-stipulative selection.[52]

3.4 Conclusion

I believe the argument from perceptual variation makes a powerful case for color relationalism. Still, there are ways of resisting the argument that deserve investigation. What we have seen in this chapter is that several of the most important forms of resistance (ways that involve denying premise (2), premise (3), or rejecting the inference from (3) to (4)) give out under scrutiny. In light of this situation, I suggest that we should accept the argument, and, in particular, its relationalist conclusion (4).

Of course, this recommendation will fail to command assent if, as many have thought, there are outstanding and compelling reasons for rejecting color relationalism. Indeed, there are a variety of linguistic, ontological, and phenomenological objections (among others) that have been offered as reasons for thinking that relationalism could not be true. My task over the next several chapters will be to argue that these objections are unpersuasive, and thereby

[52] Shoemaker (2006) objects to the Fregean strategy on the further grounds that the view misrepresents the phenomenology of color experience:

> To say that [perceptual variation with respect to color] is only a variation in the *how* of perceptual representation, and in no way a variation in *what* is represented, seems to me at odds with the phenomenology. When the light-brown object in shadow and the dark-brown object not in shadow look the same to me, the sameness is experienced as being *out there* — and in such a case the perception can be perfectly veridical. Similarity in the presenting manifests itself in represented similarity in what is represented, and in the absence of perceptual illusion requires that there be similarity in what is represented. More generally, the best gloss on the Moorean transparency intuition is that the qualitative character that figures in the perception of the color of an object is experienced as in or on the perceived object (Shoemaker, 2006, 475).

I am reluctant to endorse Shoemaker's complaint, since I think it turns on endowing phenomenology with more metaphysical insight than is deserved (I'll return to this theme in Chapter 6). But if Shoemaker is right, then we have another reason for rejecting the Fregean strategy.

to clear the way for us to accept color relationalism with a clear intellectual conscience.

PART II

DEFENSE AND ELABORATION: A RELATIONALIST'S GUIDE TO REPRESENTATION, ONTOLOGY, AND PHENOMENOLOGY

4

RELATIONALISM DEFENDED: LINGUISTIC AND MENTAL REPRESENTATION OF COLOR

> ...a good deal of such analysis seems required before we can draw any ontological conclusions from the things we say — before we can 'read off' any feature of the world from our ways of speaking about it.
>
> — (Varzi, 2007, 5).

In Part I of this book I argued for the view that the color properties represented by our visual systems are best understood as (relatively fine-grained) relational properties. The present chapter is directed at a related but distinct issue: how should we understand the semantics of (linguistic and mental) color ascription? These issues interact, of course, because the semantics for color ascription one accepts must bridge the gap between token linguistic and mental representations, on the one hand, and the ontology of color properties one accepts, on the other. Indeed, this fact can make for serious trouble for relationalists in particular in so far as there are a number of reasons for doubting that our color ascriptions *could* be connected with the fine-grained relational properties argued for in Part I. For example, there are reasons for worrying that ascriptions such as (1) are of the wrong form to pick out such properties or that they are insufficiently determinate to pick out such properties.

(1) This ripe lemon is yellow.

Moreover, many have worried that if our uses of color predicates did pick out such fine-grained relational properties, then our practices of color ascription would be much more permissive than they appear to be, that color ascriptions could never be wrong, and that interlocutors could never agree or disagree in ascribing colors to objects.

My goal in this chapter is to offer a semantics that bridges what might initially seem, on account of these and similar reasons, to be an unbridgeable chasm between ordinary color ascriptions and relational color properties. The solution I'll be offering works from both ends of the semantic relation: symbol and world. Beginning with the side of the symbol, I'll argue that contextual enrichment adds to the information supplied in the explicit material in our color ascriptions, and thereby gets us part of the way across the semantic gap. On the side of the world, I'll propose that, while this is something that varies between contexts, the properties that are the semantic values of color ascriptions are typically much less determinate — less fine-grained — than the fine-grained color properties discussed so far. This, too, will help bridge the gap by making the properties picked out by our ascriptions less remote.

Thus, my main proposal in this chapter will be that our ordinary thought and talk about color attributes relatively coarse-grained relational properties to objects, and does so in a way that is context-sensitive. Specifically, I propose that the predicate 'is yellow' in (1) as uttered in context K expresses the property *yellow for the perceivers relevant in context K under the perceptual circumstances relevant in context K*.[1] Similarly, 'is red', uttered in context K, expresses the property *red for the perceivers relevant in context K under the perceptual circumstances relevant in context K*. Likewise for other natural language color predicates. Moreover, I propose that the our ordinary mental (general cognitive) representation of colors works in a similar way, so that it ends up attributing the very same, typically coarser-grained properties to objects. Thus, when I perceive a ripe lemon, and thereby come to hold a belief in context K about its color — a belief to which I would normally give verbal expression (were I so inclined) by an utterance of (1) in context K — my belief attributes to the lemon the property *yellow for the perceivers relevant in context K under the perceptual circumstances relevant in context K*. *Mutatis mutandis* for thought about other colors.

(For convenience in what follows, I'll refer to these individual properties by the abbreviated names '*yellow simpliciter*', '*red simpliciter*', etc., and I'll talk about them collectively under the label 'coarse-grained colors'. I'll continue to follow the convention of italicizing property names, including abbreviated property names.)

In the rest of this chapter I'll elaborate and defend this proposal. I'll begin by arguing that our color predicates are pragmatically or semantically enriched in some way by the contexts in which they are uttered (§4.1). Next I'll urge that, even with this contextual enrichment, color attributions pick out relational properties that are typically less fine-grained than those recognized in earlier chapters; I'll address a series of questions about the nature of these coarse-grained properties and conclude that they deserve acceptance by relationalists (§4.2). I'll round out my proposal by sketching a context-sensitive semantics that makes such coarse-grained colors the semantic values of ordinary uses of color predicates (§4.3). Finally, I'll show how my proposal gives the relationalist resources to respond to a number of otherwise pressing objections that have their roots in facts about language and the mind (§4.4). I'll conclude that these objections can be answered once we have in hand an adequate relationalist-friendly semantics for color ascriptions.

[1] In §4.1.1 I shall address (but not resolve) the question whether this property is semantically expressed by the corresponding color predicate, or whether it is merely conveyed by that predicate through some extra-semantic mechanism. For now, and for purposes of expository convenience, I'll treat the relationship between the predicate and the property as one of semantic expression. As far as I can see, none of my arguments turns on this *pro tanto* choice.

4.1 Enriching Unrelativized Predicates

Consider a quotidian color attribution in natural language, such as an utterance of (1). It is hard to believe that ordinary utterances of (1) and other natural language color attributions attribute to objects the highly specific fine-grained relational color properties of the kind argued for in Chapters 2–3.

There are two simple and related reasons this is so hard to believe.

The first involves a mismatch of form. The plain fact is that the surface form of (1) and other color attributions in natural language lack argument places for the parameters that, if color relationalism is true, are relata of both color properties. When we linguistically ascribe colors to ripe fruit, lights, tables, and chairs, we frequently make no explicit mention of subjects or viewing conditions.[2] There is, then, a mismatch between the (overt) structure of color predicates, on the one hand, and the structure of the relationalist's color properties, on the other. Assuming, plausibly, that color predicates have color properties as their semantic values, this means that there is a mismatch of form between color predicates and their semantic values.[3]

Besides this mismatch of form, relationalism (as developed so far) results in a second, closely related mismatch — a mismatch of information. It comes from the observation that the relational color properties discussed earlier are extremely fine-grained — so much so that it takes a good deal of information to distinguish one of them from another. And while it is certainly plausible that utterances often both semantically encode and extra-semantically convey more information than what can be read off the explicit linguistic material they employ, it is not plausible that utterances of (1) generally encode or convey enough additional information to single out just one of the fine-grained color properties, and to attribute just that one to an object. After all, on the view of Chapter 2, the parameters relevant to the specification of the fine-grained colors include detailed information about the perceiver's visual system and visual circumstance, including state of adaptation, viewing distance and angle, ambient illuminant, simultaneously seen objects, and so on. But it is hard to believe that the mechanisms responsible for supplementing the explicit linguistic material of our color attributions have access to all the different

[2] One might make the same allegation about the form of color ascriptions in thought. But I don't believe we have perceptual or introspective access to the format of our conscious (or unconscious) mental representations, as opposed to (at least some aspects of) our linguistics representations. (In my view, much of the introspective evidence to the contrary marshaled by e.g., Carruthers (1996) is better understood as evidence about the format of the auditory imagery that often accompanies conscious thinking.) If this is right, then we lack evidence for the analogous allegation of mismatch between our ontology and the format of mental ascriptions of colors.

[3] This point does not depend on my particular choice of semantic ontology; for example, the same point could be put by saying that there is a mismatch of form between color predicates and their propositional constituents, or between color predicates and the contribution they make to the truth conditions of sentences containing them. Indeed, the worry about mismatch can be raised even if we take the relation between color predicates and color properties to be extra-semantic (see note 1).

parameters that (on the relationalist view presented) need fixing. The result is that the explicit material in color attributions underdetermines *which* relational color property is being ascribed. If an answer is available, it is not an answer that is supplied by the explicit material in (1).

If relational color properties have any hope of serving as the semantic values of our color predicates, then, we need to see how these mismatches can be overcome. A more expansive look at our linguistic practices, however, will bring the relationalist some comfort; for mismatches of the sort we are discussing are hardly unprecedented. For one sort of example that has been discussed extensively, consider these perfectly acceptable sentences ascribing motion:

(2) Car c was traveling at 60 miles per hour.

(3) The sun rose.

As with (1), it seems that the predicates in (2) and (3) are not (overtly) relativized to the parameters that, according to our best metaphysics of motion properties, are mandatory relata of those properties — viz., frames of reference. Assuming, plausibly, that motion predicates have motion properties as their semantic values, this means that there is a mismatch of form between motion predicates and their semantic values. Moreover, as in the case of color predicates and color properties, this mismatch of form comes with a concomitant mismatch of information: the absence of explicit parameters in natural language motion predicates corresponding to relational motion properties has the result that the explicit material in motion attributions underdetermines *which* relational motion property is being ascribed. Does 'was traveling at 60 miles per hour' in (2) attribute to car c the relational property *traveling at 60 miles per hour relative to frame* R_1 or the distinct relational property *traveling at 60 miles per hour relative to frame* R_2? Or some other relational motion property? If an answer is available, it is not an answer that is supplied by the explicit material in (2).

Indeed, it is tempting to think of the mismatches involving color and motion as instances of a much wider phenomenon that we might call *semantic incompleteness* (/*semantic underdetermination*), wherein overt linguistic material leaves out elements needed to fix semantic values of that material. Alleged examples of this kind of incompleteness that have been discussed in the literature include:

(4) I am on fire (NP omits specification of agent of the context).

(5) That is pretty (NP omits completing demonstration).

(6) Sylvester's wedding occurred on 1 April 2006 (VP omits reference to time-zone).

(7) This dumb-bell is heavy (VP omits reference to body size and strength of lifter).

(8) The elephant is small (VP omits comparison class).

(9) There's no beer left (S omits quantifier scope restriction).

(10) It's raining (VP omits reference to a location).[4]

(Moreover, philosophers have argued that this kind of incompleteness in expressions such as 'knows', 'goodness', 'believes', and 'heap', is the key to resolving a range of philosophical problems about epistemological skepticism (Lewis, 1996; DeRose, 1992; Cohen, 1991), moral properties (Drier, 1990; Unger, 1995), belief attributions (Crimmins and Perry, 1989), and vagueness (Fara, 2000; Soames, 1999), *inter alia*.)

Although it is certainly debatable whether these are all genuine instances of semantic incompleteness, I think it is reasonably clear that motion ascriptions such as those in (2) and (3) present us with other (non-color) instances of mismatch between an overtly unrelativized predicate and a relational property. Indeed, not only are there reasonably uncontroversial (non-color) instances of mismatch of this kind, but there are (non-color) instances of *mandatory* mismatch between overtly unrelativized predicates and the relational properties they express: for example, attempting to make overt the extra relatum of the relation picked out by 'foreigner' in (11) results in the ungrammatical (12):[5]

(11) John is a foreigner.

(12) *John is a foreigner to the United States.

I take these points to show that the existence of a mismatch between overtly unrelativized color predicates and relational color properties in (1) and its ilk is not a particular cause for alarm. In particular, the existence of a mismatch in the domain of color should no more compel us to abandon a relationalist metaphysics of color properties than the mismatch in the domain of motion compels us to abandon a relationalist metaphysics of motion properties.

Indeed, there is a perspective from which the occurrence of mismatches in both cases seems not only unsurprising, but predictable given both linguistic history and the results of metaphysical inquiry. For it is plausible that both our motion and color predicates predate the outward-looking (empirically informed) metaphysical investigations that lead to the conclusion that the properties answering to those predicates are relational. For that reason, the unrelativized forms of the relevant predicates may have accurately reflected views about the world that were corrected by those metaphysical investigations. Given the outcomes of those metaphysical investigations, our choice to

[4] Needless to say, there is controversy about whether these examples (except (4) and (5)) manifest genuine (semantic) incompleteness. Cappelen and Lepore (2005), in particular, have mounted a trenchant and thoroughgoing recent challenge to allegations of linguistic incompleteness. It is worth noting that much of their response to the problems we are facing (their chapter 11) is devoted to showing that, if there is a genuine problem of mismatch, it is a result of the metaphysics of the relevant properties rather than their semantics for the predicates, and therefore not a problem that semanticists (as such) need to solve. But this is consistent with the approach I am pursuing, in so far as the reasons for believing in mismatch that I have presented come from comparing the form of our predicates against a theory about the way the world is (the relationalist color ontology of Chapter 2).

[5] I owe this point to Chris Barker.

retain the pre-existing predicates (i.e., to retain these lexical items together with their morphologies and argument structures, *inter alia*) resulted in mismatch.

Such quasi-historical speculations aside, the point I wish to emphasize is that the mere fact of mismatch is no obstacle to relationalism. But, of course, this doesn't begin to answer the question how we should understand the semantics of ordinary color ascriptions such as (1). It is to this question that I now turn.

4.1.1 *A Menu of Options*

Unfortunately, this is currently a topic of heated debate, so I cannot point to a settled answer. And it is beyond the scope of this book to settle these issues. Nonetheless, I think it is useful to set out, in a general way, a taxonomy of the options available to the theorist in the face of mismatch.[6] For expository convenience, I'll label the sentences in which such unrelativized predicates occur *mismatched sentences*.

4.1.1.1 *Strategy 1: Deny Mismatch* The first option would be to deny that there is a genuine mismatch in the semantics of (so-called) mismatched sentences. Since it doesn't seem promising to insist on the overt presence of parameters that (as a matter of empirical fact) are not there, the most promising way of denying mismatch would be to insist that the relevant properties are not, after all, relational (see, for example, Cappelen and Lepore (2005, chapter 11)). Thus, as applied to (2), for example, the claim would be that the predicate 'was traveling at 60 miles per hour' expresses a property that is not constituted in terms of a relation to a frame of reference, but instead expresses a non-relational property.

If the mismatch under consideration is construed as a *prima facie* clash between the structure of language and the structure of the world, then accepting strategy 1 is, in effect, to respond to the apparent clash by siding with language. It is to take the structure of the overt linguistic material as a guide to the properties (in the relevant domain) that one accepts in one's ontology. Having adjusted one's ontology in this way to bring it back into coordination with the structure imposed by language, there will no longer be any such clash.

4.1.1.2 *Strategy 2: No Semantic Value* A second option for responding would be to claim that mismatched sentences fail to express semantically any propositions at all. To see the idea here, consider (2) as an example once again. The thought would be that, in so far as the predicate 'was traveling at 60 miles per hour' is not (overtly) parametrized, it does not have as its semantic value a relational property. But if the properties eligible to be the semantic values are all relational, this can only mean that the predicate in question lacks a semantic value altogether. Consequently, on this view, the mismatched sentences in which they occur (such as (2)) do not semantically express propositions, and are

[6] Although I think the geography of options is largely the same for many other kinds of incompleteness, I'll confine myself to discussing incompleteness arising from a mismatch between relational properties and unrelativized predicates.

strictly speaking truth-valueless. In response to the intuition that mismatched sentences are meaningful and indeed truth-valued, the theorist who adopts this line will add that, despite not semantically expressing any proposition, such sentences succeed in non-semantically conveying propositions (e.g., propositions that ascribe to the subject a relational property). Presumably this response could be elaborated in a number of different ways corresponding to different proposals about what proposition is non-semantically conveyed by utterances of mismatched sentences.

If, again, we think of mismatch in terms of an apparent clash between language and the world, we might best characterize strategy 2 as one that accepts the clash as genuine, but then sidesteps it. It accepts that there is a clash between language and the world, but goes on to say that the clash generates (through the operation of extra-semantic mechanisms of some sort) additional content that does not clash with the world, and that is itself the focus of communicative interest.

4.1.1.3 *Strategy 3: False Semantic Value* A third, related option would regard atomic mismatched sentences as (not truth-valueless, but) uniformly false. The proponent of this response would say that there *is* a non-relational property eligible for being the semantic value of the unrelativized predicate — in the case of the predicate in (2), this would be the property of (absolutely) moving at 60 miles per hour, but that empirical-cum-metaphysical investigation has revealed that such non-relational motion properties are uninstantiated. Therefore, atomic mismatched sentences that ascribe such non-relational properties to objects (such as (2)) are false. Again, in response to the intuition that some atomic apparently mismatched sentences are true, this theorist will claim that our intuitions are in fact responsive to the propositions that are non-semantically conveyed by mismatched sentences (e.g., propositions that ascribe to the subject a relational property). And once again, this form of response could be spelled out in a variety of ways, depending on how we understand what propositions are extra-semantically conveyed by mismatched sentences, and also how we understand the details of extra-semantic conveyance.

I think strategy 3 is, like strategy 2, best characterized as responding to the clash represented by mismatch by admitting the genuineness of the conflict and then sidestepping it.

4.1.1.4 *Strategy 4: Context-Sensitivity* A fourth alternative is unlike the strategies considered so far in that it attempts to restore matching to the semantics of mismatched sentences, and does so by appeal to some kind of context-sensitivity. On this alternative, the unrelativized predicates in apparently mismatched sentences manage to have as semantic values relational properties because of the systematic contribution made by context to fixing the semantic values of linguistic material. Thus, for example, this view would have it that the predicate in (2) expresses something like the property *moving at 60 miles per hour relative to the frame of the road*. If so, then (for everything we have said) mismatched sentences can express propositions that are true. Putting this alternative in terms of the clash we have discussed, we might characterize it as appealing to context to enrich the linguistic material, with the result that there is no longer a clash between the (enriched) linguistic material and the world.

Of course, the most important question faced by a proponent of this fourth view is how a context operates to enrich an overtly unrelativized predicate (e.g., 'was moving at 60 miles per hour') so that it can have a relational property as its semantic value. There are, as near as I can tell, three classes of answers to this question, each of which corresponds to a different version of the alternative we are considering.[7]

First, one might hold that the overt predicate in a mismatched sentence is an indexical to be considered alongside more familiar indexicals such as 'I', 'here', and 'now'. Now, examples like (4) have been used to show that what indexicals semantically encode goes beyond what is spelled out overtly in the linguistic material. In terms of the canonical treatment of the topic by Kaplan (1989), this is because each indexical expression has a stable "character" that maps from a context of use to a content; thus, 'I' has a character that maps

[7] An orthogonal dimension of variation between semantic theories that appeal to context to enrich overtly unrelativized predicates so as to make them match (in form and information) with relativized predicates concerns the interpretive stage at which context plays its enriching role. This is worth mentioning because in a recent, and extremely provocative paper, Lasersohn (2005) argues that taking context to operate in two different stages (rather than, as is more traditional, in one stage) secures semantic benefits worth having (see also MacFarlane (2003, 2005); Egan (2007); Egan *et al.* (2005), and for criticism, von Fintel and Gillies (2008); Glanzberg (2007)). Lasersohn's view is that context first operates on sentences to produce propositions/contents, and then operates a second time to determine a truth value of those propositions/contents, relative to further contextual parameters. Lasersohn argues that this double appeal to context allows us to simultaneously (i) recognize that your assertion of (1) contradicts my denial of (1), and nonetheless (ii) accept that your assertion of (1) and my denial of (1) are both true. This is possible, on Lasersohn's view, because your use of (1) asserts the very same contextually supplemented proposition/content that is negated by my denial of (1) (whence the contradiction), even though the *truth-value* of our utterances depends on a further contextual parameter (an individual judge, who is typically but not always the speaker). (Lasersohn does not develop this semantics for color predicates, so here I am extending his system in the obvious way.)

Since, as I remarked, Lasersohn's proposal is orthogonal to the variations I am reviewing, I won't focus on it in what follows. However, I do want to point out that Lasersohn's aims are significantly narrower than mine, and therefore that his proposal is not, as it may seem, a simpler (hence preferable) alternative to the views I am defending. Lasersohn's project is a project in semantics: his goal is to give a semantics that both permits interpersonal agreements and disagreements about sentences like (1) and nonetheless allows that (1) can be true in your mouth and false in mine. Significantly, this project is carried out without any commitments at all about the nature of the properties that color predicates (etc.) express — indeed, Lasersohn's formal model treats contents as unstructured functions, and consequently omits mention of properties altogether. Although it is also among my goals to secure the desiderata that Lasersohn wants, there is much more that I am aiming for in addition. Unlike Lasersohn's proposal, my view is about both semantics and ontology. Specifically, it is about what the semantics for (1) should look like against the background of (at least) three assumptions that he doesn't explicitly endorse: (i) the relationalist ontology of color properties argued for in earlier chapters, (ii) the assumption that color predicates express properties, and (iii) the assumption that the properties that color predicates express are, or at any rate are closely related to, the relational color properties.

from contexts to the agents of those contexts, so that the NP in (4) picks out the agent of the context. Crucially, the indexical expression here can semantically encode more than what is overtly expressed because its semantic value is determined not only by what is overtly expressed, but also partly by the context. Applying similar ideas to the unrelativized predicates in mismatched sentences, the thought would be that each has a character that maps from contexts of use to contents, and thereby allows context to contribute to what they semantically encode. Thus, the view would be that 'was moving at 60 miles per hour' in (2) has a determinate Kaplanian character, and that that character, when applied to the context, determines the property *moving at 60 miles per hour relative to the frame of the road*.

For those unhappy with expanding the traditionally recognized class of overt indexicals in the way just envisaged, there is a second version of the view according to which unrelativized predicates in mismatched sentences are not themselves indexicals, but instead mimic the context-sensitive behavior of indexicals. They do this by containing a covert, phonetically null, indexical element at some level of linguistic representation (e.g., at LF). Thus, on this proposal, it is not that the overt predicate 'was moving at 60 miles per hour' in (2) is an overt indexical in the way that 'I' is in (4); instead, the predicate contains a non-inspectable element at some level of its representation, and this non-inspectable element makes a systematic, indexical-like contribution to the semantic value of the predicate (see Stanley, 2004). In any case, the full predicate (with its overt and covert components working in concert), when set in the actual context, ends up semantically encoding the property *moving at 60 miles per hour relative to the frame of the road*.

A third version of the strategy has it that the context-sensitivity of unrelativized predicates in a mismatched sentences is encoded neither in their overt linguistic material (as on the first version of the strategy) nor in covert elements at any level of their linguistic representation (as on the second version of the strategy). Nonetheless, on this view, the semantic values of the predicates in question is partially determined by context — without the contribution of context, these predicates simply fail to have a semantic value (see Perry, 1986; Bach, 1994).

4.1.2 *Mismatch and Color*

Having set out this taxonomy of options, I wish to remain as neutral as I can in the dispute over which is the right response to the problem of mismatch for color properties/predicates as it arises in examples like (1). The point I wish to stress, however, is that (with one exception to be discussed) any of these strategies provides the materials needed by a color relationalist to solve the problem of mismatch.

Amongst the views cataloged above, there is only one that I wish to reject — namely, the first, described under the heading 'Strategy 1', and which involves claiming that the relevant predicates (in our case, color predicates) express non-relational properties. This view, of course, amounts to repudiating color relationalism, and so it will come as no surprise that I am unsympathetic to it. My reason for this lack of sympathy is metaphysical (rather than semantic), and familiar: accepting the non-relationality of color properties would seem to require, implausibly, that there is a uniquely veridical variant in cases of perceptual variation. Strategy 1 comes with this implausible entailment, and offers nothing in the way of reason to believe that it is true. Moreover, strategy 1 strikes me as methodologically suspect: it strikes me as a poor way of proceeding to expect to be able to read the correct metaphysics off the structure of natural language predicates. In particular, I don't think it is appropriate to revise one's ontology (reached by otherwise convincing metaphysical arguments) merely because that ontology contains properties that mismatch against the structure of natural language predicates. For this reason, I shall assume henceforth that strategy 1 is off the table.

That said, several other strategies for responding to mismatch (as it arises in sentences such as (1)) remain on the table. On any of these other strategies, we will regard (1) as communicating the ascription to the ripe lemon of some relational color property (either by semantically encoding or non-semantically conveying that relational property). Any of these strategies, then, explains how overtly unrelativized color predicates can be used to ascribe relational color properties to objects, and thereby resolve the mismatches of both form and information.

4.2 The Ontology of Coarse-Grained Colors

Suppose, then, that we adopt one of the views listed in the menu of §4.1; then we are in a position to agree that ordinary color predicates might pick out relational color properties. But which ones? It is hard to believe that uses of our color predicates, even if supplemented by a non-trivial contextually determined contribution, can single out anything as determinate as the fine-grained color properties recognized in Chapter 2. For while it is ultimately an empirical question just how finely individuated those properties will have to be, our best indication is that they will be individuated more finely than they could be on the basis of the information accessible to cognitive/perceptual systems in ordinary contexts of attribution. It is plausible, therefore, that the semantic values of our color predicates are less determinate than the fine-grained colors. Moreover, it is plausible that if context makes a contribution to the determination of such relatively coarse-grained colors, the level of further specificity that it contributes is something that can vary across contexts. These considerations are what lead me to suggest that the predicate 'is yellow' in (1) as uttered in context K expresses the property *yellow for the perceivers relevant in context K under the perceptual circumstances relevant in context K.*

This proposal merits a number of comments.

4.2.1 *Properties*

The first thing to note is that, as I am understanding it, this proposal means that an ordinary color predicate ('red', 'yellow', 'blue', etc.) can pick out a range of distinct properties (viz., coarse-grained colors) depending on the context in which it is uttered. Now, there may be another way of thinking of the proposal on which, rather than saying that a particular utterance of 'red' picks out one of a range R of distinct properties depending on the context, we instead say that every utterance of 'red' picks out the very same property, but that the latter is in some sense schematic and works together with a context to pick out a further (non-schematic) property in R. However, I favor the first construal over the alternative for two reasons. First, it's not clear how to make sense of a property's being schematic (not just unspecific, but with some kind of a slot that needs saturation) in the way required by the alternative. Second, the first construal better mirrors the usual ways of understanding context-sensitivity involving expressions that refer to individuals. On the usual view, what a context-sensitive pronoun like 'I' picks out (for example) is not a schematic individual that acts with context to pick out a distinct non-schematic individual; rather, the pronoun has a schematic *character* that is not itself an individual, but that, together with with a context, picks out an individual that is its content (Kaplan, 1989). For these reasons, I'll be ignoring the alternative construal in what follows.[8]

Additionally, it is worth saying that I take *yellow simpliciter* and other coarse-grained colors (*red simpliciter*, *green simpliciter*, etc.) to be properties, in the relatively unspecific sense of 'property' that I've been using in claiming that the fine-grained colors are properties.[9] Namely, the coarse-grained colors (like the fine-grained colors) are qualities of things, and are exemplified by individuals. Moreover the coarse-grained colors are just as good (and just as bad) candidates as the fine-grained colors for being multiply exemplified; consequently, whether one is inclined to treat the fine-grained colors as universals or tropes, the very same treatment can be extended to coarse-grained colors as well.

4.2.2 *Color Properties*

If *red simpliciter* and its ilk are indeed properties that are expressed by utterances of color predicates, this gives us good *prima facie* reason for taking them to be *color* properties — albeit typically less determinate/specific color properties than the fine-grained colors. Another *prima facie* reason for taking the coarse-grained properties to be color properties is that it's hard to see what else they could be. They are presumably properties whose exemplification by particulars it is possible to notice (*ceteris paribus*) by visual perception; but among the sorts of properties to which visual perception is attuned, they are certainly not

[8] On the other hand, I don't believe that this choice will affect any of my main conclusions; thus, proponents of the alternative construal are invited to translate what I say into that idiom.

[9] Here, as elsewhere, I use 'property' in a way that extends to relations.

size, shape, or texture properties. It is natural, then, to take them to be color properties.

4.2.3 *Relationality*

The properties under consideration are (in the sense expounded in Chapter 1) relational. This is so because they are constituted in terms of relations to perceivers (*inter alia*).

4.2.4 *Determinacy*

We just noted that the coarse-grained colors, like fine-grained color properties discussed in Chapter 2, are relational. They are constituted in terms of relations that their bearers have to perceivers and perceptual circumstances. In particular, these properties are constituted in terms of relations that their bearers have to contextually relevant perceivers and contextually relevant perceptual circumstances. But I take it that the types of perceivers and perceptual circumstances that are relevant with respect to many if not most ordinary contexts are far less specific — less determinate — than those in terms of relations to which the fine-grained colors are constituted. I allow, of course, that there may be contexts relative to which the contextually relevant perceivers and perceptual circumstances are extremely specific or determinate; for example, it is plausible that this is true for contexts in which we are engaging in detailed psychophysical comparisons. Indeed, relative to such contexts, the so-called coarse-grained colors might turn out to be just as fine-grained as the fine-grained colors. However, I claim that in many of the contexts in which we find ourselves, the perceivers and perceptual circumstances that are contextually relevant are much less determinate. Consequently, the coarse-grained colors that we pick out by our uses of color predicates are, relative to many contexts of use, themselves less specific — less determinate — than the fine-grained color properties. It is for this reason that the coarse-grained colors are potentially useful in resolving the puzzles of mismatch with which I opened this chapter (§4.1), and it is for this reason that they deserve the name I have given them.

It is important to see that the relative indeterminacy of coarse-grained colors (relative to fine-grained colors) is not an obstacle to their being counted as properties (in the relatively unspecific sense of 'property' at issue). By way of analogy, notice that the property *bigger than a breadbox* is less determinate than the property *bigger than 4.0 cubic meters*. But the relative lack of determinacy of the former does not appear to disqualify it from counting as a property in the relevant sense: it is a quality of things, it is exemplified by individuals, and is no better or worse a candidate for multiple exemplification than the latter, more determinate property. Likewise, then, the relative indeterminacy of coarse-grained colors is compatible with their status as properties.

Do the coarse-grained stand to the fine-grained properties in the relation of determinables to determinates? They do not. For one thing, for reasons we have noted, coarse-grained colors can, relative to some contexts, be just as determinate as fine-grained colors. But even confining ourselves to coarse-grained colors that are less determinate than fine-grained color properties, the envisaged relationship fails to hold. This is because something could be an instance of the fine-grained property *yellow for S in C* (for some specific *S* and *C*) without being an instance of the S-color *yellow simpliciter*: this could happen if *S* is not a contextually relevant perceiver or *C* is not a contextually relevant circumstance. Indeed, it may turn out that many fine-grained colors are not determinates of *any* coarse-grained color. For example, there may be fine-grained colors that relate objects to perceivers and perceptual circumstances that are not relevant with respect to any context.

4.2.5 *Normality*

As defined, *yellow simpliciter* and its ilk relate their bearers to contextually relevant perceivers and contextually relevant circumstances. Whatever else this comes to, the perceivers and circumstances that are contextually relevant in many contexts may reasonably be thought to approximate what philosophers have had in mind in talking about *normal* perceivers and circumstances (e.g., in discussions of traditional secondary quality or response-dependent accounts of color). However, I do not mean to retract the argument in Chapter 2 that there are no metaphysically principled specifications of normal perceivers and normal circumstances. Rather, and for the same reasons already discussed, I would also deny that there are metaphysically principled specifications of the perceivers and circumstances that are contextually relevant in a given context.

This means, of course, that the boundaries of the coarse-grained colors are metaphysically unprincipled. Nonetheless, I think the notions of contextually relevant perceivers and perceptual circumstance (hence, perhaps derivatively, the notions of normal perceivers and normal perceptual circumstance) can be given some minimal (if unprincipled) sense. In particular, I suggest that, at the very least, perceivers who have a receptoral structure that is significantly statistically anomalous (as revealed by standard color discrimination tests, for example) will be counted as contextually irrelevant perceivers of color in many ordinary contexts. Likewise, at the very least, perceptual conditions under which our discriminatory capacities are significantly suppressed relative to statistical norms will be counted as irrelevant with respect to many if not most of the ordinary contexts in which we find ourselves.

If so, then part of the force of the claim that our practices of color attribution are responsive to the coarse-grained colors (rather than the fine-grained colors) is that these practices focus on a subset of the colors that objects exemplify. Namely, they focus on the subset of colors that relate those objects to contextually relevant perceivers and perceptual circumstances, and ignore the (*bona fide*) colors that relate those objects to contextually irrelevant perceivers and perceptual circumstances — as it might be, dichromats and conditions of very low illumination. In effect, the restriction to contextually relevant perceivers and perceptual circumstances sets a boundary around the relational colors to which our practices of color attribution are sensitive. Objects may exemplify relational colors that fall beyond that boundary, but (in ordinary contexts, at any rate) such colors are irrelevant to our linguistic and mental ascriptive practices.

To see this point, it may be helpful to consider an analogous, more or less standard, context-sensitive account of the meaning of 'tall':

(Tall) A use of 'is tall' in a context picks out the property of being taller than the contextually relevant delineation (cf. Klein (1991); Larson and Segal (1995, 130ff.)).

It is compatible with (Tall) that a particular ant should be taller than (infinitely) many delineations; but if that ant remains not taller than the delineation d relevant in a particular context K, then (Tall) has the effect of setting a boundary around d such that uses of 'tall' in K are simply not assessed in terms of delineations other than d. These other (perfectly good) delineations are irrelevant to our practices in K.

In the same way, the contextually set boundary lines at work in our uses of color predicates delimit the properties that we ascribe with those predicates. In this connection, it is significant that even color attributions made by statistically abnormal perceivers — those who themselves fall beyond the boundaries in many contexts — can be responsive to the boundaries that they themselves violate. For example, there is evidence that the attributions made by dichromats and achromatopes (whom I take to be contextually irrelevant perceivers in ordinary non-comparative settings) are focused on the colors that relate objects to trichromats (i.e., not themselves). Thus, Roger Shepard reports that in the course of his experiments on dichromats, "One particularly articulate protan insisted that although he could not distinguish the (highly saturated) red and green we showed him, neither of these papers came anywhere near matching up to the vivid red and green he could imagine!" (Shepard, 1992, 339). Further evidence for the importance of statistically normal perceivers in the color attributions of statistically non-normal perceivers comes from a conversation, reported by Oliver Sacks, in which an achromatope recognizes a distinction in color not marked by his visual system:

> "But what about bananas, let's say — can you distinguish the yellow from the green ones?" Bob asked.
>
> "Not always," James replied. "'Pale green' may look the same to me as 'yellow'" (Sacks, 1996, 32).

Finally, evidence for the same conclusion comes from Jameson's and Hurvich's astonishing report that protanopes and deuteranopes whose performance on color similarity orderings reveals their lack of red-green discrimination "nevertheless use reddish and greenish hue terms appropriately when instructed to name the same test colors..." (Jameson and Hurvich, 1978, 146).[10] This

[10] Obviously there is room for dispute about the interpretation of these findings. Nonetheless, I take them as *prima facie* support for my contention that color ascriptions made by non-normal perceivers are responsive to the colors discriminated by the statistically normal perceivers who are relevant (for them too) in most ordinary contexts.

treatment of the color attributions made by dichromats and achromatopes might plausibly be extended to color attributions made by the blind as well.

4.2.6 *Anthropocentricity*

Part of what I mean in saying that many coarse-grained color properties are not metaphysically principled is that these color properties (/their extensions) will not carve nature at anything like the joints recognized by a principled metaphysical theory constructed from God's viewpoint, as it were. To say this is to say that these properties will not be "natural" (in the sense of Lewis (1983*a*)), but instead "anthropocentric" (in the sense of Averill (1985); Hilbert (1987)). For that matter, the same is presumably true about the fine-grained color properties. For these properties carve nature at joints specified by types of visual systems and perceptual circumstances, and there is little reason to expect these joints to coincide with those recognized by a principled fundamental metaphysics (given the plausible assumption that minds, perceivers, and visual systems are unlikely to be recognized as such in that sort of fundamental metaphysics). Both the fine- and coarse-grained colors, then, are anthropocentric properties, albeit perfectly real for all that (cf. Hilbert, 1987; McDowell, 1985; Wiggins, 1987*a*).

There is, however, a second, and potentially more worrisome, sense in which the coarse-grained colors in particular are anthropocentric. Namely, the coarse-grained colors, because they are constituted in terms of relations to the perceivers relevant to human beings rather than other sorts of organisms (and the perceptual circumstances that are relevant to human beings rather than other sorts of organisms) are shot through with a kind of species-chauvinism. Admitting that the coarse-grained colors are anthropocentric in the first sense considered means holding that they sort the world in mind- or perceiver-centric ways. But the point now before us is that the coarse-grained colors sort the world in *human*-centric ways in particular. And several authors have objected strenuously to theories that make human concerns central to color ontology (Matthen, 1999, 2005; Thompson *et al.*, 1992; Thompson, 1995).

I think the species-chauvinism present in my proposal is justifiable. We should bear in mind that the charge of species-chauvinism arises specifically with respect to the coarse-grained colors, which have been introduced to account for our thought and talk about color — i.e., the thought and talk about color undertaken by human beings. It is unsurprising and unobjectionable to be told that human thought and talk is responsive to properties that are of parochial human concern. Hilbert puts this point aptly in writing that,

> Discussions of color ontology, as well as a large part of color science, are, after all, primarily concerned with a property that human beings perceive, reflect on, and talk about. If it turns out that this property is not perceived by some other kinds of organisms that is neither surprising nor a challenge to the adequacy of our accounts of this property of particularly human interest (Hilbert, 1992*a*, 39).

However, it is a further significant feature of the view I'm defending that it makes room in its ontology for color properties that are not of parochial human concern. Namely, it admits into its ontology those fine-grained colors constituted in terms of relations to non-human perceivers (or, for that matter, various coarse-grainings of the fine grained colors that are constituted in terms of relations to members of non-human species).

I want to suggest, then, that the species-chauvinism present in my account is of just the amount, and just the kind, that we should want. It appropriately gives pride of place to species-chauvinist elements in our thought and talk, but makes this anthropocentrism limited in metaphysical importance, and does not lean on the anthropocentrism to mark distinctions of the sort that, I argued in §2.3.1, cannot be sustained.

4.2.7 *Dual Properties, Dual Representations: Parsimony Lost (Twice Over)?*

Whatever its merits, the proposal that we should recognize both coarse- and fine-grained colors in our ontology will likely strike many readers as grossly unparsimonious in so far as it makes use of two different sets of color properties rather than one. Likewise, fans of representational economy are likely to complain about a lack of parsimony in my recognition of two different levels of representation corresponding to the coarse- and fine-grained colors in the total cognitive-cum-perceptual system. Although I feel the weight of these worries about parsimony, I am ultimately unmoved by them. Let me say why.

The first and most important part of my response is that, whatever the cost in parsimony in recognizing both coarse- and fine-grained colors in our ontology (likewise, in recognizing representations of both sorts of properties), doing so carries benefits that are worth having.

There are two senses in which the coarse-grained colors and representations of them are indispensable. First, (1) and other natural language color attributions presumably represent (or convey) the exemplification of some or other properties; but the very fineness of the fine-grained colors makes them unsuitable for being attributed by such utterances, whereas the coarse-grained colors are potentially apt for this role precisely because they are less finely individuated. For, to repeat what was said in the beginning of this chapter, the fine-grained properties are too fine-grained — too determinate — to be represented in our thought and talk: it is just implausible that the mechanisms responsible for supplementing color predicates (whether construed as semantic or extra-semantic) have access to the state of adaptation of the perceiver, the viewing distance and angle, ambient illuminant, simultaneously seen objects, and so on). Whether the supplementation in question is construed as a semantic or extra-semantic process, it is in any case cognitive. And there is good reason to doubt that, in general, we have cognitive access to all the different parameters that (on the relationalist view presented) need fixing.[11] A second sense in

[11] Just where to draw the boundaries of our cognitive access to such parameters is a complicated matter. On the one hand, naïve subjects may have cognitive access to the need for fixing at least some of the relevant parameters — perhaps conditions of illumination, for example. On the other hand, it seems reasonably clear that our cognitive access falls far short of the specification of all the relevant parameters; that is why we need to do the empirical science, and not simply introspect, to

which it seems to me that recognizing coarse-grained colors and representations of them is indispensable is that, as I'll argue in §4.4, taking our thought and talk about color to represent coarse-grained colors resolves a cluster of otherwise pressing problems for relationalism — problems not solvable with the apparatus of fine-grained colors alone.

On the other hand, I think the considerations about perceptual variation from Chapters 2–3 continue to give us reason to accept the existence of the fine-grained colors and to take our visual systems to represent these properties. One might think otherwise if one held that the availability of the coarse-grained colors itself provides a means for choosing between variants in cases of perceptual variation. For example, in a case where x looks unique green to S_1 in C_1 and looks bluish green (hence, not unique green) to S_2 in C_2, one might hold that x's exemplification of the coarse-grained property *unique green simpliciter* supports the view that the way x looks to S_1 in C_1 represents x veridically at the expense of the way x looks to S_2 in C_2. If so, then there is no need to accept ecumenicism as a way of accommodating both variants, and so no need to accept the relationalist's fine-grained relational colors as a way of sustaining ecumenicism. However, on reflection, there is no reason to take x's exemplification of *unique green simpliciter* as grounds for siding with the way x looks to S_1 in C_1 to the detriment of the way x looks to S_2 in C_2. After all, there are alternative coarse-grained colors (based on coarse-grainings of the fine-grained colors relative to contexts in which the contextually relevant perceiver is S_2 and the contextually relevant circumstance is C_2) that lend as much support for the opposite choice (see §4.3.1). Needless to say, S_1's thought and talk about color is organized around certain of these available coarse-grainings rather than others; but there is no motivation for taking this fact about S_1's thought and talk as reflecting a preference for certain coarse-grainings over others in the world's ontology itself.

In sum, then, neither the coarse- nor the fine-grained colors (nor representations of either sort of property) are dispensable; consequently, we should accept both kinds of properties (and representations of them).

A further reason for not being worried about ontological profligacy is that the the fine- and coarse-grained properties are so intimately joined that, having accepted the former, the latter represent no further cost to our fundamental ontology. The two sets of properties impose partitions on the world that differ only in their level of determinacy: the coarse-grained properties are, as their name suggests, coarse-grainings over the fine-grained properties. Consequently, once one has paid the price of accepting fine-grained colors into one's ontology, adding the coarse-grained colors does not require any further additions to the supervenience base. (Analogy: once one has accepted the relatively fine-grained properties *divisible by three* and *divisible by two*, there

determine just which parameters are psychophysically relevant, and why it is surprising to learn the results of these empirical inquiries.

is no further cost in fundamental ontology to accepting the relatively coarse-grained property *divisible by six*.) Accepting the coarse-grained properties over and above the fine-grained properties means accepting further ways of cutting up our fundamental inventory; but it does not require any addition to that inventory. But I take it that parsimony is an appropriate constraint in choosing between ontologies only (at best) when those ontologies differ in the size of their fundamental inventories. Since the present choice between an ontology of fine-grained colors with coarse-grained colors and one with fine-grained colors but without coarse-grained colors is not a choice of that kind, I suggest that considerations of parsimony offer no guidance with respect to it.

Finally, it is worth noting that, besides being unobjectionable, a commitment to both less and more determinate color properties is not limited to color relationalists. Plausibly *any* acceptable color ontology will have to allow for counting as colors less determinate (*green, red, blue*) and more determinate (*chartreuse, crimson, aqua*) ways of cutting up whatever it takes as the basic inventory (cf. Kalderon, 2007*a*, 15–16). If so, then it is not a particular cost of relationalism (or some version of that view) that it makes room for coarse- as well as fine-grained colors.

For these reasons, I don't believe that parsimony considerations ultimately tell against the proposal that relationalists should appeal to both coarse- and fine-grained colors (and representations thereof).

4.2.8 *Representational Interaction*

I believe that the two sorts of representations (representations of fine-grained and coarse-grained colors) interact in perception. In a typical perceptual episode, my visual system will begin by representing the lemon as exemplifying the fine-grained property *yellow for S in C* (where 'S' is a schematic letter standing in for a relatively detailed specification of my visual system, and 'C' is a schematic letter standing in for a relatively detailed specification of the circumstance I am in at the time). Next, that representational state of my visual system will normally cause me to hold a belief (in a context K) that attributes to the lemon the coarse-grained property *yellow simpliciter*.[12] And, if I am suitably disposed, this belief can cause me to utter (1) in K, whose content in K is identical to the content of the belief in K.

On this view, then, we represent two different sorts of color properties: our visual systems represent the fine-grained color properties such as *yellow for S in C*, while in thought (i.e., general cognitive representation) and talk about color we ordinarily represent coarse-grained colors such as *yellow simpliciter*.

[12] We can think of the causal transition from the visual representation of *yellow for S in C* to the mental representation of *yellow simpliciter* as a kind of inference, so long as it is understood that this kind of inference is sub-doxastic.

4.3 Semantics for Color Attribution

4.3.1 *Context-Dependence and Shifting Standards*

The semantics for the use of color predicates that I have proposed is explicitly context-sensitive.[13] It is, in this respect, analogous to a familiar kind of context-sensitive semantics for expressions such as 'tall', 'here', 'this', 'nearby', and perhaps many others.

There is a cluster of questions that can be raised for any such theory that depends crucially on the notion of contextual parameters (such as contextual relevance) to single out semantic values. What is a context? What are its parameters? Which of its parameters is or are relevant to the determination of what is contextually relevant? And just how does this type of determination work?

The (unfortunately limited) good news is that these questions arise for a wide variety of popular semantic theories for a wide variety of expressions in a wide variety of languages; thus, the explanatory burdens are not mine alone to suffer. The bad news is that, alas, I cannot give a fully satisfactory answer to these questions (and not only for reasons of space). However, it seems to me that two important pieces of the puzzles about context-dependence are fairly well-known and uncontroversial, and can be extended straightforwardly to the cases of concern. The first is the thought that what counts as a relevant respect of comparison (for tallness, for locations, for perceivers and perceptual circumstances, and so on) can vary between cases, partly as a function of the common set of presuppositions between interlocutors (cf. Dretske, 1970; Cohen, 1988; Heller, 1989). The second is that standards for comparison along these respects of comparison adjust by what Lewis (1979) calls a principle of accommodation; the idea is that speaker-hearers adjust their standards of comparison in a context so as to make true/acceptable the utterances of their interlocutors (*ceteris paribus*). Applied to the present instance, these ingredients suggest that what perceivers and perceptual circumstances count as relevant to the evaluation of an utterance of (1) will be in some way governed by the common knowledge and beliefs of the speakers and hearers in the context, but will evolve in accord with a principle of accommodation as the need arises.[14]

That standards can be shifted in this way means that our mental and linguistic color predications can pick out extremely specific properties — and possibly even the fine-grained colors on some occasions. One way in which this can happen is that we can explicitly relativize our ascriptions to highly determinate sorts of perceivers and visual circumstances. Thus, we use

[13] I am especially grateful to Adam Pautz, Tarun Menon, and an anonymous referee for pressing me to get clearer on this aspect of my view.

[14] Of course, these two ingredients do not by themselves amount to an adequate account of semantic context-sensitivity. However, as noted, the present account of color predications is context-sensitive in familiar ways, and so is apt for treatment by familiar methods. I will be happy if I can show that the semantics for color predications is in no worse shape than the semantics for gradable adjectives, for example.

sentences like (13)–(17) when, for example, we discuss comparative color vision or the sorts of psychophysical variations considered in Chapter 2:

(13) x is yellow for a pigeon when viewed under illuminant D_{65} at a distance of one meter against a flat achromatic background.

(14) x is yellow for David Hume.

(15) x is yellow for a pigeon.

(16) x is yellow for me, but not yellow for you.

(17) x is yellow in the viewing condition of the store, but not yellow in my living room.

I suggest that we should understand the ability of our color ascriptions to ascribe either coarse- or fine-grained color properties in terms of a context-dependent system that has both default behavior and override mechanisms. When color predicates occur in contexts where there is no explicit or inexplicit specification of the relevant parameters, as in many unadorned uses of (1), they express relatively unspecific (coarse-grained) color properties. However, this default behavior of our color predicates can be overridden. When explicit linguistic material or other features of the context provide values for parameters that are different from (or even simply more specific than) those that would be provided by default in the context, as in (13)–(15), the properties expressed by our color predicates become more fine-grained, in so far as they will relate objects to explicitly marked, and therefore more fine-grained, relata. Thus, because an utterance of (13) mentions, and thereby makes relevant in the context in which it is uttered, certain kinds of perceivers (pigeons) and perceptual circumstances (those involving illuminant D_{65} when viewing the stimulus at a distance of one meter against a flat achromatic background), the property attributed to x by an utterance of (13) is plausibly something like *yellow for a pigeon when viewed under illuminant* D_{65} *at a distance of 1 meter against a flat achromatic background*. This is as expected, given the present proposal, since explicitly mentioning in a context such parameters of perceivers or perceptual circumstances is one particularly effective way of constraining the class of contextually relevant perceivers and perceptual circumstances.

Once again, it may be helpful to compare this proposal about color ascriptions to an analogous view about how context helps to fix semantic values — this time in the case of motion ascriptions. On that analogous view about motion ascriptions, which I take to be more or less canonical, an utterance of (2) in a context attributes to car c something like the relational property *traveling at 60 miles per hour relative to the contextually relevant frame of reference*. Thus, context must contribute a value for the parameter of the contextually relevant frame of reference. In contrast, (18) attributes to c the relational property *traveling at 60 miles per hour relative to the frame of reference of the train*.

(2) Car c was traveling at 60 miles per hour.

(18) Car c was traveling at 60 miles per hour relative to the frame of reference of the train.

If so, then context does not have to make the same sort of contribution to the semantic value of the motion ascription in (18) that it does in (2). The best account of the difference between (2) and (18) is very similar to what I have said with respect to color ascriptions. Namely, the context-sensitive semantic behavior of motion predicates can be overridden when explicit linguistic material (or whatever else) provides values for parameters that would otherwise be set by contextual features.

What about examples in which explicit material signals the need for departure from the default behavior for only some of the relevant parameters?[15] The most natural suggestion is that we depart from the default context-sensitive behavior where this is signaled, and revert to the default where it is not. Thus, we should read (14) as attributing the property *yellow for David Hume in contextually relevant perceptual circumstances.*

Indeed, it is plausible that such non-default behavior can be triggered by contextually salient constraints even when this sort of explicit linguistic material is absent, although it is a matter of substantial controversy (which I won't resolve here) to say whether, and if so then just how, this process works. Thus, the motion predicate in (2) expresses *traveling at 60 miles per hour relative to the frame of reference of the train* when uttered in a context in which it contextually salient that the frame of reference that matters is that of the train. Likewise, then, the color predicate in (14) expresses *yellow for David Hume when viewed under illuminant D_{65} at a distance of 1 meter against a flat achromatic background* when uttered in a context in which it contextually salient that the perceptual circumstance that matters is one of viewing the stimulus under illuminant D_{65} at a distance of 1 meter against a flat achromatic background.

The account I am proposing explains how it can be that two subjects can use distinct and non-overlapping color predicates to ascribe colors to a given object. To see this, suppose John, an ordinary trichromat who passes the standard psychophysical tests for color vision, sincerely and reflectively utters (A_{John}) in context K:

(A_{John}) : Lemon l is pure yellow.

The property he thereby ascribes to l is *yellow for the perceivers relevant in context K under the perceptual circumstances relevant in context K*. If K is a more or less ordinary context in which there are no special presuppositions in force about what perceivers are contextually salient, it is plausible that the contextually relevant perceiver is something like what traditional secondary quality theorists have had in mind in talking about a normal perceiver. Likewise, if there are no special presuppositions in force in K about what perceptual circumstances are salient, it is plausible that the contextually relevant perceptual circumstances are something like what traditional secondary quality theorists have had in

[15] In fact, (13) is one such example — it contains no linguistic material relevant to the visual angle subtended by the stimulus, among many other unmentioned but psychophysically relevant parameters (see §2.3.3).

mind in talking about normal circumstances (cf. Lewis, 1997, 327). Thus, John's utterance of (A_{John}) in K attributes to l something like the coarse-grained color property *pure yellow for a normal perceiver in normal perceptual circumstances.*

But now suppose, as is indeed possible, there is a distinct trichromatic observer, Jane, who passes the usual tests for color vision and who makes a sincere and reflective utterance of (A_{Jane}) in a a context K' where, as in K, there are no special presuppositions in force about what perceivers and perceptual circumstances are contextually salient:

(A_{Jane}) Lemon l is green-yellow.

Following a line of reasoning analogous to the one above, we reach the conclusion that Jane's utterance of (A_{Jane}) in K' attributes to l the coarse-grained color property *green-yellow for a normal perceiver in normal perceptual circumstances.*

Now, if it were true that (A_{John}) and (A_{Jane}) attributed just those properties in whatever context in which they were uttered, then it would follow that those two strings could not both be truly uttered in a single context. For nothing can (*a fortiori*, l cannot) bear both *pure yellow for a normal perceiver in normal perceptual circumstances* and *green-yellow for a normal perceiver in normal perceptual circumstances*: x's bearing the first property precludes, and x's bearing the second property requires, that x should be greenish for a normal perceiver in a normal circumstance.

But because (A_{John}) and (A_{Jane}) are semantically context-sensitive, it is not true that they attribute the very same property in every context in which they are uttered. On the contrary, if they are both uttered in a single context, then it could well happen that mechanisms of accommodation shrink the class of perceivers and perceptual circumstances relevant to the evaluation of (A_{John}) and (A_{Jane}) so that the two are no longer overlapping. In particular, it might happen that the contextually relevant perceivers for the evaluation of (A_{John}) and (A_{Jane}) include just those with the very precise perceptual systems of John and Jane, respectively, and that the contextually relevant perceptual circumstances include just those under which John and Jane perceive l, respectively. In a context where this occurs, John's utterance will attribute to l something like the property *pure yellow for a perceiver with an instance of John's precise perceptual system type in an instance of the precise type of perceptual circumstance that John is in,* while Jane's utterance will attribute to l the property *pure yellow for a perceiver with an instance of Jane's precise perceptual system type in an instance of the precise type of perceptual circumstance that Jane is in.* Since these distinct properties are compatible, both utterances can be true with respect to a single context.

In addition, we should also notice that it is compatible with the view presented that distinct perceivers can ascribe the very same coarse-grained color to the lemon (I'll discuss this issue in more detail in §4.4.3). Suppose that Jim and June both utter (1) in a single context. Unlike the case of John and Jane just discussed, here there is no threatened clash between these utterances, so accommodation is not triggered. Consequently, absent special presuppositions to the contrary, it is plausible that the perceivers and perceptual circumstances contextually relevant for the evaluation of Jim's utterance, like those contextually relevant for the evaluation of June's utterance, are simply normal perceivers and normal perceptual circumstances. But then the property attributed to l by Jim's utterance is just the property attributed to l by June's utterance: *yellow for normal perceivers in normal perceptual circumstances*. And this explains how the coarse-grained colors these different perceivers ascribe to the lemon by their utterances of (1) can coincide.[16]

4.3.2 *Vagueness*

I have claimed that the predicate 'is yellow' in (1) uttered in K expresses the property *yellow for the perceivers relevant in context* K *under the perceptual circumstances relevant in context* K. It seems clear, however, that the extension of this predicate is vague — and likewise for many other color predicates, for the same reason. For example, fixing on my current context, there are clear cases of contextually relevant perceivers (normal trichromatic human beings), clear cases of contextually irrelevant perceivers (mantis shrimp whose visual systems contain ten different kinds of cones (Cronin and Marshall, 1989) or dichromatic squirrels (Thompson, 1995, 145)), and perceivers who are borderline relevant (normal trichromat human beings who disagree with us about the spectral locus for unique green). Similarly, there are clear cases of contextually relevant perceptual circumstances (from 90 degrees at a distance of one meter under flat illumination of 7000 degrees Kelvin with uniform surround), clear cases of contextually irrelevant perceptual circumstances (at a depth of 3 miles underwater, say), and borderline cases of contextually relevant perceptual circumstances (lit by a candle, or with a surround field consisting of thin diagonal blue lines).[17] Indeed, it would be surprising if there were sharp boundaries for the perceivers and perceptual circumstances relevant to any context. Consequently, our ordinary uses of color predicates are vague.

[16] In this respect, ascription of coarse-grained colors is unlike ascription of fine-grained colors; for, as discussed in §4.4.3, it is plausible that distinct perceivers cannot ascribe the very same fine-grained color to a stimulus. What drives the difference between the two sorts of properties is that, as I have set out matters, the parametrization of fine-grained colors is (plausibly) at least as fine-grained as the individuation of perceivers or perceiver-time-slices, whereas the parametrization of coarse-grained colors can be, depending on context, less fine-grained than the individuation of perceivers or (*a fortiori*) perceiver-time-slices.

[17] It is inessential to the claim I am making that the vagueness of these comparisons runs along several independent dimensions (e.g., typicality of viewing angle, light source, atmospheric composition). In any case, it's worth noticing that, although discussions of vagueness in the philosophical literature often proceed under the pretense that the cases they discuss are vague only along one dimension (number of grains that compose a heap, number of hairs on a head), this assumption is false even in the paradigm cases. After all, heapness depends on such additional vague factors as shape and spatial proximity of the collection, and baldness depends on such additional vague factors as length of the hair and size of the head (cf. McLaughlin, 1997, 216).

The claim that ordinary uses of color predicates is vague in these ways is, I suggest, confirmed by reflection on our ascriptive practice. In particular, this is just what typical reactions to the cases in §§2.3.1–2.3.3 reveal: although we are prepared to apply the unadorned predicate 'is green' to some of these cases and to withhold it in others, there are many cases where we are not clear what to say.

In addition, the view I have proposed allows us to understand the various scientific and industrial specifications of standard observers and viewing conditions as precisifications designed for particular purposes (which is just what they appear to be) rather than as absolute standards for fixing the extensions of the color properties. Again, this is what we should expect if color language is vague in the respects I have claimed; analogously, we might establish stipulative boundaries for the extension of a vague term such as 'bald' for particular industrial or scientific reasons (perhaps we need to assemble an army to fight an enemy who happens to be particularly skilled at capturing bald soldiers, and therefore decide to draft all men with at least 10,000 hairs on their heads) without thereby claiming to have found determinate boundaries between the negative and positive extensions of the term.

4.4 Problems and Solutions

In this section I want to argue that there are substantial advantages for relationalists in adopting the main proposal of this chapter. In particular, I'll argue that accepting this view provides the relationalist with the resources she needs to solve a cluster of otherwise pressing problems.

4.4.1 *Permissiveness*

If relationalism is right, then relational properties constituted in terms of relations between objects and visual systems very different from our own, or in very strange viewing circumstances, will be counted as genuine (fine-grained) colors that ordinary objects do in fact exemplify. But attributions of these fine-grained colors to objects can strain credulity; for example, it can seem odd to say that how things look to dichromats reveals colors that those things have, or that a ripe raspberry is really gray in situations of extremely low illumination. This suggests that the practice of ordinary color attribution is less permissive than color relationalism, by itself, would predict — our practice of attribution is constrained by more than the requirement of truthfully attributing to objects the fine-grained colors that (given relationalism) they in fact exemplify.

Given only an ontology of fine-grained colors and the assumption that color predicates have colors as their semantic values, it is hard to see what additional factors could be operating to constrain our ordinary color attributions. On the other hand, the suggestion that ordinary mental and linguistic color attributions represent coarse- rather than fine-grained colors makes it easy to locate the extra constraints needed. On this suggestion, these additional constraints come from our restricting our attributions to those of the colors that relate objects to contextually relevant perceivers and contextually relevant perceptual circumstances.[18]

Relationalists who adopt the semantics proposed in this chapter, then, have a ready answer to the problem of permissiveness. To wit, the reason that our practices of color attribution appear to be less permissive than we would expect given color relationalism by itself is that those practices are concerned with only some of the relational colors recognized by relationalism — viz. those that relate objects to contextually relevant perceivers and contextually relevant perceptual circumstances.

4.4.2 *Proliferation*

A closely related objection alleges that relationalism proliferates color attributions too liberally. The objection here is not, as in the case of the previous worry about permissiveness, that color relationalism warrants color attributions that fall outside what is allowed by normal practice. Rather, the present worry is numerical: it is that, even if all of the attributions licensed by relationalism were individually plausible on their own, it would still seem unreasonable to accept all of them at once. According to the relationalist, an object is not merely yellow to a perceiver in a circumstance — it is yellow to one perceiver in one circumstance, blue to a second perceiver in a second circumstance, green to a third perceiver in a third circumstance, and so on into the night. Indeed, since relationalism puts few if any restrictions on the kinds of perceivers and circumstances relations to which constitute colors of ordinary objects, the view arguably allows for an infinite proliferation of colors of a single object (cf. §5.1). But, the objection goes, this proliferation of colors (whether finite or infinite) goes too far; in most cases we are typically inclined to attribute only a few colors to ordinary objects — certainly only finitely many, and perhaps only one. This, too, can be viewed as a case where our practices of attribution are more constrained than what relationalism, by itself, would predict.

Again, it is hard to see how a relationalist who takes ordinary color predicates to pick out fine-grained colors will be able to bring her views into line with our ascriptive practice; but the problem can be resolved by the semantics offered in this chapter. It is true that, according to relationalism, a particular ripe lemon will exemplify many — perhaps infinitely many — fine-grained colors. But if, as I am proposing, our practice of ascription is

[18] Lewis endorses a similar view in this passage:

> 'Normal light' can be explained in terms of the range of illumination that most people — actually, nowadays, and hereabouts — mostly encounter. Likewise, *mutatis mutandis*, for normal capacities and normal surroundings.... I do not suppose it is incumbent on folk psychophysics to do much by way of listing abnormal cases — if it tried, it would soon outrun common knowledge. A statistical conception, rigidified to actuality and nowadays and hereabouts, should suffice (Lewis, 1997, 327).

Unlike Lewis, however, I think we can explicitly relativize our color ascriptions to abnormal visual systems and viewing conditions when we so choose (see §4.2.8.)

organized around coarse-grained colors, then the plurality of the lemon's fine-grained colors is not immediately to the point. What is immediately to the point, as far as that practice is concerned, is the class of coarse-grained colors the lemon exemplifies that relate it to contextually relevant perceivers and perceptual circumstances. Since this class of the lemon's colors is far smaller in cardinality than the class of the lemon's fine-grained colors, the number of coarse-grained colors in the running is far smaller than the number of fine-grained colors the lemon exemplifies. Moreover, coarse-grained colors, even within their range, can collapse distinctions between numerically distinct observers and numerically distinct perceptual circumstances. Relative to most contexts, the relative indeterminacy of contextually relevant perceivers and perceptual circumstances means that the coarse-grained colors in the running will impose a coarse grid on the candidate relations between objects, perceivers, and circumstances. Consequently, the number of coarse-grained colors we truly ascribe to the ripe lemon in such contexts is quite small. Indeed, in many contexts the grid imposed by what is contextually relevant will be so coarse as to permit speakers to talk about *the* (unique) color of an object without any trouble. Trouble arises only when ascribers compare these ascriptions against ascriptions that involve other sorts of perceivers or conditions — i.e., when we engage in systematic psychophysical comparisons of the sort discussed in Chapter 2. Only when confronted with the range of variation revealed by such psychophysical comparisons do we make contextually relevant more determinately specified perceivers and perceptual circumstances. And at this point our practice of color attribution shifts to the attribution of relatively determinate (perhaps even fine-grained) colors (as discussed in §4.2.8).

Much the same seems to be true of the cases of motion and meteorological attribution considered above. In ordinary discourse we typically ascribe one velocity to an object (presumably, relative to a single frame of reference that is left inexplicit), and talk about *the* occurrent meteorological condition (presumably, relative to a single location that is left inexplicit). Trouble arises only when we compare these attributions against those we would make relative to other frames of reference/other locations — i.e., when we engage in systematic physical/meteorological comparisons. Only when directly confronted with the range of variation revealed by such physical/meteorological comparisons do we recognize the need for explicit relativization to more determinately specified relata, at which point our practice shifts to the attribution of relatively determinate motions and meteorological conditions (as discussed in §4.2.8).

Indeed, the same factors allow the relationalist to explain why we make the attributions we do rather than others that would be allowed, given appeal only to fine-grained colors. For example, if presented with salmon steaks that looked indigo to us, we would ascribe to them the color *indigo simpliciter*, even after learning that the steaks are pink for other sorts of visual systems or for our visual systems under different (non-actual) viewing conditions. Moreover, and most importantly, we would persist in our disinclination to enjoy salmon steaks bearing the color *indigo simpliciter*, despite learning about other colors that the steaks bear. The reason for this, on the present account, is that our decisions about what to eat are guided (in part) by the effects we expect those things to have on the very relata that figure in the coarse-grained colors — *we*, and not some other kinds of perceivers, are the kinds of perceivers contextually relevant in the context of the dinner table, for it is *our* nutrition that is at stake in that context. This shows that our behavior, like our ordinary thought and talk about color, is sensitive to the coarse-grained colors, rather than to the proliferating fine-grained colors recognized by the relationalist.

All of this goes to show that the problem of proliferation is not a problem for the relationalist who accepts the semantics for color ascription on offer.

4.4.3 *Heraclitean Flux*

Plato's Socrates famously reports Heraclitus as having held a doctrine of universal flux: "Heraclitus says somewhere that 'everything gives way and nothing stands fast,' and, likening the things that are to the flowing of a river, he says that 'you cannot step into the same river twice' " (*Cratylus 402a*, in Cooper (1997, 120)).[19] The relationalist who accepts only fine-grained colors is forced to the Heraclitean consequence that perceivers cannot step in the same perceptual river twice (as it were) — that distinct perceivers, or even distinct time-slices of a single perceiver, could not attain perceptual contact with the very same color property. For, given that the fine-grained colors are as fine-grained as they are, what seemed to be distinct instances of one color property will often turn out, for the relationalist, to be instances of distinct color properties.[20]

But a commitment to such a Heraclitean flux of color properties seems unattractive for a number of reasons.

First, it certainly seems that organisms can and do recognize (i.e., *re*-cognize) later instances of one color. Indeed, the behavior of organisms often depends crucially on this sort of property recognition — which, presumably, would be invoked to explain object re-identification, the possibility of classical conditioning, and so on. Thus, if relationalism is indeed committed to a Heraclitean flux, it thereby makes unavailable the most straightforward explanation of several important behaviors of organisms. Byrne and Hilbert press this point against relationalism by asking us to imagine ourselves as Old World monkeys who first eat a tasty crimson fruit and immediately thereafter perceive and then reach

[19] The extant Heraclitean fragment most closely corresponding to the view Socrates ascribes to Heraclitus comments that, "On those stepping into rivers staying the same other and other waters flow" (DK 22B12).

[20] This is slightly too quick. According to the relationalist methodology I've urged, the question whether colors should be construed in terms of a relation to a particular parameter is broadly empirical. Thus, it could turn out as a consequence of the empirical findings that the relationalist individuation of colors is less fine-grained than I am assuming — and, in particular, not so fine-grained as to result in the kind of Heraclitean flux under discussion. But, in light of the discussion of particular parameters in §2, I think it likely that relationalism will indeed lead to a reasonably fine-grained individuation. As such, the problems about flux are worth taking seriously, even if only as a worst-case scenario.

for a second fruit of the same kind. The straightforward explanation of our reaching behavior, they point out, surely invokes the claim that we recognize the second fruit as exemplifying the very same color as the first. Unfortunately, they continue,

> this simple explanation of your behavior is not available to the color [relationalist]. Call the first [perceptual circumstance] C_{F1} and call the second C_{F2}. Unless the relativization to types of circumstances is to be pointless, the [relationalist] must concede that the details of the example could be filled out so that C_{F1} and C_{F2} are *different*.... According to the [relationalist], the color the fruit first appeared to have was what we can call "crimson for you in C_{F1}," and the color the second fruit appeared to have was "crimson for you in C_{F2}" .... Because $C_{F1} \neq C_{F2}$, the the expressions are supposed to pick out *different* properties.... According to the [relationalist], the first fruit seemed to you to have a *different* color than the second, and hence the [relationalist] cannot endorse the simple and obvious explanation of your fruit-eating behavior (Byrne and Hilbert, 2003, 58).

A Heraclitean flux of colors also threatens to undercut the possibility that distinct perceivers (/distinct stages of one perceiver) could agree about the colors of objects.[21] For if perceiver S_1 in condition C_1 only perceives those colors of x that relate x to S_1 in C_1, while perceiver S_2 in condition C_2 only perceives those colors of x that relate x to S_2 in C_2, then (notwithstanding the homophonous color words that S_1 and S_2 might use in making color attributions), these perceivers can agree in representing the colors of x in the highly constrained case where $S_1 = S_2$ and $C_1 = C_2$.

On the other hand, the very same flux threatens to undercut the possibility that distinct perceivers (/distinct stages of one perceiver) could disagree about the colors of objects. Suppose that S_1 views a ripe raspberry under extremely low illumination (circumstance C_1) and S_2 views it under direct sunlight (circumstance C_2). There is a strong pre-theoretical intuition (I take it) that S_1's perceptual report (19) and S_2's perceptual report (20) disagree about the color property (/a color property) of the ripe raspberry:

(19) This ripe raspberry is gray.

(20) This ripe raspberry is not gray.

(The intuition that color attributions can disagree may be at its strongest in the case where $S_1 = S_2$, and where the subject makes a second attribution as a way of correcting a first.) But the relationalist who accepts only fine-grained colors is unable to accept this intuition: if we treat this case in the way most naturally arising out of the metaphysics presented and defended in Chapter 2, we will naturally take S_1's utterance of (19) as ascribing the property *gray to S_1 in C_1* to, and S_2's utterance of (20) as withholding *gray to S_2 in C_2* from, the ripe raspberry. And it goes to the heart of the relationalist's response to cases of

[21] The problem of accounting for agreement and disagreement has been pressed against relationalists in many places; a particularly lucid discussion (directed at the relationalist-inspired semantics for "predicates of personal taste" such as 'fun' and 'tasty', as opposed to color predicates *per se*) occurs in Lasersohn (2005, 648–650).

FIG 2.2. The two center strips are qualitatively identical, but there is an obvious difference in their color appearance.

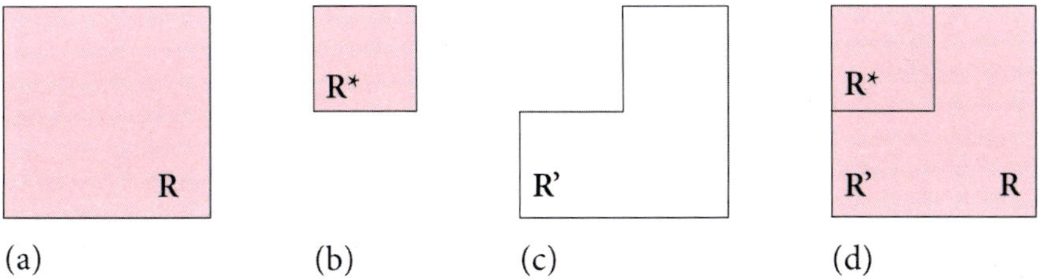

FIG 2.4. (a) Square R. (b) Subregion R^* ($\subseteq R$). (c) Subregion R' ($\subseteq R$), such that $R' \cap R^* = \{\}$. (d) $R = R^* \cup R'$.

FIG 3.1. Partially sunlit coffee cup.

FIG 3.2. Common objects under different daylight illuminants.

perceptual variation that those attributions don't conflict, just as the following meteorological attributions don't conflict (and for the same reason):

(21) It is raining in Vancouver.

(22) It is not raining in San Diego.[22]

It should be clear that the Heraclitean perceptual flux I've been discussing, and the problems that come in its wake, are products of a fine-grained individuative standard for the semantic values of color predicates. As such, these problems are serious obstacles for the relationalist who takes such predicates to pick out only fine-grained colors; on the other hand, they are easily resolved by the introduction of coarse-grained colors.

Consider, for example, Byrne's and Hilbert's problem of explaining the monkey's reaching for a second fruit of the same kind. Let it be that the first fruit exemplifies (and is represented by the monkey's visual system as exemplifying) the fine-grained color *crimson for* S *in* C_{F1} while the second exemplifies (and is represented by the monkey's visual system as exemplifying) the distinct fine-grained color *crimson for* S *in* C_{F2}. It is compatible with all this — and indeed plausible — that the two fruits can exemplify (and are represented by the monkey's cognitive system in some particular context K as exemplifying) the very same coarse-grained color *crimson for perceivers relevant in context* K *in perceptual circumstances relevant in context* K. This will be possible if it is true that the very same kind of coarsely-specified creature (e.g., that very monkey) and perceptual circumstance (e.g., amongst trees under daylight illumination) are relevant to the monkey on the two occasions. The explanation of the monkey's reaching behavior on the second occasion, then, would cite the exemplification by the two fruits of a common coarse-grained color — viz., that one common color represented by his cognitive system, as per the straightforward recipe for explanation that Byrne and Hilbert think is appropriate to the case.

The same point can be used to answer the objection that relationalism would preclude agreement with respect to color attributions. Although the visual systems of different perceivers (one perceiver in different circumstances) might be confined to the attribution of non-overlapping ranges of fine-grained colors to a single stimulus, their cognitive and linguistic representations of the colors of objects attribute properties from a common range of coarse-grained colors. Thus, even though Sam's and Pam's visual systems represent the ripe lemon's distinct colors *yellow to Sam in* C_{Sam} and *yellow to Pam in* C_{Pam} (respectively), Sam's and Pam's cognitive systems can agree in representing the lemon as bearing the single coarse-grained color *yellow simpliciter*. Similarly, should Sam and Pam choose to make verbal reports of the lemon's color, their utterances will both represent the lemon as bearing the one coarse-grained color *yellow simpliciter*.

Likewise, the relationalist can explain disagreement in color attribution by appeal to the coarse-grained colors. Since the coarse-grained colors attributed

[22] It is inessential to the example that (21) and (22) are analytic.

by different perceivers in different circumstances nevertheless match against one another, distinct attributions of coarse-grained colors to a single stimulus can conflict with one another. That is, (19) and (20) should be understood not as analogous to the obviously independent pair (21) and (22), but to the obviously not independent pair (21) and (23):

(21) It is raining in Vancouver.

(23) It is not raining in Vancouver.

Because their locational parameters agree, two people who utter (21) will be in agreement, and someone who utters (21) will disagree with someone who utters (23). Likewise, then, for (19) and (20).

In sum, while relationalists may be forced to accept that there is a Heraclitean perceptual flux of fine-grained colors, by accepting coarse-grained colors she can make that flux harmless with respect to the needs of our ordinary thought and talk about color.

4.4.4 *Error*

A final benefit of appealing to both fine- and coarse-grained colors is that this allows the relationalist to give a satisfying account of erroneous color ascription that would not otherwise be possible.[23]

It seems clear enough that our practices of color attribution are committed to the possibility of error: for example, a perceiver will typically offer a second perceptually informed color attribution in an effort to correct an earlier one (by herself or someone else) that she thinks is mistaken. Surely the most direct way of explaining these practices would sustain the second reporter's thought that the first perceptually informed color attribution, and also the perceptual state that informs that first attribution, is erroneous.

On the other hand, it can seem hard to see how the relationalist who accepts only fine-grained colors can allow for such errors. As we have seen in Chapter 2, relationalism is motivated by the need to reconcile distinct perceptual variants when (i) each purports to represent the color of a single stimulus, and (ii) there seems to be no non-arbitrary way of singling out one of those variants as veridical at the expense of the others. Relationalism allows us to accept all of the variants — to allow that each represents the stimulus veridically. But this treatment of perceptual variation threatens to over-generalize: the proposal seems so liberal in accepting perceptual variants that it is unclear how it could allow that any variant is *not* veridical.[24] On reflection, this is unsurprising;

[23] The complaint that relationalism (typically some particular version of relationalism) precludes the possibility of error has been made by Hilbert (1987, 88), Watkins (2002, 93), Matthen (2001, note 10), and Byrne and Hilbert (2003, 57–58), *inter alia*.

[24] This is too quick. As I have explained elsewhere (Cohen, 2007), the relationalist who eschews coarse-grained colors can after all accommodate two relatively abstruse sorts of erroneous color attributions: (i) those involving hallucination (e.g., while suffering from *delirium tremens* I hallucinate an elephant in the room and attribute *pink for me in the circumstances I am then in* to that represented elephant) and (ii) those involving deviant causal chains (e.g., I represent a tomato as

relationalism is designed to be inclusive about perceptual variants, so it is hardly shocking to find that it is ill-placed to exclude variants at the end of the day.[25]

In contrast, by appealing to coarse-grained colors, the relationalist is able to give an attractively unified account of errors in the attribution of colors. Here's how. Let it be that Sally the subject is invited to the psychophysics lab and is asked to view the stimulus — a ripe lemon as it happens — under viewing condition C in a context K. The stimulus, let us suppose, bears the fine-grained color *yellow for Sally in condition* C. Now, Sally will normally report on her visual experience by something like the ascription (1) in K. On the view of this chapter, this ascription attributes to the lemon (not the fine-grained color *yellow for Sally in condition* C, but) the coarse-grained color *yellow for the perceivers relevant in context* K *under the perceptual circumstances relevant in context* K. Now, without special presuppositions in force, and absent detailed comparative psychophysical evidence about perceptual variation, the kinds of perceivers and perceptual circumstances that are likely to be contextually relevant for Sally in K are likely to be fairly anodyne and unspecific — perhaps they are, respectively, something like normal human perceivers and normal daylight illumination at medium viewing distance. Of course, Sally tacitly believes that she herself is a normal human perceiver, and that her

bearing *red for me in the circumstances I am in* on the basis of its affecting my visual cortex directly — i.e., not via acting on my retina). But these sorts of errors are presumably rare at best; in any case, they won't extend to most cases we ordinarily classify as erroneous. Therefore, the relationalist who hopes to capture ordinary cases of error needs to say more.

[25] Although he is not a color relationalist, McLaughlin (2003*a*) proposes a further type of error for his relativist (realizer functionalist) view that relationalists might wish to accept. On McLaughlin's realizer functionalist form of relativism, "Redness for a visual perceiver of type P in circumstances of visual observation C is that property which disposes its bearers to look red to P in C, and which [is] had by everything so disposed" (122). According to McLaughlin, the final (commonality-requiring) clause of the quoted proposal provides an extra road to errors of color perception: a state representing that x is red for P in C can be erroneous even if x looks red for P in C if it turns out that x fails to share the property required of red things. In principle, relationalists might adopt something like the commonality requirement, and thereby find another route to the explanation of perceptual error.

Unfortunately, I think the contemplated account of error would commit relationalists (and, for that matter, relativists) to color irrealism. In order that McLaughlin's final clause can have any teeth, he must be construing 'property' in a way that two objects with different bases for the disposition to look red to P in C will count as having different properties. For if not, it will be trivially true that bearers of the disposition satisfy the commonality clause by having the disposition — in which case nothing could satisfy the first clause without satisfying the second clause, so there could be no additional path to errors of color perception here after all. But it seems clear as a matter of empirical fact that the class of things that have the disposition to look red to P in C are heterogeneous at every level of description lower than 'all of them have the disposition in question' (cf. Nassau, 1980). Or, in other words, it seems clear that the disposition is realized by a range of distinct basis properties. Consequently, given McLaughlin's proposal, it looks like the empirical facts force the conclusion that nothing is red.

Since, as I shall argue, there are other ways of recapturing error that do not lead to irrealism, it seems to me that relationalists should not accept the McLaughlin-inspired account of perceptual error under consideration.

present perceptual circumstance C is that of normal daylight illumination at medium viewing distance. Therefore, it is natural that she believe, on the basis of her visual representation of the lemon as exemplifying *yellow for Sally in condition C*, that the lemon also exemplifies the coarse-grained color *yellow simpliciter*. It turns out, however, that Sally has been fooled: C was constructed by the clever psychophysicist so that (i) C would lie outside the range of the contextually relevant perceptual circumstances, (ii) the lemon's appearance in C to Sally would be entirely distinct from the very same lemon's appearance in contextually relevant perceptual circumstances, and (iii) there would be no visual clues to tip off Sally to these facts about C. (Psychophysicists have many techniques for implementing such subtle manipulations; they include the use of contrast effects, unusual illumination, and so on; see Hardin (1988) for discussion of some of the parameters of the perceptual circumstances that affect color appearance. This is old hat to psychophysics, and it is no surprise that Sally can be fooled.)

In this case, I claim, Sally represents the color of the lemon erroneously. As it happens, the lemon *is* yellow for Sally in C; so if she had represented only that it is yellow for her in C, she would have avoided error. But she did not so confine herself. Rather, because the experimental manipulation was subtle enough not to tip her off, she represented it less cautiously as being yellow *simpliciter* — which it was not. This is just to say that Sally's representation of the lemon's color is erroneous; and since (we are supposing) there really is a lemon that Sally perceives, the error is a textbook case of perceptual illusion.

A similar recipe for illusion would manipulate Sally herself, rather than the perceptual circumstance under which she perceives the lemon.[26] Suppose that the experimenter alters Sally's visual system (e.g., by causing chromatic adaptation in her retina, or, for that matter, by slipping something in her coffee) and then asks for her report in context K' about the lemon's color in the (unaltered) perceptual condition C'. Assume that the lemon is yellow for Sally in C'. If Sally is unaware of the manipulation, she is likely to assume that she is a normal human perceiver of the type that is, by default, contextually relevant for the attribution of coarse-grained colors in K'; but the experimental manipulation has made it the case that that is not true. Because of her false assumption, then, Sally will represent in K' not merely that the lemon is yellow for her in C' (which is true) but that the lemon is yellow *simpliciter* — i.e., yellow for perceivers relevant in context K' in perceptual circumstances relevant in context K' (which is false). Here, too, we have a case of illusory representation of the tomato's color.

It is worth observing that the sort of illusion discussed above is not confined to the psychophysics lab. For example, it arises in cases that are naïvely described as color illusions, such as those in popular books of illusions

[26] There's a natural sense in which manipulations to the subject can be redescribed as manipulations to the perceptual condition, and vice versa. Consequently, its unclear whether what follows is a second recipe for illusion, or just a redescription of the first.

(e.g., Seckel, 2002). One such case is the famous Benham disk, depicted in Figure 4.1.[27] When the Benham disk is rotated about its center at a rate of about

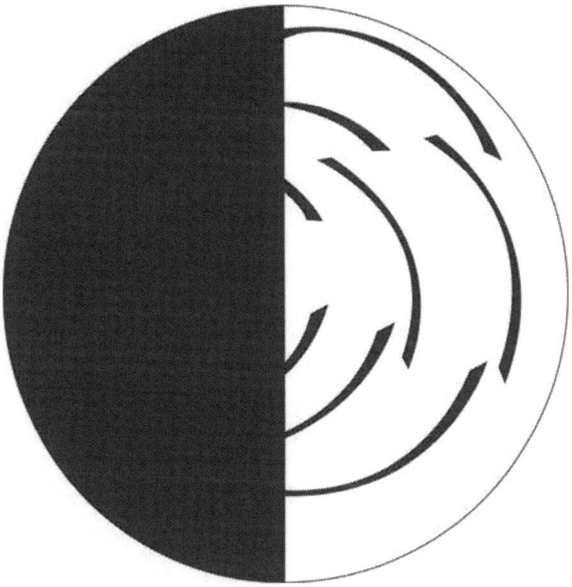

FIG. 4.1. The Benham disk.

6–8 Hz, rings of desaturated chromatic colors appear on its surface. I think there is a reasonable pre-theoretical case for counting our perceptual representation of desaturated chromatic bands on the surface of the spinning Benham disk as illusory: this is, for example, why the effect is surprising to learn about. Moreover, the case seems amenable to the (relationalist-friendly) account of illusion now under discussion. The story would be that, when you look at the spinning disk, some region of it *is* blue for you under the highly constrained perceptual circumstance you're in. As it happens, you represent in a context K the region of the disk's surface under discussion as being blue *simpliciter* — viz., blue for perceivers relevant in K and in perceptual circumstances relevant in K. But, again given the usual absence of special presuppositions and comparative data, the confined perceptual circumstances you happen to be

[27] I've chosen the Benham disk because the chromatic effects it produces are often counted as illusory, and because it can be reproduced here without incurring the cost/difficulty of chromatic printing. But there are many other cases that are amenable to the account in the text. Some examples in Seckel (2002) are the Hermann grid illusion (title page), neon color spreading (p. 245), the Bezold effect (p. 299), etc. On the other hand, there are several cases in this book that, on the account propounded here, are not illusions of color perception (e.g., the Rubik's cube "illusion" (p. 287; cf. the demonstrations at http://www.purveslab.net/)), and even several that seem (independently of the views about color I'm defending) not to be illusions at all (e.g., Jastrow's ambiguous duck-rabbit figure, p. 145).

in are different from the perceptual circumstances relevant in K, since the latter don't require that that sort of disk be rotating at a rate in the 6–8 Hz range. Thus, your representation of the disk's color is correctly classified by the account I'm defending as an illusion of color perception.

An even more naturalistic example of this sort of illusion caused me great frustration one night when I walked up and down the parking lot, searching for (but repeatedly walking past) the Chevrolet I had rented.The Chevy had been red *simpliciter* when I parked it in daylight illumination, so I was looking for something red to me in the nighttime perceptual circumstance; unbeknownst to me, the nighttime circumstance involved illumination by sodium vapor lights, and consequently the rented Chevy looked (not red, but) grey to me in that perceptual circumstance. Because I was unaware of relevant facts about the perceptual circumstance, I erroneously represented the rented Chevy as being grey *simpliciter*, and wrongly judged that it could not be the car I had parked earlier in the day (after all, that car had been red *simpliciter*). It is natural to describe the error I made in the parking lot as an error of color perception. Since accepting coarse-grained colors allows the relationalist to accept that natural and pre-theoretical description of this and other commonplace cases, I think we should accept them.

4.5 Conclusion

I have argued that relationalists should adopt a context-sensitive semantics according to which our mental and linguistic representations of color typically have as semantic values relatively coarse-grained relational color properties. It seems to me that such properties better account for the relative unspecificity of our ascriptive practices than do the fine-grained relational colors (§4.1), and that the disadvantages of admitting them to our semantics and ontology are minimal (§§4.2–4.3). Moreover, I believe that a semantic theory of this kind provides the relationalist with resources to resolve a number of otherwise serious objections to her view (§4.4). If I am right in this assessment, then it seems to me that relationalists should embrace such a context-sensitive semantics with open arms.

5

RELATIONALISM DEFENDED: ONTOLOGY

Or if perhaps [artists] manage to think up something so new that nothing remotely similar has ever been seen before — something which is therefore completely fictitious and unreal — at least the colours used in the composition must be real.

— Descartes, *Meditations on First Philosophy*, CSM I, 13.

In Chapter 4 I defended relationalism against a number of objections concerning linguistic and psychological representation of color properties. In this chapter, I want to respond to three sets of more directly ontological objections against relationalism. The first set of ontological objections has to do with the large plurality of color properties recognized by color relationalism (§5.1). The second concerns the accusation that (despite my claim that the two positions are orthogonal in Chapter 1) relationalism is committed to irrealism about color (§5.2). The third, related set, alleges that relationalism is an error theory of color that contravenes (and so revises) requirements on colors imposed by semantics of our color terms and concepts (§5.3). In what follows I'll argue that none of these threats makes for a persuasive case against color relationalism.

5.1 The Many and The One

5.1.1 *The Many: Multiplicity*

In §4.4.2 we considered (and ultimately rejected) an objection to the effect that the relationalist is committed to too many color attributions — more color attributions, that is, than seem reasonable by the standards of our ordinary thought and talk about color. However, putting matters of linguistic and mental representation aside entirely, one might persist in objecting on purely ontological grounds that relationalism populates the world with too many colors — more colors, that is, than seem reasonable by the standards of any plausibly parsimonious ontology.

For, again, relationalism says that a ripe tomato is not merely red, but red to one perceiver in one circumstance, blue to a second perceiver in a second circumstance, green to a third perceiver in a third circumstance, and so on. Indeed, it is plausible that the relationalist is committed to the existence of — and exemplification by ordinary objects of — *infinitely* many colors. We can derive this result by a valid argument relying on an entailment of relationalism (P1), plausible principles of modal plenitude (P2–P3), and a commonly accepted necessary condition on property identity (P4):

(P1) For any actual or possible perceiver of the ripe tomato S and any actual or possible perceptual circumstance C under which the ripe tomato can be perceived, *red for* S *in* C is a color that the ripe tomato exemplifies.

(P2) There are infinitely many actual or possible perceivers of the ripe tomato and infinitely many actual or possible circumstances under which the ripe tomato can be perceived.

(P3) If $S_1 \neq S_2$ or $C_1 \neq C_2$, then there is some possible object that exemplifies *red for* S_1 *in* C_1 while failing to exemplify *red for* S_2 *in* C_2.

(P4) For any colors P and Q, $P = Q$ only if, necessarily, P and Q coincide in extension.

(C) Therefore, the ripe tomato exemplifies infinitely many colors.

Arguably, then, the relationalist is committed to recognizing infinitely many color properties, and to attributing infinitely many colors to every ordinary object.

One could be forgiven for suspecting that this sort of chromatic explosion is objectionable. However, I want to suggest that this suspicion is ultimately unfounded. For while there might be reason for concern about such an explosion in intrinsic properties, it seems to me that there is nothing unreasonable in the relationalist's recognition of infinitely many colors (or in her attribution of infinitely many colors to ordinary objects), precisely because she understands colors as relational rather than intrinsic properties. Let me explain.

I can think of two potential reasons for worrying about an explosion of intrinsic properties. First, accepting such an explosion flies in the face of the apparently widespread preference for desert landscapes that has long been taken as a regulative ideal on ontological inquiry (explicitly since Quine (1953*a*), and less explicitly from much earlier), and does so in as severe a form as can be imagined. For good reasons or bad, many have been extremely reluctant to accept that there could be lots and lots of — certainly that there could be infinitely many of — numerically distinct intrinsic properties appearing in our fundamental description of the furniture of the universe. Second (and perhaps relatedly), the intrinsic properties of tomatoes and the like are presumably constrained by the intrinsic way that they are made up, and it is plausible that the intrinsic makeups of such objects, while surely more complex than a surface inspection would reveal, are not unlimited in their complexity.

But these reasons for rejecting the recognition and attribution to ordinary objects of infinitely many intrinsic properties should give us no qualms about the recognition and attribution to ordinary objects of infinitely many relational properties. The relational properties x has, of course, supervene on the relations that x bears to things other than x. Therefore, so long as one is reasonably liberal in recognizing things other than x, an explosion of relational properties that x bears will ensue. Interestingly, this will be true no matter how tightly constrained one's fundamental ontology turns out to be, and no matter how simple or complex the intrinsic description of x turns out to be.

To see the point, consider the following silly analogy. There is a relation that holds of an object and a number just in case the set of fingers attached to the object has a cardinality less than the number. This relation holds between pairs — pairs of objects and numbers; but by fixing a number, we single out a relational property that relates objects to that number.[1] For example, fixing the number seven, we single out the relational property *having fewer than seven fingers* that relates things to the number seven in a particular way; call this relational property 'F_7'. Your left hand is in the extension of F_7, assuming it has fewer than seven fingers — your left hand is related to the number seven in the way required of things that exemplify F_7. If so, then your left hand also exemplifies the relational property F_8 = *having fewer than eight fingers*, and it exemplifies the relational property F_9 = *having fewer than nine fingers* — your left hand is related to the numbers eight and nine in the ways required of things that exemplify F_8 and F_9. Indeed, it seems clear, we could continue this banal exercise forever. That is, there seem to exist infinitely many relational properties that relate things to numbers in the way we are imagining (viz., F_7, F_8, F_9, ...), and it seems that your left hand will exemplify infinitely many of these relational properties.

I submit that the recognition and attribution to your left hand of these infinitely many relational properties is ontologically innocent. It follows merely from suitably liberal standards for acceptance of objects other than your left hand (in this case, the numbers) and relations between hands and those objects (in this case, the relations F_i), together with a plausible individuative standard according to which properties that differ in extension are necessarily distinct. Significantly, the recognition and attribution to your left hand of all these relational properties does not offend against the ontological motivations for eschewing infinitely many intrinsic properties considered above. For it is compatible with taking our fundamental ontology, and our intrinsic description of your left hand, to be finite and highly constrained. Thus, even those sympathetic to such ontological motivations should be open to the recognition of and attribution to your left hand of infinitely many relational properties.

But if that is the right conclusion to draw about the left hand, then much the same is true of what the color relationalist says about the ripe tomato. As in the case of the left hand, the relationalist's recognition and attribution to the tomato of infinitely many relational color properties follows merely from suitably liberal standards for acceptance of objects other than the tomato (in this case, actual and possible perceivers and actual and possible circumstances, and actual and possible bearers of colors) and relations between hands and those objects (in this case, relational colors of the form *red for S in C*) (as stated in P2–P3), together with a plausible necessary condition on property individuation (P4). Significantly, and once again, the recognition and attribution

[1] This is an instance of the procedure for generating relational properties from binary relations that Humberstone (1996, 213–215) calls 'place-fixing'.

to the tomato of all these relational properties does not offend against the ontological motivations for eschewing infinitely many intrinsic properties considered above, for it is compatible with taking our fundamental ontology, and our intrinsic description of the tomato, to be finite and highly constrained. Therefore, as before, granting these ontological motivations for the sake of argument should leave us open to the recognition of and attribution to the tomato of infinitely many relational color properties.

5.1.2 *The One: Unity*

Even if the threat of ontological explosion — the mere fact of (large or infinite) plurality — is ultimately unpersuasive as an objection against color relationalism, that explosion invites a further concern about the unity of the colors. Hardin (2004) has pressed a version of this criticism against relationalism by drawing on Socrates's response to (Meno's explication of) Gorgias's pluralist account of virtue given in the *Meno*. Here Socrates lays down a requirement that he thinks must be met by an account of virtue, and on which he will build his criticism of Gorgias's pluralist view:

> Even if they are many and various, yet at least they all have some common character which makes them virtues. That is what ought to be kept in view by anyone who answers the question, What is virtue? (72d).

Socrates's objection to Gorgias is not that his view results in a mere plurality of virtues, but that there is no principled criterion for inclusion in the plurality. Similarly, one might reasonably hold that there should be something — and something that it is the central task of a theory of color to elucidate — shared by the several colors recognized by the theory in virtue of which they do (and other properties do not) count as colors. That is, it seems fair to insist that an adequate account of color should provide a principled and projectible criterion that unites those things it recognizes as colors and distinguishes them from those it does not.

I want to agree that an adequate account of color should provide such a principled and projectible criterion. Moreover, and significantly, I want to concede that relationalism, by itself, does not provide one. That means that relationalism, by itself, is not an adequate account of color. But this is not a surprising conclusion — it only repeats something that I have insisted on since Chapter 1, where I acknowledged the schematic character of color relationalism. In particular, I observed that relationalism, in claiming that color properties are constituted in terms of relations between objects (surfaces, volumes, lights, etc.) and perceiving subjects, is agnostic between a range of views about just what kinds of relations between these relata constitute the colors. (I'll present and assess several views about the nature of these relations in Chapters 7–8.)

That said, I do not see that Socrates's criticism should cause concern for color relationalists. For if relationalism requires supplementation by a story about the nature of the relevant relations in order to serve as an adequate color ontology, then that very story will also suffice to answer Socrates's criticism.

I'll illustrate this point by considering a more specific form of relationalism — the dispositionalist view (first mentioned in Chapter 1 and that that will be discussed in more detail in §8.1) on which something counts as exemplifying *red for S in C* iff it is disposed to look red to S in C. This account is a form of relationalism that construes the relevant relations as dispositions of objects to look certain ways to certain subjects in certain circumstances. Proponents of this view begin to answer Socrates's request for a principled and projectible criterion by saying that a relational property counts as a color just in case the exemplification of that relational property by its relata (an object x, a subject S, and a circumstance C) consists in x's being disposed to look a particular way to S in C. This answer, however, just pushes back Socrates's question by a step: the dispositionalist still won't have an answer to that question until she can explain (in a principled and projectible way) what it is for the object to look one of the relevant particular ways to a subject in a circumstance. To answer this further question the dispositionalist must not only go beyond relationalism, but indeed beyond her dispositionalism, and give an account of the nature of color experiences. Now, as I shall emphasize in §7.1.4, several types of answer seem to be open to the dispositionalist at this point, including intentionalist, sense-data, primitivist, neural type-identity, and functionalist answers. Just for the sake of concreteness, however, consider a neural type-identity answer: we can understand what it is for x to look one of the relevant ways to S in C in terms of S's being appropriately caused, by visually attending to x in C to undergo a token opponent-process system state type — types which are themselves neurocomputationally individuated (Hurvich and Jameson, 1957; Boynton, 1979; Hurvich, 1981; Hubel, 1988).

Putting all of this together does, I suggest, provide a dispositionalist answer to Socrates's question. For this sort of dispositionalist, the principled and projectible criterion that distinguishes colors from non-colors is derivative (but no less principled and projectible for that): it is derived from the principled and projectible criterion that distinguishes states that are color experiences from states that are not. And on the identity-theoretic account of color experiences, this latter criterion is itself to be understood in terms of the principled and projectible type-individuations made available by a well-known neurocomputational theory (viz., opponent-process theory). The dispositionalist is therefore in a position to meet Socrates's challenge, for she has a principled and projectible criterion for being a color experience, and (derivatively) we have a principled and projectible criterion for being a color.

The lesson I wish to draw from the foregoing is not merely that the dispositionalist has at her disposal the resources to answer Socrates's question (although that is true). Rather, I want to emphasize that something analogous to the pattern of explanation just considered can be used by any relationalist (or, any rate, any relationalist who has worked out a full account of the nature of color) to meet Socrates's demand. For every relationalist who has worked out a full account of the nature of color is, by virtue of that full account, committed to an answer to the question of just what sorts of relations to perceivers and viewing conditions constitute colors. But since any answer to the question will amount to a principled and projectible criterion for being a color, this means that every relationalist (who has worked out a full account of the nature of color) can provide for the sort of unity that Socrates complains is lacking from Gorgias's account of the virtues. Even if there is no single response to Socrates that would be acceptable to every relationalist, no relationalist (who has worked out a full account of the nature of color) will be without one.

5.2 The Many Faces of Property Realism

In Chapter 1 I argued that the choice between relationalism and non-relationalism is (as are other choices between substantive theories of the nature of color properties) orthogonal to the choice between realism and irrealism. This seems to me correct so long as we understand color irrealism as the view that ordinary actual objects do not exemplify colors (as per §1.1). For, to repeat, color relationalism (or any other substantive view about the nature of the colors) — *qua* theory of the sorts of properties colors are — is uncommitted on the further issue of whether ordinary actual objects exemplify properties of that sort. In this sense, then, it seems absolutely clear that color relationalism does not entail color irrealism (although, in so far as it makes no commitment on the realism/irrealism issue, it is open to relationalists to endorse irrealism about color as an independent commitment).

Unfortunately, however, because 'realism' is such a rampantly ambiguous term, things are not quite so simple. As it happens, relationalist views of different forms have often been criticized for failing to live up to the requirements of realism about color, given particular understandings of the realism/irrealism distinction (e.g. Stroud, 2000). What, if anything, should we make of these criticisms? This question will occupy us in the rest of this section.

Now, 'realism' is a term as vexed as they come in philosophy, so it is often hard to see just what is meant by the charge of irrealism. If our assessment of color relationalism is to amount to more than name-calling, the question we must answer is whether there is some construal of 'realism' on which relationalism is an irrealist theory of color *and* such that there are good reasons for rejecting irrealist accounts of that kind. To answer this question, I'll consider a number of ways of construing the realist/irrealist distinction that have some currency in philosophical discussion, and ask two further questions about each. First, on each understanding, does color relationalism count as a form of irrealism about color? Second, if it does, are theories that are irrealist in these alternative senses committed to unacceptable costs (e.g., do they entail the revisionary conclusion that colors are not exemplified by ordinary objects)?

I hope to acquit relationalism of the charge of irrealism in any objectionable sense, and to show that the forms of irrealism that it might entail provide no basis for rejecting the view.

5.2.1 *Mind-Independence*

Our first historically salient candidate for distinguishing the real from the unreal involves an appeal to the notion of mind-independence. We might motivate this criterion by putting ourselves in the imaginative situation of one who is faced with the threat of veil-of-ideas skepticism, and who wants to use the real/unreal distinction to mark a divide between ideas that correspond to bits of extra-mental reality behind the veil and ideas that are unassociated with things behind the veil. Members of the former class of ideas (e.g., my idea of the coffee cup before me) pick out things that are real, on this view, in that their existence is independent of what happens on the mental side of the veil. In contrast, members of the latter class of ideas (e.g., my idea of a unicorn) do not pick out anything mind-independent; therefore, we can conclude that unicorns count as unreal.

Such invocations of mind-independence have continued to flourish in discussions of realism in several areas of philosophy. Thus, Wright claims that, for the scientific realist, "the real progress of science is measured by the extent to which our theories represent a reality whose nature owes nothing to our natures or the standards that inform our conception of reasonable discourse about it" (Wright, 1992, 200). A more iconoclastically linguistic version of this view is Dummett's famous construal of realism as "the belief that statements of the disputed class possess an objective truth-value, independently of our means of knowing it: they are true or false in virtue of a reality existing independently of us" (Dummett, 1978, 146).

Suppose something like this is the right way to understand property realism; if so, it follows that relationalism about color is a form of irrealism. For the relationalist will claim that colors constitute a portion of reality whose nature (by relationalists' own lights) owes greatly to our natures. Or, again, according to color relationalism, whether color ascriptions (sincere, cooperative statements of the form 'x is red to S in C') are true depends crucially on how x affects subjects, which is just to say that statements about this and other color properties are not true or false in virtue of a reality existing independently of us — rather, they are true or false in virtue of a reality that very much depends on us (by including us within it).

A related reason for thinking of relationalism as a form of irrealism arises from the famous discussion of color in Locke (1975). Locke claims about colors and other secondary qualities that "Such qualities ... in truth are nothing in the objects themselves, but powers to produce various sensations in us by their primary qualities ..." (II.viii.10). A straightforward interpretation of this passage takes Locke here as identifying colors with powers, or dispositions, to affect subjects — i.e., as adopting a (dispositionalist) species of relationalism about color. That said, Locke also seems to endorse an apparently irrealist view about colors and other secondary qualities in claiming that such qualities (as opposed to primary qualities) are not really in bodies: "The particular bulk, number, figure, and motion of the parts are really in them; and therefore they may be called *real* qualities, because they really exist in those bodies. But light, heat, whiteness, or coldness, are no more really in them than sickness or pain is in manna" (II.viii.17).

Now, on one standard (but controversial) interpretation, the way to reconcile these remarks is to understand Locke's apparent irrealism in II.viii.17 as more or less equivalent to the dispositionalist relationalism he endorses in II.viii.10; on this reading, the force of the claim that colors are not really in bodies is (not that they fail to be exemplified by bodies, but) merely that they are powers — i.e., that they are relational (see Bennett (1971, 107), Mackie (1976, 13)). Putting aside the question of whether this interpretation is correct as a reading of Locke, the position it ascribes to him is that the relational, or mind-dependent, status of colors and other secondary qualities *ipso facto* precludes them from being really in bodies, and therefore provides instant warrant for the inference from the relationalism of II.viii.10 to the apparent irrealism of II.viii.17.

We can now see that the reading of Locke just considered is of a piece with the views about realism we have been discussing in using mind-independence as a touchstone for realism, and consequently in legitimating the inference from color relationalism to color irrealism. However, I now want to urge that color irrealism, understood in terms of the mind-independence criterion for realism, is no threat to relationalism.[2]

The first point to make is that color irrealism (in the sense in which realism requires mind-independence) does not entail the worrisome and revisionary irrealism according to which ordinary actual objects (fruit, lights, tables) fail to exemplify colors. The perceiver-/subject-/mind-dependence of colors entailed by relationalism has no such consequence; it has only the consequence that, in order to exemplify colors, such ordinary objects must be appropriately related to perceivers/subjects/minds. No reason has been given for supposing that standing in those relations should fail to count as the exemplification of a *bona fide* property (in the broad sense that includes relations). The second point to make is that no *other* obvious cost accrues to theories that make colors unreal in the present sense.

I conclude that relationalism will count as an irrealist theory in the technical sense of Wright, Dummett, and Locke, but that there is no convincing reason for resisting this form of irrealism.

[2] I am convinced by Rickless (1997) that Locke was aware of this point, and would not accept the conclusion that colors fail to exist or fail to be exemplified in bodies (/be in bodies), even allowing that he holds that colors are not *really* in bodies. For the view of Locke as a color eliminativist is difficult to reconcile with his explicit claims (in II.viii.10) that secondary qualities are powers that bodies have. Instead, Rickless urges, Locke's point is only that secondary qualities are not in bodies in the same sense that primary qualities are: secondary qualities are in bodies (but not *really* in bodies) by being exemplified relationally by those bodies and our minds, while primary qualities are both in bodies and *really* in bodies by being exemplified non-relationally by those bodies alone. Moreover, Rickless argues that the force of the quotation from II.viii.10 is that that secondary qualities are *nothing but — i.e., nothing other than — powers to produce sensations* (as opposed to: *nothing in the object, but rather powers to produce sensations*). It is for this reason that I have labeled Locke's position from II.viii.17 as an *apparent irrealism* in the main text.

5.2.2 *Convergence*

A second criterion for property realism that has often shown up in philosophical discussion concerns interpersonal convergence in ascribing the property or properties in question.

To see the thought behind this criterion, consider the ascription of a property about which realism is uncontroversially the right view: *cowhood*. While there are surely false positive and false negative ascriptions of *cowhood* that fall outside normal usage, there is a remarkable degree of convergence in the ascription of this property to particulars; moreover, it is plausible that many of the false positive and negative ascriptions can be explained away in terms of factors such as ignorance, distraction, poor lighting, borderline cases, and so on. A very plausible explanation of the remarkable convergence that remains once these factors are taken into account (i.e., set aside) is that *cowhood* is a genuine property that is indeed exemplified by some particulars and not others, and that, *ceteris paribus*, undistracted, cooperative subjects are capable of discriminating the instances from the non-instances and ascribing the property to all and only the instances (again, borderline cases aside). Since this plausible explanation for the observed convergence presupposes the reality of *cowhood*, the convergence is itself (at least) a good indication of its reality. In contrast, consider a (putative) property about which irrealism is pretty clearly the right view, such as *ghosthood*. Here we find an equally remarkable lack of convergence in its ascription to particulars; and this lack of convergence is naturally explained by the hypothesis that there is no such property or that it is nowhere actually exemplified. Thus, the thinking goes, we can use convergence in property ascriptions as at least a guide to, and perhaps even a criterion of, the reality of properties.

Now, in light of what was said in Chapter 2, one might suspect that an understanding of property realism based on convergence of ascriptions will lead immediately to the conclusion that color relationalism is a species of color irrealism. But it is worth being cautious about this verdict, since relational properties are susceptible to a special sort of merely apparent non-convergence for reasons that stem from indexical expressions sometimes occurring in the predicates used to pick out those properties. To see this point, consider what happens when we apply a convergence-based test for property realism using the predicates 'enemy' and 'my enemy'. On the one hand, we expect to see a high degree of convergence in application of the predicate 'enemy'; although this predicate presumably picks out a relational property, different subjects will apply the predicate to any individual who stands in the relevant relation to some or other person. On the other hand, the predicate 'my enemy' effectively fixes one relatum, assigning to it the speaker; thus, as the ascriber/speaker (hence the context) changes, different ranges of individuals will satisfy the very same (orthographically individuated) predicate, and will do so by standing in the same relevant relation to the speaker of each particular context (not to just any old person). Consequently, a convergence-based standard for property realism will appear to classify the property *being my enemy* as unreal. But this is surely the wrong way of interpreting the test as applied to the case at hand. Instead, it is reasonable to suggest that, despite the orthographic stability of the indexical-containing predicate, subjects are actually testing the application of distinct relational properties (*being the enemy of* S_1, *being the enemy of* S_2, etc.). If this is the right treatment of the case, as I think it is, then two morals follow: (i) the lack of convergence in the application of the (orthographically individuated) predicate 'my enemy' is not particularly useful with respect to deciding any relevant questions about property realism;[3] and (ii) the convergence test should in fact be run on the properties *being the enemy of* S_1, *being the enemy of* S_2, and so on, which will plausibly satisfy convergence-based standards of realism perfectly well.

With this cautionary lesson in mind, we can now ask how well the relationalist's colors satisfy such standards for property realism. To answer this question, we must distinguish between the relationalist's fine-grained colors (properties of the form *green for* S *in* C and coarse-grained colors (properties of the form *green for the perceivers relevant in context* K *under the perceptual circumstances relevant in context* K (see Chapter 4 on this contrast).

Considering the fine-grained colors first, the data about interpersonal intrapersonal variation discussed in Chapter 2 may give *prima facie* reason for believing that there is a serious lack of convergence in ascription of these properties. But, on reflection, those application data seem to be effectively indexical in just the way that data about the application of the predicate 'my enemy' are. For while these data show that two subjects might disagree about whether to apply the predicate 'unique green' to a given chip, as it might be, the relationalist diagnosis of the case has it that these subjects are in fact applying and withholding distinct properties to the chip: subject S_1 is using the predicate to claim that the chip bears the property *unique green to* S_1 *in* C_1, while subjects S_2 is using the predicate to forbear application of the property *unique green to* S_2 *in* C_2 to the chip. As in the case considered above, these considerations seem to me to suggest two important morals: (i) that lack of convergence in the application of the (orthographically individuated) predicate 'unique green' is not particularly useful with respect to deciding any relevant questions about property realism; and (ii) that the convergence test should in fact be run on the properties *being unique green to* S_1 *in* C_1, *being unique green to* S_2 *in* C_2, and so on, which will plausibly satisfy convergence-based standards of realism perfectly well.[4]

[3] Does this lack of convergence show, at least, that *being my enemy* (as opposed to *being the enemy of* S_1 and the like) is unreal? Not in the sense that this property fails to exist or is unexemplified (see below).

[4] Of course, it may happen that in practice S_2 ascribes the property *being unique green to* S_1 *in* C_1 only infrequently if at all: unless she engages in comparative psychophysics, matters involving this property are unlikely to come up for her. But this is irrelevant to the question of convergence in application of that property, just as it would be irrelevant that city-dwellers apply *cowhood* to fewer objects than do farm-dwellers. In both cases, we overcome the ordinary limitations on what

We can turn now to ask whether the relationalist's coarse-grained colors (e.g., *green for the perceivers relevant in context K under the perceptual circumstances relevant in context K*) satisfy a convergence-based test of property realism. While it is hard to answer this question precisely, I think it is likely that there is some substantial degree of non-convergence in the application of such properties. One result that supports this conclusion (and that was cited in Chapter 3 in a related context) is the finding, reported by Malkoc *et al.* (2005), that subjects (classified as normal on standard psychophysical color tests) diverge non-trivially in how they sorted 34 hue samples among eight (lexicalized) color categories. In particular, these authors report that seven different hue samples were assigned to the label 'blue' by at least one subject, but that there was 80% consensus on only two, and that all seven samples were assigned to coarse-grained color labels other than 'blue' at least once.

Although there is more to say about these results, and although they don't settle the matter by themselves, I think they provide good reason to suspect that the relationalist's coarse-grained colors might well fail to meet a convergence-based standard for property realism. Therefore, I am prepared to concede, at least for the sake of argument, that they do not satisfy that standard. Nonetheless, I want to argue that this concession is undamaging to color relationalism.

First, once again, the criterion under discussion fails to speak to the sort of irrealism according to which colors are not exemplified by ordinary actual objects. For, despite our initial discussion of the way this criterion distinguishes between plainly exemplified properties such as *cowhood* and plainly unexemplified properties such as *ghosthood*, it is inappropriate to take convergence as more than a *prima facie* guide to the reality of disputed properties. Certainly convergence is not a necessary criterion, lest actually exemplified properties whose exemplification is never observed, observed very rarely, or observed by only a small range of subjects be uniformly classified as unreal. But neither should we take convergence to be sufficient for realism. After all, the reality of the disputed property is but one possible explanation for such convergence as we find, and not always the most plausible — for example, I propose that realism about the physical appearance of alien abductors of human beings is not warranted by the uniformly converging descriptions given by alleged victims of such abductions. I take this to show that a lack of convergence in color ascriptions is no evidence against the existence of exemplified relational color properties. Moreover, and once again, if there is another reason for resisting theories according to which colors are unreal in the sense that they fail to exhibit convergence, I am not aware of it.

subjects are exposed to by running the convergence test in experimental conditions under which we can control their rates of exposure to different stimuli-types.

I conclude that, while critics are welcome to use convergence as criterial for a neologistic usage of 'realism', color relationalists should be unembarrassed by the failure of colors to count as real in this technical sense.

5.2.3 *Objectivity*

'Objectivity' is yet another deeply vexed metaphysical term that has been used to criticize relationalist accounts of color. Some critics of relationalism have appealed to objectivity on its own (as in Hardin (2004, 36ff.)), complaining that relationalism (or some specific form of the view) makes colors insufficiently objective. Alternatively, one might use the notion of objectivity in understanding the real/unreal distinction, and then argue that the relationalist's colors are insufficiently objective as a way of showing that they are unreal. In my view, such criticisms of relationalism offer little that goes beyond the criticisms we've already examined in this section, so I'll treat them more briefly.

'Objectivity' is sometimes understood merely to label a version of the requirement of interpersonal convergence discussed in §5.2.2; on this reading, P is an objective property just in case undistracted and knowledgeable subjects agree in judging whether x is P for a wide range of x. However, for reasons given in §5.2.2, the accusation of non-objectivity (hence irrealism) based on considerations of convergence should be nonthreatening to relationalists.

Other writers have used the notion of objectivity in a way that is built on the traditional subject–object contrast, and according to which a property P is objective if and only if it is constituted independently of subjects. Of course, color relationalism just amounts to denying that colors are objective in this sense. That said, while this understanding of objectivism entails that the relationalist's colors are not objective, we have been given no reason for regarding this is an undesirable outcome (indeed, I have argued for the opposite conclusion in earlier chapters). In particular, notice that, once again, the non-objectivity (in the sense now under consideration) of a property P does not entail that it fails to exist or lacks instances: I take it that such relational properties such as *being an uncle*, *being humorous*, and, *being beautiful* exist and have non-empty extensions, despite being non-objective in the current sense. That said, we don't even need relational properties to make this point. After all, a criterion for realism that rules out properties constituted in terms of subjects (or the minds of subjects) would entail the unreality of subjects, minds, perceivers, beliefs, and desires, among other things (cf. Railton, 1995); presumably, however, we wouldn't want this terminological choice to commit us to banishing subjects, minds, perceivers, beliefs, and desires from our ontology. But if the present sense of objectivity leaves room for (exemplified) non-objective properties in our ontology, then for the relationalist to admit that colors are non-objective in that sense contravenes no part of her view.

Finally, property objectivity is sometimes understood as a criterion for those properties whose role in nature (e.g., whose causal role) is independent of and unmediated by parochial human interests, concerns, and conceptual and perceptual faculties (Smart, 1963; Mackie, 1976; Williams, 1978). On this construal, mass or charge properties count as objective in that they have a role in the causal-natural order that transcends (and survives the imagined obliteration of) our interests: a Martian physicist with very different interests and cognitive and perceptual capacities would make false predictions about future events if she did not recognize these properties and take them into account in her causal models. In contrast, a relationalist's color properties are non-objective in the sense that they are anthropocentric: their causal profiles are more or less exhausted by their effects on creatures with our perceptual faculties. Consequently, a differently equipped Martian physicist might well leave colors out of her models, and in doing so would err at most in her predictions about effects on subjects like us. Fair enough; but, as argued convincingly by Hilbert (1987), properties that are non-objective in this sense can be real and exemplified for all that.[5] Put bluntly, reality includes both subjects and things that stand in relations to subjects; that these portions of reality would be of little interest to other sorts of creatures does nothing to impugn their ontological status.[6]

In sum, I see no reason, on any of the understandings of 'objective' considered, for a color relationalist to fear the conclusion that colors are non-objective.

5.2.4 *Summing Up: Relationalism and Reality*

I have been arguing in this section that, while relationalism may qualify as an irrealist theory of colors in some senses of that term that have gained philosophical currency, it is not committed to any objectionable form of irrealism. In particular, I have been concerned to argue that relationalism does not commit one to the view that color properties are inexistent or unexemplified (a view sufficiently revisionary that I am inclined to reject any color ontology that entails it at least until other theoretical options have been exhausted).

Color relationalism may be incompatible with color realism if we adopt one or another restrictive conception of the real (e.g., one that makes no room for mind-dependent properties, non-convergent properties, non-objective properties). But this result, I suggest, should serve to discredit those restrictive conceptions of the real rather than the sorts of properties that they repudiate (cf. Sayre-McCord (1988); Sober (1982); McDowell (1985); Railton (1995); Matthen (2001, 198–200)). One lesson of color relationalism (or, for that matter, relationalism about other properties) is that reality is complex and variegated: among many other things, it consists of some properties that are relational, and

[5] Indeed, even theorists who reject relationalism about color (e.g., Hilbert) take colors to be anthropocentric, so if one found fault with that conclusion, then this would pose no special obstacle for the relationalist in particular.

[6] Quite apart from the question of how questions about causal roles of relational properties might or might not stand as obstacles to realism about those properties, there is a further issue about just how various versions of color relationalism can secure causal efficacy of any sort for the colors. I take up this issue on behalf of my preferred (role functionalist) flavor of color relationalism in §7.3.

some that are not. If this conclusion is at odds with some restrictive theoretical conception of realism, then so much the worse for that conception.

5.3 Is Relationalism An Error Theory?

The worries about irrealism considered in §5.2 all take the form of a concern that the colors, as conceived of by relationalism, fail to respect some particular theoretical criterion for property realism (a criterion that, I have urged in each case, is itself open to criticism). A distinct but related, and potentially more troubling, worry about irrealism has its source in the "error theory" of moral properties defended by Mackie (1976). What distinguishes this worry about irrealism from those considered in §5.2 is that Mackie did not simply argue that moral properties fail to satisfy a criterion for property realism stipulated by the ontologist. On the contrary, he argued that moral properties (if there are any) fail to satisfy criteria that are imposed by our very moral concepts/terms, and that this results in an interesting kind of irrealism about moral properties.

Mackie's view can be seen as the conjunction of two theses. The first is a thesis about the semantic function of moral concepts/terms to the effect that they purport to pick out properties that are objective (by which he means something like interest-free) and intrinsically reason-giving. The second, and more ontological thesis — supported by Mackie's "argument from queerness" — is that there are no properties that are objective and intrinsically reason-giving (or, if you prefer, that such properties are unexemplified in our world). Given that this is so, Mackie offers an account of our moral discourse that assigns different (revisionary) semantic functions to our moral concepts and terms. He calls this an error theory of moral discourse because it corrects the naïve theory, which Mackie claims is embodied in our naïve moral concepts, according to which our moral concepts and terms pick out exactly the kinds of properties they purport to pick out.

While it is obviously beyond the scope of this book to assess Mackie's substantive metaethical views, his pattern of argument bears consideration in the present context. In particular, I want to ask whether one might mount a parallel argument to the effect that relationalism amounts to an error theory of color.

An argument targeting color relationalism that parallels Mackie's case would include both a semantic thesis about what our color concepts and terms purport to pick out, and an ontological thesis to the effect that nothing actually succeeds in meeting those standards. We can represent these two theses as follows:

(ST) It is part of the meaning of our color concepts and terms that they purport to pick out properties meeting one or more of the standards for property realism considered in §§5.2.1–5.2.3 (mind-independence, convergence, objectivity).

(OT) If relationalism is true, then the colors don't meet any of the standards for property realism mentioned in (ST).

It follows from these two premises that if relationalism is true, then color concepts and terms fail to refer to the sorts of properties that they purport to refer to; and this would mean that relationalism is revisionary, and so a form of error theory.

This form of argumentation is potentially threatening to color relationalism even if, I have maintained in §§5.2.1–5.2.3, the standards for realism on which the argument turns are misplaced. For (as in Mackie's own discussion of moral properties), the argument does not depend on the all-things-considered tenability of the relevant standards. It depends rather on the claim that these standards (tenable or not) are in fact imposed by our own concepts, as per (ST), and the claim that moral properties don't meet them, as per (OT). If these claims are correct, then we would be justified in concluding that, whatever its other virtues, color relationalism is in one way or another somewhat revisionary — or, in Mackie's terms, that it is an error theory of color.

Now, the envisaged argument against color relationalism turns on the two substantive premises (ST) and (OT), and consequently our evaluation of that argument will turn on our assessment of those two premises. However, in §§5.2.1–§5.2.3 I have already conceded the truth of (OT). Consequently, the only issue that remains is whether our color terms and concepts impose the standards on their referents that (ST) claims they do; it will come as no surprise that I want to answer this question negatively.

As it happens, many philosophers have held that our color terms and concepts do impose such standards; in particular, many have asserted this position on the strength of the claim that colors are represented in our experience as being non-relational (see, for example, Dancy (1986, 181); Boghossian and Velleman (1989, 85); McGinn (1996); Armstrong (1987, 36); Chalmers (2006, 56–77ff); Shoemaker (2006, 464)).[7] Now, these writers don't elaborate on exactly how, in their view, our color experience provides subjects with evidence for what, they claim, is the nature of color concepts; instead they typically advance the claim as an obvious truth that should be available to ordinary subjects — presumably by some combination of undergoing color phenomenology and fairly minimal reflective ratiocination.

In my view, this line of thought goes wrong in (at least) three ways. First, and most directly, there is evidence to the effect that thinkers do not take non-relationality as a conceptually central requirement on the colors in the way these writers have suggested. Second, the phenomenological evidence cited by these thinkers does not show unequivocally, as it is alleged to show, that colors are presented to us as non-relational. A third difficulty is that the appeal to non-

[7] Armstrong (1987, 342–343) makes the additional claim that direct introspection on our concept of redness (i.e., some kind of *conceptual* introspection, rather than introspection of our experience of redness) reveals that this concept is "empty" — in particular, that there is no conceptual connection between colors and perceivers of the sort that there would be if our concepts of colors revealed their (putative) relationality ((cf. Armstrong, 1999)).

relationality in our color concepts places unjustified confidence in our ability to distinguish essential from accidental ingredients of our concepts.

I'll elaborate on these criticisms in turn.

5.3.1 *Folk Color Concepts*

My first criticism is simple. Ordinary subjects, to whom ordinary color phenomenology and minimal reflective ratiocination is certainly available, just do not seem to have the commitment to non-relationality as a conceptual requirement on color properties that philosophers have often alleged. Shaun Nichols and I showed this by presenting subjects with a series of (counterbalanced) cases of representational variation involving shape properties, color properties, and gustatory properties, and asking them how to assess the variations with respect to these properties; in particular, in such cases of representational variation with two variants, we asked these subjects to decide to choose which, if either, variant, is veridical at the expense of the other (Cohen and Nichols, 2007).[8]

For example, here is one of our questions that involved color properties:

Andrew the alien and Harry the human view a ripe tomato in good light, at a distance of 1 meter. Harry says that the ripe tomato is red, while Andrew says that the very same ripe tomato is not red (in fact, he says it is green). Which of the following do you think best characterizes their views? (Check one and give a brief justification for your answer.)

- The tomato is red, so Harry is right and Andrew is wrong.
- The tomato is not red, so Andrew is right and Harry is wrong.
- There is no fact of the matter about unqualified claims like 'the tomato is red'. Different people have different visual experiences when they look at the same object, and it is not absolutely true or false that the tomato is red.

It should be clear that the third answer would be favored if color properties were relational, as per color relationalism (see Chapter 2), and that non-relationalist understandings of color properties (at least, those open to naïve subjects on the basis of undergoing color phenomenology and minimal reflection) would point subjects away from this answer. In contrast, if ordinary subjects' color concepts ruled out relationalist accounts of color properties, then presumably they would eschew the third answer.[9]

It turns out that many subjects found this third answer the most plausible. Interestingly, however, these subjects found the analog of the third answer to

[8] Our subjects were drawn from an undergraduate introductory logic course taught by Rick Grush in spring 2005 at the University of California, San Diego. Thanks to Rick Grush for allowing us to subject his students to this peculiar form of (IRB-sanctioned) torture, to the students for putting up with this, and to Paul Pistone for administering the questionnaire.

[9] I am not claiming that the *only* explanation of subjects' answers is that their color concepts allow for the relationality of colors; but it seems to me that this is a very plausible and direct explanation for the data that should be taken seriously. In particular, this means that we should demand of anyone who claims that subjects' color concepts preclude the relationality of colors that they supply an alternative explanation of these results.

be significantly less attractive when faced with analogous cases of perceptual variation with respect to shape.[10]

I suppose that one who took non-relationality to be a central feature of color concepts might dismiss the responses of these subjects (or, at least, of those subjects whose answers are in conflict with their philosophical views); but surely we should demand a persuasive and independently motivated reason for such a selective treatment of the data. Suffice it to say that no such reason has been suggested so far.

All this suggests strongly that philosophers who have emphasized non-relationality as a conceptual requirement have, at the very least, overstated the extent to which this feature figures in our concept of color.

5.3.2 *What Phenomenology Reveals*

My second criticism concerns the reliance on introspective phenomenology to support the contention that our concepts require of colors that they be non-relational. In Chapter 6 I'll return in greater detail to the issue of whether and how phenomenology can bear on the relationality or non-relationality of color. Still, I think it is worth registering at this point a serious doubt about whether phenomenology is the sort of thing that can in any simple or obvious way reveal colors to be relational or non-relational.

One important reason to be doubtful is that very many reflective and intelligent subjects who have enjoyed normal color phenomenology — subjects including philosophers, scientists, and riders of the Clapham omnibus — seem not to hold any views about whether colors are relational or not. Moreover, even among those reflective and intelligent subjects who have enjoyed normal color phenomenology and who do hold views about whether color are relational or not, there seems to be a spread of opinion on this last issue. (Evidence for this last claim, in case it is needed, is provided by the results reported in § 5.3.1.)

If color phenomenology revealed colors to be non-relational (or, at least, revealed this in any simple way), then one would expect that reflective and normally endowed subjects would pretty uniformly adopt some kind of anti-relationalism about color on the strength of this phenomenological evidence soon after encountering their first ripe tomatoes. That they have not, then, gives us reason for doubting that phenomenology reveals colors to be non-relational in the way that many have supposed.

5.3.3 *Skepticism About Conceptual Requirements*

My final reason for skepticism about the appeal to non-relationality as an allegedly central feature of our color concepts connects with Quine's warnings

[10] We used a sign test, comparing the number of positive and negative differences between the cases, and excluding ties; $p < .05$. Another way to look at the data is by comparing the mean rate at which subjects chose the relationalist-friendly answer. Our subjects preferred this answer 30.9% of the time in cases involving shape, 47% of the time in cases involving color, 72.5% of the time in cases involving gustatory properties (sweet, bitter), and 98.5% of the time in cases involving disagreement about *delicious*.

about the difficulty of identifying the essential elements of our concepts. An important lesson of Quine (1953*b*), which I take to be correct and extremely important, is that widespread and entrenched beliefs about xs can often be misidentified as conceptually necessary features of xs. I have already pointed to evidence suggesting that belief in the non-relationality of color is less ubiquitous than many philosophers have alleged. But even putting this evidence aside and supposing the belief in question were universal, it seems to me that we would nonetheless be well-advised to heed the Quinean warning against inferring from this that non-relationality is required by our color concepts.

For, on the contrary, the intuition (apparently widely held among philosophers, but not among the subjects questioned by Cohen and Nichols (2007)) that our concepts of color purport to pick out non-relational properties might reflect nothing more than a widespread and entrenched preference for simpler structures rather than complicated ones. This is, to be sure, a deflationary explanation of the intuition; but it seems to me that, subsequent to Quine's lesson, we have no choice but to admit that this deflationary explanation may be correct. At the very least, we must admit that citing even widely shared intuitions (should there turn out to be any) about the centrality of non-relationality to our color concepts does not establish that our color concepts and terms purport to pick out non-relational properties.

For these reasons, I think the claim that our color concepts and terms purport to pick out non-relational properties is, at best, seriously undermotivated. Therefore, the failure of the relationalist's colors to meet that standard does not show that those properties fail to satisfy requirements built into our color concepts. Consequently, the present argument to the effect that relationalism is an error theory of color is unsuccessful.

5.3.4 *Error Theory Defanged*

I have maintained that the argument for treating relationalism as an error theory (in the sense in which Mackie's view is an error theory of moral properties) is unsuccessful. But suppose, for the sake of argument, that I am wrong, and that relationalism is an error theory of color in that sense. I suggest that even this conclusion should cause no alarm for relationalists.

For supposing that nothing strictly satisfies the presuppositions of our color terms and concepts, this leaves it open that these terms and concepts refer to (existent, exemplified) properties that only approximately satisfy these presuppositions. That is to say that even if relationalism amounted to a revision of some of our beliefs about colors (a conclusion that, I have argued, is at best seriously undermotivated in any case), this would not support the worrisome kind of irrealism according to which color properties are inexistent or unexemplified. By way of analogy, while the concept of whales may at one time have included the presupposition that whales are fish, the discovery that nothing is both a whale and a fish need not (and in fact did not) lead thinkers to conclude that there are no whales. To suppose otherwise — to insist that our naïve beliefs about colors, whales, or anything else are *definitional* of their targets, is to imagine (contrary to the lesson of Quine (1953*b*)) that our beliefs are immutable in the light of discovery, and that we can only replace, and never revise, our concepts.[11] I don't see any reason to suppose this view is correct; therefore, I don't see any reason to believe that relationalism — even if construed as an error theory — should amount to a worrisome form of irrealism about color.[12]

5.4 Conclusion

In this chapter I've considered three classes of ontological objections against color relationalism. The first, discussed in §5.1, alleges that relationalism countenances too many colors — where that means either too many colors full stop, or too many colors that bear no systematic relationship to one another. As I tried to show, these numerical objections are unpersuasive. For one thing, standard motivations for parsimony in counting properties are unpersuasive when applied to relational properties. For another, relationalists in fact have the resources to explain the systematic relationships among the colors; consequently, it is false that the relationalist's colors form an unconstrained list. The second class of ontological objections, considered in §5.2, consists of various formulations of the worry that relationalism is ultimately a form of irrealism about color. Here I argued that, while there are some construals of the real/unreal distinction according to which that conclusion is warranted, there is no compelling and philosophically substantive reason to reject those kinds of irrealism. On the other hand, the most revisionary kinds of irrealism — those that deny a place in nature to colors — simply do not follow from color relationalism. Finally, I considered the accusation that color relationalism is an error theory in the sense described by Mackie (1977). I argued that this accusation fails, and that the accusation would be untroubling even if true.

I conclude that the ontological objections against color relationalism considered in this chapter are unsuccessful.

[11] Cf. Railton (1989, 158–159) for analogous comments about revision and replacement with respect to evaluative concepts.

[12] In the event contemplated (for the sake of argument), relationalism and irrealism would be alike in contravening at least some of the conceptual requirements on color properties. Even so, not all contraventions are equal. In particular, if it came to such a choice, I would favor the revisionary theory according to which colors are relational over the revisionary theory according to which colors are unexemplified by actual objects on the grounds that the former revision seems substantially less of an affront to our beliefs about the world than the latter.

6

RELATIONALISM DEFENDED: PHENOMENOLOGY

Colors are visibilia, or they are nothing.

— (Strawson, 1979, 56).

But any statement as to what it is that our immediate experiences makes us know is very likely to be wrong.

— (Russell, 1912, 7).

Perhaps the most frequently pressed forms of opposition to relational theories of color turn on issues about color phenomenology. I have in mind two different types of phenomenological complaints against color relationalism. The first, and more common, type alleges that relationalism represents colors in a way inconsistent with the way in which phenomenology represents them. Although this complaint has been developed in a number of ways, the basic thought is that there is here a clash between theory and data — between relationalism as a proposed metaphysics of color and the manifest evidence of color phenomenology — that should be resolved by giving up the theory. A second worry grounded in phenomenology alleges that relationalism suffers from a more theoretical shortcoming: here the concern is that relational theories of color are unable to provide an account of what color experience amounts to, or at any rate, that they cannot be combined with important and widely held theoretical claims about the metaphysics of color experience without giving rise to incoherence, regress, or uninformativeness.

Now, most of the objections of both types that occur in the literature are directed against dispositionalist theories; this is unsurprising, since the elaboration and defense of non-dispositionalist forms of relationalism is a relatively recent development. However, it seems clear that many of the arguments we'll be considering are applicable to forms of relationalism other than dispositionalism. Of course, it is my goal for this part of the book to defend relationalism generally speaking, rather than this or that particular form of relationalism; consequently, while it will sometimes smooth exposition for me to treat the objections in this chapter in the anti-dispositionalist form in which they come, I'll also comment on the potential extension of my defenses to other forms of relationalism as well.

My aim in this chapter will be to defend relationalism against both types of phenomenological objections. It will be my contention that color relationalism is not in conflict with our phenomenological evidence about color (§§6.1–6.3), and that it presents no special difficulties regarding the metaphysics of color experience (§§6.4–6.5).

6.1 Do Colors Look Relational?

A wide variety of writers with otherwise sharply divergent views have agreed that relational understandings of colors are at odds with the way colors are presented in ordinary phenomenology because — with notable exceptions such as the colors of holograms and highly glossy materials — phenomenology represents colors as non-relational properties of their bearers (Dancy (1986, 181); Armstrong (1987, 36); Boghossian and Velleman (1989, 85); Averill (1992, 556); Johnston (1992, 226–227); Yablo (1995, 489–490); McGinn (1996, 543–544); Tye (2000, 152–153); Chalmers (2006, 56); Gibbard (2006, 10); Averill and Hazlet (2009); and Johnston (2002, chapter 5)).[1] McGinn puts this anti-relationalist worry eloquently (and in a refreshingly explicit way) in the following passage:

> ... when we see an object as red we see it as having a simple, monadic, local property of the object's surface. The color is perceived as intrinsic to the object, in much the way that shape and size are perceived as intrinsic. No relation to perceivers enters into how the color appears; the color is perceived as wholly *on* the object, not as somehow straddling the gap between it and the perceiver. Being seen as red is not like being seen as larger than or to the left of. The "color envelope" that delimits an object stops at the object's spatial boundaries. So if color were inherently relational, ... then perception of color would misrepresent its structure — we would be under the illusion that a relational property is nonrelational. Contraposing, given that perception is generally veridical as to color, colors are not relational (McGinn, 1996, 541–542).

Thus, whatever successes they have along other dimensions, relationalist accounts are accused of representing colors in a (relational) way that unacceptably clashes with the phenomenology of color.[2]

[1] This objection, of course, presupposes that phenomenology has an intentional content. As in earlier chapters, I am assuming that presupposition is correct. However, the objection does not presuppose (and I won't presuppose) that color phenomenology can be reductively understood in terms of its intentional content, or that it supervenes on its intentional content.

[2] In the course of (usefully) attempting to elaborate this complaint, McGinn fleshes out the worry by reference to four distinct features: simplicity, monadicity, locality, and intrinsicness. But it seems to me that the challenges posed by some of these features are more serious than those posed by others.

For example, the claim that phenomenology is at odds with various forms of color relationalism in representing colors as simple seems false; on the contrary, phenomenology represents (surface) colors as having at least the dimensions of hue, saturation, and lightness (Clark, 1993), and perhaps more. (It is a topic of ongoing controversy how many dimensions are needed to encode color appearances.) On the other hand, if phenomenology represents colors as monadic, so do dispositionalism and other forms of color relationalism. These theories claim that colors are constituted in terms of relations to various relata, but those relata have determinate values and so are not open variables in need of saturation by individuals. Just as *to the left of* is non-monadic, and *to the left of Sally* is not, so, too, *disposed to look x to y in z* is non-monadic (if $\ulcorner x \urcorner$, $\ulcorner y \urcorner$ and $\ulcorner z \urcorner$ are variables), but *disposed to look red to S in C* is non-monadic (if $\ulcorner S \urcorner$ and $\ulcorner C \urcorner$ pick out determinate individuals and viewing conditions relative to a context).

I take the most serious of McGinn's worries here to concern the allegation that phenomenology does, and relationalism does not, represent colors as intrinsic (given, perhaps, the view that intrinsic

However, all of this raises an important puzzle, some answer to which is presupposed by all of the authors mentioned above, and whose solution is necessary before we can properly assess the phenomenological objection to relationalism: how, if at all, could phenomenology represent the relationality or non-relationality of color properties in the first place?[3]

To see the force of the question we are pondering, notice that corresponding claims about the phenomenology of non-color properties can seem somewhat bizarre. For some non-color properties (e.g., *being water*, *being square*, or *being a table*) it just seems implausible that phenomenology represents their constitution (*a fortiori*, their relationality or non-relationality) at all. On the contrary, discerning the essences of such properties seems to require much more than simple phenomenology. The additional information needed might be empirical (as in the case of natural kind properties), mathematical (as in the case of shape properties), psychological (as, arguably, in the case of artifact properties), or something else; but in no such case would the simple enjoyment of ordinary phenomenology suffice.[4] The relevance of phenomenology to discerning essence is somewhat less clear for paradigmatic relational properties, such as velocity properties.[5] However, I take it that it is our best theories of the world, and not phenomenology, that tell us that each velocity property is constituted in terms of a relation to a reference frame. (Were this not true it would be

properties are those shared by perfect duplicates (Lewis, 1986*b*)). Accordingly, this is the form of the objection I'll be concerned with in what follows. It is also worth remarking that leading identity theories of color such as those of Byrne and Hilbert (1997*a*, 2003) and Tye (1995, 2000) that treat colors as dispositions to affect light — theories that don't count as relational in the sense explained in Chapter 1 — also have the consequence that colors fail to be intrinsic in Lewis's sense, and so face versions of the present objection.

[3] One might hope to answer this puzzle by accepting the thesis Johnston (1992) calls Revelation: "The intrinsic nature of canary yellow is fully revealed by a standard visual experience as of a canary yellow thing" (223). This principle would have it that undergoing color phenomenology brings with it concomitant knowledge of the intrinsic nature of the colors it represents. (It should be noted that Johnston ultimately denies Revelation, although he takes it as a regulative constraint that is part of commonsense conceptions of color, and should be respected as much as possible. Proponents of Revelation-like views include Russell (1912, 47), Strawson (1978, 224), Campbell (1993, 178ff), and arguably Moore (1903, 7, 10).)

Unfortunately, this is an unsatisfactory response to our puzzle. For one thing, nothing has yet been said to motivate Revelation, and it would seem that motivating this thesis is at least as challenging as answering the original puzzle. Second, knowledge of the intrinsic nature of a property may not reveal whether that property is constituted in terms of a relation to subjects (although this will turn on one's theory of intrinsicness). But if not, then even the truth of Revelation would do nothing to explain how undergoing color phenomenology would confer upon one evidence about the relationality of colors.

[4] While some have maintained that phenomenology exhausts the essence of certain kinds of phenomenal properties such as *being in pain* (Kripke, 1980), this conclusion won't generalize to color properties unless, implausibly, the latter are construed as phenomenal as well.

[5] In saying that velocity properties are relational I mean that velocity properties are constituted in terms of relation to reference frames — something I take to be an uncontroversial lesson of 20th-century physics. Note that this claim is *prima facie* compatible with (but not required by) the view, defended by Tooley (1988), that velocities are intrinsic to individual instants.

hard to explain how non-relativistic conceptions of velocity properties could have had the long scientific life that they did; after all, Newton presumably enjoyed motion phenomenology roughly as often as Einstein did.) One might conclude from these considerations either that (i) phenomenology is entirely non-committal about the relationality or non-relationality of velocity properties or else that (ii) phenomenology represents velocity properties as non-relational but we take phenomenology to be revisable in the light of further (broadly empirical) inquiry. On either reading of the situation with velocity properties, however, it does seem clear that there is some story that needs to be told about when and how phenomenology can have any bearing on questions about property constitution in general, and on questions about the relationality or non-relationality of the properties it represents in particular.

As a way of approaching an answer to this question, let us continue to reflect on the case of velocity properties to see what lessons can be gleaned. If, as I have suggested, phenomenology is not the route to discerning the relationality of velocities, then what is? While the answer surely involves a complicated mix of empirical observation and ratiocination, one ingredient of this mix, in particular, strikes me as highly relevant to the answer: comparison. A strong clue to the relationality of velocities — and a clue that Einstein (1905) relies on crucially in arguing for the relationality of motion properties — is that their exemplification by a particular object depends on variations in the reference frame chosen. That is, comparison reveals that the velocity of x with respect to frame F_1 is different from the velocity of x with respect to frame F_2. Now, it must be emphasized that this sort of evidence is only one piece of a complex chain of reasoning leading to the conclusion that velocity properties are relational; in particular, this evidence won't establish that conclusion unless we can rule out (by some combination of evidence and ratiocination) the alternative hypothesis that one or the other otherwise incompatible representations of x's velocity (one representation in F_1, the other in F_2) is erroneous. But if that alternative hypothesis is rejected, then comparative data of the sort we are considering provides strong (but defeasible) support for the view that velocities are relational.

I now want to suggest that this lesson can be generalized more widely. The idea would be that, for other target families of properties, too, comparative evidence of this sort is crucial (but, as always, defeasible) in testing for the relationality or non-relationality of its members. Namely, as in the motion case, we can test for relationality of a property (in a family of properties) to a parameter by altering the value of that parameter and checking to see whether this change has the effect of modifying which (if any) member of our target family is exemplified. To see the power and correctness of this method, consider its application to a few test properties. The method correctly predicts that shape properties are *not* constituted in terms of a relation to viewing angle, for example, because square objects (say) continue to be square regardless of the angle from which they are viewed (or so we think). The same method correctly predicts that the "meteorological" properties we ascribe by saying 'it's raining' or 'it's sunny' are constituted in terms of a relation to location and time, since their applicability is a function of those two parameters. Likewise, as Shoemaker (1994*b*, 254–255) notes, this test shows that *being heavy* is constituted in terms of a relation to a (potential) lifter and gravitational field. This comparative test, then, delivers the right verdicts about a range of properties other than colors.

Of course, phenomenology seems largely irrelevant to the application of the comparative test to the cases we've considered so far; all that that test demands is that we assess whether an object persists in its exemplification of a target property as we modify the value of some parameter. But phenomenology could play a role in this test if it should turn out that the object's exemplification of the target property is somehow essentially tied to phenomenology.

To see what this amounts to in a concrete case, consider the so-called shimmering or unsteady colors such as those on the backs of CDs or in holograms — colors that are often put forward as examples of colors that (unusually) are represented phenomenally as being relational (e.g. Johnston, 1992, 226–227).[6] Applying the comparative test to these unsteady colors (with respect to the parameter of viewing angle) means testing to see whether an object maintains or varies its unsteady color as it is viewed from different viewing angles. Crucially, however, in this case, we assess the object's unsteady colors from each viewing angle primarily (perhaps only) by attending to the way in which it is phenomenally presented when viewed from that angle. Here, then, application of the comparative test means engaging in *comparative phenomenology*. And what the test reveals is that unsteady colors are relational (constituted in terms of a relation to viewing angle). That is so because even very slight variations in viewing angle of the kind that we engage in — often involuntarily — in ordinary perceptual circumstances show up in the phenomenal representation of their colors: by very slight and often involuntary motions, we obtain in quick succession a visual representation of x's color when viewed from angle α and a visual representation of x's color when viewed from angle β, and find that these two representations differ phenomenally.

These considerations involving comparative phenomenology explain three related facts. First, that unsteady colors behave this way explains the widely held view (even among those who take steady colors to be non-relational) that the unsteady colors of surfaces are constituted in terms of a relation to the viewing conditions under which they are perceived. Second, the fact that the conditions under which we view shimmering surfaces gives us (often involuntarily) the comparative information we need to carry out the comparative test explains why the latter view is widely held in the first place — typical perceptual circumstances provide us with the needed data, and once the data

[6] The distinction between "unsteady" and "standing" colors is made by Johnston (1992, 141), who attributes it to Rossotti (1983, chapters 3–4).

are in our possession, it is hard to avoid drawing the obvious conclusion from them. Third, and even more significantly, these considerations address our initial question by showing how phenomenology can speak to the relationality or non-relationality of a target property. Namely, when phenomenology provides our evidence about the exemplification of that property, then comparative phenomenological data collected across variations in relevant parameters can serve as grounds for inferences about the relationality/non-relationality of the target property.

But now I want to suggest that the so-called steady colors meet this criterion, so the comparative phenomenological test just used to assess the relationality of the unsteady colors should be applicable to the steady colors as well. The significant difference between the two is that, in the case of steady colors, we need systematic psychophysical comparison, rather than just the conditions of typical perception, to bring out the relevant comparative data. In particular, we need to compare the visual representation of x's color when viewed by S_1 in conditions C_1 against the visual representation of x's color when viewed by S_2 in conditions C_2. Now, it turns out that ordinary, everyday color phenomenology doesn't provide the materials needed for these kinds of comparisons all by itself. For one thing, ordinary phenomenology can't (by itself) facilitate comparisons between subjects S_1 and S_2. For another, what distinguishes "steady" colors from shimmers is that one can easily obtain a phenomenal representation of x's color for oneself in C_1 without obtaining a phenomenal representation of x's color for oneself in C_2. This means that testing for the relationality of "steady" colors will require more than the unsystematic, ordinary phenomenology we undergo outside the psychophysics lab.[7] Or, in the words of Janet Levin,

> Ordinary perception of color may *seem* to reveal colors to be simple monadic properties, just as a quick glance may seem to reveal an object with color highlights to be an object that is "steadily" striped. But in both cases, the "glances" are too quick to be definitive, given the sorts of experiences required for making the distinction; in neither case can these judgments be expected to reflect what perception in the proper circumstances would in fact reveal (Levin, 2000, 157).

[7] Boghossian and Velleman (1989) miss this point, and therefore apply (what seems to me to be) the wrong criterion to test whether phenomenology represents colors as relational/dispositional:

> If colours looked like dispositions, however, then they would seem to *come on* when illuminated, just as a lamp comes on when its switch is flipped. Turning on the light would seem, simultaneously, like turning on the colours; or perhaps it would seem like waking up the colours, just as it is seen to startle the cat. Conversely, when the light was extinguished, the colours would not look as if they were being concealed or shrouded in the ensuing darkness: rather, they would look as if they were becoming dormant, like the cat returning to sleep. But colours do not look like that; or not, at least, to us (Boghossian and Velleman, 1989, 85).

In fact, if Boghossian's and Velleman's observations are correct, then they show only that (non-shimmering) colors are not constituted in terms of relations to parameters whose values shift under ordinary conditions of perception by a single subject. And, of course, this falls far short of showing that colors are not relational/dispositional.

Levin is, in my view, quite right about this: isolated and momentary phenomenal presentations ("glances") are insufficient to bring out the relationality of both so-called steady and unsteady colors, because the comparative information needed to make their relationality apparent is more than such isolated and momentary phenomenal presentations make available.[8]

Luckily, we do not need to look very far for the needed supplementation; the systematic comparisons we need are made available by precisely the kinds of psychophysical methods exploited in Chapter 2. Namely, these methods allow us to ask S_1 and S_2 to make phenomenal matching judgments of x's color relative to various perceptual conditions, and thereby to compare the phenomenal representation of x's color for S_1 in C_1 against the phenomenal representation of x's color for S_2 in C_2. And, as we saw in Chapter 2, carrying out those comparisons shows that the pair of phenomenal representations *differ* as a function of the subject and the perceptual circumstances. As in other applications of the comparative method, this finding gives (defeasible) support for the idea that our target property (in this case, x's color) is constituted in terms of a relation to the parameters under consideration (in this case, the subject and the perceptual circumstance).

What all of this shows, I think, is that phenomenology represents the steady colors of tables and chairs as relational to exactly the extent and in exactly the way that it represents the unsteady colors of CDs and holograms as relational. This can be taken in two ways, depending on how expansively we think about what phenomenology amounts to. If phenomenology is restricted to single, isolated representations that are not integrated with ratiocinative reflection (Levin's "glances"), then I think phenomenology reveals neither steady nor unsteady colors as being relational. On the other hand, if we take a broader view of what phenomenology includes — in particular, if we take within the purview of phenomenology both systematic (psychophysical) and ordinary comparisons between phenomenological representations, together with inferences reached on the basis of such comparative data, then it seems to me that phenomenology reveals both unsteady and steady colors to be relational.

Why, then, have many theorists agreed that phenomenology differs in what it reveals about steady and unsteady colors, and therefore endorsed the phenomenological objection against color relationalism? Part of the answer, I suspect, is that they have been unclear between the narrower and broader understandings of phenomenology spelled out above. As noted, ordinary perceptual circumstances make it difficult to avoid carrying out comparative

[8] Levin focuses on the kinds of interpersonal comparisons that are never made available by ordinary perception (by itself), and concludes that the conditions under which colors would be phenomenally represented as relational, "alas, are not available even in a lifetime of normal perceptual experience" (157). In my view, the phenomenal representation of relationality can be brought out more readily by intrapersonal comparisons, so the difficulty is not quite so severe as Levin makes it out to be. In any case, it seems clear that the most direct and systematic methods for making the relevant comparisons are those of systematic psychophysics.

phenomenology with respect to "unsteady" colors, and I believe this fact has prevented many from seeing that they were engaging in comparisons (or ratiocination based on these comparisons) at all. And this has encouraged many to believe that phenomenology in the narrower sense reveals the relationality of unsteady colors, when, in my view, it is phenomenology in the broader sense that is responsible. In effect, then, such thinkers have gone looking for phenomenological evidence in the wrong place. This, in turn, has led to the erroneous expectation that, were so-called steady colors relational, then phenomenology understood in the narrower sense would also reveal this fact. As it happens, it does not. Moreover, since the manipulations required to bring out the relationality of steady colors do not occur "all by themselves" in ordinary perception, subjects are left without the phenomenological evidence they would need to come to a suitable conclusion on this matter. But since they lack the requisite evidence, and also (wrongly) believe they would possess such evidence if it existed, they have concluded (wrongly) that steady colors are phenomenally represented as non-relational. Which is to say that, after having looked for phenomenological evidence in the wrong place, such thinkers have compounded their error by mistaking an absence of evidence for evidence of absence.

This diagnosis is supported by the observation that exactly the same sort of error can arise in the case of non-color properties that are less controversially relational. Thus, to use Shoemaker's example, the natural limitations on the comparative evidence available to us in assessing the heaviness of objects can lead us (at least initially, until we seek out comparative evidence and take it into account) to think that phenomenology represents *being heavy* as non-relational. For, at least initially, I might ascribe or forbear the property *being heavy* just on the basis of the narrow phenomenal episodes I undergo when I lift them, given the (relatively stable over time) strength and physical build that I happen to have, and in the context of a relatively unchanging gravitational field (it changes so little mainly because, in the course of my ordinary travel, I don't alter significantly my distance from the center of the earth). As before, restricting myself to non-comparative phenomenological evidence of this kind will not show up the relationality of the target property; indeed, my contention is that narrow, isolated episodes of phenomenology ("glances") neither reveal *being heavy* to be relational nor to be non-relational. Someone who (wrongly) expected her narrow phenomenology to represent all and only relational properties as being relational would wrongly conclude on the basis of her narrow phenomenology that *being heavy* is not relational. But, as before, this would be an erroneous conclusion reached by taking into account the wrong kind of phenomenological evidence (viz., narrow rather than broad phenomenology).

I take these considerations to show that there is both a good sense in which phenomenology can speak to the question of whether colors (steady and unsteady alike) are relational or not, and another good sense in which phenomenology won't speak to that question. The sense in which it will is the sense in which phenomenology includes systematic comparisons of the sort made available by psychophysical methods, combined with ratiocination. The sense in which phenomenology will have nothing to say about the relationality or otherwise of colors is one in which phenomenology is restricted to introspection on isolated, momentary experiential episodes. Of course, the narrower brand of phenomenology won't reveal colors as relational — but that is only because it is unsuited to discovery of relationality where it exists at all. In contrast, employing the broader conception of phenomenology leads to the conclusion that colors *are* relational, as we saw in Chapter 2. On neither conception, however, are we justified in concluding that phenomenology represents colors as being non-relational.

6.2 Are Relational Properties Visible?

A second potentially powerful and generalizable phenomenal objection against relational theories of color builds on the platitudinous claim that colors are visible — i.e., that instances of colors (if not color properties themselves) can be seen. However, critics have alleged, (instances of) dispositional/relational properties are not the sorts of things that can be seen, even if it is allowed that their relata can be seen. Rather, these critics urge, the exemplification of such dispositional/relational properties by particulars is something we *infer*, possibly on the basis of the exemplification of other properties that we do see.[9] If that worry is correct, then relational accounts of color would entail the absurd conclusion that colors are not visible.[10] [11]

Once again, this objection is given a particularly clear exposition by McGinn (1996), who frames the issue in terms of the question of what can be a direct object of the seeing relation:

> When you look at an object you do not see (de dicto) its dispositions to act in certain ways in certain circumstances, but you do see what color it is. Here, of course, I mean direct object perception, not just seeing-that — seeing the property itself, not merely seeing that it is instantiated. You may see *that* something is soluble by watching it dissolve, but you do not see its solubility — that property itself. You can see the manifestation of the disposition, and you may also see the categorical basis of the disposition in the object's molecular structure, but your eyes do not acquaint you with the property of being *disposed* to dissolve.... And now the point about colors is that they enter the very

[9] Obviously this objection presupposes the viability of a distinction between what we see and what we infer. While this presupposition is controversial (see Churchland, 1979; Fodor, 1984), it's appropriate for me to grant it for concessive reasons (if no other).

[10] Mark Johnston attempts to extend the absurdity here by arguing that, if we didn't see (instances of) colors, we would not see objects (Johnston, 1992, note 1). This argument, however, is unconvincing as it stands: even if we could not see instances of colors, it is left open that we could (veridically) see objects by undergoing color illusions — i.e., we could see objects by seeing that they look colored, even if it turns out that we never see any veridical instances of colors (say, because nothing is colored, as per color irrealism).

[11] Again, a version of the same worry arises for those non-relational theories of color that identify colors with dispositions to affect light.

content of primitive visual experience, being part of how objects appear, but dispositions of whatever kind cannot themselves enter visual content in this way (McGinn (1996, 540); cf. Mackie (1976, chapter 1)).

Although McGinn presents this objection in the first instance as a reason for rejecting the dispositionalism he had endorsed earlier (McGinn, 1983), the threat he poses clearly generalizes to other forms of relationalism as well: if colors are possible direct objects of seeing, then any relationalist account of color will be threatened by the worry that relational properties — as opposed to their relata — cannot be direct objects of seeing.

Now, one possible line of resistance to this argument turns on a thought developed by McGinn himself, in his earlier defense of dispositionalism (McGinn, 1983, 133–135). This line of resistance turns on the idea that 'sees' introduces a highly intensional context — one where even sameness of both sense and reference does not guarantee intersubstitutability *salva veritate*.[12] If true, this claim would explain why 'I see redness' could be true while 'I see the disposition to look red' could be false even if (as per some forms of dispositionalism) 'redness' and 'the disposition to look red' are alike not only in reference but also in sense. Unfortunately, this answer strikes me as unconvincing. For while I take it to be extremely plausible that (the phenomenal use of) 'looks' introduces such a highly intensional context (see §6.3), it seems (at least, to my linguistic intuition) not only that the context created by 'sees' is not so highly intensional, but that it is *extensional*; but if so, then the current proposal is just inapplicable to the case at hand.

On the other hand, I do not believe that the present objection against relationalist views is decisive. In particular, I do not see a reason for accepting the premise that colors, if dispositions or otherwise constituted in terms of relations to perceivers, are *ipso facto* not suitable for being the direct objects of seeing. (For ease of expression, in what follows I'll discuss this point only in terms of dispositional versions of relationalism, but I hope it is clear that the response can be generalized.) At least in McGinn's presentation above, the case for this conclusion rests almost entirely on the analogy with the dispositional property *solubility*. Although this is controversial, I am prepared to spot McGinn the assumption that dispositions such as *solubility* and *fragility* are not — or, are not directly — objects of the seeing/looking relation.[13] However, this might be thought to overlook relevant differences between dispositions, some of which can be the direct object of seeing, and some of which cannot.

The reason we should take this possibility seriously, it seems to me, is that the dispositions identified with colors by dispositionalists — in dramatic contrast to paradigm dispositions like *solubility* or *fragility* — have visual experiences as their manifestations. And the reason this matters to the question

[12] A version of this response to the objection is also considered by McLaughlin (2003*b*), although he doesn't put much weight on it.

[13] For dissent on this point, see Anscombe (1981); Cartwright (1989).

about whether dispositions can be seen is that it is plausibly constitutive of seeing a disposition to look red (as it might be) that one undergoes the visual experience that is the manifestation of that very disposition. In this spirit, McDowell asks, "What would one expect it to be like to experience something's being such as to look red, if not to experience the thing in question (in the right circumstances) as looking, precisely, red?" (McDowell (1985, 112); cf. Levin (2000, 154–155)). We can buttress this thought by locating it against the following sufficient condition for property seeing: S sees property P if, by visually attending to an exemplification of P by x, S is (non-deviantly) caused to undergo a visual experience that represents x as exemplifying P.[14] On the working hypothesis that colors are dispositions to look colored, because these dispositions in question have visual experience as manifestations, it will be possible to see colors in just this sense. For example, suppose a ripe tomato exemplifies the disposition to look red, and suppose the viewing conditions are propitious; then precisely in so far as the disposition manifests itself, it will be true that by visually attending to the tomato's redness I am (non-deviantly) caused to undergo the particular visual experience that represents the tomato

[14] A couple of remarks about this condition for property seeing are in order. (Thanks to Brian McLaughlin for urging me to clarify my thoughts on these matters.)

First, the condition explicates seeing a property in terms of seeing one of its instances. I take this to be appropriate, since I assume we causally interact with properties only in virtue of causally interacting with their instances.

Second, some readers might object to the idea that we see properties (/their instances) by visually attending to them, and instead hold that we visually attend to these things only by seeing them. While there may be some understanding of visual attention that substantiates this objection, I am here understanding visual attention as an early and encapsulated mechanism that selectively allocates the resources of the visual system to objects/regions; so understood, it seems to me that property seeing should depend on visual attention rather than vice versa.

Third, the condition is only offered as a sufficient condition, rather than a necessary and sufficient condition, for property seeing. One respect in which it fails to be a necessary condition involves misrepresentation: in cases where, by visually attending to an exemplification of P by x, S is non-deviantly caused to undergo a visual experience that (mis-) represents x as exemplifying Q, I am inclined to hold that S nonetheless sees property P.

Finally, many philosophers have worried that dispositions — as opposed to their categorical bases — can't cause their manifestations. If they are right about this, then the present account won't allow that subjects can see dispositional properties (hence, given dispositionalism about color, won't allow that subjects see colors), since it won't be possible for dispositions to look red (for S in C) to cause objects to look red (for S in C). This concern, of course, is only as good as the underlying assumption that dispositions are unable to cause their manifestations. But I think the extant arguments for this assumption, which turn mostly on Kim-style considerations about the threat of causal overdetermination by multiple factors each causally sufficient for the outcome, are unconvincing. One reason for this, brought out by Loewer (2007), is that, contrary to what proponents of such arguments often maintain, the multiple factors involved (here, the base property and the disposition) are *not* causally sufficient for the outcome (here, the manifestation of the disposition). Indeed, nothing less than the total state of the universe at a time is causally sufficient for the outcome; but there seems no reason to fear causal overdetermination by a pair of factors each of which is *not* causally sufficient for the outcome. (I'll return to this issue in much greater depth in §7.3.)

as red.[15] For this reason, it is plausible for a dispositionalist to hold that the occurrence of the disposition's manifestation is constitutive of my seeing the tomato's (by hypothesis, dispositional) color property.

Of course, this won't make it the case that we see all dispositions; in particular, and as desired, this account won't make it the case that we see dispositions whose manifestations are not visual experiences, for they won't meet the sufficient condition for property seeing given above (although this allows that we might succeed in seeing those properties or their instances in some other way — the condition is only a sufficient condition for property seeing). If, for example, a vase exemplifies *fragility*, even if I attend to this state of affairs, the manifestation of the disposition leaves entirely open whether I'll undergo a visual experience that represents the vase's fragility. This is because, in this case, the disposition's manifestation (here, a shattering) is independent of the occurrence of any visual experience at all.

What all this shows, I suggest, is that the unsuitability of some dispositions to be objects of the seeing relation is compatible with the claim that colors, if dispositions, can be the objects of the seeing relation.

And now we should notice that forms of the response I am recommending are also available to non-dispositionalist relationalists for whom the current threat about the invisibility of colors arises. Although the details of the analysis will differ depending on the form of relationalism on offer, the key insight on which the answer depends is general: namely, it is that we can understand how a relational property R is seen by a subject S if the relevant relation eventuates in a visual experience in S that represents R's exemplification.

I conclude, then, that, contrary to the present worry, color relationalists can endorse the platitudinous view that colors are visible.

6.3 Phenomenology about Phenomenology?

According to dispositionalism and several other forms of color relationalism, colors are constituted in terms of relations to subjects that involve those very subjects undergoing phenomenal experiences.

For example, suppose with the dispositionalist that *redness for* S *in* C = the disposition to look red to S in C. If (plausibly) something's looking red to S in C requires that S undergo a phenomenal experience of some sort, it would seem that what it is to be red involves constitutively an episode of phenomenology. Now suppose S has a phenomenal experience that represents x as red. Assuming dispositionalism, this means that her phenomenal experience has as its content that x is disposed to look red. And, given what we've said above,

15 The claim here is not that we see the disposition *by* seeing the visual experience that is the manifestation of the disposition — indeed, I deny that we see our visual experiences except in highly abnormal circumstances (such as those involving invasive neurosurgery). Rather, the claim is that the visual experience itself (when it is appropriately caused by something to which we are visually attending) is the manifestation of the disposition, and that undergoing (rather than seeing) such a visual experience constitutes seeing the disposition (in the direct object sense at issue).

this means that the phenomenal experience has as its content something like this: that x is disposed to produce in S phenomenal experiences of a certain kind. This means that, assuming the truth of dispositionalism (and the relatively uncontroversial claim that x looks red to S only if S undergoes a certain phenomenal experience), phenomenal experiences of x's being red will have as part of their content a claim about phenomenal experience. Moreover, and for the same reasons, an analogous conclusion follows from non-dispositionalist forms of relationalism according to which the relation between subjects and objects that constitutes color properties is one that requires the subject to undergo a certain phenomenal experience. All of these relationalist views have the consequence that color phenomenology represents phenomenology (*inter alia*).

However, some have found this consequence implausible. Reflecting on their own color phenomenology, they simply do not find that their experiences have any representational commitments about phenomenology. Thus, McGinn complains that,

> I do not have experiences *of experiences* when I see something red. When I see an object as red I see *it* as having a property; I do not see any sensations that might be occurring in perceivers.... My experience type does not enter its own content (McGinn, 1996, 542).

According to this thought, my ordinary experience of a ripe tomato, as it might be, represents the fruit's size and shape, but is just not committed in any way to any claims about visual phenomenology. One might be sympathetic to this claim because one shares the oft-cited "Moorean" intuition to the effect that phenomenal experience *always* represents distal objects and their properties rather than mental entities and their properties (see Harman, 1990). Alternatively, one might take the weaker view that, at least in ordinary, non-reflective settings, the contents of phenomenal experiences (or phenomenal color experiences in particular) do not involve mental entities, *a fortiori* do not involve phenomenal experiences. Either way, once again, the worry is that relationalism (in at least some of its forms) seems to have an entailment that is at odds with the data of ordinary color phenomenology.

It is important to note that the worry under consideration is *not* that the invocation of phenomenology in a phenomenal representation is by itself viciously circular or otherwise objectionable (I'll return to that concern in §6.4). That is to say, the difficulty is not merely that the invocation of phenomenology in a phenomenal content is itself somehow incoherent. It is that the invocation of phenomenology as the content of the particular sort of phenomenal representations at issue is, it is claimed, erroneous as a description of that content.

How should relationalists respond to the objection now before us? In my view, they should respond by rejecting the alleged phenomenal datum on which it is based. In particular, relationalists should reject the claim that phenomenology cannot represent properties whose nature is explicated in terms of phenomenal experience. What the relationalist should claim is that such experience-involving properties are constituents of the contents of color experience, but that their experience-involving natures are hidden from those who undergo color phenomenology, even when those subjects attend carefully to their experiences. That is, a subject who undergoes color phenomenology thereby has an experience that represents a color property whose nature involves color phenomenology as a component; but in undergoing that phenomenal episode, the (experience-involving) nature of the represented color property is not made apparent to the subject even upon careful reflection on her experience.

This response, of course, presupposes that it is possible to represent in one's phenomenal experience properties whose essence is not known to one; but I think that that commitment is perfectly reasonable and well-precedented. After all, even if you and I know the essence of water, presumably Homer was able to enjoy — and carefully attend to — water phenomenology despite lacking this piece of knowledge. Had someone proposed to Homer that water is H_2O, it would not have been reasonable for him to object that water couldn't have hydrogen as an essential constituent on the grounds that his water phenomenology failed to disclose the involvement of hydrogen upon careful attention. That this is so should not be thought to depend solely on Homer's failing to have a concept of hydrogen (cf. Rodriguez-Pereyra, 2002, 93–94). For it seems that someone who knows quite a lot about hydrogen might also reflectively undergo water phenomenology without thereby coming to know the constitution of water. Again, it would be unreasonable for such a subject to object that water couldn't have hydrogen as an essential constituent on the grounds that her water phenomenology failed to disclose the involvement of hydrogen upon careful attention. Likewise, then, it seems to me that it would unreasonable to object to the identification of *being red to S in C* and the disposition to look red (to S in C) on the grounds that one's red phenomenology fails to disclose the involvement of visual phenomenology upon careful attention.

Another way to put the foregoing is to say that phenomenal occurrences of 'looks' in locutions of the form 'x looks red (to S in C)' create highly intensional contexts — contexts within which substitution of extensionally (or even analytically) equivalent expressions is not truth-preserving (cf. McGinn, 1983, 134ff.).[16] Thus, although to be wet just is to be covered in a certain way with H_2O, it is illegitimate to infer from 'x looks wet' to 'x looks to be covered in a certain way with H_2O'. Or, again, although to be humorous just

[16] I think this is so because color experiences (like water experiences) present the properties that are constituents of their contents under modes of presentation. Proponents of non-relationalist theories of colors (e.g. Tye, 1995, 133) have sometimes held this view as well (although Tye (2000, 56–57) later repudiates it). As Tye points out, if there are modes of presentation involved, they should be the kinds of modes of presentation that are available to infants and non-human animals (assuming, plausibly, that things can look colored to such creatures). And this gives some reason — depending on one's theory of concepts, to be sure — for denying that the modes of presentation in question are conceptual. However, I see no reason that they would have to be conceptual; instead, one might regard them as perceptual (non-conceptual) modes of presentation.

is to be disposed to cause characteristic amusement reactions in appropriately situated cognizers, it is illegitimate to infer from 'x looks humorous' to 'x looks disposed to cause characteristic amusement reactions in appropriately situated cognizers'. So, too, the failure of the inference from 'x looks red (to S in C)' to 'x looks appropriately related to a (certain type of) phenomenal experience' should not be taken to impugn the color relationalist's identification of color properties with experience-involving essences.

I claim, then, that careful reflection on one's color phenomenology by conceptually competent subjects can fail to disclose the nature of the properties that are constituents of the contents of those experiences. Experience of colors does not amount to an unmediated, acquaintance-like connection with the colors.[17] That this is so explains why, as I suggested in §6.1, isolated episodes of color phenomenology must be supplemented by (sometimes extensive) comparison and ratiocination before they can teach us about the nature of colors. Color phenomenology does relate us to the colors, but it is no substitute for the hard, broadly empirical, work necessary for determining how colors are constituted.[18]

I conclude that the absence of phenomenal evidence of experience-involving elements in the color properties one represents phenomenally cannot be taken as evidence of the absence of such elements in the natures of colors. But since the objection now before us turns on treating our phenomenal evidence as just such a criterion, it is unsuccessful as a complaint against color relationalism.

6.4 Relationalism and Regress

So far in this chapter I have concentrated on arguments to the effect that the manifest data of color phenomenology come into conflict, in one way or another, with the entailments of color relationalism. In this section I want to consider a different, and more theoretical, form of phenomenological argument against relationalism. Whereas the earlier objections held that relationalism and phenomenology disagree in what they say about colors, the present concern is that relationalism cannot coherently be combined with a satisfactory account of color phenomenology, because such a combination leads to regress.

The regress objection, which has been pressed against dispositionalism by several authors (Sellars, 1956; Boghossian and Velleman, 1989; McGinn, 1996; Stroud, 2000), comes directly from the schema dispositionalists use to specify the essence of colors, which is typically formulated in something like this form:

[17] For reasons discussed in note 3, this claim should be accepted even by those who endorse Revelation.

[18] For this reason, I take the identity between colors and experience-involving relations to subjects to be an *a posteriori* identity — one for which I am offering broadly empirical support in the current work. Were this not so, it would be possible to establish the conclusions about color ontology I'm after by phenomenal experience together with armchair reflection. While dispositionalism and perhaps other forms of color relationalism have sometimes been presented by their advocates as *a priori* theses, I do not regard them in this way.

(D) Red (for S in C) is the disposition to look/appear red (for S in C).

The objection turns on noticing that 'red' occurs on both the left- and right-hand sides of (D). Critics have objected, therefore, that if the two occurrences of 'red' are univocal in meaning, then it would seem to follow from the truth of (D) itself that one can substitute *salva veritate* the entire right-hand side expansion of the term for occurrences of 'red (for S in C)'; in particular, the thought is that one could substitute the right-hand side expansion into the occurrence of that term within the right-hand side of (D) itself. And because the right-hand side contains the term 'red', substituting in this way introduces yet another occurrence of the term. But then *this* occurrence is apt for replacement by the right-hand side expansion, and so on into the night. Boghossian and Velleman provide one much-cited formulation of this complaint in writing that,

> In order for an object to appear red rather than blue, it must appear disposed to appear red, rather than disposed to appear blue; and in order to appear disposed to appear red, rather than disposed to appear blue, it must appear disposed to appear disposed to appear red, rather than disposed to appear disposed to appear blue; and so on. Until this regress reaches an end, the object's appearance will not amount to the appearance of one colour rather than another. Unfortunately, the regress never reaches an end (Boghossian and Velleman, 1989, 89).

Although the regress objection is aimed at dispositionalism in the first instance, it (like other objections we have confronted in this chapter) can be raised against several other forms of relationalism as well (cf. Averill and Hazlet, 2009). I'll show this by demonstrating that the objection turns on three key commitments that are more general than dispositionalism.

The first commitment, which is accepted by many if not most relationalists, is the claim that the relevant color-constitutive relations involve the ways objects look/appear to subjects. Relationalists who accept this commitment hold that for x to be red (for S in C) is constituted in part by xs looking red to S in C. In holding this, these relationalists accept that we will understand colors in terms of ways objects looks/appears to subjects — i.e., such ways of looking/appearing will appear on the right hand sides of the identity statements that make up the relationalist theory of color at issue.

The second commitment, which is accepted by many relationalists and non-relationalists alike, is to a form of relational conception of color appearances — a view according to which what it is for an object to look/appear some way to a subject is constituted in terms of a relation that the subject bears to the properties exemplified by that object.[19] Thus, for example, many relationalists (and non-relationalists) hold that for x to look red to S in C is for S to stand in some relation to x's property of redness.[20] This second commitment, then,

[19] For discussion and defense of this conception of appearances, see Pautz (2008, §1).

[20] I've formulated the relational conception of appearances in a deliberately schematic way so as to show that the problem-generating commitment is shared by a wide variety of theorists who would differ in how they elaborate the schema. Relational theories of the sort under discussion include the popular intentionalist/representationalist view of (Harman, 1990; Tye, 1995; Dretske, 1995), the theory of appearing of Alston (1999), and the property-complex theory of Johnston (2004).

ensures that we will understand the relevant ways of looking/appearing (ways of looking/appearing colored) in terms of the color properties of objects — i.e., such color properties will appear on the right-hand sides of the identity statements that make up the relational theory of color appearances at issue.

Putting the first and second commitments together results in a theory of color properties given by identity statements with the names of colors (viz., color terms) on their left-hand sides and relations to color properties (expressed using color terms) on their right-hand sides. But regress does not follow immediately from this combination without a third commitment to a principle that would (on the strength of the identity statements themselves) license the substitution of the material on the right-hand sides of such identity statements for relevant occurrences of color terms. That is, the final ingredient needed to generate regress is a principle to the effect that such identity statements themselves license the substitution *salva veritate* of their right-hand side expansions for the embedded occurrences of color terms on their right-hand sides.

I claim that these three commitments, taken together, are sufficient to generate a regress. For, as we have said, the first and the second commitments result in identity statements with color terms on their left-hand sides and looks-involving relations to color properties (expressed in terms of color terms) on their right-hand sides. And the third commitment allows us to substitute into the color term occurring in the right-hand side of such an identity statement the entire right-hand side. But, of course, allowing that substitution introduces another occurrence of the very same color term on the (now expanded) right-hand side. And now we can invoke the third commitment again to substitute for that color term the entire right-hand side of the original identity statement, which will again introduce yet a further occurrence of a color term that is apt for replacement. Alas, no end to this process appears to be in sight.

Might a relationalist attempt to avoid this regress by holding that the property invoked in the relational understanding of color appearances — that in terms of which we understand x's looking red — is distinct from the color property occurring on the left-hand side of her identity statement (viz., x's redness)? This expedient does not seem promising so long as we persist in accepting both color relationalism and a relational theory of color appearances. For endorsing the latter means accepting that x looks red to S only if S (or S's visual system) stands in relation R to x's exemplification of P. But it seems to me that color relationalists will be forced to conclude that P is identical with *redness to S in C*. Presumably P should be a visually accessible property if its exemplification will suffice for something's looking some way to a subject. But among the visually accessible properties, only color properties seem appropriate: we wouldn't say that x looks red (for S in C) as opposed to, say, rough or large unless the property to whose exemplification the subject is visually related is a *color* property. Which color property? For the relationalist, the color property in question cannot be the non-relational property *red*, for the simple reason that, for her, color properties are all relational. This suggests that the property in question must be a relational color property. Which relational color property? It would seem perverse to claim that x's looking red (for S in C) consists in S's standing in a relation to the property *blue to* S' *in* C' or *green to* S'' *in* C'' — S's being related to any of those properties seems a particularly poor candidate for constituting x's being red for S in C. In fact, by relationalist lights, there is only one color property (and so only one property) relation to whose exemplification by x is appropriate for this constitution relation — and that is *red for* S *in* C. For being related to any other property — even any other color property — will not plausibly be the sort of relation that makes x count as looking red to S in C, just as S's being related to x's size, texture, or temperature won't suffice for x's looking red to S in C.

What I take all this to show is that the regress objection is reasonably general — that it is something that threatens not just dispositionalists, but other relationalists as well. What, then, should color relationalists say about the threat of regress?

The first thing a relationalist should say is that, although (as noted) the objection can be raised against several forms of relationalism, it does not get a grip against every form of the view. Relationalists agree that colors are constituted in terms of relations to subjects (possibly *inter alia*), but disagree about just which such relations constitute the colors. The regress objection we are now considering won't have purchase against relationalisms that reject the first of the regress-generating commitments considered above — that is, relationalisms according to which the color-constituting relations avoid mention of color properties. Since, on such views, color properties are never enlisted in the explication of color properties, the regress never gets off the ground.

Now, even these forms of color relationalism will make it the case that there is a close connection between x's being red (for S in C) and x's looking red (for S in C). For, as we have seen in Chapter 2, one of the most powerful motivations for relationalist accounts generally speaking is their capacity to respect visual attributions of color — to make it the case that (cases of error discussed in §4.4.4 aside), when x looks red (for S in C), x *is* red (for S in C). But what this requires is only that (again, cases of error aside) relationalism makes the latter two properties coextensive, not that they be analytically or metaphysically nested within one another in a way that would lead to regress (see note 8 in Chapter 2).[21]

Thus, the regress objection is no obstacle for forms of relationalism that deny the first regress-generating commitment by avoiding mention of colors in their specifications of the color-constituting relations. As it happens, most relationalist views with which I am familiar (with the exception of Matthen's

[21] Compare: the properties *triangularity* and *trilaterality* are (necessarily) coextensive, but no regress threatens the standard geometric accounts of either property.

sensory classificationism; see §8.3) do appear to mention color properties in specifying what they take to be the color-constituting relations, and so cannot escape the regress objection so easily.[22] However, if the recent expansion of relationalist options continues, there is reason to think this situation might change.

The second point to make in defending relationalism against the regress objection is that the relational understanding of color appearances that forms the second regress-generating commitment is (of course) a substantive theoretical assumption that a relationalist may be inclined to reject. To mention just a few examples, one might hold that an appearance of red is (not a relation to the property red, but) a neural state type (Hill, 1991), an "adverbial" type of modification of the subject (Sellars, 1975; Tye, 1984), a sense datum type (Jackson, 1977; Peacocke, 1984), or a primitive phenomenological type (Chalmers, 1996). These are obviously quite different views about the nature of color appearances, and it is beyond the scope of the present work to defend — or, for that matter, even state — any one of them. What matters for present purposes is that each of these views offers an account of color appearances that is (unlike relational theories of color appearances) not spelled out in terms of the color properties represented by those experiences. Consequently, and supposing (as it seems to me, anyway) that at least some of these views are viable, theorists who invokes color appearances in understanding color properties (as many relationalists do) can escape the contemplated threat of regress by adopting some such account of color appearances (cf. Cohen, 2003*a*, §1.3).

Putting these points to one side, the most important relationalist defense against the regress objection (in my view) is that the third commitment necessary for generating the regress is false: the substitutions needed to get the regress going are not truth-preserving, and so should not be accepted.[23] This is so because, as I have already maintained (§6.3), the context for the contemplated substitution — that created by 'looks/appears' on the right-hand side of the relationalist's schemata for color properties — is highly intensional.

Why believe that the context created by the phenomenal 'looks/appears' is highly intensional? Because, on the face of it, substitution of extensionally equivalent expressions within that context fails to preserve truth value. For example, something can look/appear Morning-Starish (viz., the way the Morning Star looks/appears) without looking/appearing Evening Starish (viz., the way the Evening Star looks/appears), even though the Morning Star is the Evening Star. Something can look/appear wet without looking/appearing covered in the appropriate way by H_2O, even though being wet just is being covered in

[22] But appearances may be deceptive. For even relationalists who take the color-constituting relations to involve things like looking red and looking blue might reasonably claim not to have mentioned color properties in their accounts if they combine their relationalisms with a denial of the relational theory of appearances; see below.

[23] I am especially indebted to Andé Gallois for advice in developing this idea.

the appropriate way by H_2O. Something can look/appear humorous without looking/appearing disposed to cause characteristic amusement reactions in appropriately situated cognizers, even though being humorous just is being disposed to cause characteristic amusement reactions in appropriately situated cognizers.[24]

These data seem to show that phenomenal occurrences of 'looks/appears', such as those within which color terms occur on the right-hand sides of the relationalist identity statements we are considering, create non-extensional contexts. Consequently, the substitutions on which the regress argument against relationalism depends are not permissible, even granting (per the relevant forms of relationalism) the extensional equivalence of the substituends. I conclude that the regress argument against relationalism fails.

6.5 Mutual Dependence and Understanding

Even if the regress objection fails, there is a closely related concern that merits discussion. Namely, one might worry that, even if one cannot derive from relationalism an infinite regress, still, the apparatus used in setting out the theory fails to be independently grounded in a way that would permit one who lacks understanding to come to it. After all, regress or no regress, it is still true

[24] A second piece of evidence in favor of the non-extensionality of 'look/appear' is that making the very substitutions on which the contemplated instance of the regress objection depends — e.g., substituting 'the disposition to look red (for S in C)' for 'red' in (1) without further syntactic changes results in the ungrammatical string (2):

(1) x looks/appears red (for S in C).

(2) *x looks/appears the disposition to look red (for S in C).

But if the substitution in question is not *salva* grammaticality, presumably it cannot be *salva veritate*. (As far as I can see, this point applies to substitutions involving right-hand sides of other relationalist schemata, so it generalizes to versions of the objection aimed at non-dispositionalist forms of color relationalism as well.)

A proponent of the regress objection might respond by adding syntactic material in the course of carrying out the substitution. Most obviously, she might attempt to infer from (1) and (D) to (3), or from (1) and (D) to (4):

(3) x looks/appears to be the disposition to look red (for S in C).

(4) x looks/appears to exemplify the disposition to look red (for S in C).

(3) and (4) have the advantage that they are not obviously ungrammatical in the way that (2) is, but have the offsetting disadvantage that they appear not to follow (at least, not by principles to which the dispositionalist is committed) from (1) and (D).

The specific formulation of the objection quoted above from Boghossian and Velleman (1989) is odd in a related way. Their formulation appears to rely on an inference from (5) to (6):

(5) x appears red.

(6) x appears disposed to appear red.

If this inference results from substituting the expression on one side of an identity statement for the expression on the other side, then the identity statement in question must be:

(D′) * red = disposed to appear red.

But (D′) is ungrammatical, so nothing follows from it at all.

that color relationalism proposes to understand *red* in terms of *looks red*, while the relational account of color experiences has it that *looks red* is to be unpacked in terms of *red*. Because each element in the combination depends on the other, one might object that the combination as a whole couldn't be understood by someone who lacks any way of cognitively entering into it. The question, then, is one of how someone who doesn't already understand the combination of relationalism about color and a relational theory of color experience might come to understand that combination. If this question can't be answered, then the worry is that no one could be in a position to entertain, let alone endorse, the proposed combination.

Once again, I should remark that this complaint only gets off the ground against those color relationalists who accept a relational conception of color experience. So long as alternative accounts of color experience are available, color relationalists might avoid the worry we are now considering altogether.

On the other hand, I want to suggest that, even for those color relationalists who accept a relational theory of color experience, the kind of mutual dependence under consideration is unobjectionable. This is because, I claim, we can break into the circle of mutual dependence by making use of knowledge we have in place prior to engaging in metaphysical theory construction — knowledge of what it is like for things to look red, knowledge of what it is like for things to look green, and so on (cf. McLaughlin, 2003*b*, 484). I allow that, without such prior knowledge (or some other way of breaking into the circle) we could not understand the contemplated combination of views. Nonetheless, it seems to me that, at least for subjects who have such prior knowledge, the pair can be understood.

I claim that normal, sighted subjects know what it is like for things to look red — and, for that matter, they also know what it is like for things to look green, and what it is like for things to look blue, and so on. Saying this does not entail that such subjects are in possession of the correct metaphysical account of what it is for something to look red (etc.).[25] Indeed, it does not entail that they have any metaphysical views whatsoever. But it does confer on them a capacity to distinguish things that look red from things that look green, and from things that look other, non-coextensive ways as well. And I hold that it thereby enables them to understand the combination of theories we are discussing.

To see this, suppose a normal, sighted subject who knows what it is like for something to look red, and therefore can identify things that look red, is confronted with the color relationalist view that *red* is constituted in terms of *looks red*. She will be in a position to understand this view as proposing to understand the color property *red* in terms of being a certain way with which she is already familiar (despite being unable to provide a correct metaphysical account of that certain way). If you like, her knowledge of what it is like for something to look red provides her with a kind of nominal definition of one

[25] Still less does it entail Revelation about *looks red* and the rest; see note 3.

term used in the analysis — one that fixes for her that particular property (*looks red*, as opposed to, as it might be, *looks green, looks scarlet, looks square, feels rough*, etc.) a relation to which the relationalist claims is constitutive of a thing's exemplifying *red*.

At this point she will already be in a position to understand quite a lot about color relationalism. Among other things, she will understand that the relationalist is proposing to understand *red* in terms of one property with which she has some familiarity and whose instances she can identify (*looks red*) rather than other properties with which she has some familiarity and whose instances she can identify (e.g., *looks green, looks scarlet, looks square, feels rough*). But she may wish to know more. Specifically, she may wish to know what is the essence of *looks red* — that property invoked in the relationalist analysis. For, as we have said, her familiarity with that property amounts to less than an adequate account of its metaphysics.[26]

To satisfy her further curiosity about the essence of this property, she can (if she wishes) consider a relational account — one that understands *looks red* in terms of the property *red*. At this point she will be in a position to understand quite a lot about this relational theory of *looks red*. Among other things, she will understand this view as proposing that something looks red in virtue of being related in a certain way to *red* — a property that she can understand by her prior understanding of the relationalist theory of color. Moreover, assuming she is sufficiently reflective, she will, in the envisioned circumstance, appreciate that the relationalist theory of color and the relational theory of color experience interdefine colors and color experiences. But she will not take that fact to show that she could not come to understand or endorse the combination of views.

The foregoing proposed explanation of our ability to understand the combination of color relationalism and a relational theory of color appearances turns crucially on the use of pre-theoretical knowledge of what it is like for things to look red (etc.) as a way of breaking into the circle of mutual dependence. It may therefore be asked: how, if not by coming to accept some theoretical account, do subjects gain this knowledge? Unfortunately, I am not in a position to answer this empirical question.[27] However, I wish to emphasize that my proposal amounts to an extremely weak constraint on such answers: the form of explanation I have proposed will fail only if it should turn out that our

[26] Compare: One might begin with a superficially grounded capacity to instances of *water* without holding any views about the constitution of that kind. If, subsequently, one comes to desire an understanding of the essence of the kind, one will need to learn more.

[27] I can, however, engage in some highly schematic armchair speculation. It might be that our knowledge of what it is like for something to look red is part of our innate perceptual/cognitive endowment. Alternatively, it may be that that knowledge is not innate but acquired as a part of some (causal, rather than cognitive/rational) developmental cascade in the course of ontogenesis. A more cognitive/rational explanation that is potentially applicable at least to human beings might invoke some kind of inductive learning from ostensive examples in the context of our desire to coordinate our linguistic and non-linguistic behavior with locally prevailing conventions (see Lewis (1997); Boghossian and Velleman (1991, 106)).

knowledge of what it is like for something to look red (etc.) is acquired as a result of learning the correct metaphysics of color and color experience. I take it that it would be very surprising indeed if that were so.[28]

Thus, it seems to me that the mutual dependence between relationalism about color and a relational theory about color appearances need not prevent us from coming to understand those theories, and even endorsing them.

6.6 Conclusion

For many writers, the most important shortcomings of relationalist accounts of color are phenomenological. While they (sometimes) acknowledge its other virtues, these writers allege that color relationalism represents colors in a way that conflicts with the way in which color phenomenology represents colors, and that the only intellectually virtuous response to this clash is to reject the offending theory rather than the data. Moreover, many argue that relationalism cannot be combined with plausible and widely held views about the metaphysics of phenomenal color experience without leading to regress or uninformativeness. Once again, they urge that we respond to this situation by giving up color relationalism.

However, I have argued in this chapter, the phenomenological objections pressed against relationalism by its critics are unconvincing. Once we make clear just what and how color phenomenology can and cannot tell us about the nature of color properties, it turns out that phenomenal data support, rather than detract from, the case for relationalism. Furthermore, I have argued that the threat of regress dissolves once we see that it depends crucially on substitution instances that we have reason to reject, and that relationalism is not ungrounded in any sense that would prevent understanding of the theory. I conclude that color phenomenology is not the stumbling block for relationalism that many have held it to be.

[28] It is also worth noting that, on the current proposal, those who lack prior knowledge of what it is like for something to look red would be unable to come to understand the combination of views under consideration in the way that I have proposed. Such subjects might come to know that relationalist theories of color and relational theories of color experience interdefine colors and color experiences, but they could not (or, at least not in the same way) break into the circle of mutual dependence to gain the kind of substantive understanding I think the rest of us can.

PART III

ROLE FUNCTIONALISM

7

A ROLE FUNCTIONALIST THEORY OF COLOR

What you think color is (your model) depends on what you think colors does for you (the task).

— (Dannemiller, 1992, 33).

I have emphasized repeatedly in the foregoing that color relationalism — the view that colors are constituted in terms of relations to subjects — is agnostic about just what sorts of relations to subjects constitute the colors. And, as we have seen, there's a lot that can be said (pro and con) about relationalism without compromising this agnosticism. Until now I have clung steadfastly to this agnosticism so as to keep my arguments for and defense of relationalism free from more particular commitments to one or another species of the view. But the time has come for me to say more about the more particular form of relationalism about color that I find most plausible, which I call *role functionalism*. That will be the task of this chapter.

I'll pursue this task in three phases. The first phase is expository: I shall lay out the role functionalist view, comment on its components, and present some of its most important consequences (§7.1). In the second phase (§7.2) I'll discuss the relationship between role functionalism about color and the related but distinct realizer functionalist position, and then bring out several ways in which it seems to me that role functionalism is preferable to realizer functionalism. In the third and final phase (§7.3) I'll consider, and attempt to neutralize, a cluster of objections concerning causation that some have thought favor realizer over role functionalism, and that seem to me, in any case, to be the most significant obstacles for the particular role functionalist species of relationalism that I favor.

After having presented and defended the theory in this chapter, I'll compare role functionalism to other forms of relationalism in Chapter 8. Ultimately, I'll conclude that role functionalism is the most promising species of relationalist color ontology — and therefore, given the arguments for and defense of color relationalism presented in earlier chapters, the most promising color ontology *tout court*.

7.1 Role Functionalism

As its name suggests, the view I wish to propose is grounded in the idea that the relations that constitute colors are *functional* relations — relations involving the performance of a certain functional role that connects surfaces, lights, and the like, to visual systems.

In particular, I favor the view according to which *red for S in C* is the functional role of disposing its bearers to look red to S in C, and *green for S in C* is the functional role of disposing its bearers to look green to S in C. *Mutatis mutandis* for the other colors.[1]

7.1.1 *Motivation*

The role functionalist view I have proposed takes its initial motivation from the following uncontroversial platitude: certain objects are disposed to look colored to subjects.[2] For example, the ripe lemon before me now has such a disposition: when I attend to the lemon (under the conditions I am now in), it looks yellow to me. By this I mean that the lemon produces in me, under these conditions, the characteristic kind of visual experience of looking yellow. More generally, it seems hard to deny that color properties (assuming they exist) occasion particular visual experiences in certain kinds of subjects under certain circumstances, and that things that have color properties are disposed to occasion particular visual experiences in certain kinds of subjects under certain circumstances. Of course, theorists will disagree about (at least) the proper understanding of the visual experiences and dispositions invoked, and just which subjects and visual conditions are relevant. Nonetheless, I take the above platitude (in both specific and general forms) to be a banal and therefore secure starting place.

This secure, if platitudinous, starting place states that things that are colored have the dispositions to look colored — i.e., to occasion certain visual experiences (to certain subjects in certain conditions). It gives us reason for believing, then, that colors and dispositions to look colored (often) coincide in extension. This point, in turn, gives us reason for wanting a theory of color that explains this extensional coincidence. Role functionalism about color is intended to offer just such an explanation: it proposes to account for the nature of color precisely in terms of the dispositions to look colored. In particular, it entails that exemplifying a color just is exemplifying some or other property that realizes the disposition to look colored, and so exemplifying the disposition to look colored. By explaining the extensional coincidence in this way, role functionalism answers an important theoretical need.[3]

[1] In earlier work (e.g., Cohen, 2003*a*) I expressed role functionalism in a different (and, it now seems to me, inferior) way: I claimed that *red for S in C* is the property that disposes its bearers to look red to S in C (and likewise for the other colors). This formulation has the serious shortcoming that the definite description used on the right-hand side is very plausibly improper, and in any case might reasonably be thought to pick out the realizer rather than the role (or, as I would suggest, to be ambiguous between the realizer and the role). While I think there is more to be said in defense of the older formulation, it seems to me simpler, and therefore preferable, to use the formulation in the main text since it avoids these difficulties.

[2] Here and below I intend a phenomenal reading of 'looks' locutions (cf. Jackson (1977, chapter 2), Chisholm (1957)).

[3] Indeed, we might say even more than this. For if, as I shall contend in §8.1, the best theory of dispositions is one according to which dispositions just are the functional role properties of

7.1.2 *Role Functionalism as a Functional Analysis*

In discussions of perception and philosophy of mind, 'function' is ambiguous between a teleological/adaptive reading (on which, roughly, something is functional for an organism by virtue of bringing about an increase in the adaptive fitness of its species) and a non-teleological reading (on which, roughly something is functional by consisting in the accomplishment of a certain task, abstracting from issues about its implementation). The intention to follow the latter disambiguation is sometimes signaled by the expression "Cummins-function," named after its explication and defense by Robert Cummins (1975, 1983).

In light of this potential ambiguity, let me disambiguate my usage. As I intend it, role functionalism about color is entirely independent of and agnostic about teleology and adaptivity; as such, my discussion of colors in terms of their functional roles should be understood as adverting to the non-teleological (Cummins) notion of function. Thus, according to role functionalism, *red for S in C* is identical with a particular (non-teleological) functional role — viz., that of disposing its bearers to look red to S in C. I make no commitment about whether colors are connected with any adaptive function.

This agnosticism about adaptivity notwithstanding, role functionalism analyzes colors in terms of their functional roles, and is therefore (as its name suggests) a functional analysis of color. This point has several significant consequences.

First, like any functional analysis, role functionalism about color understands the properties it analyzes in a way that is independent of their structural or material constitution: what determines whether something has the property *red for S in C* is not whether it has some particular structural or material constitution, but whether it has the relevant functional role. In this sense, role functionalism can be thought of as quantifying over first-order structural configuration types that realize the relevant functional role: *red for S in C* is the property of having some or other structural configuration type that realizes the functional role of disposing its bearers to look red to S in C.[4]

A reflex of this point is that, on role functionalism, a color such as *red for S in C* will be realized by different structures in different possible worlds: instances of a structural type that realizes the functional role of disposing x to look red to S in C in world w_1 may not realize the functional role of disposing x to look red to S in C in world w_2, depending on the degree of similarity between

having some or other basis property that realizes the functional role of causing their manifestations, then the role properties identified with colors by role functionalism just are the dispositions to look colored. And this would, of course, amount to an especially tidy account of the extensional coincidence between colors and color dispositions. Nonetheless, I do not want to rely too heavily on this particularly tidy explanation at this point (instead I will content myself with the explanation of the coincidence given in the main text), because I want to allow, at least in principle, for alternative views about the metaphysics of dispositions.

[4] Although functionalism makes colors second-order properties in this sense, it makes colors first-order in the distinct sense that they are exemplified by concrete particulars rather than types.

the physics (and psychology) of w_1 and w_2. By way of comparison, note that if (as is plausible) the property *being a can-opener* receives a functional analysis, it may be that a given structure counts as an instance of this property in w_1 and fails to count as an instance of this property in w_2; this will happen if the physics and the cans of w_1 and those of w_2 are sufficiently unlike that what fills the functional role of opening cans in w_1 does not fill the functional role of opening cans in w_2. Moreover, and for the same reasons, color functionalism leaves it open that there may be many distinct structures that count as realizers of *red for S in C* within world w; this will happen if the different structures all realize the functional role of disposing their bearers to look red in w. And again, this is just what we expect from a functionally analyzed property: if *being a can-opener* is analyzed functionally, we expect that property to apply to many different structural and material configuration types (can openers made of steel, can openers made of gold, mile-long can openers, newly conceived structural types that you invent in your basement one afternoon) within a world w just so long as all of them realize the functional role of opening cans in w.

A further, and related, feature of role functionalism about color is that the view is officially neutral on whether colors are disjunctively realized properties in world w, whether colors are physically realized properties in world w, and so on. If it should turn out that, in world w, the functional role of disposing things to look red to S in C is non-disjunctively or non-physically realized, then role functionalism will entail that the property *red for S in C* is, in w, non-disjunctively or non-physically realized. I take it that, on the best current scientific evidence, the realizers of the roles in question are physical (on any of the usual understandings of that term) and disjunctive, hence (on role functionalism) that colors are realized physically and disjunctively in the actual world (see Nassau, 1980). But this fact (if it is a fact) is not required by role functionalism. I take it that the neutrality of role functionalism on such questions is a virtue, since it allows for a possibility that is actual — namely, that we can make sense of the very color properties with which we denizens of the actual world have perceptual contact applying to objects in worlds very different from our own.

Notice, however, that if it is true (as it seems to be) that things that are red for S in C can have any of a number of physically quite disparate structural makeups, then this gives us reason for preferring a view on which colors are not tied to particular structures. For in this case we should prefer an account that vindicates the claim that these physically disparate structures all share one and the same color. As noted already, role functionalism about color allows for this outcome. Moreover, role functionalism, unlike many views about color (e.g., Hilbert, 1987; Lewis, 1997), needn't restrict itself to surface color, but applies straightforwardly to the colors of luminous sources, volumes, and so on; for, so long as a luminous source or a volume has the functional role of disposing its bearers to look colored, role functionalism will count that luminous source or volume as an instance of a color. Role functionalism even makes sense of the (pre-theoretically plausible) claim that a surface and a volume can share one and the same color: for example, the surface of a banana and a volume of beer share the same yellow color just in case they both have the functional role of disposing their bearers to look yellow. In this sense, role functionalism permits a completely unified treatment of surface color, volume color, source color, aperture color, and film color — it explains why they are all species of *color*.

Is role functionalism about color the view that colors are the categorical bases for the dispositions to look colored? Not if we accept the widely held view that a basis is only contingently connected with the disposition for which it is a basis (read *de re*). For, on role functionalism, the colors are essentially — constitutively — connected with the dispositions to look colored. According to role functionalism, the bases for the dispositions to look colored are not *identical* with the colors, but are *realizers* of the colors (in particular possible worlds). For example, suppose physical configuration P is a basis for the disposition to look red to S in C in the actual world. For the role functionalist, *red for S in C* is (not P but) the functional role of disposing its bearers to look red to S in C; and this functional role happens to be realized, in the actual world, by P. But since the functional role of disposing its bearers to look red to S in C fails to be realized by (indeed, fails to coincide with) P in other possible worlds, the former cannot be identified with the latter. Analogously, if the description 'the inventor of bifocals' applies to whatever individual invented bifocals, and if it so happens that Benjamin Franklin satisfies that description in the actual world, it does not follow that 'the inventor of bifocals' picks out Benjamin Franklin in every world, or that that description is synonymous with 'Benjamin Franklin'. Rather, 'the inventor of bifocals' expresses a descriptive content that happens to be satisfied, in the actual world, by Benjamin Franklin.

Finally, role functionalism provides a clear explanation of the relation between the philosophical project of attempting to specify the nature of colors, on the one hand, and the scientific project that goes by the same description, on the other — i.e., it will give us a way of answering Sellarsian questions about the relation between the description of the world given by our experience and that given by science. Namely, if we follow role functionalism in identifying the colors with certain functional roles, we can understand the scientific project of attempting to specify the nature of colors as the empirical project that attempts to determine the physical (or, if it should turn out that way, non-physical) structures that happen to fill those functional roles in the actual world.[5]

[5] The scientific project in question sometimes goes by the name 'color physics'. This terminology will seem somewhat clumsy in worlds where non-physical structures fill the relevant functional roles, for in these worlds it will be part of the job of color physics to tell us about certain non-physical structures. But perhaps a certain amount of terminological inaptness is inevitable when we use our language to describe such (presumably remote) worlds.

7.1.3 *Role Functionalism and Perceptual Variation*

Like other forms of relationalism, role functionalism is well-suited to account for instances of perceptual variation of the kind discussed in Chapter 2. Role functionalism holds that *red for S in C* is the functional role of disposing its bearers to look red to S in C. As I discussed in Chapter 2, there is a wide range of cases in which a single stimulus can look red to S_1 in C_1 despite not looking red to S_2 in C_2, and in which it is implausible to regard one of these variants as veridically representing the stimulus to the exclusion of the other. The role functionalist has a ready description of these cases that (unlike non-ecumenical theories) does not require holding out hope for the existence of a uniquely veridical variant. Namely, the role functionalist can say that both variants are (compatibly) veridical, in so far as the stimulus both (i) bears the color property *red for S_1 in C_1* and (ii) does not bear the color property *red for S_2 in C_2*. Thus, like other relationalists, the role functionalist is able to accommodate the observed range of perceptual variation without either unmotivated stipulations in favor of a distinguished variant or blind faith in an unknown fact of the matter.

All of this is to say merely that, because it is a form of relationalism, role functionalism can enjoy all the benefits of an ecumenical relationalist response to problems of perceptual variation.

7.1.4 *Being Red and Looking Red*

Color functionalism holds that *red for S in C* is the functional role of disposing its bearers to look red to S in C (and likewise for the other colors). Thus, this view, like several other forms of relationalism, gives us an account of the property *red for S in C* in terms of the property *looks red to S in C*. The natural next question is what it means to say that something looks red to S in C.[6]

I propose to answer this question by holding that x looks red to S in C just in case, by visually attending to x in C, S is appropriately caused (in C) to have an experience of red. (*Mutatis mutandis* for the other colors.)

Several features of this proposal are in need of comment.

First, on this proposal, the sort of relation we bear to objects when they look red to us in a circumstance involves a certain kind of attention (namely, a visual kind). Objects might bear the property *red for S in C* even when S is not visually attending to them, but in this case they will not (occurrently) look red to S in C. On the present account, this is possible because their having the color property *red for S in C* confers on them a disposition to look red to S in C, but leaves open that the latter disposition might be unmanifested. As in my earlier invocation of visual attention in §6.2, I don't want to commit to any particular view of the nature of visual attention here, except to say that I take visual attention to be

[6] In the current context, this question is, of course, linked to the issue of whether theories that unpack *red for S in C* in terms of *looks red to S in C* lead inevitably to regress; for reasons discussed in §6.4, I hold that the threat of regress is not ultimately damaging to such theories.

an early, informationally encapsulated, psychological mechanism that selects certain objects/regions in the space around the perceiver.[7]

A second feature of the proposal deserving of comment is its invocation of a notion of appropriate causation. I believe this invocation is ineliminable in order to avoid problems about deviant or wayward causal chains (Peacocke, 1979; Davidson, 1973, 78ff.). To see the sort of problems at issue, consider the (admittedly fanciful) case of the telekinetic tomato. This tomato, T, is in most respects similar to other ripe tomatoes. However, T has, in addition, a very unusual telekinetic capacity: it has the capacity to affect nearby visual cortices directly — i.e., without retinal stimulation of any kind; indeed, the way in which T affects those cortices is to induce in them the state they normally undergo when they experience a very unripe tomato of the same size and shape as T. When I visually attend to T, its telekinetic capacity instantly swamps the effect of its ordinary, non-telekinetic capacity, so I end up representing that T is green to me in my perceptual circumstances. Despite this fact, I am inclined to say that T does *not* look green to me in those circumstances. In support of this claim, note that T would have the same telekinetic effect that it has on me on an entirely blind subject (say, one with no retinas); assuming we would not want to say that T looks green (or any other way) to such a subject, we should neither say that T looks green to me. Rather, I think we should say that T looks red (to me, but of course not to a retina-less subject) but that its non-standard telekinetic effect prevents me from apprehending the way T looks in respect of color to me in the circumstances (namely, that it looks red to me in those circumstances). My restriction to the non-deviant causes in my understanding of *looks red to S in C* allows for this outcome, and so delivers what seems to me the right verdict about the case.[8] Unfortunately, I have no specific proposal to offer about how the deviant/non-deviant distinction

[7] My appeal to visual attention helps in avoiding a worry discussed by Gold (1999). Gold worries that statements of the form 'x is pale blue just in case x looks pale blue' result in our seeing too many instances of color properties, since both x and the light coming from x to the visual system can be said to be disposed to look pale blue:

> If something is colored just in case it has a disposition to look colored, then when we look at a pale blue urn, we are actually seeing an identical disposition in two distinct things, namely, the color of the urn and the color of the light reflected by the urn (Gold, 1999, 30).

But if we hold, as I propose, that x cannot look pale blue unless *visually attending* to x appropriately causes a visual experience of the right sort, then we can make the necessary distinctions among instances of colors. For although, in this case, we can say that the light is disposed to look pale blue to S in circumstances in which S is visually attending to the light, it will not be true that the light manifests this disposition — that it looks pale blue to S — in circumstances in which S is visually attending to the urn rather than the light. Thus, both the light and the urn may be disposed to look pale blue to S in the relevant circumstance; but it is false that both look pale blue to us whenever one of them does. And if, plausibly, we don't see the color of an object that doesn't look colored to us, it will be false that we see both instances of the color whenever we see one of them.

[8] Plausibly the deviant/non-deviant distinction is unprincipled: I can imagine many possible causal pathways that diverge from the standard one less dramatically than does the telekinetic

should be cashed. However, I take it that some such distinction is needed to make plausible more or less any philosophical theory that invokes causation. Since the need for such a distinction is so general, I don't consider its provision a special burden for my account of *looks red to S in C*.

The final significant but as yet unexplained component of my understanding of the property *looks red to S in C* is the notion of an experience of red. By this notion, I mean to pick out a type of mental state of subjects — namely, that type whose tokens are the (typical) effects of those subjects' attending to red things. Saying only this much, however, is bound to be unsatisfying. Beyond this, one might reasonably wonder what is the essential nature of the state type in question. Is the type constituted by its members' having a common functional or representational profile (Harman, 1990; Dretske, 1995; Tye, 1995), a common neural realization (Hill, 1991), a common irreducible phenomenological feel (Chalmers, 1996), or some other feature? I have not yet answered this question, and I do not wish to answer it. This is because I want the role functionalist theory of color that I have proposed to remain neutral on the important and controversial question of the metaphysics of color experience. I see the detachability of color functionalism from views about color experience as a benefit of the former, because it means that proponents of many different answers to the latter question can (in principle) accept role functionalism about color.

7.2 Role and Realizer Functionalism

The role functionalist view of color I have been setting out in the foregoing is, of course, modeled on the more familiar application of role functionalism to the ontology of mental states — a view defended by Putnam (1967), and Block and Fodor (1972), among others. Thinking of the position in this way, however, invites comparison to a related position about color based on the realizer functionalist ontology of mental states defended by such authors as Armstrong (1968, 1970) and Lewis (1972). Indeed, the view that results from extending Armstrong–Lewis style realizer functionalism about mental states to the domain of colors (henceforth, *realizer functionalism about color*) has been defended ably in recent years by authors such as Jackson and Pargetter (1987), Jackson (1996, 1998*a*), and McLaughlin (2000). Role and realizer versions of functionalism about some domain (mental states, colors, whatever) are two different attempts to harness the general functionalist idea of explaining elements of that domain in terms of functional roles.[9] However, they disagree about the details of how these functional roles figure in the nature of their analytic targets. As we'll see below, this seemingly small difference turns out to have many important consequences.

pathway by which T acts, and I doubt that there is a crisp line past which a pathway counts as deviant. If so, then there will be borderline cases of something's looking red to S in C.

[9] On the contrast between the two positions in philosophy of mind, see Block (1980, 177–181).

Now, the close relationship between role and realizer functionalism, and the historical interplay between these two positions, give ample reason for exploring realizer functionalism in the context of the present defense of role functionalism about color. There are, however, two additional reasons for being interested in realizer functionalism that have to do with the dialectical strategies I've adopted in this book.

First, realizer functionalism remains an as-yet-unclosed loophole in my case for relationalism from Chapters 2–3. As noted in §3.3.1, one could block the case for relationalism by finding an adequate but non-relational relativist theory of color; and, as I pointed out at the time, realizer functionalism seems to offer the most promising option for a theory of this kind. Second, the motivation I offered for role functionalism in §7.1.1 supports both role and realizer functionalism equally well; for *both* forms of functionalism are in a position to offer an explanation of the coincidence between color properties and the dispositions to look colored. As noted, role functionalism can explain the coincidence by entailing that instances of colors will exemplify the functional role of disposing those instances to look colored, and so will exemplify the dispositions to look colored. But realizer functionalists can also explain the coincidence: they will say that instances of colors must exemplify some realizer of the functional role of disposing those instances to look colored, and that by exemplifying some realizer of that functional role, they will also exemplify the functional role, and therefore the disposition.

What this means, then, is that the arguments I have offered so far in favor of relationalism and role functionalism leave realizer functionalism unscathed. Therefore, if I wish to defend relationalism and role functionalism about color (and I do), then I need further reasons for rejecting realizer functionalism and for retaining role functionalism in its stead.

In the rest of this section, then, I'll first attempt to characterize the relationship between role and realizer functionalism more precisely (§7.2.1), and then turn to the task of providing arguments for favoring role functionalism over realizer functionalism about color (§§7.2.2–7.2.4).[10]

7.2.1 *Compare and Contrast*

The difference between role and realizer functionalism can perhaps best be explicated as a disagreement about the referents of terms for mental states, or colors, as the case may be.[11]

[10] In revising the material in this section I have drawn extensively on comments from an anonymous referee.

[11] It might initially seem surprising that this contrast is drawn in such a linguistic form — i.e., as a disagreement about the referents of certain terms (even though this way of presenting the contrast has become somewhat traditional). After all, realizer and role functionalism are, in the first instance, ontological positions — views about the nature of mental states or colors, rather than about pieces of language. But I don't think the linguistic formulation of the contrast should be taken to empty the contrast of ontological significance. For the referents of mental terms and

Realizer functionalists think of the task of giving an account of color names in two stages.[12] In the first, philosophical, stage, one identifies and spells out the functional role associated with the referent of a color name such as 'red (for S in C)'. In the present instance, realizer and role functionalists agree that the relevant functional role is (something like) that of disposing bearers to look red (to S in C). In the second, empirical stage, one looks to empirical investigation to discern what entities actually play the functional role articulated in the first stage, and identifies the target with these realizers of the role. Thus, if it should turn out, as a matter of *a posteriori*, contingent fact that having a certain spectral reflectance distribution ϕ is what occupies (in the actual world α) the functional role of disposing bearers to look red to S in C, then the realizer functionalist will conclude that 'red (for S in C)' refers to ϕ. Moreover, since ϕ only contingently satisfies the relevant functional description, the realizer functionalist will hold that 'red (for S in C)' refers *non-rigidly* to ϕ.[13] Crucially, on this view, the functional role is merely an intermediary aid to the identification of the target; the role is not itself the referent of the color name, it is neither a constituent nor element of that referent, and it is only contingently satisfied by that referent.

It is just here that role functionalism differs crucially from realizer functionalism. Role functionalists hold that the referent of 'red (for S in C)' is the property of having some or other property (distinct from *red (for S in C)*) that fills or realizes the role of disposing its bearers to look red (to S in C). The referents of color names are, on this position, higher order properties that involve quantification over realizers of a certain functional role. That role is, therefore, no mere inessential identificatory aid for the role functionalist, as it is for the realizer functionalist. Quite the contrary: role functionalism earns its label by making the role a central, essential element of the referents of color names. Moreover, role functionalists will hold that color names refer rigidly. For although the properties that satisfy the relevant functional roles vary between possible worlds, the functional role properties themselves do not; and since the role functionalist maintains that color names refer to role properties rather

color terms are (respectively) mental states and colors; thus, in disagreeing about the referents of the terms, realizer functionalists and role functionalists are disagreeing about what non-linguistic entities are mental states or colors. In that sense the two sides are engaged in a genuinely ontological dispute. (In this connection, Williamson (2007, chapter 2) argues persuasively that questions about non-linguistic and non-conceptual matters sometimes require for their resolution arguing about linguistic or conceptual matters, and that, when this occurs, it does not render the original questions themselves linguistic or conceptual.)

[12] This two-stage process for realizer functionalism about color comes out especially clearly in Jackson and Pargetter (1987, 69).

[13] This is so if the realizer functionalist holds that 'red (for S in C)' designates whatever satisfies the functional role of disposing its bearers to look red (to S in C). On the other hand, if we adopt a rigidified version of the view according to which 'red (for S in C)' designates whatever actually satisfies the functional role of disposing its bearers to look red (to S in C), then it will follow that that color term designates rigidly (see §7.2.4). I'll continue to work with the unrigidified version of the view here for simplicity.

than role satisfiers, she will maintain that the referents of color names are stable across worlds.

It is worth, at this point, emphasizing a further difference between role and realizer functionalism that is especially important given the overall argumentative strategy of this book: role functionalism is, and realizer functionalism is not, a species of relationalism about color. It is easy to see why role functionalism is a form of relationalism: the former identifies color properties with functional roles that are constituted in terms of relations to subjects, and thereby entails that colors are constituted in terms of relations to subjects. In contrast, the realizers of the functional roles under discussion are not constituted in terms of relations to subjects. For what realizes these functional roles are various material constitutions; and, as I hope all parties to the present debate will agree, it would be deeply and implausibly idealistic to suppose that such material constitutions are constituted in terms of relations to subjects.

The conclusion that realizer functionalism is not a form of color relationalism may be surprising.[14] After all, realizer functionalists about color have traditionally made much of considerations about perceptual variation very much like those I used to motivate color relationalism in Part I of this book (Jackson and Pargetter, 1987; McLaughlin, 2000, 2003*b*). On reflection, however, it seems clear that the way in which realizer functionalists make use of these considerations stops short of identifying colors with relational properties. Realizer functionalists talk about perceptual variation because the functional roles that particular color stimuli play vis-à-vis subjects and circumstances do indeed vary, and because realizer functionalists appeal to these functional roles in deciding what to identify with the colors. Crucially, however, what they ultimately decide to identify with the colors are not the functional roles, which are constituted in terms of relations to subjects, but the realizers of the functional roles, which are *not* constituted in terms of relations to subjects. It is true that realizer functionalists fix what colors are partly by specifying the functional roles that colors play; but they then identify the colors with the realizers rather than the roles. The functional roles in question are neither identical to, nor constituents of, their realizers. Consequently, the relationality of the former is not inherited by the latter.[15] But if realizer functionalism entails that colors are not constituted in terms of relations to perceiving subjects, then it is not a species of color relationalism (as I have been using the term). It is, instead, a conceptually (but inessentially) dressed up form of identity theory — a theory on which colors are identical to physical types, although they

[14] In saying this I do not mean to suggest that proponents of realizer functionalism have themselves been laboring under the illusion that their view is a form of relationalism. For example, McLaughlin (2003*b*) makes this particularly clear in conjecturing that colors are certain types of spectral reflectance distributions. Alas, McLaughlin's clarity about this matter has not prevented some commentators (e.g., Cohen, 2004) from wrongly describing realizer functionalism as an instance of relationalism. *Mea culpa maxima.*

[15] Analogy: Kaplan (1989) teaches that the character of an expression, when supplemented by a context, fixes its content; but an expression's character is not a constituent of its content (498, 523).

may happen, contingently, to be conceived of as satisfying particular functional roles.

With this characterization of the differences between role and realizer functionalism about color in hand, I am now in a position to offer several arguments for the superiority of role functionalism over realizer functionalism.

7.2.2 *The Argument from Commonality*

The first concerns a plausible platitude that Yablo (1995) calls *commonality*. This is the demand that the nature of a target property F (whatever it turns out to be) should explain why F "is shared by all and only Fs" (Yablo, 1995, 482).[16] This demand is important in the present instance because, as Yablo goes on to note, on the best physical evidence (Nassau, 1980, 1983), the realizers that satisfy the role of looking red to S in C appear to vary substantially within the actual world (and, of course, the variation is, if anything, more wide-ranging between worlds):

> When Armstrong says that the red-role is played by a physical property, he is only playing a scientific hunch; there *could*, he admits, be "*irreducibly* diverse causes in the physical surfaces bringing about identical colour-appearances for human observers." But where Armstrong puts this forward as a sort of doomsday scenario in which colors are reduced to the status of pseudo-qualities, nowadays it is thought to be more or less the situation.... Something similar is of course the standard line on suffering things — they too have nothing but a causal syndrome in common (Yablo (1995, 481), 481; (cf. Cohen, 2003*a*, 29–30)).

Now, it is not hard to find a plausible unifying explanation of why all and only the physically diverse red things count as *red (for S in C)*: namely, they and only they satisfy a particular functional role (viz., the role of disposing the bearers of this property to look red to S in C). However, recall that realizer functionalists deny that that functional role is essential to *red (for S in C)*. In saying this, realizer functionalists are adopting a theory that locates the needed explanatory resources outside of the nature of colors. For this reason, then, they make it impossible to explain why the target property at issue is shared by all and only Fs in terms of the nature of F, and thereby give up on the commonality demand. This, it seems to me, is a serious *prima facie* problem for realizer functionalism.

How might a realizer functionalist respond to this problem?

One option would be to deny that colors are, in fact, as physically heterogeneous as the data initially suggest. In this spirit, Jackson (1998*a*, 108)

[16] The commonality platitude is intended to allow that there might be some other explanations not invoking the nature of F-hood — as it might be, historical or causal explanations — of why F is shared by all and only the Fs. The claim is only that the nature of F-hood should provide the materials for one such explanation.

Yablo treats commonality as the basis of one half of an anti-functionalist dilemma. He thinks realizer functionalists are unable to provide for commonality, while role functionalists about F are unable to secure the causal powers of F in bringing about the effects in terms of which the functional role is elaborated. If my arguments in §7.3 are correct, then the horn of Yablo's dilemma that targets role functionalism can be answered.

writes that, even if colors are physically disjunctive, perhaps "the disjunction is not excessively disjunctive". Likewise, McLaughlin (2003*b*, 479) adds a final clause to his realizer functional characterization of colors to ensure that a form of commonality is satisfied. Significantly, and to their credit, Jackson and McLaughlin accept forthrightly that, should the realizer properties fail to be unified, then they would give up their view in favor of some kind of irrealist color projectivism (Jackson (1998*a*, 112); McLaughlin (2003*b*, 481)). That said, these writers hope to avoid this irrealist endpoint by claiming that, while the diverse realizers of the redness role are indeed heterogeneous in their (physical) makeup, they are nonetheless unified in respect of the way (as a matter of contingent fact) they happen to affect light (cf. Jackson (1998*a*, 109ff.); McLaughlin (2003*b*, 497–499)).

Unfortunately, this reply is unresponsive to our worry. For the commonality desideratum is plausibly understood as requiring not merely that the Fs turn out, *de facto*, to have something or other in common; it should be taken as requiring that the essential nature of F, as spelled out by a candidate account of that property, should explain what is common to all and only Fs; and here the suggestion at hand is unhelpful. Here is an analogy. Suppose I desire to own every can-opener ever made in order to complete my collection. It goes little distance toward satisfying the commonality desideratum with respect to the property *can-opener* to cite the fact that all of its physically heterogeneous instances contingently have the property of being desired by me. What is wrong with that attempt to secure commonality with respect to *can-opener* is that what it cites as common between instances is a feature that is plainly not constitutive of *can-opener* (on anybody's account). But the present suggestion on behalf of the realizer functionalist fails in the same way. It doesn't show that the physically heterogeneous realizers share that which, according to the realizer functionalist, is constitutive of *red (for S in C)*. Rather, it shows that the realizers share something else — a feature that is (by the realizer functionalist's own lights) not constitutive of *red (for S in C)*.

There is another curious point about the response now under consideration. On that response, the something else in terms of which the diverse realizers are said to be alike is a causal syndrome/functional role that involves their effect on light. But, come to think of it, there is a more obvious (less conjectural) causal syndrome/functional role that is uncontroversially shared by the diverse realizers: they are all, after all, realizers of the red-for-S-in-C role. For the realizer functionalist, that latter shared functional role isn't enough to answer the commonality desideratum; it won't provide an answer unless we take that functional role to be constitutive of *red (for S in C)*, which would mean giving up on realizer functionalism in favor of role functionalism. But it seems that the proposal we're now considering is no better. For the shared functional role (assuming it is, indeed, shared) that involves the effect distinct realizers have on light isn't enough to answer the commonality desideratum unless we take *that* functional role to be constitutive of the target property, which, as before, would mean giving up on realizer functionalism in favor of role functionalism.

The same problems apply to a related realizer functionalist response to the current worries about commonality that involves appealing to the semantic values of nearby linguistic expressions. The thought here would be that, while realizer functionalists take 'red (for S in C)' to refer to the realizer property (which does not satisfy the commonality demand) rather than the role property (which does), there are nearby cognate expressions that might take the role property as semantic values, and that could be enlisted to answer to whatever intuitions underwrite the commonality desideratum. In particular, realizer functionalists have sometimes suggested that, while property names ('F'/'red (for S in C)') refer to realizer properties, the closely related predicates ('is F'/'is red (for S in C)') and gerunds ('being F'/'being red (for S in C)') formed from these names instead have role properties as their semantic values.[17] Thus, Lewis addresses the issue of commonality (in his defense of realizer functionalism about pain) this way:

> Don't we think that there is one property of being in the state M — one property that is common to all, actual or possible, of whatever kind, who can truly be said to be in state M? — There is. It is the property of being such that, for any possible X, X has it just in case X is in the state that occupies the M-role for X's kind at X's world. The gerund 'being in M' can be taken, at least on one good disambiguation, as a rigid designator of this property (Lewis (1994, 420); cf. Jackson and Pettit (1988, 384–385)).

[17] An alternative strategy, suggested by the realizer functionalist treatment of pain by Lewis (1980), would have it that color terms are either lexically ambiguous or polysemous. (Here the idea would be to find both candidate semantic values for the one color predicate, rather than appealing to a nearby neighbor expression.) Perhaps the most interesting version of this view would hold that such terms make a context-sensitive semantic contribution with parameters filled by features of the context. But I think we can rule out all forms of this strategy.

First, I doubt that color terms are lexically ambiguous in the simple way that 'bank' is, since there are, as far as I know, no languages that lexicalize the distinction between role and realizer, as one would expect for a bank/bank ambiguity (Kripke, 1977).

On the other hand, tests involving VP ellipsis tell against treating color predicates as polysemous in any more interesting way. Where there is polysemy (including context-sensitive variation), expressions must maintain a consistent interpretation under VP ellipsis (Stanley, 2003). This explains why, for example, (1) lacks an interpretation on which Mary and Sally kick different individuals, and (2) lacks an interpretation on which the place that Mary likes is distinct from the place that Sally likes.

(1) Mary kicks me and Sally does too.

(2) Mary likes it here and Sally does too.

But we do not find similar restrictions against such "crossed" readings under VP ellipsis involving color predicates. To see this, let a Martian-tomato be a tomato that exemplifies the red role in virtue of having a new and heretofore unencountered realizer, and let a mad-tomato be a tomato that exemplifies the very property that in a standard ripe tomato is a realizer of the red role, but such that this object does not exemplify the red role. And now notice that (3) is not anomalous:

(3) The Martian-tomato is red and the mad-tomato is too.

Pending some reason for thinking that the standard VP ellipsis test is defective in its application to the case, this gives us reason for rejecting the Lewis-inspired ambiguity/polysemy proposal in any form.

My reason for rejecting this strategy of response on behalf of realizer functionalism is that, once again, it appears not to answer the demand that commonality makes. Commonality requires that an account of the colors — of the properties that are referents of color names — should explain what is common to the diverse instances of each color in terms of the nature of the colors as understood by that theory. The realizer functionalist strategy we are now considering explains what is shared by all and only the diverse realizers of a color *not* in terms of the essence of that color, but in terms of some other property that is *not* the essence of that color.[18]

Perhaps a realizer functionalist sympathetic to either of the strategies just considered might reply that, despite what has been said above, there is a version of (necessary) commonality that they can accommodate. For, while the realizer functionalist accepts that what is common to the diverse realizers of the red (for S in C) role is not part of the essence of the color *red (for S in C)*, she will nonetheless maintain that:

(4) Necessarily all the red (for S in C) things have the red-for-S-in-C role.

As we have seen, this claim can only be relevant to the present discussion if the necessity at issue is *de re*. But I claim that (4) does not express a *de re* necessity.[19]

While it is controversial how best to flesh out the *de re/de dicto* distinction, I can make my point by relying on (at least) two different ways of understanding the distinction that one finds in the literature.[20] One such common usage, which is reflected in the Latin terminology, and which arises from a metaphysical understanding of the distinction, can be put somewhat roughly in terms of the idea that necessities *de re* are necessities that hold in virtue of the

[18] A further worry about the present strategy is that, on the one hand, standard philosophical usage treats the relevant expression types as semantically on a par (indeed, often freely substituting each for the others as I have in this work), and, on the other hand, its proponents have offered no evidence to substantiate a differential semantic treatment for property names and their related predicates/gerunds. While I am not certain what to say about this matter at the end of the day, it is at least potentially relevant (and supportive of the strategy under consideration) that there are distributional differences between names and gerundives for colors or mental states (especially with regard to their occurring in a direct object position):

his behavior caused pain/being in pain.

I could see pain/*being in pain on her face.

I can see red/*being red in the pattern.

there was pain/*being in pain on her face.

there was red/*being red in the pattern.

And of course color/mental predicates are distributionally unlike both names and gerundives in that they can only occur in predicative positions. However, these distributional differences fall short of showing that the expressions involved should be treated differently by the semantics. (Thanks to Ivano Caponigro for discussion of these matters.)

[19] I'll discuss this strategy and its shortcomings as applied to a different set of modal claims about the colors in §7.2.3.

[20] For discussion and some other ways of thinking about the distinction, see McKay and Nelson (2006).

essential nature of the *res*, while necessities *de dicto* are always relative to a particular (linguistically expressed) way of thinking of those *res*. As I say, something like this metaphysical understanding of the distinction appears to be in philosophical currency; moreover, and more importantly, the metaphysical understanding of the distinction connects nicely with the thought, argued for above, that commonality should get at what is constitutive of the colors rather than at features that colors merely happen to have. A second, and also common (but controversial) way of thinking of the *de re*/*de dicto* distinction is in terms of scope. The idea is that a modal sentences is *de re* iff (i) it contains a pronoun or free variable inside the scope of a modal operator that is bound by an element outside the scope of that operator, or (ii) can be accurately paraphrased by a sentence that is *de re* in the sense of (i). Thus, (5) is *de re* on the current criterion, while (6) is ambiguous between a reading that is *de re* reading and one that is *de dicto* (depending on whether (5) adequately paraphrases (6)):

(5) The shortest spy in the universe is such that necessarily she loves cheese.

(6) Necessarily the shortest spy in the universe loves cheese.

Suppose we understand the *de re*/*de dicto* distinction in either of these common ways. Then I claim that (4) does not express a true *de re* necessity.

Consider the metaphysical construal of the distinction first. Now, it is is true about the entities that are realizers of the red-for-S-in-C role that, relative to the conception of them *as* the realizers of the red-for-S-in-C role, they necessarily exemplify the red-for-S-in-C role. For if they did not exemplify that role, then these entities wouldn't be realizers of the role and so wouldn't fall under the subject term. This is just to say that (4) does appear to express a true claim about what is necessary relative to a certain (linguistically expressed) way of thinking about the relevant entities. On the other hand, if we consider those *res* as entities on their own, independently of any specific way of thinking about them, it does not appear to be necessary of those entities that they have the red-for-S-in-C role. On the contrary, it appears that, at least for some of the entities in question (perhaps one of them is a particular volume of blood), it is possible that it fail to exemplify the red-for-S-in-C role. For there appears to be nothing in the constitution/essence of that *res* that mandates its satisfying that role.

The same result falls out if we construe the *de re*/*de dicto* distinction in terms of scope. For while there appears to be a true reading of (4), this won't help in the current context unless that reading is *de re*. As formulated, (4) does not contain a free variable or pronoun inside the scope of its modal operator, so it can only count as *de re* if it can be accurately paraphrased by (7):

(7) all the red (for S in C) things are such that necessarily they have the red-for-S-in-C role.

I take it that (7) is obviously false. But if so, then even if (4) has a true reading, that reading is not a *de re* reading (because accurate paraphrase must, minimally, preserve truth value).

I take these considerations to show that, while there may be a weak (*de dicto*) formulation of commonality that is respected by realizer functionalism about *red (for S in C)*, this is not an interesting conception of the demand, and not one that could possibly have motivated its introduction. After all, to return to the analogy used above, my desiring all and only the can-openers would satisfy a *de dicto* necessary understanding of the commonality demand about the property *can-opener*. (Metaphysical version: relative to the conception of can-openers as things that I desire in order to complete my collection, it is necessary *de dicto* that I bear an intentional relation to these objects — for if not, they wouldn't be things that I desire to own, and so wouldn't fall under the subject term. Scope version: there is a true, *de dicto*, reading of 'Necessarily all and only the can-openers are things that I desire to complete my can-opener collection'.) But surely that sort of *de dicto* necessity is too cheap — too easily attained — to be what the proponent of commonality had in mind. The demand for commonality could not have had much interest in the first place had such easily attainable answers counted as satisfying it. Likewise, I suggest that the commonality demand would be of little interest as a constraint on accounts of color if taken only to require common features as a matter of necessity *de dicto*. The commonality thesis is interesting because it demands more than this: namely, it requires commonality amongst the instances of each color, *qua res*. The current response does nothing to address that requirement, and I don't see any other response available to the realizer functionalist that is more successful.

7.2.3 *The Argument from Necessity*

The next difficulty I want to consider for realizer functionalism concerns its ability to capture a class of widely accepted modal claims about the colors — modal claims attributing to colors the features of being unique or binary, or of bearing certain similarity relations to other colors.[21] For example, consider the following sorts of modal claims about colors:

(8) Necessarily orange is binary.[22]

(9) Necessarily orange is more similar to red than to green.

Of course, there are variants of these modal claims corresponding to colors other than orange as well, and it seems likely that what substantiates or fails to substantiate the versions involving orange will generalize to versions corresponding to other colors as well; consequently, we can expect that all such modalized attributions to colors of the status of being binary or unique, or their position in a similarity and difference network, will stand or fall together.

[21] Recall that, as noted in §2.3.2, it is possible to understand the unique/binary distinction as applying to colors (and not, or not only, as a distinction among color experiences). The argument that follows presupposes that some such understanding of the distinction is available.

[22] Here and below I shall sometimes suppress relativization to perceivers and circumstances for expository convenience; unrelativized color names can be taken to refer to the coarse-grained relational colors discussed in Chapter 4.

The problem for realizer functionalism brought out by (8)–(9) and their ilk is simple enough. It turns on the thought that the properties identified with colors by realizer functionalists — viz., the realizers of particular experience-involving functional roles — are material structures that, on the face of it, are only *contingently* binary or unique, and only *contingently* stand in the relevant similarity relations. For, as Hardin (1984, 1988) points out in the context of his argument against identity theories of color, there seems to be nothing in the essence of the relevant material structures that, by itself, could explain these features (cf. Boghossian and Velleman, 1991; Johnston, 1992; Maund, 1995; Thompson, 1995).

Given this situation, it seems that realizer functionalists can best explain the similarity relations between colors and the unique/binary distinction in terms of the features of the color experiences elicited by these colors in subjects. Thus, on the proposed form of explanation, a particular material structure that happens to realize the experience-involving functional role suitable for orange (as it might be) counts as binary rather than unique because the color experience that that material structure causes in appropriate subjects in appropriate circumstances is binary. Likewise, the realizer functionalist would account for the similarity relations between the particular material structures that she identifies with the colors in terms of the (more fundamental) similarity relations that obtain between the color experiences caused in appropriate subjects in appropriate circumstances.[23] Unfortunately, however, just because realizer functionalism makes the relationship between a color and the experience-involving functional role that it realizes contingent rather than necessary, the contemplated form of explanation secures the relevant features as contingent rather than necessary as well. For this reason, it appears that realizer functionalism predicts that modal claims of the form of (8) and (9) are false.[24]

Now, McLaughlin (2003*a*,*b*) has argued that the realizer functionalist can vindicate (8)–(9) (and similar necessities). McLaughlin proposes to recapture

[23] This strategy of explanation (on behalf of realizer functionalism and other views) has been suggested by Shoemaker (1990, 107–108); Matthen (1992); Lewis (1997); Byrne and Hilbert (1997*a*, 274–279); Byrne and Hilbert (2003); Jackson (1998*b*, 2000); McLaughlin (2003*a*,*b*); Cohen (2003*b*).

[24] I am awkwardly placed to criticize realizer functionalism for failing to capture these necessities, since I am not confident that they are true. On the contrary, and as I have argued elsewhere (Cohen, 2003*b*), it seems to me that the kinds of features ascribed necessarily to orange in (8) and (9) may very well hold contingently rather than necessarily of the colors (cf. Kurth, 2008). However, I am clearly in the minority on this point: writers as diverse as Campbell (1969), Hardin (1988), Boghossian and Velleman (1991), Johnston (1992), Maund (1995), and Thompson (1995), as well as realizer functionalists McLaughlin (2003*a*,*b*), all endorse versions of (8)–(9). Since at least some realizer functionalists (at least one!) are prepared to take the constraint seriously, it is fair play for me to ask whether they can indeed respect it, as McLaughlin claims they can.

Just to be clear about my own view: I am an agnostic, not an atheist, about whether the properties attributed by (8) and (9) are essential features of colors. Since I think the view according to which such features are contingent rather than necessary has not been ruled out satisfactorily, my own inclination is to view the vindication (or otherwise) of modal sentences such as (8) and (9) as what Lewis (1986*d*, 194) (following Armstrong) calls "spoils to the victor" (where victory should be established on independent, and hopefully less contested, grounds).

these necessities in two steps. First, he holds that color terms not only designate the realizers of color roles, but that they are *synonymous* with the definite descriptions expressing those color roles: "The description 'that property which disposes . . . ' is used in a content-giving sense, rather than merely in a reference fixing sense, in our functional analysis of redness" (McLaughlin, 2003*b*, 485). And second, given this relation of synonymy between color terms and descriptions, he proposes to recapture necessities such as (8) and (9) as true relative to a *de dicto* (*/de conceptu*) reading (486–491). That is, McLaughlin is accepting that there is nothing essential to the *res* that he identifies with orange (the material structure that, as it happens, realizes a certain experience-involving functional role) that secures the truth of (8) and (9). Instead, and as usual, McLaughlin believes that that *res* has its status as binary and its location in the similarity network between colors only because of the contingent relations it bears to particular experiences. However, McLaughlin wants to suggest, (8) and (9) express true necessities relative to a *de dicto* reading.

To appreciate McLaughlin's suggestion, it may help to consider the following analogy. On the one hand, it is false of the *res* who happens to be the shortest spy in the universe that necessarily she is a spy. On the other, the modal sentence (10) has a true *de dicto* reading where the individual in question is specifically conceived of as the shortest spy in the universe — or, in terms of scope, where the description is given narrow scope relative to the modal operator:

(10) Necessarily the shortest spy in the universe is a spy.

Likewise, then, McLaughlin contends, (8) and (9) may be false relative to a *de re* reading, but are true relative to a *de dicto* reading where the *res* in question (some material structure) is specifically conceived of as the realizer of an experience-involving functional role — or, in terms of scope, where the role-description with which 'orange' is allegedly synonymous is given narrow scope relative to the modal operator.[25]

While this is an ingenious proposal, I now want to suggest (with Pautz (2006*a*, 560ff.)) that it doesn't go far enough. For, by means of a technique of Lewis (1986*b*, 250), the original problem about (8) and (9) can be restated using modal sentences to which the proposed solution is inapplicable. To see this, suppose we are engaged in a discourse in which it is clear that the topic under discussion is the color orange. In the midst of this discourse framework, suppose I utter these sentences:

[25] One might object to this solution by noting that, even if it provides a true reading of the target necessities, it predicts that there should also be a false, *de re* reading of (8) and (9). But those who think (8) and (9) are obviously true might allege that there is *no* available reading that makes (8) and (9) come out false. McLaughlin might defend his proposal against this objection by suggesting that the expected false readings are absent because, for the kinds of modal sentences at issue, *de dicto* readings are obligatory. One way of explaining this, relying on the scope construal of the *de re/de dicto* distinction, would be to say that color terms with descriptive content mandatorily take narrow scope when embedded inside modal operators. (This move is analogous to Dummett's suggestion that names with descriptive content under modal operators always take wide scope (Dummett, 1981).)

(11) Necessarily it is a binary color.

(12) Necessarily it is more similar to red than to green.

It seems to me that our confidence in (11) and (12) will be exactly the same as our confidence in (8) and (9); if we are taking (8) and (9) to be true, then, we should say the same about (11) and (12). However, the solution McLaughlin offered to explain the truth of (8) and (9) is unavailable here, since there is no color term under the scope of a modal operator in (11) and (12); rather, in these sentences, there is only a bare (anaphoric) pronoun that lacks descriptive content. Given that this is so, even if we accept McLaughlin's contention that color terms are synonymous with descriptions, there is no linguistic *dictum* under which to conceive of the relevant *res* or that can take narrow scope with respect to a modal operator in the sentences (11) and (12). Therefore, the only reading available for (11) and (12) should be the *de re* reading — the reading that, as we have seen, realizer functionalists must predict is either unavailable or false. But since (11) and (12) seem both meaningful and no less true than (8) and (9), this prediction is at odds with the data. And, indeed, given the similarity between the cases, the failure of this realizer functionalist strategy with respect to (11) and (12) gives us reason to doubt it as an explanation of (8) and (9). I take all this to show that the *prima facie* difficulty posed by (8) and (9) for realizer functionalism stands: realizer functionalism seems unable to capture what many have taken to be essential features of the colors, as expressed by modal sentences such as (8) and (9).

In contrast, it is worth noting that role functionalism predicts that these and other ascriptions to colors of a necessary unique/binary status and a necessary location in a similarity network are true.[26] The role properties that realizer functionalists and role functionalists take to be associated with colors constitutively involve the manifesting experiences that subjects undergo when perceiving the colors. And since role functionalists identify colors with those role properties, they will claim that the connection between colors and the color experiences that are constitutively involved in those role properties is *de re* necessary.[27] Moreover, significantly, role functionalists will say that *both* 'orange' in (8)–(9) and 'it' in (11)–(12) designate the very same role property that constitutively involves a manifesting experience for that color. This is because, for the role functionalist, the connection at issue here is one between a *res* and

[26] This should motivate the adoption of role functionalism among those who accept (8)–(11). On the other hand, this prediction should not be objectionable to those who, like me, are agnostic about such modal claims and are willing to take predictions about their truth or falsity as spoils to the victor; see note 24.

[27] Johnston makes a version this point (as a way of enumerating the attractions of dispositionalism) when he notes that,

> ...if teal is essentially the disposition to manifest a certain appearance Te and turquoise is essentially the disposition to manifest the appearance Tq then teal and turquoise will be essentially ...similar if these two manifestations are similar (Johnston, 1992, 240).

All of this applies, *mutatis mutandis*, to role functionalism about color as well.

an experience that is part of its constitution, not between a *res* under a particular linguistic or conceptual guise and some contingently associated experience. This is just to say that, for the role functionalist, all of (8)–(9) and (11)–(12) should be true relative to a *de re* reading (as well as a *de dicto* reading if one is available).

Thus, realizer functionalism predicts about the necessities under discussion that they are false, whereas role functionalism predicts that they are true. To the extent that intuition supports the view that they are true, it thereby gives us yet another reason for preferring role functionalism over realizer functionalism about color.

7.2.4 *The Argument from Rigidity*

A final class of arguments that I believe supports role functionalism over realizer functionalism centers on the question of whether color terms designate rigidly. As we have spelled out the two views above, role and realizer functionalists agree that the functional role relevant to determination of the reference of color terms is that of disposing their bearers to look colored. Moreover, proponents of the two views will agree that those color roles are multiply realized across worlds (and for that matter within worlds). Consequently, and again given the above characterization of the two positions, these theorists will then disagree about whether this interworld variation affects the referents of color terms. For role functionalists will hold that color terms refer to the roles, which are themselves stable across worlds, even though their realizers shift across worlds, and so conclude that the references of color terms are modally stable, or rigid. (Analogy: the condition of being the shortest spy doesn't change into some other condition when we evaluate it with respect to a different world, although the individual that satisfies that condition will vary as a function of the world with respect to which the condition is evaluated.) In contrast, realizer functionalists will hold the referents of color terms are identical with the modally unstable realizers of the modally stable color roles. Therefore, they will conclude that color terms vary in reference between worlds — which is just to say that, for realizer functionalists, color terms refer non-rigidly.

To put the matter slightly differently, while both role and realizer functionalists accept the interworld variation in the satisfaction of the color role properties, role functionalists locate the variation in the realization relation rather than the reference relation, while realizer functionalists make the opposite choice. And this leads role functionalists to hold that color terms are rigid designators, while realizer functionalists hold that color terms are non-rigid designators.

Now, I will offer a series of arguments below that are intended to show that color terms designate rigidly. *Prima facie*, this gives a further reason to accept role rather than realizer functionalism. Unfortunately, matters are not quite so simple. For it is not that hard to imagine that, in response to such considerations, a realizer functionalist might propose a slightly modified "rigidified" version of her account — one according to which color terms refer to whatever properties *actually* realize the subject-involving functional roles of disposing their bearers to look colored.[28] Since rigidified realizer functionalism entails that color terms designate rigidly, it escapes some of the difficulties raised for the unrigidified form of realizer functionalism below. Unfortunately, however, it seems to me that at least some of the arguments I'll discuss make trouble for rigidified realizer functionalism as well. Therefore, I'll conclude, these arguments can be used to rule out both rigidified and unrigidified realizer functionalism.

To begin, then, let us put aside rigidified realizer functionalism, and just ask whether we should accept the proposition, entailed by unrigidified realizer functionalism, that color terms designate non-rigidly. I shall argue that we should not. (Here again I am agreeing with Pautz (2006*a*, 559–560).)

One initial motivation for this conclusion comes from the by-now widely accepted thesis that names (and, for that matter, most designating expressions other than descriptions) designate rigidly rather than nonrigidly (Kripke, 1980; Neale, 1993). This is relevant because the terms under discussion have often been thought by both role and realizer functionalists to be *names* — or, at least, not descriptions — of colors. If this is true, and assuming what is generally thought to be true about names and other designating expressions other than descriptions, it would be quite surprising if it turned out that color terms designated nonrigidly.[29] While this consideration is only as strong as the (widely accepted) assumptions on which it is based, it seems to me that it gives at least an initial advantage to role functionalism.

However, I think this initial advantage can be made much more compelling by consideration of variants of the famous modal, epistemic, and semantic arguments initially pressed against descriptive theories of reference for names by Kripke (1980); these variant arguments will all contribute to the case against the claim that colors terms designate non-rigidly, and so against realizer functionalism.

We can begin with the modal version of the argument for the rigidity of color terms. The guiding idea behind this argument is just that standard modal tests for rigidity — tests that deliver the correct verdicts about uncontroversial cases such as proper names and (unrigidified) definite descriptions — appear to show that color terms are rigid as well. Let it be that an expression is rigid iff it designates the very same individual in all worlds in which it designates at all.

[28] In fact, some defenders of realizer functionalism have held neither the rigidified nor the unrigidified form of the view: in particular, McLaughlin (2003*a*, 485) and Jackson (1996) have claimed that color terms are ambiguous between the meanings given by the rigidified and non-rigidified descriptions. But if the arguments of this section work at all, then they give us reason for thinking that color terms can *never* have the meanings of the non-rigid descriptions. Accordingly, I think there is very little to be gained (with respect to these arguments) from moving to the hybrid position advocated by McLaughlin and Jackson, and so will ignore it in what follows.

[29] For what it is worth, Kripke himself takes the view that color terms designate rigidly (Kripke, 1980, 140, note 71), although of course he does not endorse role functionalism about color.

Then a rough operational test for the rigidity of an expression $\ulcorner e \urcorner$ comes from asking whether the sentences obtained by replacing ϕ with $\ulcorner e \urcorner$ in schemata (13) and (14) are true.

(13) the actual ϕ might not have been ϕ.

(14) something other than the actual ϕ might have been ϕ.

If $\ulcorner e \urcorner$ is rigid, then the sentence resulting from substituting $\ulcorner e \urcorner$ into (13) should be false (because the individual designated by $\ulcorner$the actual $e\urcorner$ = the individual designated by $\ulcorner e \urcorner$ with respect to any possible world at all). Whereas, if $\ulcorner e \urcorner$ is nonrigid, then the sentence resulting from substituting $\ulcorner e \urcorner$ into (13) should be true (because the embedded clause $\ulcorner$the actual e is not $e\urcorner$ is true with respect to any world in which the individual designated by $\ulcorner e \urcorner$ is distinct from the individual designated by $\ulcorner$the actual $e\urcorner$). Correlatively, if an expression $\ulcorner e \urcorner$ is nonrigid, then the sentence obtained by substituting $\ulcorner e \urcorner$ into (14) should be true (because the embedded sentence $\ulcorner$something other than $e \neq$ the actual $e\urcorner$ is true with respect to any world in which the individual designated by $\ulcorner e \urcorner$ is distinct from the individual designated by $\ulcorner$the actual $e\urcorner$). And if $\ulcorner e \urcorner$ is rigid, then the sentence resulting from the substitution of $\ulcorner e \urcorner$ into (14) should be false (because the individual designated by $\ulcorner$the actual $e\urcorner$ = the individual designated by $\ulcorner e \urcorner$ with respect to any possible world at all).

The propriety of these intuitive operational tests is confirmed by their agreeing with the standard judgments that 'the winner of the 1968 US presidential election' is non-rigid (because (15)–(16) are true), while 'Nixon' is rigid (because (17)–(18) are false):

(15) The actual winner of the 1968 US presidential election might not have been the winner of the 1968 US presidential election. (true)

(16) Something other than the actual winner of the 1968 US presidential election might have been the winner of the 1968 US presidential election. (true)

(17) (The actual) Nixon might not have been Nixon. (false)

(18) Something other than (the actual) Nixon might have been Nixon. (false)

What happens when we apply these operational tests — which, as we have seen, deliver the standard verdicts about standard examples — to color terms? It appears that (19) and (20) are false, and so pattern with (17)–(18), rather than (15)–(16):

(19) (The actual) red might not have been red. (false)

(20) Something other than (the actual) red might have been red. (false)[30]

[30] Realizer functionalists such as McLaughlin (2003*b*, 484–485) have sometimes heroically accepted these entailments (cf. McLaughlin (2003*a*, §6); similarly, Lewis (1980, 125) accepts the analogous conclusion that there is a true reading of 'pain might not have been pain'). All I can say is that I find these results highly counterintuitive.

Because these tests reveal color terms to function semantically like canonical rigid designators rather than canonical nonrigid designators in the relevant ways, they provide evidence that color terms also designate rigidly.

Indeed, there is a related consequence that brings out the difficulty for treating color terms as nonrigid designators even more starkly. We have just seen that, because realizer functionalists hold that color terms refer non-rigidly to the realizer properties, and because the realizer of (as it might be) the role associated with red is something that its actual realizer might have failed to realize, their theory leads to the prediction that (19) is true. But presumably it is also true that the (actual) realizer of the red role might have failed to realize the functional role associated with green, the functional role associated with blue, and the functional role associated with yellow. Therefore, since the possibility of the actual realizer's failing to satisfy the functional role associated with red leads realizer functionalists to endorse (19), exactly analogous reasoning should commit realizer functionalists to (21), (22), and (23):

(21) (The actual) red might not have been green.

(22) (The actual) red might not have been blue.

(23) (The actual) red might not have been yellow.

(24) (The actual) red might not have been n.

In fact, this pattern clearly generalizes: presumably it is true of the actual realizer of the red role that it might have failed to realize *any* of the functional roles associated with any color. Consequently, the realizer functionalist should endorse every substitution instance of (24) obtained by replacing its occurrence of $\ulcorner n \urcorner$ by the name of a color. And since realizer functionalists are committed to the conjunction of all of these substitution instances, they should likewise be committed to (25), which is entailed by that conjunction:

(25) Red might not have been a color.

But (25) is deeply implausible; indeed, the negation of (25) (or its variants) is arguably among the most historically popular candidates for a non-logical analyticity. That realizer functionalism runs so decisively against this longstanding philosophical current gives us a strong reason for doubting its correctness.[31]

I turn now to an epistemic argument (again modeled on a well-known argument Kripke (1980) uses against the description theory of reference) in favor of the rigidity of color terms. Kripke's famous epistemic argument is strikingly simple. He points out that, if the name 'Aristotle' designates nonrigidly whatever entity best satisfies an allegedly reference-constitutive cluster of descriptive conditions, then sentences attributing elements of that descriptive cluster to the bearer of the name, such as (26), should be *a priori*.

[31] This argument mirrors Kripke's accusation that, if pain is a non-rigid designator of a realizer property, then it follows that pain — this very quality — might not have played the pain-role or the role associated with any relevant mental state, and so (absurdly, he thinks) might not have been a mental state (Kripke, 1980).

(26) If Aristotle exists then he was teacher of Alexander.

Alas, Kripke points out, this prediction seems incorrect: (26), and indeed any similar sentence attributing descriptive conditions to the bearer of the name, must be confirmed or disconfirmed on the strength of *a posteriori* historical inquiry rather than *a priori* reflection. Many have followed Kripke in taking this result to tell against the idea that the name nonrigidly designates the best satisfier of a cluster of descriptions.

Once we recognize, however, that the property of realizing a certain functional role is simply a special kind of descriptive condition that an entity might satisfy or fail to satisfy, then it becomes apparent that an argument exactly analogous to the one we've just reviewed can be used against the realizer functionalist's claim that 'red' nonrigidly designates whatever best occupies a particular functional role. For if, *per* (un-rigidified) realizer functionalism, 'red' designates nonrigidly whatever entity satisfies the allegedly reference-constitutive description of being the property that realizes the red role, then (27), which attributes to the bearer of 'red' the property of realizing the red role, should be *a priori*.

(27) If red exists then it realizes the role of disposing its bearers to look red.

Alas, this prediction seems incorrect. After all, as noted in §1.1, some color irrealists hold that red and other colors are among the properties that exist, but are actually unexemplified, even though certain actual objects do have the dispositions to look red. Since these irrealists hold that actual objects have the dispositions to look red without also exemplifying the (on their view, extant) property *red*, then they must claim either that no property realizes the dispositions in question in those actual objects, or that some property other than *red* realizes the dispositions in question in those actual objects, contrary to (27). Therefore, if (27) were indeed *a priori*, then the sort of color irrealism under consideration would be (not simply erroneous, but) a trivial, *a priori*, falsehood. Of course, I am inclined to reject this form of color irrealism; but the position does not appear to be a trivial, *a priori* falsehood. This, it seems to me, gives us another reason for thinking that realizer functionalism about color has gone wrong.[32]

[32] Objection (*ad hominem*): The form of role functionalism advocated in the present book is vulnerable to a variant of this objection. For I argue in §8.1 that, on the best (functionalist) theory of dispositions, dispositions to look colored are just identical to the role properties, and so, given my role functionalism, identical to the colors. But if so, then it follows that objects could not have their dispositions to look colored and yet fail to be colored, as per the kind of color irrealism we are discussing (cf. Tye, 2000, 169).

Response: First, notice that the objection now pressed against role functionalism is not quite parallel to the objection against role functionalism in the main text, and indeed that a parallel objection can't be generated. The objection against realizer functionalism works by finding a descriptive condition (viz., the realization of a certain role) whose satisfaction by an entity the realizer functionalist takes to be necessary and sufficient for 'red' to refer to that entity, and then forming a sentence (viz., (27)) that predicates that very descriptive condition of the subject term 'red'. Since satisfying the descriptive condition attributed by the sentence formed in this way

Finally, I'll turn to ways in which the semantic arguments Kripke (1980) uses against the description theory of reference can be turned against realizer functionalism about color. As I read them, Kripke's semantic arguments are empirical: they claim that, as a matter of empirical fact (to be tested against the data of native speaker judgments) the entities we would refer to by our uses of names in respect to certain controlled (often imagined) cases are *not* the best satisfiers of the cluster of associated descriptions. In particular, Kripke contends that as a matter of empirical fact (i) we manage to refer with the name in imagined cases where the cluster of descriptions is best satisfied by no one at all (Kripke's Jonah case), (ii) we manage to refer to a single determinate individual with the name in imagined cases where the cluster singles out more than one individual (Kripke's Feynman case), and (iii) we manage to refer to one individual by using the name even in imagined cases where the cluster singles out an entirely different individual (Kripke's Gödel case). These arguments are, of course, old news, and I am siding with an extremely widespread consensus in saying that I take them to comprise a persuasive indictment of the description theory of reference.

But it seems to me that there are equally persuasive variants of these arguments that tell against realizer functionalism about color. The key to extending Kripke's semantic arguments in this direction lies in an observation we've already made: having a certain functional role is just another descriptive feature that an entity may or may not exhibit. Therefore, all we have to do to apply Kripke's semantic arguments to the case at hand is to fix as the relevant descriptive cluster the having of the relevant functional role — in the case at hand, this is the functional role of disposing its bearers to look red. Then we can consider what 'red' denotes under imagined conditions where (i) nothing

is, according to realizer functionalists, reference-constitutive for 'red', the realizer functionalist is committed to holding that the sentence is *a priori*. But because role functionalists explain the reference of color terms in a quite different way, this procedure cannot be extended to their view. Role functionalists hold that 'red' refers rigidly to a certain role property — not (non-rigidly) to whatever entity happens to satisfy some descriptive condition. Consequently, there is no sentence corresponding to (27) that is formed in terms of such a descriptive condition, and that the role functionalist is committed to treating as *a priori*.

That said, it is true that role functionalism conflicts with the contemplated form of color irrealism in another way. For, given role functionalism and the functionalist theory of dispositions, it does indeed follow that objects could not have their dispositions to look colored and yet fail to be colored. Thus, I hold that the version of irrealism that says that objects could have those dispositions and yet fail to be colored is necessarily false. I take that view to be conceivably true, however, in just the sense that ⌜water $\neq$ H_2O⌝ is conceivably true. Namely, while (given role functionalism about color and the functionalist theory of dispositions) there is no possible world where things have their dispositions to look colored and fail to be colored, there are possible worlds where things have distinct properties that are "superficially" like their dispositions to look colored and yet fail to be colored (for example, worlds in which objects have "bare dispositions" to look colored, which won't amount to dispositions to look colored — or, therefore, colors — given the functionalist theory of dispositions). Moreover, I take the falsity of the kind of color irrealism under consideration to be *a posteriori*, since (as I have emphasized throughout) my case for color functionalism is broadly empirical.

fills this functional role, where (ii) multiple things fill this functional role, or (iii) the wrong things fill this functional role.

For example, we can consider as actual (i) a circumstance in which color irrealism is true, and therefore in which nothing exemplifies any color role. Since realizer functionalists hold that 'red' designates non-rigidly whatever fills the functional role, their view predicts that in such a circumstance 'red' designates nothing (*mutatis mutandis* for other color terms). But this prediction seems incorrect: rather, it seems more plausible to say of the envisaged scenario that 'red' designates an unexemplified but nonetheless *bona fide* property that things look to have but do not. To its credit, role functionalism supports exactly this more plausible diagnosis; for in the envisioned circumstance the role property exists, but is, by hypothesis, unexemplified. Thus, where realizer functionalists must describe the envisaged circumstance as one in which color terms fail to designate at all, role functionalists will offer the alternative (and, to my mind, more plausible) description of the scenario as one in which color terms designate unexemplified properties.

Consider now as actual (ii) a circumstance in which a variety of physically distinct structural types realize the functional role associated with 'red'. As noted in §7.2.2, realizer functionalists have clearly been (appropriately, in my view) worried about this sort of circumstance, and have typically formulated their position as requiring that the referents of color terms are not "excessively disjunctive" (Jackson (1998*a*, 108); McLaughlin (2003*b*, 479)). Moreover, Jackson and McLaughlin in particular have explicitly predicted that, if the structures in question are "excessively" disjunctive (whatever that means), then color terms would fail to designate. But this prediction strikes me as implausible once again; even if the functional role were satisfied by a very large range of disjuncts, I suggest that 'red' would designate nonetheless. (Indeed, I suggest that the envisaged scenario is actual, and take our apparently designative uses of color terms as actual, rather than merely imagined, counterevidence to the realizer functionalist's semantic predictions.) Of course, and as we have seen, role functionalism has no trouble accommodating any amount of intra-world variation between the realizers of color roles. In particular, multiple realization of the role property does not threaten to show, for role functionalists, that more than one entity is a candidate for designation by any color term — it does not threaten to make the role properties identified with colors by role functionalists at all (let alone "excessively") disjunctive. Consequently, whereas realizer functionalists must predict that color terms would fail to designate in the envisaged scenario, role functionalists will predict that color terms designate in the normal way. Here, too, I believe semantic intuition is on the side of role rather than realizer functionalism.

Finally, we can consider as actual (iii) a circumstance in which what is intuitively the wrong entity ends up satisfying the relevant functional role. We can, for example, consider as actual a circumstance in which, for some bizarre reason, what realizes the role of disposing its bearers to look red is *triangularity*.

If realizer functionalists are right in holding that 'red' designates nonrigidly whatever satisfies the latter functional role, then in the envisaged circumstance 'red' designates *triangularity*. And if so, then (28)–(29) make true predications about *triangularity*.

(28) Red is a shape property.

(29) Red is a property that entails trilaterality.

Yet again, this strikes me as an incorrect set of semantic predictions. Rather, it seems to me that, even in the envisaged (admittedly very odd) circumstance, (28)–(29) make false predications about *red* — which is to say that they make predications about something that is not a shape property, and that does not entail trilaterality, *a fortiori*, about something distinct from *triangularity*. And, of course, role functionalism allows us to say just this; for, in virtue of its commitment to holding that 'red' rigidly designates the role property, the view predicts that (28)–(29) make predications (as it happens, false predications) about that role property even with respect to the odd imagined circumstance. Here again, therefore, it seems to me that realizer functionalism makes false predictions about the semantic properties of color terms that are clearly avoided by role functionalism.

Summing up, it appears that versions of Kripke's modal, epistemic, and semantic arguments tell against the (non-rigidified) realizer functionalist's thesis that color terms designate non-rigidly, and in favor of the role functionalist's thesis that color terms designate rigidly. However, as I indicated earlier in this section, there is a way in which a realizer functionalist might attempt to accommodate this conclusion: she might claim that, contrary to the initial formulation of the position above, the color roles used to fix the reference of color terms should be rigidified. Thus, for example, a realizer functionalist might hold that 'red (for S in C)' designates whatever property actually realizes the functional role of disposing its bearers to look red to S in C.[33] The realizers of these rigidified color roles are modally stable, where the realizers of the unrigidified roles are not. (Compare: the satisfier of 'the actual shortest spy in the universe' does not vary between worlds, although the satisfier of 'the shortest spy in the universe' does vary between worlds). Consequently, this modified version of realizer functionalism (*rigidified realizer functionalism*) entails that color terms designate rigidly rather than non-rigidly, and so escapes many of the problems raised in this section for the claim that color terms designate non-rigidly.

[33] A notational variant would put the rigidifier inside the specification of the functional roles; on this variant, color terms refer to whatever properties realize the subject-involving functional roles of *actually* disposing their bearers to look colored. Since I don't see that the difference between these two formulations affects anything I want to say about rigidified realizer functionalism, I'll simply work with the formulation in the main text for convenience.

Unfortunately, however, it seems to me that slight variants of at least some of the arguments presented above tell equally against rigidified realizer functionalism.

For example, above I urged against unrigidified realizer functionalism that, because it makes (27) *a priori*, it wrongly entails the *a priori*/trivial falsity of the view irrealist view that things have the dispositions to look red but fail to be red. But a version of this difficulty can be raised against the rigidified realizer functionalist as well. For the rigidified realizer functionalist is committed to holding that (27′) is *a priori*:

(27′) If red exists then it actually realizes the role of disposing its bearers to look red.

And, just as is the case with (27), the *a priority* of (27′) would wrongly entail the *a priori*/trivial falsity of the irrealist view that actual things have the dispositions to look red and yet fail to be red.

A second problem raised above for unrigidified realizer functionalism but that applies also to rigidified realizer functionalism concerns the worry that the color roles might be realized by a plurality of physically distinct structural configuration types. We saw above that unrigidified realizer functionalists are inappropriately committed to holding that color terms would fail to designate in scenarios under which the unrigidified color roles were realized disjunctively. But an exactly parallel problem arises for the rigidified realizer functionalist if, as the empirical evidence suggests, a variety of physically distinct structural types realize the rigidified role of actually disposing its bearers to look red. If this scenario is actual (which we have empirical reason to believe), then the rigidified realizer functionalist is committed to holding that color terms fail to designate. Again, this seems (at least, to me) an incorrect description of the scenario.

Thus, the move to rigidification does not save the realizer functionalist from all of the troubles raised above for unrigidified realizer functionalism. Moreover, of course, the arguments from commonality and necessity (§§7.2.2–7.2.3) are applicable to both rigidified and unrigidified forms of realizer functionalism. I conclude, then, that both rigidified and unrigidified forms of realizer functionalism are ultimately unacceptable. If we aspire to understand color properties in the terms made available by any kind of functionalism, it is role, rather than realizer, functionalism that offers the most promising path forward.

7.3 Role Functionalism and Causation

So far in this chapter I have laid out the role functionalist account of color properties, and have argued that role functionalism holds advantages over the related realizer functionalist view. Powerful though these motivations are, I suspect that many will nonetheless be resistant to role functionalism about color because of a cluster of objections concerning causation. These objections are important not only because they will be counted by some as balancing against the case in favor of role functionalism I have presented so far, but also because they are, arguably, the most serious potential threat to role functionalism in particular — as opposed to threats that stand in the way of color relationalism more generally speaking.

The set of concerns I have in mind is familiar from discussions of functionalist theories in other areas in philosophy (e.g., functionalist theories of mental states, content, properties, laws, etc.), but has been pressed with special force in recent writings about color by Jackson and Pargetter (1987), Jackson (1996, 1998*a*), McLaughlin (2003*a*,*b*), and Shoemaker (1990). All of these writers cite worries about causation as their reasons for giving up role functionalist (or dispositionalist) theories of color, and proceed on this basis to advocate alternative accounts. Because causal worries have been seen by so many as so devastating against role functionalism, it is especially important for role functionalists to defend their view against those worries. In what follows I'll do just that.[34]

7.3.1 *Can Role Properties Be Causes?*

The objections in question stem from the pre-theoretical idea that colors cause their bearers to look colored to subjects, and so must be causally efficacious. While this idea is plausible and widely held by color realists of all sorts, role functionalists have a special reason to endorse it: their theory is one that takes colors to be constituted precisely by a role that is built from causal effects on subjects. But many have argued that functional roles cannot have this sort of causal efficacy, hence are unsuitable candidates for identification with colors. This, of course, would mean that role functionalism about color is an untenable position.

Why, then, might one believe that functional roles cannot do the relevant causal work?[35]

One prominent motivation comes from the idea that functional role properties are constituted in terms of, hence necessarily connected to, the range of effects in terms of which the relevant functional role is spelled out.[36] That functional roles are this tightly connected with the relevant effects has been thought by some to cut against their causing those effects. For example, I take it that the force of Molière's famous jape at the Aristotelians in *Le Malade Imaginaire* is that, since the effect of inducing sleep is intimately but trivially, necessarily bound up with the concept of a *virtus dormitiva*, the latter is not an appropriate candidate for being the cause of that effect. Generalizing, the

[34] My defense of role functionalism from causal worries in this section overlaps with material from Cohen (2005).

[35] Significantly, neither of the reasons I shall discuss below depends on thinking that functional roles must be entirely causally impotent; rather both reasons are alleged to show that even if functional roles are causally efficacious, nonetheless they won't have the particular causal powers that we want to grant to colors.

[36] I find versions of this motivation in the writings of Jackson (1996, 203–204), McLaughlin (2003*b*, 480), and Johnston (1998).

thought goes that properties definitionally — or, at any rate, necessarily — connected to the production of e cannot be causes of e, on pain of (i) violating Humean prohibitions on necessary causes, and (ii) draining the interest from the respectable empirical project of hunting for causes.[37]

This consideration provides a potentially devastating weapon against a wide range of role functionalist accounts in philosophy. For example, Jackson uses this idea to argue against a functional/dispositional theory of *fragility*:

> ...to allow that fragility itself, as opposed to its categorical basis, causes breaking on dropping, would be to allow that there are properties that have causal powers essentially. If fragility does or would do the causing in one world, then it does or would do the causing in any world. In every world the fact of being fragile is intimately connected with the fact of breaking on dropping, and if that intimate connection counts as fragility causing or having the power to cause breaking in any world, it will so count in every world. Clearly, the same goes for functional properties in general — to allow them as causes is to violate a good Humean principle (Jackson (1996), 394; cf. Yablo (1995), 482).

Thus, Jackson invites us to conclude, it must be the categorical basis of the disposition to break, rather than the disposition itself, that causes breaking on dropping.

And, of course, the concern here transfers straightforwardly to role functionalism about color. Role functionalism construes *red for S in C* as the functional role of disposing its bearers to look red to S in C. It therefore ties that color property intimately to its effect on S in C. To count the color property as a cause of that effect, then, is (i) to permit a necessary cause of the effect (in violation of what Jackson says is a "good Humean principle"), and (ii) to drain the (empirical) interest from the apparently respectable question 'what explains why things look red to S in C?'. If, as is widely thought, these are unacceptable consequences, it would seem that we are forced to choose between the causal efficacy of colors on subjects and a role functionalist account of colors.

A second motivation for denying the relevant sort of causal efficacy to functional roles trades on considerations about causal competition and explanatory exclusion.[38] The thought is that every particular exemplification of the functional role will coincide with an exemplification of some or other realizer of that role — a realizer that is numerically distinct from the role property. But, it is argued, only one of these coincidentally exemplified properties can be the cause of the relevant effects on pain of "a curious and ontologically extravagant kind of overdetermination" (Jackson, 1996, 202). However, since it is common ground to all parties that the realizers are *bona fide* causes of the relevant effects, the realizers would seem to render the role properties causally

[37] I wish to remain agnostic about whether this so-called Humean prohibition, as understood here and below, reflects Hume's actual views; I use the label merely out of deference to traditional philosophical nomenclature.

[38] The leading advocate of this argument against role functionalism in philosophy of mind is Jaegwon Kim (1989*a*,*b*, 1993*a*, 1998). The argument has been applied in the literature on color by Jackson and Pargetter (1987), Jackson (1996), and Jackson (1998*a*, ch. 4); cf. Shoemaker (1990, 116).

otiose.[39] Once again, although this motivation for denying the relevant sort of causal efficacy to functional role properties is fairly general, and although its most famous application is to functional role theories in philosophy of mind, it applies directly to the role functionalism about color I have proposed in this chapter by threatening to rob colors of the causal powers that we pre-theoretically recognize them as having.

To my mind, there is little hope (for functionalists or non-functionalists) in denying the pre-theoretical idea that colors cause their bearers to look colored to subjects. Therefore, I need to find a way of defusing the two arguments just given. Below I'll present such a defusing strategy that will begin by finding fault with the causal competition motivation, and then move on to respond to the *virtus dormitiva* motivation. I'll conclude that, for all that has been said, we have good reasons for believing (and no good reasons for disbelieving) that functional roles can indeed be said to cause the effects in terms of which they are adumbrated.

7.3.2 *Explanatory Exclusion and Determination*

The first point to make regarding the worries we are considering is that, as spelled out above, the causal competition motivation is overdrawn: it inappropriately excludes as causes properties having nothing to do with colors or even functional roles. To see this point, consider the following example.

Suppose a bell is set up to ring any time an object over 1000kg in mass is placed on a certain scale. And suppose that when x, which happens to have a mass of 1037kg, is placed on the scale, the bell rings (as expected). What (causally) explains the bell's ringing on that occasion? Answer number one: the event of x's exemplifying the property *being over 1000kg*. Answer number two: the event of x's exemplifying the property *being 1037kg*. Which of our two candidate answers correctly answers our question?

I take it that the best, most pre-theoretically plausible response is that *both* answers are correct: *both* of the mass properties mentioned can be cited in true, felicitous causal explanations of the bell's ringing (relative to an appropriate explanatory context). Inventing a piece of jargon to simplify exposition, we can say that a property is causally relevant to an effect in some explanatory context C if it can be cited in C in a true and felicitous causal explanation of that effect. On this terminology, our pre-theoretically plausible response can be put by saying that *both* of the (numerically distinct) mass properties mentioned can be causally relevant in the single context in which we asked the question.

But this pre-theoretically plausible response is threatened by the considerations about causal competition bruited above. For, just as in the cases discussed above in connection with causal competition, here the particular

[39] Role (and realizer) functionalists have reasons above and beyond the usual ones for insisting that the particular causal potency at issue cannot be withheld from the realizers. Namely, it is presumably required for thinking of the realizers *as realizers* of the role of bringing about the relevant effects that they do causally bring about those effects.

exemplification of one of the candidate properties coincides with the particular exemplification of the other. Thus, if ascribing causal efficacy to both coinciding properties would lead to an unacceptable kind of overdetermination in the earlier cases, it should lead to an unacceptable overdetermination here as well.[40] This suggests strongly that the argument from causal competition, as presented, is (at the very least) in need of qualification. The question that remains is exactly what form the needed qualification should take.

A promising suggestion, due to Yablo (1992), sees the roots of the problem in the relationship between the properties at issue. Returning to the example of the two mass properties, it is crucial that exemplifying *being 1037kg* is one particular way among many of exemplifying *being over 1000kg*. That is, *being 1037kg* is a more specific, hence determinate, version of the less specific, or determinable property *being over 1000kg*. More generally speaking, x's exemplifying the more specific/determinate property determines that x exemplifies the less specific/determinable property: the occurrence of the former event *constitutes* the occurrence of the latter.

This idea turns out to be extremely useful in undercutting the worry about causal competition. We can explain this in one of two ways, depending on the standards for event individuation in force. On a coarse-grained standard (see, for example, the essays in Davidson, 1980), we can say that the exemplification of the determinable *just is* the exemplification of the determinate, hence that there are insufficiently many contestants to engage in a meaningful competition for causal relevance. Given that there is no meaningful competition for causal relevance between the determinate and the determinable, we can explain the difference between explanations citing one or the other of them in this way: the two explanations will differ in their (compatible/non-competing) characterizations of the one event. It follows from this way of thinking about the situation that any property that is used to pick out that one (causally efficacious) event is causally relevant in the explanatory context at hand. Alternatively, on a fine-grained standard for event individuation (cf. Kim, 1976), there will be distinct but closely related events corresponding to the difference between determinable and determinate properties, but these events will be spatio-temporally coincident, and the occurrence of one of them will partially constitute the occurrence of the other. But if the occurrence of the one partially constitutes the occurrence of the other, it will once again seem bizarre to apportion causal relevance to one (say, the determinate) at the expense of the other (say, the determinable).

Yablo's proposal, then, is that determinables and their determinates *do not* compete for causal relevance: since the having of the one constitutes the having

[40] Lest it seem that the worry is restricted to artificial cases of little interest, a number of writers have emphasized that the argument from causal competition would seem to threaten the possibility of causal explanation in terms of the kinds of special sciences quite generally speaking (Fodor (1989, 138–141); van Gulick (1992, 325); Baker (1993, 77); Burge (1993, 102); but see Kim (1997) and Kim (1998, 77–87, 112–120)).

of the other, which of them is cited in a causal explanation is a matter of choice of how general or specific do we want to be given the communicative and explanatory needs at hand. There is not, for such pairs of properties, a zero-sum choice between mutually exclusive candidates for a particular causal job. Consequently, far from competing against each other for causal relevance, determinates and their determinables work together to achieve a kind of non-competitive efficacy — the causal relevance of the one is not precluded by, but is *constituted by* the causal relevance of the other.

7.3.3 *Explanatory Exclusion and Partial Determination*

This idea seems a promising avenue of response to the problem of causal competition; it shows how and why according causal relevance to *being 1037kg* is not incompatible with according causal relevance to *being over 1000kg* (which is, of course, exactly what we wanted to say). Yablo (1992) argues, ingeniously, that this idea can be used to secure compatible causal relevance not only for paradigm determinable/determinate pairs (e.g., *being over 1000kg/being 1037kg, being red/being scarlet*) but for mental properties and their physical realizers, in so far as the latter can be understood as standing in the determinable/determinate relation as well.

Unfortunately, however, this idea is not directly applicable to property pairs that stand in the role/realizer relation, which is the sort of pair that create problems for a role functionalist. This is because it is crucial to the application of Yablo's strategy to our two mass properties that those properties stand in the relation of metaphysical determination. In order to apply this solution for getting around the problem of explanatory exclusion, we need something like a metaphysical guarantee that the exemplification of the determinate is not a competitor to, but instead something that constitutes, the exemplification of the determinable. This guarantee is underwritten, in the case of the mass properties, by their standing in the relation of metaphysical determination. But things are otherwise with role/realizer pairs. For example, it's not metaphysically necessary (*de re*) that being a realizer of the red-for-*S*-in-*C* role comes with (much less constitutes) exemplifying the red-for-*S*-in-*C* role; whether instances of this realizer property are instances of this role depend on metaphysical contingencies such as the laws of nature, the nature of surfaces (volumes, light sources, films, etc.), and the nature of visual systems.

However, I want to suggest that there is a way of extending Yablo's idea to role/realizer pairs by finding a relation that does for role/realizer pairs what the determination relation does for determinable/determinate pairs in the context of Yablo's solution. As we have said, it's not metaphysically necessary (*de re*) that being a realizer of the red-for-*S*-in-*C* role comes with exemplifying the red-for-*S*-in-*C* role, in so far as the realizer only plays the role given contingencies about materials, visual systems, and the laws of nature; consequently, the role and realizer properties don't stand in a relation of metaphysical determination. But there is a weaker kind of determination in which they do stand — the relation of determination *relative to certain contingencies* (in the case at hand, the contingencies are contingent truths about materials, visual systems, and laws). In order to distinguish this relation from the stronger sort of metaphysical determination that applies between determinables and their determinates, call the weaker one *partial determination*, or *p-determination* for short. To say that the red-for-S-in-C realizer p-determines the red-for-S-in-C role relative to truths about materials, visual systems, and laws is to say that, holding fixed these contingent truths, it is metaphysically necessary that anything that exemplifies the realizer will exemplify the role. Moreover, and as in the case of the more stringent determination relation between mass properties, this is so not because exemplifying the realizer will cause some further event of exemplifying the role — rather, it is so because, given the contingent truths about materials, visual systems, and laws that we agreed to hold fixed, exemplifying the realizer constitutes one way (possibly among many ways) of exemplifying the role.

Here's a way to put the difference between the two sorts of cases. We need fix no further contingent facts to ensure that an instance of the more specific mass property *being 1037kg* counts as an instance of the less specific mass property *being over 1000kg*; this result follows given only what is metaphysically necessary. In contrast, where there is only p-determination, we must fix contingent facts (here facts about materials, visual systems, and laws) to ensure that an instance of the p-determining property (here the red realizer property) will also be an instance of the p-determined property (here the red role property).

However, importantly, if the further contingent facts relative to which p-determination holds *are* fixed (for whatever reason), then we are warranted in taking an instance of the red realizer property to be an instance of the red role property. And if we have that warrant, then we can say about the role/realizer pair exactly what we had said about the determinable/determinate pair: there is no causal competition between the two in so far as exemplification of the latter member of the pair partially constitutes the exemplification of the former member of the pair. Thus, again on the assumption that we have the needed warrant, we should conclude that causal explanations of e citing the realizer add nothing over causal explanations of e that cite the role except greater specificity; in particular, they don't add a second event that would then be a competitor for the title of causal relevance.

Of course, to repeat, all of the benefits discussed accrue only if we are warranted in fixing the relevant further contingencies — in our case, facts about materials, visual systems, and laws. Luckily, however, we often *are* warranted in fixing those facts. When we are engaged in giving causal explanations, it is often (though not universally) true that the explanatory context is one in which these and many other contingencies are taken for granted.

What falls out of all this, then, is that what's needed to extend the Yablo strategy to the role/realizer case is much weaker than full metaphysical determination: it is only that the target pair should hang together in the sense that x's having one constitutes x's having the other (without creating further events that would then be competitors for causal relevance). And for this, p-determination will suffice if (as is in fact frequently true) the additional constraints relative to which the first p-determines the second are presupposed in the explanatory context. This explains how the red-for-S-in-C role property and red-for-S-in-C realizer property can both be causally relevant. Since the realizer property p-determines the role property relative to certain contingencies about materials, visual systems, and laws, explanations given in contexts presupposing those contingencies that cite the realizer property won't block explanations that cite the role property. Hence, the causal relevance of the realizer property (relative to such contexts) won't be any obstacle to the causal relevance of the role property (relative to such contexts).

7.3.4 *Causal Relevance and Causation*

That realizer and role properties can be non-competitively causally relevant (in certain contexts) is, I think, an important insight that goes some distance toward resolving the role functionalist's difficulties. However, it might reasonably be thought that this falls short of what we need to respond fully to the problem about causal competition. For the difficulty we are facing is that realizer properties and role properties could not both be *causes* of the effects of interest — not that they could not both be *causally relevant* to those effects. We had said that a property P is causally relevant to an effect e (in a context C) just in case P can be cited in a true and felicitous explanation of e (given in C). But since this account leaves open that a property could be causally relevant to e (in C) without being a cause of e, the finding that roles and realizers can both be causally relevant to e (in C) leaves open the possibility that according causal efficacy in bringing about e to the realizer is incompatible with according causal efficacy in bringing about e to the role property.[41] In short, even if what we have said is sufficient to dispatch worries about competition between roles and realizers occurring at the level of *causal relevance* (understood as above), worries about competition between the two may resurface at the level of causation.

Now, many will find this suggested reason for remaining worried about causal competition unpersuasive. For one thing, the concern that exclusion could obtain at the level of causation even if it doesn't obtain at the level of causal relevance presupposes that the causal relation is something more metaphysically basic than, something less rooted in our explanatory practice,

[41] One reason for thinking that a property could be causally relevant to e (in C) without being a cause of e would involve the claim that, whereas causal explanations are (like other explanations) plausibly sensitive to contextual features of the communicative settings in which they occur, causation itself is not. Consequently, one might go on to say, causal relevance will be a much less discerning relation than causation — i.e., that the open sentence ⌜x is causally relevant to e⌝ will have satisfiers that are not also satisfiers of the open sentence ⌜x causes e⌝. Of course, this way of developing the point depends crucially on the controversial idea that causation is unlike causal relevance in not being context-sensitive; for dissent, see Schaffer (2005), Northcott (2008), and, on some readings, Lewis (1973).

than causal relevance — and one may well find that presupposition unacceptable (Baker, 1993; Burge, 1993). For another, and as we have noted above, the problem of causal competition (understood at the level of causation rather than causal relevance) has been thought by many to threaten the causal efficacy of all multiply realizable properties, including those that figure centrally in causal explanations in the special sciences; but if so, then arguably the appropriately Moorean reaction would be to reject the argument from causal competition rather than to accept its conclusion.[42]

However, and without taking anything away from these suggestions, there is an even more important reason for denying that role functionalism faces a further problem of causal competition despite having reconciled the causal relevance of roles and realizers: namely, the motivation for the worry about causal competition in the first place is plausibly taken to concern causal relevance as opposed to the causal relation itself (granting, *arguendo* the distinction between the two). To see this, recall that the problem about causal competition arose because (i) we found ourselves wanting to say that colors, whatever they turn out to be, can be cited in causal explanations of why their bearers look colored to subjects, and because (ii) role functionalists in particular found themselves wanting to say that colors are constituted in terms of their causal effects. Crucially, imposing these demands means imposing demands about what we can say. But if that is what we are aiming for, then it is the relation of causal relevance, rather than the causal relation *per se* that will satisfy our needs. For, regarding (i), what it means to find that role properties are causally relevant to their bearers' looking colored to subjects is, precisely, that we *can* truly and felicitously cite those properties in providing explanations in some context of why objects look colored to subjects. Likewise, regarding (ii), finding that role properties are causally relevant to their bearers' looking colored to subjects, and therefore accepting as true and felicitous the invocation of role properties in explaining why objects look colored to subjects, we can then go on to propose (if we so choose) that the role properties of interest are constituted in terms of the effects they causally explain — crucially including the effects of looking colored to subjects.

I am contending, then, that our motivations for ascribing causal efficacy to colors in general and color role properties in particular are agnostic between requiring mere causal relevance and requiring causation. Thus, whether or not there is an important distinction between the two — i.e., whether or not there is a further question about competition at the level of causation as opposed to causal relevance — the finding that role properties can be causally relevant is sufficient to answer our motivations, and to give us all the causal power we need.[43]

[42] Indeed, the problem generalizes to *all* properties if one holds that properties are constituted by their causal powers.

[43] If it turns out that causation is a more selective relation than causal relevance, then presumably causal relevance is a derivative relation constituted somehow in terms of causation. If so, then what

7.3.5 *Virtus Dormitiva*

What has been said so far leaves unanswered the *virtus dormitiva* argument against according causal powers to functional roles properties. Now I wish to argue that this objection, too, can be answered by the considerations already on the table.

Recall that the *virtus dormitiva* argument builds on the idea that functional roles are definitionally, hence necessarily, bound up with the effects in terms of which those roles are specified. The thought is that, given both Humean prohibitions against necessary causes and our desire to preserve the scientific interest in the project of searching for causes, this fact shows that role properties can't be causally relevant. I want to suggest that the motivations undergirding this argument are incorrect — that, given the story about causal relevance I have developed, functional role properties *can* be causally relevant after all.

Why, then, should we accept that functional role properties can be causally relevant? Recall that, on the present view, a property is causally relevant to an effect with respect to an explanatory context C just in case that property can be cited in a true and felicitous explanation (given in C) of that effect. Consider, as an uncontroversial example of a functional role property the sleeping potion's property of having a *virtus dormitiva*; moreover, grant that this property is necessarily connected to the effect of inducing sleep. But surely there are contexts with respect to which the functional role property is causally relevant to this effect. For instance, there are contexts in which there is an alternative suggested explanation of the potion's effect according to which magicians cast a sleeping spell on someone who ingests the sleeping potion (or, for that matter, on all and only those who ingest the sleeping potion); in that sort of context, citing the *virtus dormitiva* of the potion excludes a live rival explanation, and thereby tells us something we might genuinely want to know. And to say this is just to admit that, relative to the (admittedly contrived) context described, the sleeping potion's *virtus dormitiva* is causally relevant despite being necessarily connected with its effect. Generalizing a bit, this case shows us that even if a property p is definitionally bound up with an effect e, explanations of e that cite p can be informative (hence true and felicitous) in at least this way: they can rule out alternative (i.e., non-p-involving) pathways to e.

Thus, I am prepared to reject the Humean/scientific motivations that have prevented some from according causal relevance to functional role properties. The main such motivation was the desire to preserve the interest of the difficult empirical project of looking for causes: the thought was that, if it sufficed to causally explain the capacity to induce sleep by citing a *virtus dormitiva*, then it is hard to see why anyone would care as much as we manifestly do care about

I've shown is only that functional roles are causally related to their effects in some derivative way. Does this not show that, after all, roles aren't *really* (i.e., non-derivatively) causes? Not unless the intuitions undergirding the need for causality require non-derivative causes. But there is no reason to think that the intuitions come metaphysically marked in that way.

causal explanations.[44] There is the feeling that explanations citing necessary causes would always fail to give us new information, and so would always pale in comparison to the interest of explanations in terms of non-necessary causes.

But what has been said so far allows us to provide a pragmatic re-diagnosis of this feeling without denying causal relevance to role properties. It is true that explanations citing necessary causes may, in some explanatory contexts — perhaps even in many or all of the most proximate explanatory contexts — pale in comparison to the interest of explanations in terms of non-necessary causes. However, this should not be taken to show that explanations citing necessary causes can be true and felicitous relative to *no* explanatory context. Indeed, it does not even show that explanations citing necessary causes fail to be true and felicitous relative to *actual* explanatory contexts; as shown by the example of the potion considered above, whether they are or not will depend on the details of the explanatory context. Rather, what it shows is that there are salient alternative explanations that would be *more* felicitous relative to actual contexts (and perhaps some/many/all nearby non-actual contexts). In short, allowing for the causal relevance of a *virtus dormitiva* allows for the interest of the search for additional causally relevant properties. Indeed, allowing necessary causes that are role properties positively *invites* us to pursue the empirical project of looking for other (non-necessary) causes: for citing a role property as a cause leads naturally to the question of what, as a matter of contingent fact, realizes the relevant role.

If I am right, then, the motivations under consideration do not provide (as they have been taken to provide) metaphysical constraints on the sorts of properties that can be causally relevant. Instead, they provide pragmatic reasons for preferring explanations that cite other sorts of properties in many of the explanatory contexts in which we find ourselves. For all that those motivations tell us, then, there is no reason to deny that role properties are causally relevant.

7.3.6 *Causal Relevance and Profligacy*

One might object to the foregoing on the grounds that the account of causal relevance I have put forward is too permissive — that it allows that all sorts of properties should be causally relevant, and indeed potentially causally efficacious, that are not. For example, this view "makes Brutus's property of being Caesar's killer causally relevant to Caesar's death, and Drano's property

[44] The other motivation discussed consisted mainly in the approving appeal to Hume's prohibition against necessary causes. It is unclear just what (beyond the invocation of a great philosophical figure) lies behind this motivation, and correspondingly it is unclear to what extent this motivation goes beyond that just discussed. In so far as the appeal to Hume is intended as an independent consideration, it is also unclear whether and to what extent it would depend on Hume's (controversial) metaphysics and epistemology. As such, I don't see how I can evaluate the Humean prohibition in any more detail without engaging in speculative and exegetical tasks that would take me well beyond the scope of the present book.

of being plumber-recommended causally relevant to the unclogging of my drain" (Yablo, 1995, note 27).[45]

I am prepared to bite the bullet here, and to acknowledge that the account presented here will recognize as causally relevant many properties that might not have initially seemed that way. However, I take this clash between intuition and my theory of causal relevance not to show that that the theory is incorrect, but rather that the initial intuitions are sensitive to something slightly different from causal relevance. In particular, I propose that intuitions purporting to represent what could be causally relevant *tout court* are in fact intuitions about what is causally relevant with respect to salient explanatory contexts (given our actual epistemic state). It is easy enough to see how we might confuse the latter sort of intuitions for the former — roughly, by neglecting the contribution made to them by the actual epistemic state in which we find ourselves. However, I think it is possible to correct this confusion by explicitly describing a different (possibly remote) explanatory context, and then showing that the kinds of properties under discussion are plausibly causally relevant with respect to this new and different explanatory context.

Thus, for example, it is true that, on the present view, Brutus's property of being Caesar's killer is causally relevant to Caesar's death in some contexts — namely, those contexts in which that property can be cited in a true and felicitous explanation of Caesar's death. And Yablo is surely correct in reporting the presence of an intuition to the effect that this property of Brutus is not causally relevant to Caesar's death. In my view, however, this intuition reflects the thought that, at least in many of the most epistemically proximate explanatory settings, we would want to know more than that true and felicitous explanation could tell us. This is true because, given what we already know about Caesar's death, that explanation doesn't advance our understanding as much as, say, an explanation that cites Brutus's property of having stabbed Caesar (a property that p-determines Brutus's property of killing Caesar). But, again, the causal relevance of this more specific property is no obstacle to the causal relevance of the less specific property with which we began. Moreover, we can show that the less specific property of being Caesar's killer is a candidate for causal relevance (with respect to some context) after all, just as the present account entails, by noting that an explanation citing that property *would* make for a true and felicitous explanation of Caesar's death in a context where it is an epistemically live possibility that Caesar died from, say, an exercise-induced heart-attack.

In short, while it does seem to be true that our initial intuitions are more selective than is my theory of causal relevance, there is reason for believing that those intuitions incorporate additional restrictions that are not strictly to the point — in effect, that they are intuitions about *causal relevance relative to*

[45] Yablo's immediate target here is the so-called program model of causal relevance of Jackson and Pettit (1990).

contexts incorporating our actual epistemic state, rather than intuitions about *causal relevance relative to some or other explanatory context*. It is surprising neither that we are wont to confuse intuitions of the former kind for intuitions of the latter kind, nor that making this confusion would lead to the appearance that a correct account of causal relevance is inappropriately profligate. Consequently, I am inclined to hold on to my account, intuitions of the kind under consideration notwithstanding.

7.4 Conclusion

In this chapter I have presented a role functionalist theory of color — that form of color relationalism that I find most attractive — and explored several of its components and consequences (§7.1). I have also contrasted role functionalism against realizer functionalism about color, and argued that there are a range of reasons for preferring role functionalism over realizer functionalism (§7.2). Moreover, I have defended role functionalism from what I take to be the most important cluster of objections that face this particular brand of relationalism as opposed to others (§7.3).

Taken together, I think these considerations show role functionalism to be a powerful and attractive proposal about the nature of color. But before settling on this view, I want to consider and assess a range of alternative relationalist accounts in Chapter 8. In each case I'll urge that these alternative views come with serious defects. I'll conclude that role functionalism is the most plausible form of color relationalism, hence (in the context of what has been said until this point) the most plausible theory of color overall.

8

ROLE FUNCTIONALISM AND ITS RELATIONALIST RIVALS

While the law [of competition] may be sometimes hard for the individual, it is best for the race, because it ensures the survival of the fittest in every department.

— (Carnegie, 1889, 655).

In order to assess role functionalism, it will be helpful to compare the view against other forms of color relationalism. As we have noted, there are potentially many different forms of color relationalism that differ in exactly how they understand the relations between objects and subjects that (like all forms of relationalism) they take to be constitutive of color properties. Unsurprisingly, I cannot consider every possible form of color relationalism — for I cannot consider every putatively color-constitutive relation between objects and subjects. However, I want to compare role functionalism against its most important relationalist rivals, especially including those that have attracted the most interest in recent philosophical writing about color.

I'll open by considering the most well-known, historically important, and widely discussed of these rivals — color dispositionalism (§8.1). Next I'll turn to the "enactive" (/ecological relationalist) view of Thompson *et al.* (1992) and Thompson (1995) (§8.2), Finally, I'll consider the sensory classificationist view of Matthen (2005) (§8.3). I'll compare the role functionalism of Chapter 7 against each of these other positions with the goal of showing that role functionalism is the most attractive form of color relationalism on offer.

8.1 Dispositionalism

8.1.1 *Exegesis*

The most historically important form of color relationalism is the dispositionalist view that identifies colors with dispositions to look colored.[1]

Expressed in a rough and ready way, the guiding idea behind color dispositionalism is that colors are analogous to properties like *fragility* or *solubility* in having characteristic manifestations that occur only when appropriate circumstances obtain. Many have had the thought that what distinguishes fragile from non-fragile objects is, roughly, their tendency to shatter in relevant conditions. Of course, it is a difficult problem to say just what conditions count as relevant. But at a first pass we might say that fragile objects shatter when

[1] The material in this section represents a significant departure from the views of Cohen (2003*a*, §3.1).

they are struck sufficiently hard (whatever that means) but not held together by extrinsic supports (e.g., packing material, beneficent angels, etc.); I take it that it is incumbent on someone who wants to analyze *fragility* as a disposition to fill in this extremely rough schema in a more satisfactory way.

So, too, the dispositionalist about color claims that what distinguishes objects that are colored from uncolored objects is, roughly, their tendency to occasion characteristic visual states in subjects in relevant conditions. Of course, it remains a difficult problem to say just which visual states, subjects, and conditions are at issue. But at a first pass we might say that colored objects look colored when viewed by attentive subjects when the lights are up; I take it that it is incumbent on someone who wants to analyze colors as dispositions to fill in this extremely rough schema in a more satisfactory way.

Although this formulation of color dispositionalism is clearly inadequate as it stands, it serves two important purposes for us. First, it makes clear that dispositionalism construes colors as constituted by relations to subjects, and therefore that the view is a species of color relationalism. Second, by at least roughly locating the relevant kind of relation to subjects — viz., the dispositional kind, it gets us at least in the right philosophical neck of the woods. Unfortunately, this neck of the woods contains so many distinct variants that it is often difficult to know exactly what is meant by the label 'color dispositionalism'.

One dimension of variation concerns the way in which the dispositions in question are specified; as Johnston (1992) discusses, several non-equivalent formulations of the view can be generated depending on how we fill in the positions for perceivers and visual circumstances mentioned in the relevant dispositions. In what follows I'll resolve this problem by fiat; for concreteness, I'll simply work with a more or less standard form of dispositionalism according to which *red for S in C* is the disposition to look red to S in C, and *green for S in C* is the disposition to look green to S in C (*mutatis mutandis* for the other colors).[2]

A second, and for our purposes more complicated, dimension of variation in different forms of dispositionalism turns on the metaphysics of dispositions — in particular, on the question of how dispositions are related to their bases.[3] While a number of answers to this question have been defended in

[2] Saying this leaves unaddressed a still further dimension of variation: how should the dispositionalist about color understand the specification of the color manifestations (viz., what it is to look green to a subject in a circumstance)? For reasons discussed in §7.1.4, I think it is useful to leave this question open for present purposes.

[3] Obviously there are many further controversial issues about the metaphysics of dispositions that I can't address adequately here. For simplicity I'll only consider views according to which dispositions exist and have actual instances. I'll assume that all dispositions have basis properties, but I won't assume that all basis properties are categorical or that all basis properties are intrinsic. Among many related topics about which I'll have nothing to say, I make no commitments about the definability/analyzability of dispositions, the relation between dispositions and counterfactuals, the intrinsicness of dispositions, or the nature of the dispositional/categorical distinction.

the literature, perhaps the most important are those construing the relation between dispositions and their bases as one of type-identity (Armstrong (1968); Armstrong *et al.* (1996, chapter 1)), token-identity (Mumford, 1998), and a functional relation (Lewis (1986*a*, 223–224); Prior *et al.* (1982); Prior (1985)).

Why should someone interested in color feel that she has to take a stand on such issues at all? In the first place, one might want to resolve the question simply as a matter of wanting to understand the substance of color dispositionalism (which is, after all, one of the traditional philosophical theories of the nature of color). In the second place, it seems to me that how one falls on this question has implications for whether color dispositionalism is a genuine alternative to role functionalism: in particular, I claim that if dispositions are understood according to the so-called functionalist theory of dispositions (Prior *et al.*, 1982; Prior, 1985), then color dispositionalism and role functionalism about color coincide.

To see this, recall that a role functionalist holds, for example, that *red for S in C* is the functional role of disposing its bearers to look red to S in C. In Chapter 7 I said that this functional role should be understood as the second order property of having some or other first order (basis) property that realizes the functional role of disposing its bearers to look red to S in C. But according to the functionalist theory of dispositions, the disposition to look red to S in C is the second order property of having some or other first order basis property that realizes the functional role of causing its bearers to look red to S in C. On this theory of dispositions, then, the role properties identified with colors by the role functionalist just are the dispositions to look colored — which is to say that, given this view about dispositions, color dispositionalists and role functionalists are in complete agreement about the nature of color.

Of course, other theorists have proposed alternative ways of thinking about the relationship between dispositions and their basis properties such that role functionalism and dispositionalism come apart. But it seems to me that these alternative views are ultimately less attractive ways of thinking about dispositions for reasons I'll explain below. Thus, the challenge I'll be posing to the dispositionalist takes the form of a dilemma: either she can accept the functionalist theory of dispositions, and thereby accept the role functionalist theory of color I am defending, or else, in holding some alternative metaphysics of dispositions, she will render her dispositionalism vulnerable to (what seem to me, anyway) pressing metaphysical objections.[4]

[4] One irony of this result is that, although modern philosophers standardly took colors, understood dispositionally, as their paradigm case of secondary qualities, many of the historically salient criteria for the primary/secondary distinction result in classifying role functionalism (hence dispositionalism) as a (non-traditional) primary quality theory of color (Cohen, 2003*a*, §2). I am inclined to take this to show that "the" traditional primary/secondary distinction doesn't do the work in sorting theories of color that many have wanted it to do.

8.1.2 *The Argument from Absorption*

So what is wrong with non-functionalist theories of dispositions? (For convenience, I'll continue to type such theories by the way they conceive of the relationship between dispositions and their bases; and I'll follow Fara (2006) in presenting the relevant types by analogy to familiar views in the philosophy of mind between mental properties and physical properties.) Although I can't hope to argue against every possible non-functionalist alternative, the main contenders that I'll consider are the type-identity view of Armstrong (1968), the token-identity theory of Mumford (1998), and a kind of dualist theory suggested by Cartwright (1989).

The type-identity view about dispositions faces classic worries about multiple realization. The threat here comes from the simple idea that one disposition could be realized by distinct basis properties: it is possible that the crystalline structure that is the basis for a pane of glass's exemplification of *fragility* is distinct from the crystalline structure that is the basis for the vase's exemplification of the same disposition. Indeed, it is possible for multiple realization to arise in a single object: the cloth can exemplify *water absorbency* both by having threads weaved of a water absorbent material and by being weaved in such a way as to absorb water between its threads (Mackie, 1973, 148). But if there are distinct bases for one disposition, then the disposition can't be type-identical to its basis.

A modal variant of this objection parallels a well-known argument against type-identity theories in philosophy of mind by Kripke (1980): if $\ulcorner a \urcorner$ is the name of a disposition and $\ulcorner b \urcorner$ is the name of its basis property, and both names are rigid designators, then the identity statement $\ulcorner a = b \urcorner$ must be necessary if true. But it seems that, even if a disposition and its basis property are everywhere actually coextensive, this coextension is at best contingent; after all, whether a structural/material property is a basis for a given disposition will depend on the operative laws of nature. If so, then the type-identity view must be false.[5]

Consider, then, the view that dispositions are *token*-identical with their basis properties (Mumford, 1998). The idea here is that, while the disposition property and basis property are not identical (*qua* types), every particular instance of the disposition is identical with an instance of some or other basis property for that disposition. This view is well-placed to avoid the troubles about multiple realization raised for the proponent of type-identity: it allows, appropriately, that the instance of *fragility* exemplified in the pane of glass is an instance of one crystalline structure that serves as a basis for the disposition, while the instance of *fragility* exemplified in the vase is an instance of a different crystalline structure that serves as a basis for the same disposition. So far, so good. The difficulty is that, given what has been said so far, we are not yet in a position to say much about the nature of the dispositional property itself, as opposed to its instances. (One way to see this is to note that functionalists about dispositions can also agree to token-identity about dispositions as that

[5] For another version of this argument, see Prior *et al.* (1982).

thesis has been expressed: functionalists can agree that the particular token instances of the higher-order properties they identify with disposition are indeed identical to token instances of particular basis properties.) The question remains, then: what (besides functionalism) might a token-identity theorist say about the nature of dispositional properties themselves?

Given her acknowledgment of multiple realization, one thing a token identity theorist might say is that a disposition such as *fragility* is identical to the property p_1 that is its realizing basis on one occasion (say, in a pane of glass), and identical to another property p_2 (say, in a vase) that is its realizing basis on another occasion. Alas, this leads to the unpalatable conclusion that *fragility* = p_1 and *fragility* = p_2 even though $p_1 \neq p_2$. A marginally more attractive option would be to say that *fragility in the pane of glass* = p_1, while *fragility in the vase* = p_2. But this position of course entails that *fragility in the pane of glass* ≠ *fragility in the vase*. In other words, the view contemplated amounts to giving up on the idea that there is any common essence shared between (what we might have thought were) the distinct instances of one and the same dispositional property.[6] But since I take it that theories of dispositions are in the business of providing an account of just such essences, it seems that the view under consideration fails to do the things we want from a theory of dispositions. Unfortunately, I do not see any better options for the token-identity theory.

A final proposal for conceiving of the relationship between dispositions and their bases is property dualism. Just as in the philosophy of mind, the property dualist holds that the two properties under study (here, the disposition and its basis) are fundamentally different in kind, causally unrelated, and mutually irreducible — i.e., neither is constituted by or analyzable in terms of the other. It is plausible that dualism about dispositions survives worries about multiple realization (within and across worlds): since it denies the presence of any particular constituting relationship between a disposition and its basis, it does not predict that a given disposition should always be found together with (within or across worlds) a particular basis property.

Nonetheless, dualism seem unsatisfying. As I suggested in considering whether to posit primitive (/dualist) color properties in earlier chapters, it seems to me that we should be reluctant to accept primitive properties without powerful arguments in their favor: as an explanatory strategy, dualism is so unconstrained that we should resist it when possible. A special case of this difficulty for dualism can be raised concerning this question: given the dualist's view that basis properties and dispositions are unrelated, why is it that objects that exemplify a disposition always and in all possible worlds exemplify some basis for that disposition? To deny that there is such a correlation — to answer that it is metaphysically possible for an object to have a disposition without having a basis for that disposition — clashes strongly with our intuitions.[7] In

[6] See the analogous criticism of realizer functionalism about color in §7.2.2.

[7] See note 3.

contrast, to answer that there is such a correlation but that it has no further explanation is to accept an enormous collection of brute modal facts (one per disposition). Neither of these options seems appealing.

I take these considerations to show that non-functionalist accounts of the relationship between dispositions and their bases are unpromising. In fairness, it must be admitted that many philosophers (including proponents of functionalism about dispositions) have felt that functionalism about dispositions also faces an important objection in that it would render dispositions causally impotent (Lewis, 1986*a*; Prior *et al.*, 1982; Prior, 1985). This objection is not to be taken lightly; moreover, it has special importance for me, since, if I am right that this theory of dispositions makes it the case that dispositionalism and role functionalism about color coincide, then it would follow that colors are causally impotent as well. However, I argued in §7.3 that the kind of causal efficacy we have reason to want for colors can be had by the role functionalist. And since my case for this conclusion did not rest on considerations particular to the case of color, I think they can be accepted more widely by functionalists about dispositions.

In all, then, I think that the most important arguments against the functionalist theory of dispositions can be answered, but that powerful objections face alternative accounts. But given the functionalist theory of dispositions, it seems that dispositionalism about color is no longer a genuine alternative to role functionalism about color. I conclude, then, that there is no form of color dispositionalism that ultimately constitutes a serious relationalist rival to the role functionalism of Chapter 7.

8.2 Ecological Relationalism

8.2.1 *Exegesis*

Evan Thompson and his colleagues (Thompson, 1995; Thompson *et al.*, 1992) have put forward a view about the nature of color that, I think, clearly is a genuine relationalist alternative to role functionalism.[8]

Thompson (1995) offers his ecological relationalist ontology as an account of three related property-types: (i) the property of having some particular "categorical" color, where categorical colors are "visually salient equivalence classes" comprised of "physically heterogeneous distal properties"; (ii) the property of having some particular determinate color; and (iii) the more general property *being colored* (245). Since only property-types (i) and (ii) will be of interest in what follows, I'll put property-type (iii) aside. As I understand his explanations of (i) and (ii), Thompson intends that the categorical colors are relatively coarse-grained; examples of coarse-grained colors might be *being red*, or *being reddish-orange*. In contrast, I take it that Thompson's determinate colors are more fine-grained, and might include things like *being crimson* or *being*

[8] Ecological relationalism is a complex view with many working parts; for reasons of expository convenience, I'll be selective in the presentation of it that follows. I hope and believe that my simplifications do not result in any philosophically significant misrepresentations.

chartreuse. Having made this distinction, Thompson presents the heart of his account in this passage:

> ...being coloured a categorical colour is simply equivalent to [identical to?] having a spectral reflectance, illuminance, or emittance that is perceived as belonging to some specific colour category by a particular perceiver in specific viewing conditions. Being coloured a particular determinate colour or shade, on the other hand, is equivalent to [identical to?] having a particular spectral reflectance, illuminance, or emittance that looks that colour to a particular perceiver in specific viewing conditions (Thompson, 1995, 245).

While there are several things about Thompson's ecological relationalism that I find perplexing (see below), one thing that is absolutely clear about the proposal is that Thompson intends it as a species of color relationalism, in the sense in which I've been using that label. Thompson makes this lucid by drawing a pair of relationalist consequences from his view immediately after presenting it (245–246). First, he says that it follows from his view that nothing bears any color (categorical or particular) except by being related to a perceiver and viewing condition. And second, he says that his view allows for the kind of ecumenicism discussed in Chapters 2–3: "the same thing can have different colours (again in the particular or categorical sense)" (Thompson, 1995, 246). On the basis of these claims, I think it is appropriate to regard Thompson as advocating a species of color relationalism.[9]

8.2.2 *The Argument from Multiple Realization*

Ecological relationalism, construed as a metaphysics of color properties, is a hybrid of relationalist and non-relationalist elements. It requires not only that colored things are appropriately related to perceivers and viewing circumstances (as per other forms of relationalism) but also that those things are related to perceivers and viewing circumstances in virtue of exemplifying a spectral reflectance/illuminance/emittance that is appropriately related to perceivers and viewing circumstances. This formulation obviously gives a larger role to physical constitution — or, rather, to the physically grounded dispositions to affect light rather than to affect subjects — than do other forms of relationalism. But it nonetheless stops short of identifying colors with subject-independent

[9] One concern invited by Thompson's formulation is that ecological relationalism might seem to be an analysis of color concepts, as opposed to a metaphysics of color properties. This reading is encouraged by Thompson's twice using 'equivalent to' (as opposed to 'identical to') as a way of connecting his analysandum and his analysans in the quoted passage. It is encouraged further by his contrast of his own view against dispositionalism in terms of the different conceptions (of the relation between world and perceiver) each makes available: for it is not obvious how or why an ontology of color properties should have any such conceptual implications. Of course, if it turns out that Thompson is really offering a conceptual analysis rather than an ontological theory, then his view falls outside the domain that is presently our concern — viz., the domain of relationalist rivals to role functionalism *qua* metaphysical account of color properties. Since I believe Thompson intended his view as one that falls in this domain, and since his view becomes uninteresting for present purposes if it does not, I'll just treat it, henceforth, as if it does (and shall ignore the textual motivations for supposing otherwise).

physical constitutions or dispositions in the way in which Hilbert (1987), Tye (1995), and other proponents of identity theories of color do.

Now, because it makes requirements about physical constitution, ecological relationalism gives up the attractive idea that colors are multiply realizable — an idea that is a central attraction of several other forms of relationalism (see §7.1.2).[10] For example, because of this feature, his view has the result that things could not exemplify (categorical or particular) colors in (physically remote) worlds where things lack the sorts of constitutions (/light-affecting dispositions) that colored things have in α. Similarly, it forecloses the possibility that someone could discover a new physical (or, for that matter, non-physical) way of being colored.[11] I take these points as revealing costs of Thompson's view, but expect they are costs he would be willing to accept.

8.2.3 *The Argument from Non-Idealism and Location*

However, a more serious, and less easily dismissed, set of problems for ecological relationalism has to do with the way in which the view requires colored objects to be related to subjects. According to ecological relationalism, something bears a categorical color (e.g., *red*) by having a reflectance/-illuminance/emittance "that is perceived as belonging to some specific colour category by a particular perceiver in specific viewing conditions" (Thompson, 1995, 245). Now consider the following question: should we read this claim as requiring that, to be red, the reflectance/illuminance/emittance of things must be *occurrently* perceived as belonging to some specific color category (by a particular perceiver in specific viewing conditions)? Similarly, ecological relationalism has it that something bears a determinate color (e.g., *crimson*) by having a reflectance/illuminance/emittance "that looks that colour to a particular perceiver in specific viewing conditions" (Thompson, 1995, 245). Again, we must ask whether this requires that, to be crimson, the reflectance/illuminance/emittance of things must *occurrently* look crimson (to a

[10] Byrne and Hilbert (2003) make the opposite complaint against Thompson's view in saying that the latter ultimately "boils down to something not much different from traditional dispositionalism" (8) — a view they argue against elsewhere in the same paper (7). Perhaps it is unsurprising that proponents of the kinds of pure theories Thompson combines in constructing his own hybrid view (i.e., both non-relationalists like Byrne and Hilbert and relationalists like me) are dissatisfied by the resulting combination.

[11] Thompson's uses of 'particular' (and 'specific') are ambiguous between a quantificational and a specific reading, which makes it hard to evaluate just how remote these scenarios are, and correspondingly how serious the threats under discussion really are. For example, when he says that "Being coloured a particular determinate colour or shade ... is equivalent to having a particular spectral reflectance, illuminance, or emittance that looks that colour ...," does he mean that something can only be crimson by having a specific reflectance/illuminance/emittance (to which appropriate perceivers are appropriately related) that he has in mind, or that it can be crimson by having some or other reflectance/illuminance/emittance (to which appropriate perceivers are appropriately related)? If the former (specific) reading is intended, then the worrisome scenarios are not particularly remote, so the worry is extremely pressing. If the latter (quantificational) reading is intended, then the worry still arises, but perhaps it is less immediate.

particular perceiver in specific viewing conditions)? I want to argue that the ecological relationalist has no acceptable way of answering these questions.

If these questions are answered affirmatively, then the view has implausibly idealistic consequences. For example, it would follow that inattention to x by perceivers prevents x from exemplifying any categorical or determinate colors. If so, then mere shifts of attention by perceivers would have the effect of obliterating and restoring x's (categorical and determinate) colors; likewise, it would follow that nothing is colored in locations where there are no perceivers (e.g., the dark side of the moon, the earth after a nuclear holocaust). In order to avoid these presumably unacceptable idealist consequences, the obvious (and familiar) move would be to say that ecological relationalism requires of colored things only a dispositional (rather than occurrent) relation to perceivers. Thus, the view would be that, to be red, a thing's reflectance/illuminance/emittance must be disposed to be perceived as belonging to some specific color category ...; and, analogously, that to be crimson, a thing's reflectance/illuminance/emittance must only be disposed to look crimson ....

This dispositional reading of ecological relationalism is, as far as I can see, the only way in which the view can avoid the unpalatable idealistic consequences considered. It is, therefore, the most plausible version of the view. Unfortunately, it has an insuperable cost of its own. Namely, when read in this way, ecological relationalism locates the dispositions to look colored in the wrong place — it makes the dispositions to look colored properties of the reflectances/illuminances/emittances of objects, rather than the objects themselves. This, I want to suggest, is an unacceptable result. It is the ripe tomato, and not its reflectance, that is disposed to look red. Indeed, it is plausible that the reflectance of the tomato is not disposed to look any way (likewise, more generally, for the reflectances/illuminances/emittances of objects). Ecological relationalism, then, attributes the dispositions to look colored to entities that in fact lack them (reflectances/illuminances/emittances), and forbears the attribution of those dispositions to the entities that in fact bear them (tomatoes, lemons, etc.). I suggest that any color ontology that does not allow that colored objects are disposed to look colored is *ipso facto* unacceptable. If so, then we must reject the dispositional version of ecological relationalism; and, since it is the most plausible version of the theory, this means that we must reject ecological relationalism altogether.

8.3 Sensory Classificationism

8.3.1 *Exegesis*

In this section I want to consider a positions that is in some ways quite close to the role functionalism of Chapter 7. This view comes in the context of a general account of sense perception by Matthen (1999, 2001, 2005), and that I shall call *sensory classificationism* (for reasons that will soon become apparent).[12] I'll first set out the essential elements of sensory classificationism, and then proceed to evaluate the view.

Matthen begins with the uncontroversial observation that sensory perception — including, of course, color vision — sorts stimuli into what he calls sensory classes (Matthen, 2005, 24). For example, color vision sorts ripe limes and unripe tomatoes into one class, ripe strawberries and stop signs into a second class, and canaries and ripe lemons into a third class. Much more controversially, Matthen proposes to understand the nature of the colors in terms of such sortings, or sensory classifications, by the color vision system: colors just are, for Matthen, "properties that distal stimuli appear to have when color vision assigns them to classes in accordance with its own classification scheme" (Matthen, 2005, 14). The sensory classificationist view, then, is not one that begins with the color properties as features of the perceiver-independent world and then understands color vision as a system by which organisms recover those properties. Rather, the picture is just the reverse: we begin with the color vision system as one that partitions stimuli into certain classes (according to its own internally organized classification scheme), and give a derivative explication of the colors as the classes of stimuli that result from such classificatory activity. For Matthen, the classification of a particular by the color vision system results in what he calls a "colour-look," which is the observer's subjective experience of that particular (Matthen, 2005, 253). Colour-looks, then, are the outputs of sensory classification, not its inputs: similarity in subjective experience of two particulars (i.e., their having the same colour-look) is not a *basis* for co-classification of those particulars, but evidence that they have been co-classified by the visual system.

What, then, is the relation between color properties (for Matthen, classes of stimuli) and color experiences (in Matthen's argot, colour-looks)? Matthen's approach to this question is to think of the color experiences (/colour-looks) as labels provided by the visual systems that *designate* the colors.[13] Of course, Matthen wants to allow that such labels can be applied falsely to particulars — i.e., that things can look red without in fact being red. But when the appearance/label/colour-look of some particular is veridical, then (i) that particular genuinely exemplifies the corresponding color, and (ii) sentences attributing that color to that particular are true. Matthen expresses this much in his Fundamental Principle of Color Attribution: " 'x is *Col*' is true if and only

[12] Just as in my discussion of ecological relationalism in §8.2, here I content myself with a simplified and abbreviated presentation of sensory classificationism in order to facilitate a clean comparison against role functionalism. I believe that my simplifications do not misrepresent Matthen's view in any philosophically significant way.

[13] This comes out in his principle of Look Exportation:

Col is the colour property something visually appears to have when it looks *Col* (Matthen, 2005, 256).

if x really is the colour something visually appears to be when it presents the *Col*-look" (Matthen, 2005, 257).

It should be clear that while this Fundamental Principle gives the correctness condition for color attributions, it does so schematically. In particular, the right hand side of the Fundamental Principle invokes a (so far unexplicated) distinction between cases where x really is the color something visually appears to be when it presents a certain colour-look and cases where x is not the color something visually appears to be when it presents the same colour-look. Recalling that colour-looks are, according to sensory classificationism, the outputs of acts of classification, we can rephrase this as a distinction between cases where x really is red (as it might be) and has been classified as red, on the one hand, and cases where x is not red despite having been classified as red, on the other. What we need to understand, then, is what it is for an act of classification to be right as opposed to wrong. Crucially, however, the sensory classificationist cannot, on pain of circularity, answer that an act of classification is right in virtue of carving stimuli at their perceiver-independent joints, because it is part of that view that the joints in question are constituted in terms of the acts of classification themselves.

Thus, to fill out his account, the sensory classificationist needs a condition for the rightness/wrongness of acts of color classification that does not advert to the color properties induced by these acts of classification. Matthen answers this need by appealing to the teleology of acts of classification: he says that "An act of classification is *wrong* if it disrupts a specialized function that this classification is supposed to aid" (Matthen, 2005, 206). In particular, Matthen tells us that acts of color classification are supposed to aid at least the following specialized functions:

> to co-classify things for purposes of induction, for example, to make generalizations concerning the ripeness of fruit, or the health of one's conspecifics;
>
> to re-identify things on different occasions, for example, one's car in a crowded parking lot;
>
> to segment the visual scene into figure and ground, adjacent things of similar colour being both assigned to the figure or both to the ground;
>
> to find things by visual search, for instance red or orange fruit against a background of green foliage; and
>
> to match and differentiate things by the colour-looks they present, in order to be able [to] tell, for instance, which part of a uniformly coloured lawn is shaded by trees (Matthen, 2005, 230).

Putting all of the parts together, sensory classificationism has it that colors are the properties things have when they are in fact as they are classified by the color vision system — i.e., when they are *correctly* classified by that system. And they are correctly classified by that system when they are classified in a way that subserves the specialized telos that is sketched in the above list, and toward which this type of sensory classifications is directed by Mother Nature. In this way, Matthen maintains that there is a constitutive connection between colors and a range of teleologically apt actions. (Significantly, Matthen construes 'action' broadly so as to include inference, judgment, and other epistemic categories, as well as bodily motions).

Before I come to the evaluation of sensory classificationism, I want to emphasize that the view is a species of color relationalism, and therefore a potential competitor to the role functionalism of Chapter 7. This is so because sensory classificationism construes colors in terms of relations between distal objects and subjects; in particular, the relations in question relate objects to the sensory classifications made by subjects' visual systems. Indeed, there is a sense in which sensory classificationism might reasonably be counted a kind of functionalism about color (although pretty clearly a different species from the view presented in Chapter 7). For the relations in terms of which the colors are constituted, according to sensory classificationism are in fact functional relations (in the usual Cummins sense).[14] They are relations to produce a certain kind of response — namely, a response of correct sensory classification in visual systems. Consequently, sensory classificationism, like the view of Chapter 7 (and like many other functionalist theories in philosophy), permits that colors may be multiply realized within and across worlds; this will happen if there are multiple material realizations that all fill the relevant function of being correctly classified by the color visual system. The disagreement between the sensory classificationist and the role functionalist (in the narrow sense of Chapter 7), then, is not a disagreement about the merits of a functional account of colors, but instead an internecine disagreement between functionalists about exactly which function is constitutive of the colors.

Unsurprisingly, therefore, my reason for preferring the view of Chapter 7 to sensory classificationism involves worries about the function that the latter takes to be constitutive of colors. To repeat, that function is the function of producing correct sensory classifications in visual systems, which in turn is spelled out in terms of the teleologically apposite actions facilitated by these classifications. My main concern about the appeal to this function is that I am dubious that color properties are as directly connected with such functions as Matthen supposes.[15]

8.3.2 *The Argument from Stimulus-Independence*

One way to make this point is through the observation that there are many cases where different actions (epistemic or otherwise) are apt with respect to the classification of (what we might have described as) one color. Significantly, there seem to be entirely analogous cases of this sort where the classifications in question occur in organisms of different species, in different organisms of

[14] Of course, it also happens that the Cummins functions played by the colors, according to sensory classificationism, are teleological, adaptive functions; thus, it turns out that the two senses of 'functional' discussed in §7.1.2 both apply here.

[15] For the record, I am more generally worried (because of more or less standard concerns brought against adaptationism by Gould and Lewontin (1979)) about Matthen's teleological ascriptions to the perceptual system; but I'll let this pass.

one species, and even in different time slices of one organism; moreover (and as I emphasized with respect to a parallel range of cases in Chapters 2–3), the structural similarity of these cases suggests strongly that we should hope for a general treatment that applies uniformly to all of them. Unfortunately, I shall suggest, sensory classificationism does not provide for such a general treatment.

Thus, consider an inter-species case where what action (epistemic or otherwise) is apt seems to come apart from classification of color: the actions apt given a classification of redness for a creature whose prey is red are, intuitively, quite different from the actions apt for a creature whose predator is red. In this case we have *two* apt actions corresponding to (what we might have thought was) *one* color. Now, for the sensory classificationist who wishes to preserve the claimed constitutive tie between colors and the actions their classification makes apt, there are two ways of responding to such cases: one can insist that there is only one action rather than two (to match the number of colors classified) or one can insist that there are in fact two colors classified (in order to match the number of apt actions). Here Matthen emphatically favors the second alternative; one of the major conclusions Matthen (1999, 2005) stresses is that organisms of different species act differently in response to a single (neutrally described) stimulus type, and that each of these actions can be (epistemically or otherwise) apposite given the stimulus for the organism that performs it. Thus Matthen concludes about this sort of case that the two different organisms (predator and prey, in the case considered) are perceiving different colors. In other words, his response here is to reject the original characterization of the cases as one where different actions are apt with respect to one color, and thereby to retain his view that colors are individuated by the actions they make apt. Whether or not this response is plausible in this inter-species case, we should now consider how the same issue arises in other cases.

In particular, we need to consider cases in which different actions (epistemic or otherwise) are apt with respect to the classification of (what we might have described as) one color by different individuals of one species, or even different time-slices of a single individual. For example, the redness of the mother bird's mouth might be taken by juvenile birds as an apt occasion for feeding, whereas the acts apposite to the classification of red by adult birds might be quite different. Another example of the same type comes from Tinbergen's celebrated findings about the behavior of red-bellied sticklebacks. On the one hand, it appears that any classification of redness at all (whether located on a reproductive competitor or not) makes apt the action of attacking in adult male red-bellied sticklebacks during breeding season; on the other hand, the action of attacking is not apt (viz., some other action, or no action at all, is apt) with respect to the classification of redness made by juveniles of the same species, females of the same species, or even adult males of the same species at other times of the year.[16]

Once again, such cases pose a *prima facie* threat to the individuation of colors by the actions (epistemic or otherwise) their classification makes apt. And once again, one can preserve the classificationist view either by holding that there is only one action rather than two (to match the number of colors classified) or one can insist that there are in fact two colors classified (in order to match the number of apt actions). However, the second alternative, which Matthen advocated strongly in the inter-species case, seems much less inviting in the intra-species/intra-individual cases. Application of that strategy to the present case would mean insisting that the juvenile and adult birds/sticklebacks fail to perceive the same color as a way of saving the claim that colors are constitutively tied to their associated apt actions. But this conclusion has unpalatable consequences. For example, if we say that the individuals/time-slices in question perceive distinct colors, then we lose the ability to account for such important and diverse phenomena as object re-identification, classical conditioning, and agreement and disagreement about the colors of objects, *inter alia* (see §4.4.3). This, I suggest, is simply too great a price to bear.

I take these considerations to show that colors and the actions (epistemic or otherwise) made apt by their classification seem to come apart in extension in a wide range of cases, and that the sensory classificationist lacks a sufficiently general way of responding to these cases. There are, moreover, other reasons for thinking that the claimed constitutive tie between colors and the actions they make apt is not as strong or direct as the sensory classificationist would have us believe.

For instance, there is a range of cases in which different actions (epistemic or otherwise) are apt with respect to the classification of one color by a single organism depending on further thoughts/classifications of that organism. For example, it is conventionally apt for human beings both that red lights at traffic intersections compel automobile drivers to slow their vehicles and that red lights in recording studios compel those present to avoid making unnecessary noise; thus, which actions are apt responses to the stimulus of a red light depends crucially on which sort of situation I take myself to be in (which, in turn, presumably depends on further sensory classifications I have made). Moreover, it is plausible that in many cases, the epistemically or otherwise

[16] Frankie Egan suggested to me (in conversation) another possible example of this type: certain instances of redness might make romantic actions apt in an adult human beings even though those same actions would not be apt for a juvenile human being encountering the same stimuli. In response to criticisms of this type from Egan (2008), Matthen (2008) suggests that the allegedly constitutive connection between acts of classification and apposite actions should be restricted to cases where the actions in question are innate — i.e., genetically or developmentally specified responses, as opposed to conditioned responses, to stimuli. While this proposed restriction may save sensory classificationism from some otherwise troublesome cases, the view remains vulnerable to cases where there are multiple (or no) innately specified actions apposite for a particular classification such as (I claim) those in the main text.

apt action in response to a color stimulus is plausibly to do nothing. Again, whether this (null) response is apt presumably depends on other factors about the perceptual/cognitive system in question and the environment in which it finds itself.[17]

The lesson suggested by all these cases is that the actions that are apt for an organism are independent of — not under the control of — either the stimulus or even the color classifications of the stimulus performed by the organism. For it seems that the relation between color classifications and the actions they afford is one-many, potentially idiosyncratic to individuals (or even time-slices), and mediated by other perceptual and cognitive states of the organism. Consequently, it is not the case that given a classification alone one can say which actions are apt with respect to that classification. This, in turn, would seem to be a serious threat to the sensory classificationist claim that colors are constituted in terms of the correct classifications (i.e., the classifications resulting in teleologically apt actions) they afford.

Now, Matthen is aware of these worries. Under the pressure of such examples, he claims that color classifications have "non-coercive contents" — i.e., that their effect is "not to manipulate the effector systems directly, but simply to issue a signal that a certain situation obtains, leaving it to the effector system to do what is appropriate and necessary" (Matthen, 2005, 237). He does not, however, take this point to undermine his view that the correctness conditions for color classifications are constituted in terms of the contributions they make to the specific apposite actions of co-classification, re-identification, segmentation, visual search, and matching/differentiation. As I read him, then, Matthen's position is that color classifications do have these canonical functions, but issue in signals that leave some amount of freedom for the effector systems to act in the canonical way or not, as is appropriate and necessary.

But this treatment seems unsatisfying. For in this case it seems that the apt actions for a given classification give us no purchase on "what is appropriate and necessary" for the organism; and if so, I don't see any reason for thinking that the canonical actions taken to be apt with respect to particular types of classification really are apt or canonical after all. On the contrary, the lesson of the foregoing seems precisely that neither color stimuli nor color classifications are the sorts of things that, by themselves, determine what is apt for the organism. I want to suggest that sensory classificationism, in denying this lesson, falls prey to something like the mistake that Chomsky (1959) accused Skinner's behaviorist theory of language use of making: just

[17] Perhaps Matthen would say that, since the actions in question are clearly not innately linked to the classification of redness, they are unproblematic for a version of sensory classificationism restricted to innate responses (see note 16). On the other hand, this response reinforces the worry that what is apt with respect to a color classification is mostly, or even entirely, highly contingent on all sorts of post-perceptual factors and facts about the local environment, so not constitutively linked to color classifications after all.

as Skinner was wrong in claiming that linguistic action is under the control of the environmental stimulus alone, sensory classificationism is wrong in claiming that epistemic and non-epistemic action is under the control of the environmental stimulus and sensory classifications thereof alone. Correcting this mistake robs sensory classificationism of its correctness criterion for color classifications, which in turn undercuts its specification of the functions in terms of which it characterizes colors.

For this reason, I remain unconvinced that sensory classificationism is a plausible form of color relationalism.

8.4 Conclusion

In this chapter I have examined three important relationalist alternatives to the role functionalism of Chapter 7: dispositionalism, ecological relationalism, and sensory classificationism. My goal has been to assess their relative merits, and to argue that role functionalism is superior to the other forms of relationalism on offer. I have argued that dispositionalism either collapses onto role functionalism or rests on an implausible account of the relationship between dispositions and their bases; that ecological relationalism falls prey to worries about multiple realization, and is committed either to an unacceptable form of idealism or else mislocates colors; and that sensory classificationism links too tightly the perceptual classificatory responses of organisms and their subsequent epistemic or non-epistemic actions. In view of these shortcomings, I contend that role functionalism does more of the things we want a theory of color to do, and does them more successfully, than the relationalist rivals discussed in this chapter. Although my discussion has not exhausted (and cannot exhaust) the space of possible relationalist accounts of color, it has addressed the relationalist accounts that have attracted the most support and interest in recent philosophical work on color. Accordingly, unless and until an even more attractive form of relationalism emerges, the arguments of this chapter give us reason for thinking that relationalists about color should be role functionalists about color.

PART IV

SUMMARY

9

SUMMARY CONCLUSION

> It is not really difficult to construct a series of inferences, each dependent upon its predecessor and each simple in itself. If, after doing so, one simply knocks out all the central inferences and presents one's audience with the starting-point and the conclusion, one may produce a startling, though perhaps a meretricious, effect.
>
> — (Doyle, 1905, 50).

At the beginning of this essay I proposed that there was much to be gained in dividing up accounts of the nature of color in terms of a distinction between relationalist accounts — those that understand colors to be constituted in terms of a relation to perceiving subjects — and non-relationalist accounts, which deny that colors are constituted in terms of such relations. This put me in a position to provide a novel taxonomy of the theoretical landscape that (I hope) offers advantages over more standard treatments (Chapter 1).

With this taxonomy in hand, I offered an extended argument for color relationalism in Part I. This argument infers from empirical findings about perceptual variation and the difficulty in fixing a uniquely veridical variant when there are other candidates to the conclusion that objects have many of the colors they are represented as having by different visual systems and in different conditions of observation; it then puts forward color relationalism as the best way of making sense of this ecumenical treatment (Chapter 2). I next defended this argument against a series of challenges — some that suggest treating our inability to single out a distinguished variant as a mere epistemic shortcoming with no ontological import, some that suggest accepting irrealism about color, and some that suggest non-relationalist ways of accepting ecumenicism with respect to multiple perceptual variants (Chapter 3). I found these challenges unsuccessful, and therefore endorsed the relationalist conclusion of the argument from perceptual variation.

Having argued for (and defended my argument for) the claim that we should embrace a relationalist ontology of color, I turned in Part II to defending relationalism from objections. The first class of objections concerned the possibility of reconciling a relationalist metaphysics of color with data about the semantics of (mental and linguistic) color ascription. I attempted to meet these challenges by providing a context-sensitive semantics for color ascription that made use of both fine- and coarse-grained relational color properties, and argued that this proposal confers substantial benefits with only minimal costs (Chapter 4). Next, I considered a series of ontological challenges to relationalism concerning the unity of the colors, worries about realism, and the charge that relationalism is an error theory; I claimed that relationalism contains the resources to meet these worries (Chapter 5). I then moved on to explore the accusation that color relationalism is inconsistent with our ordinary color phenomenology, or that it cannot be coherently combined with plausible theories of the nature of color phenomenology. I contended that relationalism is not in conflict with — indeed, that it is supported by — the evidence of color phenomenology, once we are clear about just how phenomenology can be useful in addressing questions of color ontology, and that the alleged theoretical incompatibility between color relationalism and popular views about phenomenology is illusory (Chapter 6).

After carrying out the foregoing argument for and defense of relationalism at a general level in Parts I and II, I finally turned to arguing for the particular — role functionalist — form of relationalism that I wish to defend in Part III. First I laid out this role functionalist view, argued that it is superior to realizer functionalism about color, and attempted to show how role functionalism can be reconciled with standard intuitions about the causal efficacy of colors (Chapter 7). Finally, I attempted to motivate role functionalism about color by comparing it against other forms of color relationalism that have attracted philosophical adherents, and by arguing that these alternative forms of relationalism all have serious drawbacks (Chapter 8).

The separate Parts of the essay fit together to comprise a larger argument for role functionalism about color. For if my argument for, and defense of, a relationalist treatment of color in Parts I and II is successful, then we should accept the most plausible form of relationalism there is. And if I am correct in maintaining, in Part III, that role functionalism is the most plausible form of relationalism there is, then role functionalism is the most satisfying color ontology full stop.

Of course, I must leave it to others to assess the strength of this larger argument and the smaller ones that comprise it. But even if my arguments fail to carry conviction in every case, I hope they will have the collective effect of giving relationalism and role functionalism about color a larger share of philosophical attention than they have had until now.

Bibliography

Abbott, Edwin A. (1884). *Flatland: A Romance of Many Dimensions*. Seeley, London.

Albers, Joseph (1963). *Interaction of Color*. Yale University Press, London.

Allen, Keith (2009). Inter-species variation in colour perception.

Alston, William P. (1999). Back to the theory of appearing. *Philosophical Perspectives*, **13**, 181–203.

American Society for Testing and Materials (1968). *Standard Method of Specifying Color by the Munsell System*. ASTM, Philadelphia. Designation D 1535–68.

Anscombe, G. E. M. (1981). Causality and determination. In *Metaphysics and the Philosophy of Mind: Collected Papers, Volume II* (ed. G. E. M. Anscombe), pp. 133–147. University of Minnesota Press, Minneapolis.

Arend, Lawrence and Reeves, Adam (1986). Simultaneous color constancy. *Journal of the Optical Society of America A*, **3**(10), 1743–1751.

Arend, Lawrence, Reeves, Adam, Schirillo, James, and Goldstein, Robert (1991). Simultaneous color constancy: patterns with diverse Munsell values. *Journal of the Optical Society of America A*, **8**, 661–672.

Armstrong, David (1968). *A Materialist Theory of the Mind*. Routledge, London.

Armstrong, David, Martin, Charlie B., and Place, U. T. (1996). *Dispositions: A Debate*. Routledge, London.

Armstrong, David M. (1970). The nature of mind. In *The Mind/Brain Identity Theory* (ed. C. V. Borst). MacMillan, London. Reprinted in Block (1980), 191–199.

Armstrong, David M. (1987). Smart and the secondary qualities. In *Metaphysics and Morality: Essays in Honour of J. J. C. Smart* (ed. P. Pettit, R. Sylvan, and J. Norman). Basil Blackwell, Oxford. Reprinted in Byrne and Hilbert (1997*b*), 33–46.

Armstrong, David M. (1999). *The Mind–Body Problem: An Opinionated Introduction*. WestviewPress, Boulder.

Austin, John L. (1962). *Sense and Sensibilia*. Clarendon, Oxford.

Averill, Edward Wilson (1985). Color and the anthropocentric problem. *The Journal of Philosophy*, **82**, 281–304. Reprinted in Byrne and Hilbert (1997*b*), 11–32.

Averill, Edward Wilson (1992). The relational nature of color. *The Philosophical Review*, **101**(3), 551–588.

Averill, Edward Wilson and Hazlet, Allen (2009). A problem for relational theories of color. *Philosophy and Phenomenological Research*. Forthcoming.

Bach, Kent (1994). Conversational implicature. *Mind and Language*, **9**, 124–162.

Baker, Lynne Rudder (1993). Metaphysics and mental causation. See Heil and Mele (1993), pp. 75–95.

Bäuml, Karl-Heinz (1999). Simultaneous colour constancy: how surface color perception varies with the illuminant. *Vision Research*, **39**(8), 1531–1550.

Bennett, Jonathan (1968). Substance, reality, and primary qualities. In *Locke and Berkeley: A Collection of Critical Essays* (ed. C. B. Martin and D. M. Armstrong), pp. 86–124. Anchor Books, Garden City, New York.

Bennett, Jonathan (1971). *Locke, Berkeley, Hume: Central Themes*. Clarendon Press, Oxford.

Block, Ned (ed.) (1980). *Readings in the Philosophy of Psychology, Volume 1*. Harvard University Press, Cambridge, Massachusetts.

Block, Ned (1999). Sexism, racism, ageism and the nature of consciousness. In *Philosophical Topics 26 (1&2), The Philosophy of Sydney Shoemaker* (ed. R. Moran, J. Whiting, and A. Sidelle). University of Arkansas Press, Fayetteville.

Block, Ned and Fodor, Jerry A. (1972). What psychological states are not. *The Philosophical Review*, **81**(2), 159–182. Reprinted in Block (1980), 237–250.

Boghossian, Paul A. and Velleman, J. David (1989). Colour as a secondary quality. *Mind*, **98**, 81–103. Reprinted in Byrne and Hilbert (1997*b*), 81–103.

Boghossian, Paul A. and Velleman, J. David (1991). Physicalist theories of color. *The Philosophical Review*, **100**, 67–106.

Bowmaker, J. K. and Dartnall, H. J. A. (1980). Visual pigments of rods and cones in a human retina. *Journal Physiologica*, **298**, 501–511.

Boynton, Robert, Schafer, W., and Neun, M. (1964). Hue-wavelength relation measured by colornaming method for three retina locations. *Vision Research*, **29**, 115–128.

Boynton, Richard M. (1979). *Human Color Vision*. Holt, Rinehart and Winston, New York.

Bradley, Peter and Tye, Michael (2001). Of color, kestrels, caterpillars, and leaves. *The Journal of Philosophy*, **98**, 469–487.

Broackes, Justin (2009). What do the colour-blind see? In *Color Ontology and Color Science* (ed. J. Cohen and M. Matthen). MIT Press, Cambridge, Massachusetts.

Brown, Derek H. (2006). On the dual referent approach to colour theory. *The Philosophical Quarterly*, **56**(222), 96–113.

Burge, Tyler (1993). Mind-body causation and explanatory practice. See Heil and Mele (1993), pp. 97–120.

Burnyeat, Myles (1979). Conflicting appearances. *Proceedings of the British Academy*, **LXV**, 69–111.

Byrne, Alex (2002). Intentionalism defended. *The Philosophical Review*, **110**, 199–240.

Byrne, Alex (2003). Color and similarity. *Philosophy and Phenomenological Research*, **66**, 641–665.

Byrne, Alex (2006). Comments. *dialectica*, **60**, 337–340.

Byrne, Alex and Hilbert, David R. (1997*a*). Colors and reflectances. In *Readings on Color, Volume 1: The Philosophy of Color* (ed. A. Byrne and D. R. Hilbert), pp. 263–288. MIT Press, Cambridge, Massachusetts.

Byrne, Alex and Hilbert, David R. (ed.) (1997*b*). *Readings on Color, Volume 1: The Philosophy of Color*. MIT Press, Cambridge, Massachusetts.

Byrne, Alex and Hilbert, David R. (ed.) (1997*c*). *Readings on Color, Volume 2: The Science of Color*. MIT Press, Cambridge, Massachusetts.

Byrne, Alex and Hilbert, David R. (2003). Color realism and color science. *Behavioral and Brain Sciences*, **26**(1), 3–64.

Byrne, Alex and Hilbert, David R. (2004). Hardin, Tye, and color physicalism. *The Journal of Philosophy*, **CI**(1), 37–43.

Byrne, Alex and Hilbert, David R. (2007*a*). Color primitivism. *Erkenntnis*, **66**, 73–105.

Byrne, Alex and Hilbert, David R. (2007*b*). Truest blue. *Analysis*, **67**(293), 87–92.

Byrne, Alex and Hilbert, David R. (2009). What do 'color blind' observers see? In *Color Ontology and Color Science* (ed. J. Cohen and M. Matthen). MIT Press, Cambridge, Massachusetts.

Byrne, Alex and Tye, Michael (2006). Qualia ain't in the head. *Noûs*, **40**(2), 241–255.

Campbell, John (1993). A simple view of color. In *Reality, Representation, and Projection* (ed. J. Haldane and C. Wright). Oxford University Press, New York. Reprinted in Byrne and Hilbert (1997*b*), 177–190.

Campbell, Keith (1969). Colours. In *Contemporary Philosophy in Australia* (ed. R. Brown and C. D. Rollins). Allen & Unwin, London.

Cappelen, Herman and Lepore, Ernest (2005). *Insensitive Semantics: A Defense of Semantic Minimalism and Speech Act Pluralism*. Blackwell, Oxford.

Carnegie, Andrew (1889). Wealth. *The North American Review*, **CCCXCI**, 653–665.

Carruthers, Peter (1996). *Language, Thought and Consciousness: An Essay in Philosophical Psychology*. Cambridge University Press, Cambridge.

Cartwright, Nancy (1989). *Nature's Capacities and Their Measurement*. Clarendon Press, Oxford.

Chalmers, David (1996). *The Conscious Mind: In Search of a Fundamental Theory*. Oxford University Press, New York.

Chalmers, David (2004). The representational character of experience. In *The Future for Philosophy* (ed. B. Leiter). Oxford University Press, New York.

Chalmers, David (2006). Perception and the fall from Eden. In *Perceptual Experience* (ed. T. S. Gendler and J. Hawthorne), pp. 49–125. Oxford University Press, New York.

Chang, Hasok (2005). *Inventing Temperature: Measurement and Scientific Progress*. Oxford University Press, Oxford.

Chisholm, Roderick (1957). *Perceiving: A Philosophical Study*. Cornell University Press, Ithaca.

Chomsky, Noam (1959). Review of B. F. Skinner, *Verbal Behavior*. *Language*, **35**, 26–57.

Chomsky, Noam (1965). *Aspects of the Theory of Syntax*. MIT Press, Cambridge, Massachusetts.

Churchland, Paul M. (1979). *Scientific Realism and the Plasticity of Mind*. Cambridge University Press, Cambridge.

Churchland, Paul M. (2009). On the reality of objective colors. In *Color Ontology and Color Science* (ed. J. Cohen and M. Matthen). MIT Press, Cambridge, Massachusetts. Forthcoming.

Cicerone, C. M. and Nerger, J. L (1989). The relative number of long-wavelength-sensitive to middle-wavelength-sensitive cones in the human fovea. *Vision Research*, **26**, 115–128.

Clark, Austen (1993). *Sensory Qualities*. Clarendon Press, Oxford.

Cohen, Jonathan (2003*a*). Color: A functionalist proposal. *Philosophical Studies*, **112**(3), 1–42.

Cohen, Jonathan (2003*b*). On the structural properties of the colors. *Australasian Journal of Philosophy*, **81**(1), 78–95.

Cohen, Jonathan (2004). Color properties and color ascriptions: A relationalist manifesto. *The Philosophical Review*, **113**(4), 451–506.

Cohen, Jonathan (2005). Colors, functions, realizers, and roles. *Philosophical Topics*, **33**(1), 117–140.

Cohen, Jonathan (2006). Color and perceptual variation revisited: Unknown facts, alien modalities, and perfect psychosemantics. *dialectica*, **60**(3), 307–319.

Cohen, Jonathan (2007). A relationalist's guide to error about color perception. *Noûs*, **41**(2), 335–353.

Cohen, Jonathan (2008). Color constancy as counterfactual. *Australasian Journal of Philosophy*, **86**(1), 61–92.

Cohen, Jonathan (2010). Color relationalism and color phenomenology. In *Perceiving the World* (ed. B. Nanay). Oxford University Press, New York.

Cohen, Jonathan, Hardin, C. L., and McLaughlin, Brian P. (2006*a*). True colors. *Analysis*, **66**(4), 335–340.

Cohen, Jonathan, Hardin, C. L., and McLaughlin, Brian P. (2006*b*). The truth about "The Truth about True Blue". *Analysis*, **67**(2), 162–166.

Cohen, Jonathan and Meskin, Aaron (2004). On the epistemic value of photographs. *Journal of Aesthetics and Art Criticism*, **62**(2), 197–210.

Cohen, Jonathan and Nichols, Shaun (2007). Color, objectivity, and intuitions. Unpublished manuscript.

Cohen, Stewart (1988). How to be a fallibilist. *Philosophical Perspectives*, **2**, 91–123.

Cohen, Stewart (1991). Skepticims, relevance, and relativity. In *Dretske and His Critics* (ed. B. McLaughlin), pp. 17–37. Blackwell, Cambridge, Massachusetts.

Cooper, John M. (ed.) (1997). *Plato: Complete Works*. Hackett Publishing Company, Indianapolis.

Cornelissen, F. W. and Brenner, E. (1995). Simultaneous colour constancy revisited: an analysis of viewing strategies. *Vision Research*, **35**, 2431–2448.

Cornman, James W. (1971). *Materialism and Sensations*. Yale University Press, New Haven.

Cornman, James W. (1975). *Perception, Common Sense, and Science*. Yale University Press, New Haven.

Crane, H. and Piantanida, T. P. (1983). On seeing reddish green and yellowish blue. *Science*, **221**, 1078–1080.

Crimmins, Mark and Perry, John (1989). The prince and the phone booth. *The Journal of Philosophy*, **86**, 685–711.

Cronin, Tom W. and Marshall, N. Justin (1989). A retina with at least ten spectral types of photoreceptors in a mantis shrimp. *Nature*, **339**, 137–140.

Cummins, Robert (1975). Functional analysis. *The Journal of Philosophy*, **LXXII**(20), 741–756.

Cummins, Robert (1983). *The Nature of Psychological Explanation*. MIT Press, Cambridge, Massachusetts.

Dancy, Jonathan (1986). Two conceptions of moral realism. *Proceedings of the Aristotelian Society*, **Supplementary Volume 60**, 167–187.

Dannemiller, James L. (1992). Color is as color does. *Behavioral and Brain Sciences*, **15**(1), 33–34.

Dartnall, H. J. A., Bowmaker, J. K., and Mollon, J. D. (1983). Human visual pigments: microspectrophotometric results from the eyes of seven persons. *Proceedings of the Royal Society of London B*, **220**, 115–130.

Davidson, Donald (1973). Freedom to act. In *Essays on Freedom of Action* (ed. T. Honderich). Routledge & Kegan Paul, London. Reprinted in Davidson (1980), 63–81.

Davidson, Donald (1980). *Essays on Action and Events*. Clarendon Press, Oxford.

Davies, Martin (1993). Aims and claims of externalist arguments. In *Philosophical Issues* (ed. E. Villanueva), Volume 4, pp. 227–249. Ridgeview Publishing, Atascadero, CA.

Dennett, Daniel C. (2003). Forestalling a food fight over color. *Behavioral and Brain Sciences*, **26**, 788–789.

DeRose, Keith (1992). Contextualism and knowledge attributions. *Philosophy and Phenomenological Research*, **52**(4), 913–929.

Doyle, Arthur Conan (1905). *The Return of Sherlock Holmes*. McClure, Phillips & Company, New York.

Dretske, Fred (1970). Epistemic operators. *The Journal of Philosophy*, **67**, 1007–1023. Reprinted in Dretske (2000).

Dretske, Fred (1995). *Naturalizing the Mind*. MIT Press, Cambridge, Massachusetts. Originally delivered as the 1994 Jean Nicod Lectures.

Dretske, Fred I. (2000). *Perception, Knowledge, and Belief: Selected Essays*. Cambridge University Press, Cambridge.

Drier, James (1990). Internalism and speaker relativism. *Ethics*, **101**, 6–26.

Dummett, Michael (1978). *Truth and Other Enigmas*. Harvard University Press, Cambridge, Massachusetts.

Dummett, Michael (1981). *The Interpretation of Frege's Philosophy*. Harvard University Press, Cambridge, Massachusetts.

Dunn, J. Michael (1990). Relevant predication 2: Intrinsic properties and internal relations. *Philosophical Studies*, **60**, 177–206.

Egan, Andy (2007). Epistemic modals, relativism, and assertion. *Philosophical Studies*, **133**, 1–22.

Egan, Andy, Hawthorne, John, and Weatherson, Brian (2005). Epistemic modals in context. In *Contextualism in Philosophy* (ed. G. Preyer and G. Peter), pp. 131–168. Oxford University Press, Oxford.

Egan, Frances (2008). The content of color experience. *Philosophy and Phenomenological Research*, **76**(2), 407–414.

Einstein, Albert (1905). Zur Elektrodynamik bewegter Körper. *Annalen der Physik*, **17**, 891–921.

Evans, Ralph M. (1948). *An Introduction to Color*. Wiley, New York.

Fara, Delia Graff (2000). Shifting sands: An interest relative theory of vagueness. *Philosophical Topics*, **28**(1), 45–81. Originally published under the name 'Delia Graff'.

Fara, Michael (Fall 2006). Dispositions. In *The Stanford Encyclopedia of Philosophy* (ed. E. N. Zalta). Center for the Study of Language and Information.

von Fintel, Kai and Gillies, Anthony S. (2008). CIA leaks. *The Philosophical Review*, **117**(1), 77–98.

Fodor, Jerry A. (1984). Observation reconsidered. *Philosophy of Science*, **51**(1), 23–43.

Fodor, Jerry A. (1989). Making mind matter more. *Philosophical Topics*, **17**, 59–79. Reprinted in Fodor (1990*a*), 137–159.

Fodor, Jerry A. (1990*a*). *A Theory of Content and Other Essays*. MIT Press, Cambridge, Massachusetts.

Fodor, Jerry A. (1990*b*). A theory of content, I: The problem. In *A Theory of Content and Other Essays* (ed. J. Fodor), pp. 51–87. MIT Press, Cambridge, Massachusetts.

Fodor, Jerry A. (1990*c*). A theory of content, II: The theory. In *A Theory of Content and Other Essays* (ed. J. Fodor), pp. 89–136. MIT Press, Cambridge, Massachusetts.

Gert, Joshua (2006). A realistic color realism. *Australasian Journal of Philosophy*, **84**(4), 565–589.

Gert, Joshua (2008). What colors could not be: An argument for color primitivism. *Journal of Philosophy*, **CV**(3), 128–155.

Gibbard, Allan (2006). Moral feelings and moral concepts. In *Oxford Studies in Metaethics, 1* (ed. R. Schafer-Landau), pp. 195–215. Clarendon Press, Oxford.

Giere, Ronald (2006). *Scientific Perspectivism.* University of Chicago Press, Chicago.

Glanzberg, Michael (2007). Context, content, and relativism. *Philosophical Studies*, **136**, 1–29.

Gold, Ian (1999). Dispositions and the central problem of color. *Philosophical Studies*, **93**(1), 21–44.

Gould, Stephen J. and Lewontin, Richard C. (1979). The spandrels of San Marco and the Panglossian paradigm: A critique of the adaptationist program. *Proceedings of the Royal Society*, **B 205**, 581–598.

van Gulick, Robert (1992). Three bad arguments for intentional property epiphenomenalism. *Erkenntnis*, **36**, 311–331.

Hagstrom, S.A., Neitz, Jay, and Neitz, Maureen (1998). Variation in cone populations for red-green color vision exampled by analysis of mRNA. *NeuroReport*, **9**, 1963–1967.

Hardin, C. L. (1984). A new look at color. *American Philosophical Quarterly*, **21**, 125–133.

Hardin, C. L. (1988). *Color for Philosophers: Unweaving the Rainbow.* Hackett, Indianapolis.

Hardin, C. L. (2004). A green thought in a green shade. *Harvard Review of Philosophy*, **XII**, 29–39.

Hardin, C. L. (2006). Comments. *dialectica*, **60**(3), 341–345.

Harman, Gilbert (1977). *The Nature of Morality*. Oxford University Press, Oxford.

Harman, Gilbert (1990). The intrinsic quality of experience. Volume 4, pp. 31–52. Ridgeview Publishing Company, Atascerdo, California.

Harman, Gilbert (1996). Explaining objective color in terms of subjective reactions. In *Philosophical Issues* (ed. E. Villanueva), Volume 7. Ridgeview, Atascadero, California. Reprinted in Byrne and Hilbert (1997*b*), 247–261.

Heil, John and Mele, Alfred (ed.) (1993). *Mental Causation.* Oxford University Press, New York.

Heller, Mark (1989). Relevant alternatives. *Philosophical Studies*, **55**, 23–40.

Hilbert, David R. (1987). *Color and Color Perception: A Study in Anthropocentric Realism.* CSLI, Stanford.

Hilbert, David R. (1992*a*). Comparitive color vision and the objectivity of color: Open peer commentary on Thompson *et al.* (1992). *Behavioral and Brain Sciences*, **15**, 38–39.

Hilbert, David R. (1992*b*). What is color vision? *Philosophical Studies*, **68**, 351–370.

Hill, Christopher S. (1991). *Sensations*. Cambridge University Press, Cambridge.

Hubel, David H. (1988). *Eye, Brain, and Vision*. Scientific American Library, New York.

Humberstone, Lloyd (1996). Intrinsic/extrinsic. *Synthese*, **108**(2), 205–267.

Humphreys, William Jackson (1964). *Physics of the Air*. Dover, New York.

Hurvich, Leo Maurice (1981). *Color Vision*. Sinauer Associates, Sunderland, Massachusetts.

Hurvich, Leo M. and Jameson, Dorothea (1957). An opponent-process theory of color vision. *Psychological Review*, **64**, 384–403.

Jackson, Frank (1977). *Perception: A Representative Theory*. Cambridge University Press, New York.

Jackson, Frank (1996). The primary quality view of color. *Philosophical Perspectives*, **10**, 199–219.

Jackson, Frank (1998*a*). *From Metaphysics to Ethics: A Defence of Conceptual Analysis*. Oxford, New York. Originally given as the 1998 Locke Lectures.

Jackson, Frank (1998*b*). Review of Maund, *Colours: Their Nature and Representation*. *The Philosophical Quarterly*, **48**(191), 243–245.

Jackson, Frank (2000). Philosophizing about color. In *Color Perception: Philosophical, Psychological, Artistic and Computational Perspectives* (ed. S. Davis), pp. 152–162. Oxford University Press, New York.

Jackson, Frank and Pargetter, Robert (1987). An objectivist's guide to subjectivism about color. *Revue Internationale de Philosophie*, **160**, 127–141. Reprinted in Byrne and Hilbert (1997*b*), 67–79.

Jackson, Frank and Pettit, Philip (1988). Functionalism and broad content. *Mind*, **97**, 381–400.

Jackson, Frank and Pettit, Philip (1990). Program explanation: A general perspective. *Analysis*, **50**, 107–117.

Jacobs, Gerald H. and Deegan, J. F. (1997). Spectral sensitivity of macaque monkeys measured with ERG flicker photometry. *Visual Neuroscience*, **14**, 921–928.

Jacobs, Gerald H. and Neitz, Jay (1993). Electrophysiological estimates of individual variation in the L/M cone ratio. In *Colour Vision Deficiencies* (ed. B. Drum), Volume XI, Documenta Opthalmologica Proceedings Series 56, Chapter 11, pp. 107–112. Kluwer Academic Publishers, Dordrecht.

Jakab, Zoltán and McLaughlin, Brian (2003). Why not color physicalism without color absolutism? *Behavioral and Brain Sciences*, **26**(1), 34–35.

Jameson, Dorothea and Hurvich, Leo M. (1978). Dichromatic color language: 'reds' and 'greens' don't look alike but their colors do. *Sensory Processes*, **2**, 146–155.

Jameson, Dorothea and Hurvich, Leo M. (1989). Essay concerning color constancy. *Annual Review of Psychology*, **40**, 1–22. Reprinted in Byrne and Hilbert (1997*c*), 177–198.

Johnson, Monte (2008). Spontaneity: Democritean casuality and freedom. Unpublished manuscript.

Johnston, Mark (1992). How to speak of the colors. *Philosophical Studies*, **68**, 221–263. Reprinted in Byrne and Hilbert (1997*b*), 137–176.

Johnston, Mark (1998). Are manifest qualities response-dependent? *The Monist*, **8**(1), 3–43.

Johnston, Mark (2002). *The Manifest*. Ms., Princeton University.

Johnston, Mark (2004). The obscure object of hallucination. *Philosophical Studies*, **120**(1–3), 113–183.

Judd, Donald B. and Wyszecki, G. (1963). *Color in Business, Science, and Industry, Second Edition*. Wiley, New York.

Kalderon, Mark Eli (2007*a*). Color pluralism. *The Philosophical Review*, **116**(4), 563–601.

Kalderon, Mark Eli (2007*b*). The multiply qualitative. http://www.kalderon.demon.co.uk/mq.pdf.

Kaplan, David (1989). Demonstratives: An essay on the semantics, logic, metaphysics, and epistemology of demonstratives and other indexicals. In *Themes From Kaplan* (ed. J. Almog, J. Perry, and H. Wettstein), Chapter 17, pp. 481–563. Oxford University Press, New York. Originally circulated as a mimeograph from the Department of Philosophy, UCLA.

Kelly, K. L. and Judd, Donald B. (1976). *Color: Universal Language and Dictionary of Names*. National Bureau of Standards, Washington, DC. Special Publication 440.

Kim, Jaegwon (1976). Events as property exemplifications. In *Action Theory* (ed. M. Brand and D. Walton), pp. 159–177. Redel, Dordrecht.

Kim, Jaegwon (1989*a*). Mechanism, purpose, and explanatory exclusion. In *Philosophical Perspectives 3, Philosophy of Mind and Action Theory* (ed. J. E. Tomberlin), pp. 77–108. Ridgeview Publishing, Atascadero, California. Reprinted in Kim (1993*b*), 237–264.

Kim, Jaegwon (1989*b*). The myth of nonreductive materialism. *Proceedings and Addresses of the American Philosophical Association*, **63**, 31–47. Reprinted in Kim (1993*b*), 265–284.

Kim, Jaegwon (1993*a*). The nonreductivist's troubles with mental causation. In *Mental Causation* (ed. J. Heil and A. Mele), pp. 189–210. Oxford University Press, Oxford. Reprinted in Kim (1993*b*), 336–357.

Kim, Jaegwon (1993*b*). *Supervenience and Mind: Selected Philosophical Essays*. Cambridge University Press, New York.

Kim, Jaegwon (1997). Does the problem of mental causation generalize? *Proceedings of the Aristotelian Society*, **97**, 281–297.

Kim, Jaegwon (1998). *Mind in a Physical World: An Essay on the Mind–Body Problem and Mental Causation*. MIT Press, Cambridge, Massachusetts. Originally given as the 1996 Townsend Lectures.

Klein, E. (1991). Comparitives. In *Semantics: An International Handbook of Contemporary Research* (ed. A. von Stechow and D. Wunderlich), pp. 673–691. Walter de Gruyter, Berlin.

Kripke, Saul (1977). Speaker reference and semantic reference. In *Contemporary Perspectives in the Philosophy of Language* (ed. P. A. French, T. E. Uehling, and H. K. Wettstein), pp. 6–27. University of Minnesota Press, Minneapolis. Reprinted in Martinich (1990).

Kripke, Saul (1980). *Naming and Necessity.* Harvard University Press, Cambridge, Massachusetts.

Kripke, Saul (1982). *Wittgenstein on Rules and Private Language: An Elementary Exposition.* Harvard University Press, Cambridge, Massachusetts.

Kurth, Charles B. (2008). A deflationary account of the unity of color. Unpublished manuscript.

Langton, Rae and Lewis, David (1998). Defining 'intrinsic'. *Philosophy and Phenomenological Research*, **58**(2), 333–345.

Larson, Richard and Segal, Gabriel (1995). *Knowledge of Meaning: An Introduction to Semantic Theory.* MIT Press, Cambridge, Massachusetts.

Lasersohn, Peter (2005). Context dependence, disagreement, and predicates of personal taste. *Linguistics and Philosophy*, **28**(6), 643–686.

Levin, Janet (2000). Dispositional theories of color and the claims of common sense. *Philosophical Studies*, **100**, 151–174.

Lewis, David (1972). Psychophysical and theoretical identitifications. *Australasian Journal of Philosophy*, **50**(3), 249–258. Reprinted in Block (1980), 207–215.

Lewis, David (1973). Causation. *The Journal of Philosophy*, **70**, 556–567. Reprinted in Lewis (1986*c*), 159–172.

Lewis, David (1979). Scorekeeping in a language game. *Journal of Philosophical Logic*, **8**, 339–59.

Lewis, David (1980). Mad pain and Martian pain. See Block (1980). Reprinted in Lewis (1983*b*), 122–130.

Lewis, David (1983*a*). New work for a theory of universals. *Australasian Journal of Philosophy*, **61**, 343–377.

Lewis, David (1983*b*). *Philosophical Papers, Volume I.* Oxford University Press, New York.

Lewis, David (1986*a*). Causal explanation. In *Philosophical Papers, Volume II* (ed. D. Lewis), pp. 214–240. Oxford University Press, New York.

Lewis, David (1986*b*). *On the Plurality of Worlds.* Basil Blackwell, Oxford.

Lewis, David (1986*c*). *Philosophical Papers, Volume II.* Oxford University Press, New York.

Lewis, David (1986*d*). Postscripts to "Causation". In *Philosophical Papers, Volume II* (ed. D. Lewis), pp. 172–213. Oxford University Press, New York.

Lewis, David (1994). Reduction of mind. In *A Companion to the Philosophy of Mind* (ed. S. Guttenplan), pp. 412–431. Blackwell, Oxford.

Lewis, David (1996). Elusive knowledge. *Australasian Journal of Philosophy*, **74**, 549–567.

Lewis, David (1997). Naming the colors. *Australasian Journal of Philosophy*, **75**(3), 325–342.

Locke, John (1975). *An Essay Concerning Human Understanding (1689).* Oxford University Press, New York.

Loewer, Barry (2007). Mental causation, or something near enough. In *Contemporary Debates in Philosophy of Mind* (ed. B. McLaughlin and J. Cohen), pp. 243–264. Wiley-Blackwell, Oxford.

MacAdam, Douglas L. (1997). The physical basis of color specification. In *Readings on Color, Volume 2: The Science of Color* (ed. A. Byrne and D. R. Hilbert), pp. 33–63. MIT Press, Cambridge, Massachusetts.

MacFarlane, John (2003). Future contingents and relative truth. *The Philosophical Quarterly*, **53**, 321–336.

MacFarlane, John (2005). Making sense of relative truth. *Proceedings of the Aristotelian Society*, **105**, 321–339.

Mackie, J. L. (1973). *Truth, Probability, and Paradox.* Oxford University Press, Oxford.

Mackie, J. L. (1976). *Problems from Locke.* Oxford University Press, Oxford.

Mackie, J. L. (1977). *Ethics: Inventing Right and Wrong.* Penguin Books, Harmondsworth.

Malkoc, Gokham, Kay, Paul, and Webster, Michael A. (2005). Variations in normal color vision. IV. Binary hues and hue scaling. *Journal of the Optical Society of America, A*, **22**(10), 2154–2168.

Martinich, A. P. (1990). *The Philosophy of Language,* second edition. Oxford University Press, New York.

Matthen, Mohan (1988). Biological functions and perceptual content. *The Journal of Philosophy*, **85**, 5–27.

Matthen, Mohan (1992). Colour vision: Content and experience: Open peer commentary on Thompson *et al.* (1992). *Behavioral and Brain Sciences*, **15**, 46–47.

Matthen, Mohan (1999). The disunity of color. *The Philosophical Review*, **108**(1), 47–84.

Matthen, Mohan (2001). Our knowledge of colour. In *Naturalism, Evolution, and Intentionality* (ed. J. Macintosh), pp. 215–246. *Canadian Journal of Philosophy.* Supplementary volume 27.

Matthen, Mohan (2005). *Seeing, Doing, and Knowing: A Philosophical Theory of Sense Perception.* Oxford University Press, Oxford.

Matthen, Mohan (2008). On the diversity of auditory objects. *European Review of Philosophy*, **7**.

Maund, Barry (1981). Colour: A case for conceptual fission. *Australasian Journal of Philosophy*, **59**, 308–322.

Maund, Barry (1995). *Colours: Their Nature and Representation*. Cambridge University Press, New York.

Mausfeld, Rainer, Niederée, Reinhard, and Heyer, Dieter (1992). On possible perceptual worlds and how they shape their environments. *Behavioral and Brain Sciences*, **15**(1), 47–48.

McDowell, John (1985). Values and secondary qualities. In *Morality and Objectivity: A Tribute to J. L. Mackie* (ed. T. Honderich), pp. 110–129. Routledge & Kegan Paul, London.

McGinn, Colin (1983). *The Subjective View: Secondary Qualities and Indexical Thoughts*. Oxford University Press, Oxford.

McGinn, Colin (1996). Another look at color. *The Journal of Philosophy*, **93**(11), 537–553.

McKay, Thomas and Nelson, Michael (Winter 2006). Propositional attitude reports. In *The Stanford Encyclopedia of Philosophy* (ed. E. N. Zalta). Center for the Study of Language and Information.

McLaughlin, Brian (1995). Disposition. In *A Companion to Metaphysics* (ed. J. Kim and E. Sosa), pp. 121–124. Basil Blackwell, Oxford.

McLaughlin, Brian (1997). Supervenience, vagueness, and determination. In *Philosophical Perspectives 11: Mind, Causation, and World* (ed. J. E. Tomberlin), pp. 209–230. Ridgeview Publishing, Atascadero, California.

McLaughlin, Brian (2000). Colors and color spaces. In *Proceedings of the Twentieth World Congress Of Philosophy* (ed. R. Cubb-Stevens), Volume 5. Philosophy Documentation Centre.

McLaughlin, Brian (2003*a*). Color, consciousness, and color consiousness. In *Consciousness: New Philosophical Perspectives* (ed. Q. Smith and A. Jokic), pp. 97–154. Oxford University Press, New York.

McLaughlin, Brian (2003*b*). The place of color in nature. In *Colour Perception: Mind and the Physical World* (ed. R. Mausfeld and D. Heyer), pp. 475–502. Oxford University Press, New York.

Millikan, Ruth Garrett (1989). Biosemantics. *The Journal of Philosophy*, **86**, 281–297. Reprinted in Stich and Warfield (1994).

Mizrahi, Vivian (2007). Color objectivism and color pluralism. *Dialectica*, **60**(3), 283–306.

Moore, G. E. (1903). *Principia Ethica*. The University Press, Cambridge.

Mumford, Stephen (1998). *Dispositions*. Oxford University Press, New York.

Munsell, A. H. (1946). *A Color Notation*. Munsell Color, Baltimore.

Munsell Color Company (1976). *Munsell Book of Color*. Munsell Color, Baltimore.

Nassau, Kurt (1980). The causes of color. *Scientific American*, **243**, 124–154. Reprinted in Byrne and Hilbert (1997*c*), 3–29.

Nassau, Kurt (1983). *The Physics and Chemistry of Color*. Wiley, New York.

Neale, Stephen (1993). Term limits. *Philosophical Perspectives, Language and Logic*, **7**, 89–117.

Northcott, Robert (2008). Causation and contrast classes. *Philosophical Studies*, **39**(1), 111–123.

Papineau, David (1993). *Philosophical Naturalism*. Blackwell, Oxford.

Pautz, Adam (2006*a*). Can the physicalist explain colour structure in terms of colour experience? *Australasian Journal of Philosophy*, **84**(4), 535–565.

Pautz, Adam (2006*b*). Color eliminativism. Ms., University of Texas, Austin.

Pautz, Adam (2006*c*). Sensory awareness is not a wide physical relation: An empirical argument against externalist intentionalism. *Noûs*, **40**(2), 205–240.

Pautz, Adam (2008). A simple view of consciousness. In *The Waning of Materialism* (ed. G. Bealer and R. Koons). Oxford University Press, Oxford.

Peacocke, Christopher (1979). Deviant causal chains. *Midwest Studies in Philosophy*, **4**, 123–155.

Peacocke, Christopher (1984). Colour concepts and colour experiences. *Synthese*, **58**(3), 365–381. Reprinted in Rosenthal (1991), 408–416.

Perkins, Moreland (1983). *Sensing the World*. Hackett Publishing Company, Indianapolis.

Perry, John (1986). Thought without representation. *Proceedings of The Aristotelian Society*, **supplementary volume 60**, 263–283. Reprinted in Perry (1993), 202–225.

Perry, John (1993). *The Problem of The Essential Indexical and Other Essays*. Oxford University Press, New York.

Pokorny, Joel, Smith, V. C., and Wesner, M. (1991). Variability in cone populations and implications. In *From Pigments to Perception* (ed. A. Valberg and B. B. Lee), pp. 23–34. Plenum, New York.

Prior, Elizabeth (1985). *Dispositions*. Aberdeen University Press, Aberdeen.

Prior, Elizabeth, Pargetter, Robert, and Jackson, Frank (1982). Three theses about dispositions. *American Philosophical Quarterly*, **19**, 251–257.

Putnam, Hilary (1967). The mental life of some machines. In *Intentionality, Minds and Perception* (ed. H.-N. Castaneda). Wayne State University Press, Detroit. Reprinted in Putnam (1975), 408–428.

Putnam, Hilary (1975). *Mind, Language, and Reality: Collected Papers, Volume 2*. Cambridge University Press, New York.

Quine, Willard Van Orman (1953*a*). On what there is. In *From a Logical Point of View: 9 Logico-Philosophical Essays* (ed. W. V. O. Quine). Harper and Row, New York. Originally in the *Review of Metaphysics*, 1948.

Quine, Willard Van Orman (1953*b*). Two dogmas of empiricism. In *From a Logical Point of View* (ed. W. V. O. Quine). Harper and Row, New York. Originally in *The Philosophical Review*, 1951.

Quine, Willard Van Orman (1960). *Word and Object*. MIT Press, Cambridge, Massachusetts.

Railton, Peter (1989). Naturalism and prescriptivity. *Social Philosophy and Policy*, **7**(1), 151–174.

Railton, Peter (1995). Subject-ive and objective. *Ratio*, N. S., **VIII**(3), 259–276.

Rickless, Samuel C. (1997). Locke on primary and secondary qualities. *Pacific Philosophial Quarterly*, **78**, 297–319.

Rodriguez-Pereyra, Gonzalez (2002). *Resemblance Nominalism. A Solution to the Problem of Universals*. Oxford University Press, Oxford.

Roorda, Austin and Williams, David R. (1999). The arrangement of the three cone classes in the living human eye. *Nature*, **397**, 520–522.

Rosenthal, David (1991). *The Nature of Mind*. Oxford University Press, New York.

Rosenthal, David (1999). The colours and shapes of visual experiences. In *Conscioussness and Intentionality: Models and Modalities of Attribution* (ed. D. Fisette), Volume 62, Western Ontario Series in the Philosophy of Science, pp. 95–118. Kluwer, Dordrecht.

Ross, Peter W. (1999). The appearance and nature of color. *The Southern Journal of Philosophy*, **37**, 227–252.

Rossotti, Hazel (1983). *Color: Why the World Isn't Grey*. Princeton University Press, Princeton.

Rushton, W. A. H. and Baker, H. D. (1964). Red/green sensitivity in normal vision. *Vision Research*, **4**, 75–85.

Russell, Bertrand (1905). On denoting. *Mind*, **14**, 479–493. Reprinted in Martinich (1990), 203–211.

Russell, Bertrand (1912). *The Problems of Philosophy*. Oxford University Press, London.

Sacks, Oliver (1996). *The Island of the Colorblind*. Vintage Books, New York.

Sayre-McCord, Geoffrey (1988). The many moral realisms. In *Essays on Moral Realism* (ed. G. Sayre-McCord), pp. 1–23. Cornell University Press, Ithaca.

Schaffer, Jonathan (2005). Contrastive causation. *The Philosophical Review*, **114**, 327–358.

Schiffer, Stephen (1992). Belief ascription. *The Journal of Philosophy*, **89**, 490–521.

Seckel, Al (2002). *The Great Book of Optical Illusions*. Firefly, Toronto.

Sellars, Wilfrid (1956). Empiricism and the philosophy of mind. In *Minnesota Studies in the Philosophy of Science* (ed. H. Feigl and M. Scriven), Volume 1, pp. 253–329. University of Minnesota Press, Minneapolis.

Sellars, Wilfrid (1963). Philosophy and the scientific image of man. In *Science, Perception and Reality* (ed. W. Sellars), pp. 1–40. Routledge & Kegan Paul, London.

Sellars, Wilfrid (1975). The adverbial theory of the objects of perception. *Metaphilosophy*, **6**, 144–160.

Shepard, Roger N. (1992). The perceptual organization of colors: An adaptation to regularities of the terrestrial world? In *The Adapted Mind: Evolutionary*

Psychology and the Generation of Culture (ed. J. Barkow, L. Cosmides, and J. Tooby), pp. 495–532. Oxford University Press, Oxford. Reprinted in Byrne and Hilbert (1997*c*), 311–356.

Shoemaker, Sydney (1980). Causality and properties. In *Time and Cause* (ed. P. van Inwagen), pp. 109–136. Dordrecht Reidel, Dordrecht.

Shoemaker, Sydney (1990). Qualities and qualia: What's in the mind? *Philosophy and Phenomenological Research*, **50, Supplement**, 109–131. Reprinted in Shoemaker (1996), 97–120.

Shoemaker, Sydney (1994*a*). Phenomenal character. *Noûs*, **28**, 21–38. Reprinted in Byrne and Hilbert (1997*b*), 227–245.

Shoemaker, Sydney (1994*b*). Self knowledge and 'inner sense'. *Philosophy and Phenomenological Research*, **54**, 249–314. Reprinted in Shoemaker (1996), 201–268.

Shoemaker, Sydney (ed.) (1996). *The First-Person Perspective and Other Esays.* Cambridge University Press, Cambridge.

Shoemaker, Sydney (2000*a*). Introspection and phenomenal character. *Philosophical Topics*, **28**(2), 247–273.

Shoemaker, Sydney (2000*b*). Phenomenal character revisited. *Philosophy and Phenomenological Research*, **LX**(2), 465–468.

Shoemaker, Sydney (2003). Content, character, and color. In *Philosophy of Mind* (ed. E. Sosa and E. Villanueva), Volume 13, Philosophical Issues, pp. 253–278. Ridgeview Publishing Company, Atascadero, California.

Shoemaker, Sydney (2006). On the way things appear. In *Perceptual Experience* (ed. T. S. Gendler and J. Hawthorne), pp. 461–480. Oxford University Press, New York.

Siegel, Susanna (Summer 2005). The contents of perception. In *The Stanford Encyclopedia of Philosophy* (ed. E. N. Zalta). Center for the Study of Language and Information.

Smart, J. J. C. (1963). *Philosophy and Scientific Realism.* Routledge & Kegan Paul, London.

Smart, J. J. C. (1975). On some criticisms of a physicalist theory of colors. In *Philosophical Aspects of the Mind–Body Problem* (ed. C. Cheng). University Press of Hawaii, Honolulu. Reprinted in Byrne and Hilbert (1997*b*), 1–10.

Smith, A. D. (2002). *The Problem of Perception.* Harvard University Press, Cambridge, Massachusetts.

Soames, Scott (1999). *Understanding Truth.* Oxford University Press, New York.

Sober, Elliot (1982). Realism and independence. *Noûs*, **16**, 369–385.

Spackman, John (2002). Color, relativism, and realism. *Philosophical Studies*, **108**, 249–287.

Stanley, Jason (2003). Context, interest relativity and the Sorites. *Analysis*, **63**(4), 269–280.

Stanley, Jason (2004). On the linguistic basis for contextualism. *Philosophical Studies*, **119**, 119–146.

Stich, Stephen P. and Warfield, Ted A. (1994). *Mental Representation: A Reader*. Basil Blackwell, Oxford.

Strawson, Galen (1978). 'Red' and red. *Synthese*, **78**, 193–232.

Strawson, Peter F. (1979). Perception and its objects. In *Perception and Identity* (ed. G. F. MacDonald), pp. 41–60. MacMillan, London.

Stroud, Barry (2000). *The Quest for Reality: Subjectivism and the Metaphysics of Colour*. Oxford University Press, New York.

Thau, Michael (2002). *Consciousness and Cognition*. Oxford University Press, New York.

Thompson, Brad (2006). Colour constancy and Russellian representationalism. *Australasian Journal of Philosophy*, **84**(1), 75–94.

Thompson, Brad (2009). Senses for senses. *Australasian Journal of Philosophy*, **87**(1), 99–117.

Thompson, Evan (1995). *Colour Vision: A Study in Cognitive Science and the Philosophy of Perception*. Routledge, New York.

Thompson, Evan, Palacios, Adrian, and Varela, Francisco (1992). Ways of coloring: Comparative color vision as a case study for cognitive science. *Behavioral and Brain Sciences*, **15**, 1–74.

Tooley, Michael (1988). In defense of the existence of states of motion. *Philosophical Topics*, **16**, 225–54.

Travis, Charles (2004). The silence of the senses. *Mind*, **113**(449), 57–94.

Troost, Jimmy M. and deWeert, C. M. M. (1991). Naming versus matching in color constancy. *Perception & Psychophysics*, **50**, 591–602.

Tye, Michael (1984). The adverbial approach of visual experience. *The Philosophical Review*, **93**, 195–226.

Tye, Michael (1995). *Ten Problems of Consciousness: A Representational Theory of the Phenomenal Mind*. MIT Press, Cambridge, Massachusetts.

Tye, Michael (2000). *Consciousness, Color, and Content*. MIT Press, Cambridge, Massachusetts.

Tye, Michael (2006*a*). The puzzle of true blue. *Analysis*, **66**, 173–178.

Tye, Michael (2006*b*). The truth about true blue. *Analysis*, **66**(4), 340–344.

Unger, Peter (1995). Contextual analysis in ethics. *Philosophy and Phenomenological Research*, **55**, 1–26.

Varzi, Achille (2007). From language to ontology: Beware of the traps. In *The Categorization of Spatial Entities in Language and Cognition* (ed. M. Aurnague, M. Hickmann, and L. Vieu). John Benjamins Publishing, Amsterdam and Philadelphia.

Vimal, R. L. P., Pokorny, Joel, Smith, V. C., and Shevell, Steven K. (1989). Foveal cone thresholds. *Vision Research*, **29**, 61–78.

Walton, Kendall (1984). Transparent pictures: On the nature of photographic realism. *Critical Inquiry*, **11**, 246–276.

Watkins, Michael (2002). *Rediscovering Colors: A Study in Pollyanna Realism.* Dordrecht, Boston.

Watkins, Michael (2005). Seeing red: The metaphysics of colour without the physics. *Australasian Journal of Philosophy*, **83**(1), 33–52.

Watkins, Michael (2008). A posteriori primitivism. Unpublished ms.

Weatherson, Brian (Fall 2006). Intrinsic vs. extrinsic properties. In *The Stanford Encyclopedia of Philosophy* (ed. E. N. Zalta). Center for the Study of Language and Information.

Werner, John S. (1998). Aging through the eyes of Monet. In *Color Vision: Perspectives From Different Disciplines* (ed. W. G. K. Backhaus, R. Gliegl, and J. S. Werner), pp. 3–41. Walter de Gruyter, Berlin.

Westphal, Jonathan (1987). *Colour: Some Philosophical Problems from Wittgenstein.* Blackwell, Oxford.

Westphal, Jonathan (2005). Conflicting appearances, necessity and the irreducibility of propositions about colours. *Proceedings of the Aristotelian Society*, **105**(2), 235–251.

Wiggins, David (1987*a*). A sensible subjectivism? In *Needs, Values, Truth* (ed. D. Wiggins), pp. 185–211. Basil Blackwell, Oxford.

Wiggins, David (1987*b*). Truth, invention, and the meaning of life. In *Needs, Values, Truth* (ed. D. Wiggins). Basil Blackwell, Oxford.

Williams, Bernard (1978). *Descartes: The Project of Pure Enquiry.* Penguin, Harmondsworth.

Williamson, Timothy (2007). *The Philosophy of Philosophy.* Blackwell, Oxford.

Wright, Crispin (1992). *Truth and Objectivity.* Harvard University Press, Cambridge, Massachusetts.

Wyszecki, Günter and Stiles, W. S. (1967). *Color Science: Concepts and Methods, Quantitative Data and Formulae.* Wiley, New York.

Yablo, Stephen (1992). Mental causation. *Philosophical Review*, **101**, 245–280.

Yablo, Stephen (1995). Singling out properties. *Philosophical Perspectives*, **9**, 477–502.

Yablo, Stephen (1999). Intrinsicness. *Philosophical Topics*, **26**(1/2), 479–505.

Yamaguchi, T., Motulsky, A. G., and Deeb, S. S. (1998). Visual pigment gene structure and expression in human retinae. *Human Molecular Genetics*, **6**, 981–990.

Index